DUNDEE

DUNDEE

RENAISSANCE TO ENLIGHTENMENT

Edited by Charles McKean,
Bob Harris and Christopher A. Whatley

Dundee
University
Press

First published in Great Britain in 2009 by
Dundee University Press

University of Dundee
Dundee DD1 4HN

http://www.dup.dundee.ac.uk/

ISBN: 978 1 84586 016 5

British Library Cataloguing-in-Publication Data
A catalogue record for this book is available on
request from the British Library

Typeset and designed by Mark Blackadder

Printed and bound in Britain by MPG Books, Bodmin, Cornwall

Contents

List of Figures and Tables

List of Illustrations

Colour plates

List of Contributors

Malcolm Archibald graduated with first class honours in History at Dundee University as a mature student, before becoming a researcher on Scottish east coast ports. A lecturer first in Dundee, and latterly Moray College, he is also author of the Dundee Book Prize winning novel 'Whales for the Wizard', and the non-fiction 'Whalehunters'.

David Barrie is Lecturer in History at the University of Western Australia. His area of specialist interest is criminal justice history and he is currently working on police courts in nineteenth-century Scotland. His monograph, *Police in the Age of Improvement: Police Development and the Civic Tradition in Scotland 1775–1865* (Cullompton, 2008), was commended as 'the best first book' by the committee of the Frank Watson book prize in Scottish history (2009).

Karen J. Cullen is Lecturer in Scottish History at the Centre for History, UHI Millennium Institute, the future University of the Highlands and Islands. She is author of *Famine in Scotland: the 'Ill Years' of the 1690s* an SHR monograph (Edinburgh, 2010). Her current research interests lie in seventeenth- and eighteenth-century Scottish social, economic and demographic history.

Elizabeth Foyster spent five happy years as a lecturer in History at the University of Dundee, and is currently a Senior College Lecturer and Director of Studies in History at Clare College, University of Cambridge. She has published widely on the history of masculinity, the family and marriage in the early modern period. She is series editor (with

Christopher A. Whatley) of a *History of Everyday Life in Scotland* (Edinburgh University Press), and (with James Marten) of the *Cultural History of Childhood and Family* (Berg).

Bob Harris is Lightbody Fellow and Tutor in History at Worcester College, University of Oxford, where he has been working since 2006. Before that he was Professor of British History at the University of Dundee. He is currently working with Professors McKean and Whatley on a collaborative research project funded by the Arts and Humanities Research Council on Scottish towns in the age of the Enlightenment. His latest book is *The Scottish People and the French Revolution* published in 2008 by Pickering and Chatto.

Alan MacDonald is a lecturer in early modern Scottish History at the University of Dundee. He is author of *The Jacobean Kirk, 1567–1625: Sovereignty, Polity and Liturgy* (Ashgate, 1998), *The Burghs and Parliament in Scotland c. 1550–1651* (Ashgate, 2007), several articles on ecclesiastical, environmental and parliamentary history, and co-author, with T. C. Smout and Fiona Watson, of *A History of the Native Woodlands of Scotland 1500–1920* (Edinburgh, 2005).

Andrew Mackillop is a lecturer in Scottish History in the School of Divinity, History and Philosophy in the University of Aberdeen. His current research is on Scottish involvement in the East India Company from 1695 to 1813, with a particular focus upon the impact of Indian wealth upon Scotland's domestic economy, politics and society. His publications include *More Fruitful than the Soil: Army, Empire and the Scottish Highlands, 1715–1815* (East Linton, 2000), papers in the *Historical Journal* and *Itinerario*, and 'Europeans, Britons and Scots: Scottish Sojourning Networks and Identities in India, c. 1700–1815', in A. McCarthy (ed.), *A Global Clan: Scottish Migrant Networks and Identities since the Eighteenth Century* (London, 2006).

Charles McKean FRSE has been Professor of Scottish Architectural History at the University of Dundee since 1998. He is author, inter alia, of *The Scottish Thirties* (1987), *Edinburgh – Portrait of a City* (1990), *The Making of the Museum of Scotland* (2000), *The Scottish Chateau – the country house of Renaissance Scotland* (2001), and *Battle for the North* (2006). He is currently collaborating with Bob Harris and Christopher

Whatley on a research project funded by the Arts and Humanities Research Council on Scottish Towns in the Age of the Enlightenment.

Derek J. Patrick is a lecturer in History at the University of Dundee. His PhD, 'People and Parliament in Scotland 1689–1702' was part of the Scottish Parliament Project in 2002. He was latterly employed as a Research Fellow at Dundee 2002–2008, working with Professor Christopher Whatley on *The Scots and the Union* (Edinburgh, 2006). He has published several articles on seventeenth- and eighteenth-century Scottish political history including 'Unconventional Procedure: Scottish Electoral Politics after the Revolution', in K. M. Brown and A. J. Mann (eds.), *The History of the Scottish Parliament Vol. II, Parliament and Politics in Scotland, 1567–1707* (Edinburgh, 2005). He is currently working on his first monograph, *Scotland under William and Mary*.

Claire Swan completed her undergraduate and MPhil degrees in Modern History at Dundee University in 2003 and 2004 respectively. She is currently writing up her PhD thesis on the origins and development of Scottish investment trusts at Dundee University. In 2004, she published *Scottish Cowboys and the Dundee Investors*, and is currently employed by Baillie Gifford & Co. in Edinburgh.

Christopher A. Whatley FRSE is Professor of Scottish History at the University of Dundee, where he is also a Vice Principal, and Head of the College of Arts and Social Sciences. In 1997 he initiated the History of Dundee project, of which this volume is a product. He was one of the editors of and a contributor to *Victorian Dundee: Image and Realities* (2000), the first volume in the series, and has written extensively on Scottish history, most recently *The Scots and the Union* (Edinburgh, 2006).

Mary Young works with Archives, Records Management and Museum Services at the University of Dundee. Her research interests focus on the economic and social history of rural Lowland Scotland. The subject of her PhD thesis was 'Rural Society in Scotland from the Restoration to the Union: Challenge and Response in the Carse of Gowrie, c1660–1707'. She is the author of *Abernyte: the quiet revolution* (Perth and Kinross Libraries, 2008) and articles in the *Agricultural History Review* and the *Scottish Historical Review*.

Acknowledgements

We should like to thank, particularly, the staff at Dundee City Archives, Dundee University Archives and their Friends, and Dundee Central Library, Innes Duffus, Stuart Walker, David Walker, Gary Smith and Neil Grieve for all the help we have received. We also owe thanks to the Robert Fleming Charitable Trust which not only enabled us to employ David Barrie on researching civic governance and policing in the eighteenth century, but also enabled us to provide the generous illustrations in this volume.

Publishers' acknowledgements

The publishers thank the following for permission to reproduce copyright images:

DUNDEE CENTRAL LIBRARY: *Plate section 1.* p. 1 top; p. 4 top, bottom; p. 8 bottom right; p. 10; p. 11 bottom; p. 13 bottom; p. 14 bottom. *Plate section 2.* p. 1 top; p. 3 bottom; p. 4 bottom; p. 5 bottom; p. 7 top, bottom; p. 9 bottom right; p. 12 bottom; p. 13 top. *Plate section 3.* p. 1 top left; p. 3 top, bottom; p. 4 top; p. 6 bottom; p. 7; p. 9; p. 10 bottom; p. 11; p. 12; p. 13; p. 14; p. 15 bottom.

DUNDEE CITY ARCHIVES: *Plate section 1.* p. 8 top left. *Plate section 2.* p. 8 bottom. *Plate section 3.* p. 8 top.

D. C. THOMSON: *Plate section 1.* p. 5; top right; p. 16 bottom.

DUNDEE MUSEUMS AND GALLERIES: *Plate section 1*. p. 1 bottom 154-1987-4; p. 2 154-1987-4; p. 5 bottom 39-1987-2; p. 9, bottom 155-1987-17; p. 12 top 33-1987-2. *Plate section 2*. p. 2 33-1987-1, top left; p. 3 top 33-1987-14; p. 10, top left 37; p. 14 155-1987-3; p. 16 bottom 155-1987-5. *Plate section 3*. p. 1 bottom B.H. 1971-117a; p. 4 top and bottom B.H.1971-117-j; p. 5 bottom; p. 15 top 155-1987-2. *Colour plates 1* 7-1990; *2* 6/1925; *12* 75-1987; *15*.

EDINBURGH UNIVERSITY LIBRARY (SCRAN): *Plate section 2*. p. 15 top.

FRIENDS OF DUNDEE CITY ARCHIVES: *Plate section 2*. p. 8 bottom.

CHARLES McKEAN: *Plate section 1*. p. 6 top; p. 7 (all); p. 9 top; p. 12 bottom; p. 15 (both). *Plate section 2*. p. 1 bottom; p. 2 top right; p. 4 top; p. 5 top; p. 6 bottom; p. 8 top left; p. 9 top left; and bottom left; p. 10 bottom; p. 13 bottom; p. 15 bottom; p. 16 top. *Plate section 3*. p. 2 (both); p. 6 top; p. 8 middle and bottom. *Colour plates* 3, 4, 5, 6, 7, 8, 9, 10, 11, 16.

NATIONAL GALLERIES OF SCOTLAND: *Plate section 2*. p. 9 top right.

NATIONAL LIBRARY OF SCOTLAND: *Plate section 1*. p. 3.

NATIONAL MUSEUMS OF SCOTLAND: *Plate section 1*. p. 13 top.

NINE INCORPORATED TRADES OF DUNDEE: *Plate section 3*. p. 16 top. *Colour plate 14*

RIAS COLLECTION: *Plate section 2*. p. 11 bottom; p. 12 top.

ROYAL COMMISSION ON THE ANCIENT AND HISTORICAL MONUMENTS OF SCOTLAND: *Plate section 2*. p. 6 top.

UNIVERSITY OF DUNDEE ARCHIVES: *Plate section 1*. p. 5 top left; p. 6 bottom; p. 8 middle; p. 11 top; p. 14 top. *Plate section 2*, p. 8, top right; p. 10, top right; p. 11 top. *Plate section 3*. p. 1 middle; p. 8 top; p. 10 top; p. 16 bottom.

Abbreviations

APS	Acts of the Parliament of Scotland
DCA	Dundee City Archives
DUA	Dundee University Archives
ECA	Edinburgh City Archives
EIC	East India Company
EUL	Edinburgh University Library
GROS	General Register Office for Scotland
HL	Huntington Library
NA	National Archives (Kew)
NAS	National Archives of Scotland
NLS	National Library of Scotland
NRA(S)	National Register of Archives (Scotland)
OIOC	Oriental and India Office Collections
PER	*Parliaments, Estates and Representation*
PKCA	Perth & Kinross Council Archives
RCRBS	*Records of the Convention of Royal Burghs of Scotland*
RPC	*Register of the Privy Council of Scotland*
RSS	*Register of the Secret Seal*
TCM	Town Council Minutes
TNA	The National Archive (Kew)

Introduction

Charles McKean, Bob Harris
and Christopher A. Whatley

One challenge faced by those researching early Dundee is just how little the town appears to figure in recent Scottish historiography: indeed, in many respects, pre-jute Dundee has become invisible. Given the fact that between *c.* 1450 and 1650 the burgh had risen to be second in wealth only to Edinburgh (as judged by tax revenue), a significant player in the governance of the realm, a centre of both patronage and craftsmanship, and a major port, this invisibility is truly remarkable. It may partly be explained by the fact that not only so very little of the fabric of this Renaissance burgh survived the century-long city improvement programme unleashed in 1871, but also because its original topography was obliterated. Dundee had developed in a long, linear manner squeezed between two small hills (the Corbie Hill and the Windmill Hill that lay immediately to the north, behind the market place and the Overgate) and the shore, with its market place at the centre. The Dundee recorded in old drawings felt dense, dynamic and powerful because it was so tightly hemmed in between those hills and the sea to the south which ran along the foot of the raised beach. That town utterly vanished once both hills were quarried away. To the north, all is now flat, and space leaches away into the characterless and confusing former Meadow and Ward Lands. To the south, the sea has been distanced by over half a mile of serially reclaimed foreshore – originally docks, then railways and now roads. So, more than any other Scots town, Dundee has neither built heritage nor its setting to act as anchors for memory.

The void created by the absence of physical remains was filled by mythologies of different Dundees, exemplified by William Blain's 1946 historical novel *Witch's Blood*, which portrayed a burgh of witch burning, sacking by Cromwell, and industrial turmoil. Blain was only using materials that had been commonplace in Dundee ever since the later eighteenth century, by which time the earlier Dundee had already become obscured, as if by a gauze. So when the playwright/architect Sinclair Gauldie wrote in 1984 that eighteenth century Dundee 'never experienced that expansion of a civilised middle class which ensured the success of Edinburgh's New Town. . . a modest burgh with a fairly typical social stratification whose tone was set by merchants and skilled artisans',[1] he may have been reiterating an accepted truth; but it was not the entire historical reality. Compare Gauldie's description to John Macky's description of the town in 1723: 'The inhabitants here. . . are very genteel and have more of the Air of Gentlemen than Merchants.'[2] The reality of Dundee for most of the period covered in this volume resembled Macky's Dundee at least as much as Gauldie's.

This volume is the second in the University of Dundee's three-volume *History of Dundee* project, which was launched with the publication of *Victorian Dundee, Image and Realities*[3] in 2000 (which likewise faced the problem of comparing the reality against Dundee's well-worn mythologies). The final volume, *Dundee in the Twentieth Century*, is in preparation. The purpose of the series is to assess Dundee's changing role within the world and, particularly, within Scotland and Britain; its similarity or difference to other towns; and to identify any recurrent themes. This volume is divided into two sections. The first part addresses the role and nature of the port between the mid sixteenth and eighteenth centuries, approximately chronologically. The second part focuses upon Dundee between 1750 and 1820 by examining key themes, again approximately chronologically: its relationship with the empire, its port development, its material culture, and its reputation for radicalism and disorder. The volume ends where the next begins – with the liberation of the harbour from the town council into the more dynamic hands of the maritime interest.

During the Renaissance, Dundee was an international trading port of consequence, taking advantage of its inestimable location on a great river estuary with its enormous sheltered anchorage. Goods transhipped at Dundee would travel inland to the very heart of Scotland, providing the king with his oranges and his palaces with their timberwork. Although there are parallels with other Scots burghs, comparisons with ports such as Danzig, Lübeck and Hamburg – with which Dundee customarily traded – are more fruitful, albeit Dundee was significantly smaller than they were and enjoyed considerably less patronage. Its town plan strongly resembles that of Lübeck: its great curving street winding along a ridge, narrowing and widening where there was the town hall or parish church closely paralleling that of Dundee. The passages from the High Street down to the harbour in both ports were curved to cope with the slope and to control the tempests.

Dundee's internationally-trading merchant venturers, as they styled themselves, were so successful that the burgh's private dwellings, civic buildings and its majestic church, St Mary's, were all lavishly appointed – St Mary's even outstripping Edinburgh's St Giles Kirk in the number of its altars and chaplainries. Although it lacked a university, the evidence shows that the arts – particularly music and poetry – played a significant role; and one of the requirements of being admitted a burgess was 'good conversation'. The merchant venturer David Wedderburn, with a major interest in a number of vessels, exemplified perfectly the international trading pattern of relying upon extended kinship to safeguard his cargoes, both at sea and at destination. He is not the normal kind of figure one associates with the term 'renaissance man'; but in his range of reading, his languages, his leisure interests and his patronage, he well merits that description. Wedderburn was one of an oligarchy of at least forty, and his dwellings were certainly not as grand as those of some of his fellows, so there is no reason to believe that he was untypical.

Having rebuilt itself after the English destruction of 1549, and re-organised its public buildings on a new axis, the port of Dundee enjoyed its finest decades between 1560 and 1630. Its significance at national level, examined in Chapter 2, was reflected in the strength and frequency of its representation both at the level of Parliament and the Convention of Royal Burghs. Dundonian experience meant that the burgh's representa-tives were frequently used as senior advisers by representatives of other burghs. Although it failed at the last post in the long-running saga to establish its superiority over Perth, it achieved that de facto in the following centuries, beginning by enticing away much of Perth's textile business by offering lower duties on linen sales.

Dundee was never just a port. Textiles have long been part of Dundee's economy, albeit a less important one for the early modern period than is sometimes assumed[4] – and the burgh's bonnetmakers, and dyers and waulkers (or fullers) played a significant role – albeit waulkers had to rent mills outside the town's boundaries because of the burgh's insufficient water power.[5] The trades' organisations were central to Dundee's civic life, furnishing food and clothing to the inhabitants, regulating their members in terms of numbers employed, quality of work, and prices charged, and supporting them in sickness and old age. They elected representatives to the town council. But Dundee lacked royal, ecclesiastical or aristocratic patronage, and the access to capital and patronage they would have provided. Its elite were the merchant venturers (formed into one of the earliest guilds in Scotland – at least as early as the thirteenth century)[6], its professionals (physicians appear frequently), its craftsmen (particularly its celebrated gunsmiths), and its shipmasters.

The great asset of a safe anchorage, however, also proved a sore burden. The river Tay has the largest outflow of any river in the British Isles, and in virtually every decade, much of Dundee's available income would be used up in protecting its harbour from the ferocious current. Moreover, whereas years of peace proved profitable, the port had few resources to fall back upon if troubles emerged; and, as is explained in Chapter 3, the seventeenth century with its serial disasters was particularly unkind to the town. The plagues of 1605–07 and 1645–46 may have been shared by other towns in Scotland; but Dundee was particularly badly hit by military attacks during the civil wars: first in 1645 by the Marquis of Montrose, and then in 1651 by General Monk. For all the subsequent myth that Monk's sack in 1651 was the most damaging and brutal, Montrose's earlier 1645 attack had been worse; and just when the burgh had picked itself up again, harbour and shore were devastated by a storm in 1668; and then the town lost perhaps 20% of its population during the great famine of 1696–99. Moreover, as Scotland's overseas trade shifted to the west, to the Americas and the empire, Dundee's rank, as measured by wealth, slipped to third after Glasgow and periodically to fourth place after Aberdeen.

Popular belief holds that Dundee had been so ravaged by Monk's sack that it did not recover until the later eighteenth century. Thus the town's Enlightenment minster Dr Robert Small wrote in 1793: 'In the 16th century Dundee was esteemed, after Edinburgh, the most opulent town in Scotland; that in the 17th it was supposed to have decayed more than half, and in the 18th more than two thirds, from its former importance.'[7] It was not quite like that, for, as Chapter 4 reveals, the town remained a significant player in Scotland's history. By the 1680s, its shipping had recovered to pre-civil war volumes – albeit of much lesser ambition – and its citizens contributed substantial sums to the Darien Company. The paradox is that like many Scots burghs in the early eighteenth century, Dundee's administration was so close to bankruptcy that, at the same time that its council was being forced to sell off burgh assets and its burgesses refused to take up office, some individual merchants were building very grandly indeed. Moreover, the Guildry could find £2,287 in 1711 to invest on creating a new port on the more advantageous south shore of the Tay, and invited the then leading hydraulic engineer George Sorocold of Derby up to advise them.[8]

Dundee was the only major burgh to offer a ceremonial welcome to the Old Pretender in 1716, somewhat surprisingly given the extent of James VII's malign meddling in the town's affairs. Yet, after the failure of the rebellion Dundee, as elsewhere, showed notably little taste for revenge. The town clerk, Sir Alexander Wedderburn, who had so enthusiastically greeted the Old Pretender, lost his position – that is all. With only itself and its merchants to fall back upon, the burgh's elite appears to have concluded that to have exacted a more exemplary revenge could have split the burgh and damaged its recovery. The burgh's perceived weakness meant that, effectively, everybody rallied round.

What is even more distinctive, given the port's sixteenth century association with strong reform – 'the Geneva of Scotland' as it was put – is the extent to which Dundee remained Episcopalian, and that almost thirty years after the Glorious Revolution, the established church was still finding it difficult to find recruits to fill its pulpits in 1716. It was, however, a regional phenomenon; and as its merchant venturers – the Clayhills, Goldmans, Guthries, Fotheringhams and Wedderburns – became lairds, the port's elite merged with a new regional gentry.

So Dundee was far from being a demoralised and beaten burgh. Although Newport did not prove a success, the burgh's continuing ambition was next symbolised in the construction of the totemic Town House in 1733 designed by William Adam, the most splendid civic building in Scotland at the time, and one of the finest north of London. The town's principal streets were then refashioned to suit. Beneath the architectural rhetoric, the port's life was developing largely as one might expect. Towns were the regional centres of knowledge and professional skill, irrespective of whether they had a university or not, and Dundee's tradition had been to patronise and support St Andrews University. Medical men – physicians, lithotomists,[9] barber-surgeons – had long been prominent members of Dundee's community before the establishment of its Dispensary in 1784 and Infirmary ten years later, and so the burgh provides an excellent case study of how medical care was provided beyond the medical schools. Chapter 5 focuses upon the 'informal, unofficial and "amateur"' methods of care and medical services in Dundee, on medical relationships, how the system worked, and the increasingly important role of women – particularly in the formal recognition of midwives.

From the beginning of the century, there had been a growing association between Dundee and cloth manufacture – one of its provosts George Yeaman (1706–08, 1710–12), acting as a leading advocate for the Scottish linen industry at Westminster.[10] Between c. 1750 and 1820, the fruits of this paid off. Dundee metamorphosed first to a textile port, and then into a manufactory; not such a manufactory as it was to become half a century later as 'Juteopolis', but a town with an increasing proportion of handloom weavers whilst at the same time fostering a major industry in spinning and osnaburg weaving in the broad hinterland with a particular focus around Forfar (much to the chagrin of the town's weaving craft).

Whereas Dundee's distinctiveness as a Renaissance port, with counterparts elsewhere in Europe, can readily be understood, Georgian Dundee, as Chapter 6 explains, was fairly unexceptional in terms of population growth, civic improvement, industrial change and social habits. Yet it remained *very* exceptional both in the continuing importance of its port and maritime quarter, and in the failure of its city fathers to construct a 'new town' like its peers. This may partly explain the well-travelled English visitor Henry Skrine's disappointment on entering Dundee towards the end of the eighteenth century. Notwithstanding the burgh's 'beautiful situation', its fine townscape viewed from afar, and even its elegant townhouse and assembly room, Skrine judged the town to be 'an irregular and unpleasant place', burdened with noxious smells and a too-numerous body of inhabitants who were 'unusually coarse both in manner and figures'.[11] Yet Dundee had early begun urban improvement – ensuring that its streets and buildings were improved and regularised – and its urban ambition was symbolised by the appointment of Samuel Bell as burgh architect in the 1770s. Bell's designs were copied as far away as Banff and Irvine, he was responsible for embellishing the ancient market place with classical civic buildings, and such was his success that on his death, his wealth at £4,000 (excluding his substantial property interests) indicated that he was as wealthy as some of the Baltic merchants.

It is notable, however, that the burgh's gracious new buildings were erected at the heart of the town rather than in the elite classical suburbs that represented the new civil society of the Enlightenment – although a handful of 'ornamental houses' were constructed beyond the burgh's boundaries. Dundee remained the only substantial Scots burgh not to construct a new town.[12] Showing little taste for the fashion of 'houses after the English manner', its inhabitants left Bell and David Neave's proposals for uniform terraced houses in Tay Street and Castle Street unbuilt for decades. Perhaps the culture of a working port differs from that of a county and university town with a harbour, like Aberdeen; and Dundee's shipmasters, who had become the largest identifiable group amongst the town's elite, were conservative in their tastes. Instead, the seadogs upgraded and modernised their city centre apartments with the most contemporary and lavish plasterwork and timberwork with Adam fireplaces, as the drawings of Charles Lawson, a Dundee printer and lithographer, carried out before the buildings were demolished, record; and they furnished them with sea chests, plain chairs and plentiful bottles and glasses. Unfortunately, visitors to Dundee would compare the tall, dense, curving and very narrow medieval closes of the maritime quarter unfavourably with the new, straight, wide, regular homogeneous streets of other towns; and then conclude that Dundee had not built a new town because it had neither the people nor patronage nor the wealth to build one – a conclusion drawn in the face of Dundee having a higher percentage of its population being of the professional class than Glasgow.[13]

Although Dundonians had simply not chosen to follow fashion, this absence of a new town allowed dramatic conclusions to be drawn. When in Dundee to hear a case of incest in 1818, Lord Cockburn referred to the burgh as a 'sink of iniquity which no moral flushing can cleanse'; and the epithet stuck. Cockburn might have been taking a sideswipe at Provost Alexander Riddoch's political jobbery since he had been retained to promote burgh reform by those opposing Riddoch, but there was no

Enlightenment new town to demonstrate that the burgh's character might have been rather different. So the evidence of Chapters 8 and 9 is salutary. By the standards of the 1780s, Dundee was, despite its reputation and the occasional hat-toppling on the king's Birthday, a sedate place. Before the outbreak of the war with France in 1793, it was a town of people supporting its growing cadre of bustling cloth merchants and manufacturers, and hard-pressed journeymen, all making money and supplying the international trade passing through the lifeline of the port. Indeed, an industrious working class household, in what was to be the last phase of prosperity for the hand-loom weavers and the like, could aspire to owning a cottage if not a small plot of ground for potato growing in the Scouringburn.

As Chapters 7 and 11 show, Dundee's trading patterns had changed. Dundee was much more heavily involved in the East Indies than has been appreciated, with private fortunes and income returning from Asia between the 1770s and 1810 forming the equivalent of 42% of Dundee's harbour dues over the same period. But the majority of Dundee's goods were being shipped by coastal vessels to London, where there was a Dundee wharf, before going overseas. Moreover, the burgh benefited from unusually powerful patronage in London, not least the protection of the remarkable George Dempster of Dunnichen, to the extent that it came to enjoy close links with the directors of the Honourable East India Company. Physicians from Dundee were to be found throughout the empire, and the percentage of the skippers of the huge East Indiamen was higher from Dundee than from Glasgow. The Renaissance pattern of operating through kinship, exemplified by David Wedderburn, can be shown operating 200 years later in the networking and activities of the Jobson family – ships' brokers, bankers, shipmasters, and even soldiers in the Honourable East India Company. It is now clear that Scots generally made disproportionate contributions in the East India Company's service in India,[14] and Angus benefited hugely on their return with their fortunes.

The involvement of Dundonians and Angus gentry in the western empire – particularly the West Indies – is equally striking. Until the American Revolution, there was a steady trade with Charleston – comprising largely bespoke cargoes commissioned by agents. Throughout the period, the port of Dundee remained an entrepot – importing wines, sugars (a seven-storeyed Sugar House was opened in

1765, its manager imported from London), citrus fruit (just as it had during the Renaissance) alongside cord, tar, timber, deer and buffalo skins and whale blubber – and exporting finished cloth to America and shoes to London. The 'roads' were normally thronged with shipping and the press gang had a permanent 'rendezvous' down in the harbour . . .

One might have expected that the combination of a port and traditionally radical weavers might well have combined to produce a political volatility sufficient to alarm the lieges. Chapter 8 reveals that, instead, although the town had its radicals and informers in the early 1790s, loyalism dominated thereafter. Indeed it is curious to observe just how tame, relatively-speaking, had been the riot over the Tree of Liberty, attended by possibly no more than a few hundred; and just how little impact such a notorious radical such as George Mealmaker – weaver in the Seagate, transported for sedition in 1798 – had upon the broad swathe of the populace in the burgh. For all that Dundee's revolutionary fervour was chimerical, however, fear of the mob was on the increase. Yet, as revealed in Chapter 9 and making due allowance for periodic food riots, Dundee's crime rate (or at least the number of those prosecuted) had been 30% below the regional average before 1793, and once the young men had gone to war it reduced even further. Dundee was the only major burgh in Scotland not to institute a salaried watch between 1800 and 1815, and there was a distinct reluctance by the authorities to prosecute. Once the war ended, however, with soldiers and sailors returning, and the town speedily expanding with steam-powered textile mills, robberies increased, and people began to feel much more alarmed than they used to be at traditional expressions of displeasure such as food riots. A watching scheme was finally introduced in 1816.

Growing social anxiety appears to be at odds with what Chapter 10 refers to as the 'rising tide of respectability' in the town. Although the merging of Dundee's elite with the regional gentry at the beginning of the century had ended – for Dundee was now a mercantile place and the gentry socialised elsewhere – Dundonian lifestyles were typical of elsewhere in Britain. Its dwellings may have been comparatively modest in scale (presumably the consequence of the continuing popularity of living in apartments), but Lawson's drawings show them to have been refitted and very well appointed. In these dwellings, they took tea, coffee and chocolate from china, as elsewhere, and introduced appropriately furnished reception rooms and that key signifier – the dining room. In public, Dundonians enjoyed regular concerts, theatre and assemblies, were members of clubs, used libraries and bookshops, and enjoyed gentle strolls along urban parades and tree-lined walks. In short, from that perspective, the life style in Dundee was typical of the generality of late eighteenth century Scotland – save that between high street and harbour lay a distinctive, dense, unmodernised maritime quarter.

The burgh's success depended upon the river Tay – the port's greatest asset and its biggest problem. Rivers could silt up and ships become larger (which had the same consequence), leaving formerly prosperous towns decaying. Bruges is a principal European example, although, in a lesser Scottish context, that was the fate of Renfrew and – increasingly – of Perth. Dundee was locked in a war of attrition with the Tay, which was constantly eroding its harbour walls and filling the basin with silt. The town's sea-side location made it vulnerable to the savage storm of 1668 and the great tidal surge of 1755. Furthermore, the steadily rising tonnage of vessels increased pressure on the harbour, particularly following the introduction of the larger whalers after 1750. There was a 350% increase in tonnage between 1777 and 1805. Although it sought the advice of the greatest engineers of their age – Smeaton, Stevenson, Telford – on how to maximise the opportunity and diminish the threat, the council failed to develop a suitable strategy for its harbour. Harbour dues were applied to other purposes, and the council then pled insufficient revenue to provide the investment that the Baltic traders and their shipmasters required. The ruling clique was focused upon the economic opportunities emerging from manufacturing, and had become detached from port and shipping operations. Their failure to appreciate that their inaction was holding back trade expansion was their undoing. Dundee might have become a manufactory, but it still needed a sufficient harbour. Adding occasional piers was adequate to cope neither with the rising demand nor with the larger vessels; and in 1815 Parliament removed the harbour from council control. The story of how Dundee boomed thereafter is taken up in *Victorian Dundee*.

In its trajectory from 1500 to 1820, Dundee had shown extraordinary resilience. Although it was, by European standards, a small[15] and relatively weak community, with neither external resources nor patronage to fall back upon, it had survived four military attacks, three sackings, numerous plagues, tempests and a tidal wave. By virtue of its natives' maritime skill and mercantile acumen, it developed, then lost and then regained an international role founded essentially on seafaring. Although it slipped from second to fourth rank amongst Scottish towns, it had ended the eighteenth century ready to evolve into the linen capital of Britain. *That*, not the myths, is the history of this hitherto invisible port.

NOTES

1 S. Gauldie, 'Introduction' to C. McKean and D. Walker, *Dundee: An Illustrated Introduction* (Edinburgh, 1984), pp. 1–3.
2 J. Macky, *A Journey through Scotland* (London, 1732), p. 101.
3 L. Miskell, B. Harris and C. A. Whatley (eds.), *Victorian Dundee: Image and Realities* (East Linton, 2000).
4 See, for example, A. M. Smith, *The Nine Trades of Dundee* (Dundee, 1995), pp. 123–135, 157–168.
5 Smith, *Nine Trades*, pp. 169–177.
6 A. M. Smith, *The Guildry of Dundee: A History of the Merchant Guild of Dundee up to the 19th Century* (Dundee, 2005), p. 3.
7 Dr Robert Small, *Statistical Account of the Parish and Town of Dundee* (Dundee, 1793), p. 71.
8 I am grateful to Innes Duffus for information from the Dundee Guildry Account Book.
9 Remover of kidney stones.
10 E. Cruikshanks, S, Handley and D. W. Hayton, *The History of Parliament. The House of Commons, 1690–1715, V, Members O–Z* (Cambridge, 2002), pp. 953–955.
11 H. Skrine, *Three Successive Tours in the North of England And a Great Part of Scotland* (London, 1795), p. 108.
12 See C. McKean, 'Not even the trivial grace of a straight line' in Miskell, Harris and Whatley, *Victorian Dundee*.
13 In 1841, 4.53% of Glasgow's population were professional, as compared to 4.98 of Dundee's. R. Roger, 'Employment, Wages and Poverty in the Scottish cities 1840–1914' in G. Gordon (ed.), *Perspectives of the Scottish City* (Aberdeen, 1985), p. 80.
14 T. M. Devine, *Scotland's Empire, 1600–1815* (London, 2004), pp. 250–270.
15 See D. Nicholas, *Urban Europe 1100–1700* (Basingstoke, 2003) pp. 19–20.

CHAPTER I

What Kind of Renaissance Town was Dundee?

Charles McKean

> *Devout Dundee doughty and doubtit aye*
> *And sure to fois a pleasure to thy prince*
> *Who nether from god nor king declined away*
> *For church and country sore soldiers in defence*
> *Thy policy puissance and providence*
> *Thy ships thy strengths. What poet can furth scan*
> *Thy situation of such magnificence*
> *By nature wrought is figured like a man*
> *I say no more. Look, Albion's Isle all through*
> *Is none like thee save London & Edinborough.*
>
> Alexander Wedderburn *c.* 1590[1]

In 1587, the sixteenth century chorographer and map maker Timothy Pont surveyed Dundee at the start of his project to map the entire realm of Scotland.[2] His depiction of the burgh, albeit rudimentary by virtue of its tiny scale, is revealing for its presentation of Dundee as a port. The harbour dominates the scene with its bulwarks and lighthouses, and an unusual number of ships (for Pont's maps) ride safely at their moorings in the 'roads' or safe haven of the Tay estuary. It was that safe haven and the port – 'thy ships thy strengths' as Wedderburn put it – that were the principal causes of Dundee's prosperity.

For over a century before Pont visited it, Dundee had been the second town of Scotland (judged by tax returns) – and was to remain so for most of the next one (see Chapter 3); and its fiscal status was reflected in its high standing – second only to Edinburgh – in the government of the realm (see Chapter 2). When the Mint had to leave Edinburgh for reasons of plague in 1585, it was to Dundee that it came, where it squatted north of the Overgait.[3] The burgh was relatively large – its population in 1639 estimated at *c.* 12,000[4] – and occupied physically a very similar urban footprint to Edinburgh, albeit with a population well under half. So, whereas only in Edinburgh and Dundee would you find the dense urban fabric of apartment blocks of six storeys or more as customary in Europe (as still is the case today), Dundee was very much better endowed with spacious gardens and open land. This chapter will attempt to assess the burgh's character, ambition and culture as revealed through its urban building and remodelling, and through the networks of the internationally trading merchants who paid for it. To do so provides the opportunity to question previous histories of the burgh which have tended to play down its significance.[5]

That Dundee could rise to be the second town of the realm was extraordinary in itself, for it lacked every single one of the necessary sources of patronage – royal, ecclesiastical, aristocratic or intellectual – that a Renaissance town normally required to be successful.[6] Whatever the myth of a royal lodging down Whitehall Close,[7] Dundee had no permanent royal dwelling. Regents and monarchs made regular and sometimes lengthy visits to the burgh, and after the burgh gave James V 'a costlie entry', he visited frequently. Monarchs probably lodged in a religious house or in a prominent town house such as the Earl of Crawford's great lodging. The port was also a principal source of regal wine and citrus fruits.[8] Although Dundee's steepled Greyfriars was probably the richest in Scotland,[9] the burgh enjoyed no major ecclesiastical patronage: no cathedral, no archbishop, and no great abbey. It was not even the county town, that being Forfar, nor the location of a Sheriff Court until 1641. Finally, there was no university. Instead, Dundee was proud to patronise nearby St Andrews University, contributing 300 merks to its library, and promising to gift duplicate copies of any books in its own Town Library.[10]

Whereas Dundee's success was extraordinary, therefore, given its lack of patronage, it still lacked the investment that kings, aristocracy, prelates and courts would have brought it by fostering high-culture goods such as goldsmithing, painting or tapestry. Although its handful of goldsmiths and gunsmiths enjoyed a very high reputation, they were few in number. The burgh's elite being successful merchants, international traders and ships' captains, Dundee most closely resembled the ports of the Hanse, with whom the burgh had some affinity. It was to the Senate and councillors of Lübeck, for example, that James V wrote seeking protection for James Kinloch and his fellow merchants when the latter proposed to trade with Danish harbours in May 1532.[11] However, if its nearest counterparts were Lübeck, Hamburg or Rostock, it has to be acknowledged that Dundee was much smaller. It had neither the great Exchange nor Bourse that characterised the successful mercantile towns and ports of northern European towns – and none of the Wool Halls nor Meat Markets of the Low Countries.

THE BURGH

It sometimes requires an enemy to persuade a Dundonian of his burgh's value. On his seizure of the burgh in 1547, Sir Andrew Dudley wrote to Protector Somerset praising its fruitful gardens and clear wells but, above all, its harbour: 'It is one of the goodliest rivers that ever I saw, and the ships may ride here as they would in the Thames, and better; and is one of the plentifulest rivers of fish as ever I saw, both salmon, porpus, seal, herring and other kinds of fish. . . '[12] That was, of course, whilst he was still intending to occupy the town, and before he had his troops burn it. His judgement was shared by his enemy, the French soldier, Jean de Beaugé, who wrote that Dundee was 'one of the most beautiful and most populous towns of the country'.[13] Protected by hills from the north and west, the burgh was set on the sunny south-facing slopes facing the wide bowl of the Tay estuary upstream from the river's constricted mouth at Broughty castle. To its north, sheltered below the slopes of Dundee Law, lay the town's common meadow and recreation ground where the butts were set up,[14] known for its clear rills and wells, and crossed by the town's principal watergang – the Scouringburn (known also as the Castle Burn or Mause Burn). The burgh's Playfield (equivalent to Edinburgh's Greenside) lay just outside the Overgate Port to the north-west,[15] (its southern brow, now Hawkhill, earned its later name of the Witches Knowe after the Regent Earl of Moray had some witches burned there in 1568–69).[16] The use of Magdalen Green as a further recreational area for Dundonians on the Tay shore upstream was vindicated as of right and custom in 1582.[17]

Dundee's hinterland was stuffed with country properties and villas (see p. 23) interspersed with the occasional great house, the nearest of which was Dudhope, on the town's edge, seat of the Scrymgeours, hereditary keepers of the long-vanished castle of Dundee. To Dudhope's east, straddling the King's Highway to Forfar uphill beyond the town boundary, was the suburb of the Hilltown (known as Bonnet Hill, Bonnet Row and eventually Rotten Row). A typical urban *alsatia* growing beyond the control of the burgh's craft organisations, the Hilltown was home to 'unfree' tailors, bonnetmakers and weavers,[18] whose poorer quality products threatened to undercut goods produced within the burgh. Curiously, long before it was erected into a separate burgh of barony by the Scrymgeours of Dudhope in 1643, the Hilltown had its own tolbooth.[19] East of the burgh lay the Sklaitheughs, the primary source of not just civic slate, but also of the slates exported to Edinburgh's St Giles Kirk and the royal palaces; and slates were still being shipped daily to Fife and Lothian a century later.[20] Here also, at Seikmens' Yairds, was the Leper House, and the 'lodges for sick folks in time of pest' to which those suspected of having plague were exiled (see Chapter 5), the plague burial ground (in what is now called The Roodyards, also known as the 'Rood'), and, appropriately, the burgh's lime pots.[21]

Dundee's fringes were largely encompassed by the lands of the town's religious houses, which were to become the property of the town in 1564.[22] As normal in Scotland, they lay on the edge of the burgh boundary or just outside it: the lands of the Dominicans or Blackfriars just west of the town boundary between the Overgate and Nethergate ports;[23] the Maison Dieu, or Hospital of the Holy Trinity, founded for the old and sick, which became the town's hospital, on the west shores of the town by Monksholm; the extensive lands of the wealthy ashlar-built Greyfriars on the north side of the town engrossed into what became known as the queen's *donationem,* to the burgh in 1567,[24] and the lands of the Sisters of St Clare (the Gray Sisters) immediately to the north-west of the Overgate. Most of these lands remained under cultivation, and the Grey Sisters' acres, as well as providing the burgh playfield, became well established market gardens. For the most part, the council devoted the income therefrom to the town's hospital, school and ministers.

As normal for a Scottish burgh, Dundee was not fortified and, despite frantic attempts by the English in 1548 (see p. 16), remained largely defenceless until the troubles of the seventeenth century. Its outer ports (or gates) were heraldic structures that represented the status of the place, acting as control points for the collection of Customs and repelling undesirables – particularly in times of plague. It also had four inner, timber gates called 'barras ports'. Whereas most European cities developed centrifugally from the necessity of being encircled by protective walls, Dundee evolved in a long, linear and largely indefensible manner. Its preparation for war was restricted to a small emplacement down on St Nicholas Craig on the Shore, another on the top of Corbie Hill, and the later conversion of the Shore windmill to the burgh arsenal.[25] Weapons were otherwise stored handily in St Mary's tower or the tolbooth cellars.

Dundee's mother church was, although Scottish historians have been prone to overlook it,[26] Scotland's largest and most magnificent parish church. Dedicated to the Blessed Virgin Mary, it was 250 feet long, 174 feet wide with transepts: the tallest steeple rose to over 147 feet, and it had forty eight altars and chaplainries dating mostly from the fifteenth century. The steeple was originally capped by the stone imperial crown that symbolised the independence of Scottish monarchs; similar to those on the other principal parish churches of James IV's reign – Linlithgow, Edinburgh and Haddington and upon King's College, Aberdeen.[27] Ready for its bells in 1495, the clock was supplied by the Edinburgh royal 'knock' (clock) maker, William Purves.[28] Craft chapels included St Severus, erected by the weavers in 1492, St Cuthbert's (notable for its gorgeous furnishings of silks, gilt silver and chandeliers) by the baxters (bakers) in 1486, St Duthac's by the skinners in 1516, and St Mark's erected by the waulkers (fullers) in 1525. The two most elaborately furnished were the 1454 St Katherine's chapel, and the Guildry's own chapel of the Holy Blood founded in 1515.[29] St Mary's reflected the success and wealth of the town's merchants and crafts.

THE STRUCTURE OF THE BURGH

Dundee's town plan, like those of Baltic ports, had evolved both to maximise the use of the wind for shipping down by the harbour, and to control its force in the 'outdoor rooms' or civic meeting places of the burgh up on the plateau. Shelter was a primary consideration.[30] Consequently, closes, vennels and wynds rising between shore and plateau, off which opened even more sheltered courtyards, were curved to moderate the blast, as in Lübeck. On the plateau, the burgh took the simple form of four principal streets meeting at the market place in the middle; and this readily lent itself to Francesco di Giorgio's Renaissance concept of a town in the form of a man – exactly as notary and town clerk Alexander Wedderburn applied to Dundee and sketched onto the flyleaf of his protocol book.[31] He placed St Mary's at the head of his Dundonian humanoid, and the slaughterhouse at its loins. Its outstretched arms were the Argylisgait (now Overgate) pointing north-west to Coupar Angus, and the Fleukergate (now Nethergate) pointing along the edge of the raised beach, past the town's almshouse to Magdalen Green (this was before some pedestrian bureaucrat renamed them the Overgate and Nethergate respectively – the quotidian equiv-alent of Upper Street and Lower Street). Its legs were the Seagait running north-east along the shore to the East Port and Arbroath, and the Murraygate running north to the Wellgate where it became double-jointed, surging uphill north into the Hilltown and Forfar, or bifurcating eastwards through the Cowgate to the pasture lands of Stobsmuir and Craigie. The humanoid metaphor made it very simple to navigate round the burgh; and it must still have remained current a century later, when the Rev. Robert Edward, father of the notable architect the Rev. Alexander Edward, used it to explain Dundee's form in his description of the county of Angus in 1678.[32]

By the late sixteenth century, a principal street of 'narrows' and 'broads' like those in Lübeck and Copenhagen was evolving in Dundee. It curved from the Nethergate port into the 'Broad' of the Nethergate then back into the 8-foot wide 'Narrows' of Our Lady's Gait, out into the Broad of the Hie Gait (market place) then squeezed through the 'Narrows' of the Murraygait into its 'Broad', narrowing again for the Murraygait Port before broadening again into the Wellgait and then uphill into the broad wide sweep of the Hilltown. The Market Place at the centre was protected from wind surging down its four principal streets by those 'narrows' – Our Lady's Gait only 8 feet wide, the Overgait and Murraygait 'narrows' at 12 feet wide, and the Seagait's only 6.

Dundee's market place (or Hie Gait), with the meal market, market cross, tron and tolbooth, had always been the centre of the burgh, and at 100 feet wide, was the same width as Edinburgh's High Street, if less extended. (The legend locating the first tolbooth low in Seagate at the foot of Horse Wynd was the result of a misreading of the text of Robert

I's original charter of 1325.[33]) The tolbooth had been built on the west side of the market place, rather like that of St Andrews; but its presumably free-standing site had later been encroached on by the large mass of building called the luckenbooths (locked-up booths) as in Edinburgh. Over time, the tolbooth had become so hemmed in that when it needed more space, it could expand only by renting the neighbouring plot called Our Lady Warkstairs, and became peripheral to the market place. On the south-east side of the market place lay the Castle Hill, the town's two mills powered by the Castle Burn, and the adjoining malthouse and burgh bakehouse.[34] Farther west, wynds and closes curved down to the Shore, on which slopes Dundee's maritime district would evolve. It was in this area – on the axis between High Street and harbour – that the burgh was to locate its principal Renaissance civic buildings.

Whatever else a port town had to do, it must safeguard its harbour without which its economy would die. The condition of Dundee's harbour was of perpetual concern to the council since the river Tay, with the largest outflow of any river in the British Isles, not only perpetually threatened the stability of its bulwarks (breakwaters), but also filled the harbour with silt and blocked its entrance. Under pressure from the merchant venturers – who would regularly petition that 'the hewen Shore and bulwark of this Brugh are greatly decayed, ruined, and Able to perish in a short Tyme' as they did in 1567, the council had find the money.[35] Yet another luckless councillor would be appointed the Collector of yet more Shore Silver.[36] Maintaining a working harbour was a ceaseless struggle that was addressed properly only in the 1770s (see Chapter 11) and was finally solved only with the construction of wet docks in the early nineteenth century.

Yet for all that, the harbour was extremely busy – 'throng with ships and boats and much resorted to by divers countries', as Sir Andrew Dudley reported to Protector Somerset after the English fleet had arrived in 1547.[37] In addition to its normal trade (see Chapter 3), the port also imported building materials – particularly timber, iron and lead – from the Baltic. The building accounts of James V's palace construction programme of the 1530s record the import through Dundee of enormous quantities of joists and wainscoting for Linlithgow, joists, deals and oak for Holyrood, and oak for Falkland – which they loaded onto rafts and floated over to Lindores for onward shipment over land.[38]

Booming trade brought a flurry of regulations to keep the quays clear – enforced with added vigour whenever the harbour was crowded.[39] All foreign ships arriving 'after the noon' had to 'present their Entres' to the Burgh Court the following morning at eight, and nobody was allowed to trade with the incomer until that had taken place.[40] Nor could any ship take on cargo without the Dean of Guild being present.[41] Vessels were forbidden from blocking the passage of others, and from mooring too close to each other; and, as soon as they were unladen, they had to quit the harbour for their moorings in the roads. Damaging a pier was met with exemplary punishment.[42] Timber left lying on the Shore for more than eight days attracted a fine imposed by the Shore Officer.[43] By 1591, smuggling worried the council sufficiently to appoint William Clayhills as Searcher for Contraband.[44]

Increasing trade inexorably led to harbour improvements and the requirement for a larger harbour than the original haven. The shoreline originally ran along the foot of the raised beach, bounded on the west by the Shore windmill and on the east by Castle Wynd, and was built up as Fish Street. Since it was single-sided facing the sea, Fish Street attracted investment by the leading men of the town – Wedderburns, Rollocks, Lovells, Clayhills, Alisons, Yeamans, Gardynes, Foresters, Kinlochs – who either lived or had property there.[45] However, to tie in with the new harbour, a New Shore was constructed in the mid sixteenth century. Constructed of monastic ashlar stonework,[46] it ran between the circular fortalice of St Nicholas Craig and the chapel of the same name (both constructed by the Earl of Crawford, whose great lodging looked out toward them) and where the coal boats unloaded on the east.[47] This was the first step in Dundee's serial reclamation of its foreshore.

The New Shore's buildings eventually contained some of the finest shipmasters' apartments in the port. However, they were entirely outshone by the structure at its east end straddling the New Shore and Fish Street. One of the most elaborate public buildings of Renaissance Dundee, this fanciful structure was constructed by bailie John Pierson, council treasurer and Shoremaster, after whom it was named. Although Pierson enjoyed a fine apartment within, this edifice was not a house. With its circular stairs on each corner, its ground floor ornamented by elaborate arcading similar to that lining the Howff graveyard (see p. 18) this was a storehouse with an apartment above on the Hanseatic model. Its function was revealed by its multiple staircases and a thick cross wall that rose through its centre to the roof. Rarely were such buildings expressed in such a flamboyantly French-influenced architecture, or so vividly decorated.[48]

INVASION, RECONSTRUCTION AND REFORMATION

In 1587, much of Dundee's fabric was relatively new, for the burgh had suffered badly in the late 1540s. When Protector Somerset invaded Scotland in his pursuit of a marriage between Edward VI and the infant Mary Queen of Scots, an English fleet and army invested Scotland's second town in 1547, in the belief that Dundee and its hinterland were primed to rise in support of the Reformation, as the burning of the Blackfriars and Greyfriars four years earlier had implied.[49] The treason of Patrick, Lord Gray, in surrendering the Castle of Broughty to the English without a fight, apparently 'seduced to the faith and opinion of England' by Alexander Whitelaw, seemed to confirm it.[50]

So, on 27 October 1547, Dundee's leaders agreed with Sir Andrew Dudley, styled 'knight and captain of the Castle of Broughty Crag for the King's majesty Edward VI',[51] to be true and faithful to the English king, to supply any necessaries or merchandise at normal rates, to lock up its artillery, and – or so it implies – adopt the Reform. When the English occupied the town two months later, they were received 'very well' (Dundee's elite were all later cleared of accusations of treason, some dubiously). Finding the town indefensible, Dudley reported to England 'we are fortifying Dundee as fast as we can' focusing particularly on the 'divers places meet for forts' – namely the Castle Hill, Corbie Hill and the hill behind St Salvador's Close north of the Hie Gait.[52] The Scots army under the Earl of Argyll approached Dundee too quickly, so the English, the forts incomplete and thinking Dundee too insecure, retreated to the Broughty promontory. Finding Broughty Castle too small, they then constructed a 'a very fine fortress and spared no cost to make it admirable' (according to Jean de Beaugé)[53] on the only high ground nearby at Brackenrig (now Fort Hill) which gave them, thought de Beaugé, 'an early entry into Scotland'.[54] The fort of Brackenrigg was designed by Sir Thomas Palmer, expressly dispatched from England for that purpose.[55]

When the Scots moved against them again in late 1548, the English relinquished the idea of occupying the burgh any further, retreated back to Brackenrig on 9 November, rifled the town, and then set it on fire. It burned for eight days.[56] Broughty was finally surrendered by its captain Sir John Luttrell on 7 March 1549/50,[57] and the English returned home following the Treaty of Boulogne in 1550. The French duly occupied the fort on the ridge behind St Salvator's Close, the castle of Broughty now being in ruins.[58]

To judge from claims before the Burgh Court, damage to the burgh was widespread: its windmills and many tenements facing the principal streets, 'the whole remnant of the burgh, or the most part of it' was burned.[59] Although the flammable parts – the timber galleries, roof structures and thatched roofs of most of the town's buildings – had largely gone, their stone substructures probably remained largely intact. One gauge of the damage is that rebuilding caused such a demand for slates, that export of slates to Leith and Edinburgh for work on St Giles Kirk was expressly forbidden in 1555 and 1556.[60] The emphasis given to rebuilding may have come from Robert Mylne, recently provost, descended from, and ancestor of, a line of royal master masons, and the Shore windmill was rebuilt immediately.[61]

The principal icons of the town – St Mary's church and the tolbooth – lay in ruins. St Mary's was re-roofed, beginning with its choir in 1552; and judging from the gratitude shown that year to John Scrymgeour of the Myres, the Royal Master of Works, the distinctively modern, unGothic design of the choir with its rectangular windows might be attributed to him.[62] Timbers were obtained from Rostock, and the work was carried out by Pattone Black, wright, with his sons Andrew and George.[63] The dressings and fittings of its altars, carefully hidden from the English, were now retrieved and reinstalled in the chapels. St Mary's steeple, however, had been badly damaged, destroying both William Purves's clock and the imperial crown spire.[64] A new 'orloge for the steeple' was obtained from David Kay, but the crown was lost for good – although its footings can still be seen in the clock chamber.[65]

The tolbooth was irrecoverable, and its neighbouring tenement, Lady Warkstairs, was so severely burnt that almost total rebuilding was required.[66] The council, contemplating its longer term urban strategy, delayed rebuilding the tolbooth, and occupied a less damaged building on the corner of the market place as a temporary tolbooth – to the distress of the family that owned the Warkstairs site and were thus deprived of their former income.[67]

The rebuilding of the burgh was well under way when the Reformation burst upon the country. 'So remarkable were the people of this place for their adherence to true religion', wrote the enthusiastic Robert Edward 'that at the Reformation it was honoured with the appellation of a second Geneva'.[68] The reputation that 'the people of Dundee were foremost in zeal and activity' probably resulted as much from the independent cast of mind of its merchants, as from religious zeal. During James V's persecution of heresy in 1539–40, the timber merchant James Wedderburn composed 'in forme of tragedie the beheading of Johne the Baptist which was acted at the West Port of Dundee [presumably on the town's Playfield] wherein he carped roughlie the abuses and corruptiouns of the Papists'.[69] This was underscored by an attack upon the Greyfriars in August 1543,[70] followed by the burning of the Dominican or Blackfriars convent the following year. The mob had been led by a group of merchants and craftsmen – including coopers, weavers and waulkers (whom Mary of Guise was still respiting ten years later) – and given that their caution was set as high as £40–50, and that many of those accused stood caution for each other (and the Earl of Crawford himself had stood caution for a number), these were people of some substance.[71]

The strict control over behaviour that we normally associate with the Reformation was early introduced into Dundee, with the establishment of a swear box in 1559,[72] and the conversion of the roof space above the vault of St Andrew's Aisle, in the east end of St Mary's, into a prison for fornicators and adulterers.[73] Conversely, that the town did not entirely follow the 'killjoy' pattern sometimes presumed for the post-reformation period is illustrated by the continuing support and fostering of its Song or Music School.[74]

Save the Trinitarian almshouse, all Dundee's religious houses were in ruins by 1560, and they were swiftly put to use. Stones from the Greyfriars built the new fleshhouse, the new tolbooth and the New Shore, whereas those of the Blackfriars were used to canalise the Castle Burn through the Meadows.[75] Through Queen Mary's *donationem*, the burgh acquired, in addition to the buildings themselves, the open country that became the Meadows, the Ward Lands and the Kirklands. Following best European practice to remove potentially disease-ridden graveyards to the town's edge – 'within Ye realm of France and other foreign parts there is no dead buryit within the burrows and great towns, but have their bureall-places and sepultres outwit Ye same' – the town formed a new graveyard on the garden or orchard of the Greyfriars (trees had to be cleared from the site first) to relieve pressure on the land around St Mary's.[76] The new graveyard, later known as the Howff or meeting place, was enclosed with 'sufficient dykes' in 1601.[77] Its south wall was formed from the town's own back dykes, and the remainder were designed with curiously elaborate arcading similar to that in Provost Pierson's storehouse down on the New Shore. Similar arcades on churchyard walls framing wall-mounted tombstones can be seen in St Peter's kirkyard in Copenhagen – albeit Dundee's were far more ornate. The Howff became the principal sepulchre for the merchant elite and their kin; and its collection of seventeenth century gravestones (despite too many being carved from the only too soluble Dundee sandstone) is equalled in Scotland only by Edinburgh's Greyfriars.

The council's determination to rebuild the burgh for 'honour and decoring the policy of the town' led to a programme of self-conscious modernisation and civic aggrandisement that lasted the following twenty years. In 1560, it put three major civic buildings in hand, the largest being Dundee's civic castle – a new tolbooth on a new site facing the centre of the market place. The site was land once owned by the chapel of St Clement, patron saint of sailors; but the chapel had ceased to function in the 1520s,[78] when work had begun on foundations for a new tolbooth along the northern edge of its churchyard. Construction had been stalled for almost forty years.[79] The rest of St Clement's graveyard, occupying the slope between the south side of the market place and the Shore, was generically known as the Vault by virtue of the stone archway which led between it and the Shore. In 1560, the wright George Black was appointed to construct a new tolbooth upon these foundations using ashlar recycled from the Greyfriars, and the roof which Patrick Walker had dismantled from Lindores Abbey.[80] It was 140 feet long, and its height of 40 feet from its foot to its battlemented parapet implies that there were three storeys above its ground-floor arcades.[81]

Typically, the principal floor would have contained town clerks, the burgh court (which met almost daily), a collector's room, and the Council House, where the council met every Thursday before noon.[82] The Guildry and a great civic chamber for ceremonial purposes (in Glasgow called the King's Room, and in Edinburgh the Parliament Hall) would probably have been on the floor above, with what appears to have been a prison in the attic.[83] The tolbooth had a central clock tower, and its principal staircase projected into the street. Windows – and probably the armorials and crenellations – were vividly painted by David Scott.[84] Probably complete in time to welcome Queen Mary in 1561, it was the largest tolbooth in Scotland, and would remain so until Glasgow's behemoth tolbooth was completed in 1626.[85] When major repairs were needed thirty years later, the mason Alexander Young added a tall, two-storeyed well-windowed ashlar steeple – with string courses, and encrusted with finials – to the roof at its north-west corner.[86]

That same year, the council also appointed Black to move the burgh fleshhouse from the Vault and rebuild it on the paved area to the west of the Castle Burn, in place of the scald (or skin) market.[87] Completed with ashlar from the Greyfriars in 1565, this distinguished structure contained twelve booths within its walls, eight with lofts, a shop and various seats – not unlike Edinburgh's.[88] That same year, 1560, George Lovell began the construction of a new weighhouse in the Vault facing the main route from market place to the harbour. A joint stock venture rather than a council expenditure,[89] this significant civic building cannibalised some of the fabric of the abandoned St Clement's chapel.[90] Given that it was the council that obtained lead weights from Flanders when required, and the Guildry that had responsibility for ensuring proper weights, it is curious that the public weighhouse was privately financed.

The council's new regulations for maintaining the town in good order would have put Edinburgh to shame. It not only agreed to pave the Cowgate from the Murraygate eastwards to Our Lady's Wynd (Sugarhouse Wynd),[91] but first instructed the removal of middens from both the West Port and the Burial Wynd, and swine from all the town's closes and wynds,[92] and then decided to ban all middens from the town. To enforce this, the Town's Executioner made daily midden patrols since he had so little else to do.[93] The Castle Burn was to be kept clean and unpolluted, and anyone tossing filth onto the streets was henceforth condemned to the branks.[94]

In 1582, the king's master mason John Mylne rebuilt the town's Mercat Cross along the line of those in Edinburgh and Glasgow – namely a hexagonal plinth with a stair inside leading up to a proclaiming platform, signing it I.M.M. It is curious that his hand was not more discernible in the other civic buildings. He might well have been the designer, but the only names that have come down to us are those of the masons. When the council finally turned its attention to building a new

Grammar School, it concluded that the 'most commodious place upon which to build a Common School [was the] void place at the back of the Weighhouse' – in other words, a still vacant portion of the Vault. John Barss, appointed as Master of Work and instructed to proceed 'with all godly diligence' on 29 April 1589,[95] finished the school later that year. It was a significant investment by the burgh, for the council provided three doctors (teachers) to look after the pupils. The Master also took in the children of gentlemen who were not resident in town (at a cost over three times more than a resident child).[96] The school's standing is implied by the appointment of the distinguished Andrew Duncan as Master, for the Latin-to-Scots glossary which he published in 1595 as an appendix to a Latin Grammar is taken to herald the beginning of Scots lexicography.[97]

The burgh's new civic buildings provided Dundee with an urban axis that provided a much more imposing entrance than landing at the former Haven and negotiating the steep, narrow and squint Tyndall's Wynd up to the market place. Now, on arriving at the New Shore, visitors and ships' captains would first walk up a broad, outdoor 'merchants' exchange' (later referred to as the 'lime-tree walk'), past the Pierson storehouse on the west, then through the archway in Castle Wynd known as the Vault, where they would encounter first the new Weighhouse, then Grammar School, followed by the Tolbooth, and then – once in the High Market Gait – the Fleshhouse. The burgh's self-esteem also extended to a tennis court (catchpull) in the Overgait[98], which may – from the absence of any other territorial designation – have been a civic one; the appointment of two Serjeants to parade continually with their halberds through the Market Place;[99] and the clothing of the Town's Piper 'in the town's livery and colours' for him to pass and play every day at 4 a.m. and 8 a.m.[100] In the 1580s, the town also rebuilt its inner and outer ports.

The burgh's dwellings varied in size according to quality and location. Streets were lined by the tall blocks of apartments which could rise to six storeys or more, and most properties facing the principal thoroughfares had both ground floor booths and lower cellars or booths (as still, in, for example, Copenhagen or Amsterdam), the lower ones presenting a danger to pedestrians if not covered over at night. A lesser merchant might occupy the typical apartment of 'hall, cellar and chamber' entered from a common stair, but some were very much larger and more elaborate, and galleries were common.[101] There had been much encroachment into burgh streets by the building of 'toofalls' or lean-tos in front of the main blocks; and when these were rebuilt with timber superstructures, they jetteyed some 6 feet out from their stone tenements, carried upon columns. So when Our Lady Warkstairs was rebuilt after the English invasion, 7-feet tall stone columns 'in the form of a piazza'[102] carried the floors above – as became typical of the wider streets of major Scots towns. In the Broad of the Murraygait, arcades 6 feet deep were sufficiently continuous to afford 'a dry walk in wet weather'.[103] Rather than insisting on standard dimensions for the arcades like Edinburgh in the 1610s or Glasgow in the 1650s, Dundee was more relaxed.

Houses of particular distinction, as was common elsewhere in Scotland and in northern Europe, were set at the backs of closes where there was more space and air. Dundee was host to the town houses of the regional landowners, of which the Earl of Crawford's Great Lodging, between Nethergate and the Shore, was probably the largest (the earls having their ancestral burying plot in Dundee's Greyfriars[104]); the Abbot of Scone's lodging immediately west, with those of the lairds of Fordell, Banff, Lundie, and Strathmartine nearby; the laird of Murthly settled in the Seagate, and Claverhouse in the Murraygate.[105]

THE BURGH ELITE

In the absence of an aristocratic or religious elite, the concept of the burgh as a community of families provides a useful way of considering how Renaissance Dundee worked.[106] Comparable to the 400 of Venice or the nine of San Sebastian, whose power lasted over generations, Dundee's elite were the 'merchant venturers', a title ascribed to those who had the liberty to trade where they pleased.[107] It is too simplistic to presume that the elite would be restricted to 91 burgesses as suggested for 1580, for that simply recorded those who attended an unusually large meeting of the Guildry.[108] Moreover, it is not at all clear if the professional and shipping interests were adequately represented within them, and a number were likely to have been absent abroad. It seems likely, however, from their prominence in the records, that Dundee's elite included the prominent families of Yeaman, Mudie, Kyd, Traill, Clayhills, Forester, Guthrie, Fotheringham, Wedderburn, Rollock, Sturrock, Lovell, Strachan, Ramsay, Man, Scrymseour, (or Scrymgeour), Fleschour (or Fletcher), Myln(e), Gourlay, Halyburton and Goldman amongst them. The Goldmans, who emerged suddenly in Dundee in 1562 to become senior craftsmen, then burgesses and later landowners of Sandford (Fife),[109] have particular interest since their name is neither Dundonian nor Scots. They may either have represented a Jewish community so far invisible in Renaissance Scotland, or they could have arrived in Scotland from Silesia through Gdansk, whence derived Goldmans found in other countries. Whatever their origins, they were entirely assimilated into Dundee society by the end of the sixteenth century, Robert Goldman becoming Collector for the Crafts in 1604,[110] and William Dean of Guild some time before 1612, when he was sent to represent Scotland in reinstating the Staple at Veere.

Maintaining the standing of burgesses was a constant burgh preoc-cupation, for if inadmissible people pretended to that dignity, the burgess rank would be tarnished. Burgesses were required to possess a residence within the town boundary,[111] and were admitted to burgess-ship by acclaim and the payment of an entry fee. Acclaim was based upon paternity and character: 'no persons be received burgess, freemen and brother of Guild of this burgh without their honest conversation and manners be utterly known'.[112] Indeed, during the seventeenth century, personal qualities gradually came to take on higher importance than paternity in the right to burgess-ship. Dundee's insistence on 'honest conversation and manners', however, says something striking about the nature of the port.

Lamenting the 'daily decay of the common weal of the merchants' in 1577,[113] the council grieved that burgesses were damaging their rank through both inappropriate behaviour or dress, and through declining brotherliness in their persistent failure to attend guild meetings or funerals of brethren.[114] Four years later, the Burgh Court prohibited any freeman from standing 'to lay forth or sell their gear or merchandise in the High Gate' – since dignity required they could do so only at their own doors or booths. Moreover, no 'honest Merchant man's wife within this burgh, neither in kirk, market, nor on the High Gate' was permitted to wear plaid (common homespun).[115] Whatever a burgess could be, he could not descend to being a huckster – as witness this 1590 Guildry threat to confiscate the goods of any 'persons of their number as trade with eggs, kail, onions, apples, pears and others the like huckstery form of trade to the great dishonour of their estate', with repeat offences being met with the removal of status.[116] The Guildry then insisted that every burgess should dress as well as possible when in public, and never act in a way that might lessen their status. Only whores were permitted to dress above their rank.[117]

The council and the Guildry were preoccupied with mercantile rank whereas, to judge from the fact that the matter had to be returned to so frequently, the free-spirited Dundonians remained quite casual about it. Typically for a royal burgh, the Guild brethren met as the Guildry, and the Dean of Guild's court was responsible for the physical condition of the town's public and private buildings. Anxiety about its status is evident from the 1592 decision to meet more frequently, to toll the council bell to summon the brethren, and to fine those absent.[118] The following year, it increased the fee for admittance to burgessship to £40, and restated the requisite qualifications namely: honesty, conversation and good manners – to which it had now added religion.[119] Perhaps this sensitivity can be explained by a growing appreciation that its status was now under threat by the council.

Until 1590, the Guildry officers had been elected by the entire merchant burgesses. However, with what Alexander Warden dismissed as great supineness,[120] the Guildry agreed that year to elect their officers exactly a week *after* the council elections (one can just hear the arguments suggesting efficiency), so that Guildry officers could be elected by a combination of all burgesses *and* the council (theoretically the same since all council members had to be burgesses). Before long, the Guildry and its operations became wholly 'owned' by the council, and the plebiscite became restricted to members of the council alone, thus reducing the Guildry to a cipher. A century later, perhaps in a vain attempt to recover some initiative and independence, the Guildry sought to diversify by developing a new port on the Tay's south shore to escape the difficulties of Dundee's harbour on the north, rather in the same way that the Glasgow merchants developed Port Glasgow. It bought the lands of Inverdovat for a new port on Tay,[121] but the venture was not successful. The Guildry remained largely quiescent thereafter until the harbour wars of 1814 provided it with the opportunity of a *Risorgimento* (see Chapter 11).

Two other groups had a profound influence upon the town. The first was the shipping interest – mariners, ships' captains and the like – many of whom were also burgesses. It is difficult to establish just how great a part they played in the town's life. The contribution that they made can be inferred from the fact that when assessing for the Ministers' stipend in 1588, the entire Crafts under the Deaconry were assessed for 40 merks whereas the mariners were assessed for £20.[122] Most of the latter lived down toward the Shore in Fish Street, the New Shore, and Seagate; and one may infer from gravestones in the Howff that there was probably a tendency for them to intermarry. A perpetual stream of foreign visitors came to Dundee – Nicolas Christe, skipper from Dieppe, Martyn Boed from Copenhagen, Pierre Mallon, Clement Lies, Jacob Emden, Lodovic Gardene, William Le Low and Thomas Albertson[123] – and they would probably have lodged either with fellow mariners or the merchants with whom they were trading. Some foreigners came to stay. A group of Flemish workers arrived from Leiden in 1601,[124] and Abraham Martine, French barber-surgeon, son of a burgess of Metz, married an Auchinleck, and his success is underscored by his burial in the Howff.[125]

The other group, numerically the largest, were the members of the Nine Trades[126] – in order of precedence the bakers (baxters), shoemakers (cordiners), glovers (skinners), tailors, bonnetmakers, fleshers, hammermen, weavers (brabeners or websters) and waulkers.[127] Unlike Edinburgh, Dundee did not have individual craft associations of hatmakers, candlemakers, surgeons and barbers, coopers, wrights or masons, although litsters, maltmen, and coopers came to be grouped amongst Dundee's 'Pendicle Trades'. Masons, wrights and slaters were formed into the Three United Trades only in 1641. A guild governed entry into the craft, and conferred privileges upon the successful; and when feeling under threat from the merchants, the Trades occasionally acted collectively, appointing a Collector to speak for them.

Widows were sometimes permitted to carry on their late husbands' businesses, such as carrying on a shop, or continuing to hold shares in a ship, but usually at a cost. The Dundee provost, bailies and deacons only permitted Merron Forester, widow of David Cockburn, to continue her husband's business as the burgh's principal roofing contractor – buying, selling and transporting slates to and from Dundee – on condition that she reroofed and slated the tolbooth free of charge.[128]

Different districts of European Renaissance towns were customarily occupied by distinct crafts or guilds,[129] but Dundee's records are very unspecific about this. Although bonnetmakers and perhaps other textile trades occupied the Hilltown just beyond the control of the magistrates, they were certainly not the burgh's own bonnetmakers. Maltmen congregated near the West Port and the Scouringburn, as did the tanners and cordiners (shoemakers) who became particularly associated with the Wooden Land in the Overgate.[130] Waulkers or dyers appear to have congregated near the Murraygate, probably attracted by the wells and the burns running through the Meadows.[131] The bucklemakers – and thereby possibly armourers and gunsmiths – occupied the Wellgate rather as Edinburgh's hammermen occupied the Upper Bow. Dundee was the foremost gunmaking centre of Scotland, and the first town to use the term 'gunsmith'. In 1587, there were seven gunsmiths in Dundee – pre-eminent amongst them the families of Ramsay and Alison – and twenty-three other hammermen including five sword slippers (sharpeners), and guardmakers, lorimers and goldsmiths. Dundee guns were highly fashionable noble accessories: David Wedderburn exported them to Spain,[132] and in the inventory of Sir Duncan Campbell of Glenorchy's seat of Balloch there was 'ane long piece with snapwork that came out of Dundee'.[133] The mason's craft congregated at Our Lady Lodge at the west end of Our Lady's Gait[134] (as the Narrows of the Nethergate were origi-nally called). The wrights appeared to have congregated in Key's Close,[135] and Candlemaker Wynd almost certainly records the location of that occupation.

The number of smaller properties rather than great estates in Timothy Pont's map of Dundee's hinterland is striking, partly the conse-quence of the break-up of the ecclesiastical estates after the Reformation, and partly due to the decline of the once dominant Gray family. In the early seventeenth century, the merchant elite began to purchase properties as villas to which they could retreat, as was typical throughout Europe.[136] The seventeenth-century drawing of Wallace Craigie (see Plate section 1) indicates the nature of these houses: horizontal in proportion and lacking all faux-military rhetoric. Adorned solely by token pepperpot studies and tall stairtowers, they were embosomed in walled orchards. The Clayhills bought Invergowrie from Patrick Gray in 1642[137] and re-edified it comparably, making three estates held by that family, the others being Baldovie and Drumgeich. Wedderburn holdings of such Baltic merchant villas were even more extensive: in addition to Blackness, they occupied Forgan, Moonzie, and Kingennie. Villas like these lacked the great landholding required to maintain a country house, since their occupiers' principal source of income remained their urban activities as merchants and traders.[138]

However, if the community of a Renaissance port may be compared to a community of families, families can fall out – and as the sixteenth century ended, there was increasing acrimony between merchants and Crafts, between the council and the Guildry, between the council and some of the Crafts, and between individual craftsmen and their deacons. Insubordination was in the air. Town council minutes redound to cases where respectable bailies were damned 'lubberts' by impertinent goldsmiths; the goldsmith and deacon of the Hammermen, Patrick Ramsay, was called a 'hangman' by the pewterer David Gray;[139] and even the town's piper, Anthony Court, who had dared play 'some springs through this burgh to the miscontentment of some honest neighbours and irritating of them provoking to great anger', was instructed as to what would be permissible.[140] The underlying cause of the growing friction might have been the burgh's prosperity, for the elite pulled together when the burgh was under threat, or perhaps it was the imperialism of a grasping council seeking to take over traditional rights and liberties.

A RENAISSANCE MAN

An overview of Renaissance Dundee can be obtained through considering the life of the merchant venturer, David Wedderburn, both son and brother of Dundee town clerks. He left a sparkling account book covering Dundee's boom years of 1580–1630, when the burgh's prosperity was at its peak – reflected in it having its own soap maker.[141] This vivid man was burgess resident in the Overgait (which he persisted in calling Ergylis Geyt), the fashionable street of late sixteenth century Dundee, where he lived alongside Goldmans, Fletchers, Allardyces, Rollocks, Hunters and Newmans. From there, he wove a network of kinship extending to almost forty close relatives and distant cousins based in Dundee and its region, trading not just throughout Perthshire, Angus and Fife, but with Flanders, Norway, Dieppe, Spain, La Rochelle, Danzig, and Queensbrig (the Dutch port of Quedlinburg).

That overseas trading was a risky business is evidenced by the records being full of supplications to foreign monarchs or town councils seeking assistance, support or redress for sunk ships, plundered goods, crooked merchants or evil ships' captains. In one case, the captain marooned the entire crew and passengers and made off with the contents, and in another interminable case before the Burgh Court, a merchant desperately sought recompense from a crooked agent.[142] The means that

Dundonians like Wedderburn adopted to counteract this was to rely as much upon kin and extended kin as possible.

Wedderburn managed a wide kinship network which he extended enormously by carefully planned marriage alliances. The three godmothers and three godfathers appointed to each of his ten children, bound him to much of the elite of Dundee. First, the home base in Dundee was secured with brothers Alexander as town clerk and Robert, Dean of Guild, bailie and kirkmaster, and the surgeon Bailie William Duncan a brother-in-law. David's overseas trading was also secured by kin: cousin Richard Wedderburn was an indweller in Elsinore, brother Robert, joint partner in the ship *Nightingale*, in Bordeaux, brother George indweller in Trolsund, and son-in-law James Symsone in Flanders.[143] Security during transit was likewise assured by ownership and kin. Wedderburn was a shareholder in fifteen ships – the *Diamond, Falcon, William, Rochill, Lyon, Robert of Dundee, Clinkbells, Primrose, Swallow, Andrew, Providence, Nightingale, Pelican, Hart*, and *Lamb*.[144] His cousin Bessie accompanied one cargo to Denmark, from which David imported most of his dry goods; brother-in-law Peter Clayhills was dispatched on the ship *Lyon* in 1594, nephew William accompanied a cargo to Danzig, and nephew Alexander another to Spain.[145]

David Wedderburn was principally a dealer in cloth, fish and skins – his salmon and his linen invariably marked with his initials DW.[146] He and his partners would trade in anything from gunpowder and wheat to woven beds and jewels. He not only exported the elaborate Ramsay pistols, but frequently hired out guns, pistols, muskets and swords to friends at home. He imported whatever would sell – vinegar, butter, hemp, glasses, olive oil,[147] endless puncheons of white wine, claret, English cider, pepper, saffron, vinegar, Canary sugar, marmalade (murmblade) and barrels of confections.[148]

A cultured man, he imported paintings from Holland and France, although his commissioning pattern was unspecific: '[John Meill] has promised a fine gilt board with a picture how soon he passes to France', or 'two painted boards overgilt. . . from Flanders'.[149] He sought fine wines, 'fine grew-green silk' from Flanders,[150] French paisements, spices, gold, a doublet of fine grew-green Naplis, and he would dispatch a flagon to Elgin annually for a quart of whisky.[151] Although Dundee had a free library of which it was very proud,[152] Wedderburn preferred his own books of which he had an impressive collection, relishing their fine bindings – noting, when he lent them, if 'well-bound', 'bound in swine skin of verry braw binding', or 'overgilt', or even 'bound in red overgilt'. Merchants travelling to London were frequently instructed to buy him more – predominantly cultural rather than religious texts – with an emphasis upon literature, geography and history. His reading included Holinshed's *Chronicles*, Marlow's *Dr Faustus*, Chaucer, Ortelius's books of maps, the poems of Sir David Lindsay, Virgil and of Ovid, a book of fishes in French, and Drake's *Voyages*.[153] On 7 November 1621, he lent out twenty-one volumes including: 'Metamorphosis Ovidii in Latin with the pictouris bund in ane swynis skyn of verry braw binding sumtyme apertening to Robert Wedderburn my uncle with ane uther buik of inglis of Emblemis in meter for the space of ane moneth.'[154]

The most curious of these loaned volumes was that English book of Emblems in verse. Although it could have been Thomas Combe's 1614 *The Theater of Fine Devices* which was being used in the contemporary decoration of the gallery of Earlshall, Fife, the volume was more likely *A Choice of Emblemes* by Geoffrey Whitney, published in Leiden in 1586.[155] If so, this entry is the only record of this volume's presence in Scotland found to date – apart from the evidence of the painted walls and ceilings themselves. As if reinforcing his interest in contemporary fashion, Wedderburn lent another 'Style Book' (unspecified) to James Carmichael.[156] Given the obliteration of old Dundee since the improvements began in 1871, nothing of this decoration survives; but there is repeated description of elaborately painted decoration in buildings throughout the burgh in *Old Dundee – its Quaint and Historic Buildings*.[157] The Chorister's House facing the Overgate, for example, had woodwork painted in distemper, with 'representations of animals, birds, fruit and flowers, conventionalised', and oak panelling;[158] and Charles Lawson's drawings record ancient houses replete with painted ceilings and timberwork, elaborate fireplaces and plasterwork, and carved oak staircases and panelling.[159]

Fashionable internal decoration being essential to the character of these elite houses, Wedderburn himself selected a variety of religious or deistic mottos to be engraved or painted on the lintels above the pillars of his own gallery.[160] The importance accorded to such decoration is underscored by the painted ceilings inserted into the rear building of Gardyne's Land in the 1650s, for they were adorned with mottos by Francis Quarles which had been modified to contain a subtle attack upon the Cromwellian occupiers – a more sophisticated manner of expressing protest than insulting the English soldiers directly.[161]

The Episcopalian minister Robert Edward considered that Dundonian merchants' houses resembled palaces,[162] and given that his son Alexander was already one of the favoured architects of the Scots aristocracy, his judgement can be relied upon. In demonstration, just along from David Wedderburn's lodging in the Overgait lay the great courtyard house of the merchant and reluctant Town Treasurer, Harbour Master and Hospital Master, David Hunter (whom Wedderburn had had to sue for payment). At the head of what later became Methodist Wynd, and misleadingly assumed to have been the Gray Sisters' nunnery, Hunter's mansion was completed in 1621, dated both on the skewput and the fireplace in the first-floor hall. This stunning complex was exceptionally well-furnished and panelled, and particularly elaborate carved panelling in its hall had an identifiable 1530s character – which implies it might once have decorated a chapel in St Mary's, bought when such fittings were sold off.[163] At the head of the court, the spacious four-windowed hall was flanked by a galleried wing above a loggia on one side, and the public staircase on the other. Even in its time, Hunter's Lodging was known as a particularly desirable residence, for later owners included Alexander Wedderburn of Easter Powrie, and the Fotheringhams of Wester Powrie and Ballindean.[164]

Victorian historians, following the lead of the Enlightenment *literati*, were convinced that Renaissance Scotland was primitive, as Alexander Maxwell put it: 'The fine arts were little cultivated in the rude Scotland of those days'.[165] The evidence is entirely otherwise, Robert Edward observing in 1684: 'Dundee was a favourite of the Muses',[166] in proof of which David Wedderburn's account book was dotted with poetry – including a conceit that he may have written upon the death of Mary Queen of Scots, and which his notary cousin Alexander likewise inscribed into his own protocol book:

> *I cam of Kingys, I kyngis increst, my state a Crown did crave,*
> *Thrys weddit, and als wedow, thrie kyngdomes heir I leave;*
> *Fraunce has my welth, Scotland my birth, and Ingland has my grave.*[167]

For, despite its lack of a university, Dundonians enjoyed literature. The burgh's own printer, John Scot, established a printing press in Dundee in

1546, and undertook the earliest printing of Sir David Lyndsay's *Tragedie of the Cardinall* the following year. He is thought also to have been the printer of the *Gude and Godlie Ballatis* when the provost and constable were instructed (unsuccessfully) by the Regent to arrest him. David's namesake James Wedderburn, who had 'played the merchant in Rouen' and Dieppe, as Calderwood put it waspishly,[168] had 'a good gift of poesie', and his brother John 'turned manie bawdie songs and rhymes into godlie rymes'. Far from 'playing' a merchant, James Wedderburn was a principal timber importer for the royal palaces who devoted his leisure hours to writing 'divers comedies and tragedies in the Scottish tongue wherein he nipped the abuses and superstitions of the time'. With his brother, he was also author of the *Gude and Godlie Ballatis* in 1559. Whereas the *Gude and Godlie Ballatis* are normally taken as a sign of the burgh's stern temperament, to put all this effort into either modifying the words of old Scots songs, or producing new poems to fit them, the Wedderburns were demonstrating (as was Robert Burns to do 200 years later) just how fond they and their circle were of singing or listening to the old Scots tunes – which, by virtue of their rewriting, they were safeguarding for the future.

A large number of the gravestones in the Howff are also enriched by poems far beyond the customary religious doggerel, as witness the gravestone to Andrew Archibald, a famous lithotomist who died in 1662:

> *Here lies good Andrew Archibald; to his art*
> *Chirurgion, to the poor he did impart*
> *His helping hand; still minding God, who bids*
> *The Christian throw his bread upon the floods.*
> *He, in his art most skilful was, and he*
> *Excelled others in the mystery*
> *Of cutting the stone; for by his skill*
> *He many healed, but never one did kill.*[169]

When Sir John Scot of Scotstarvit published *Delitiae Poetarum Scotorum*, in 1637, he included a number of poems by Dundonians, including those of the celebrated Latin poet Hercules Rollock and of Peter Goldman,[170] and when James VI landed at the Roodyards in 1617 to spend the night in Dudhope, he was presented with poems by Walter Coupar and James Gleg.[171]

The burgh fostered its Library controlled by the Kirkmaster, and subjected it to an annual inspection.[172] It also nurtured its Music School, which had not only survived the Reformation but relocated to the now redundant nave of St Mary's, where virginals were bought for it.[173] A deputy music master was added in 1613 and, after the destruction of St Mary's during the Troubles, it was provided with new premises in the later seventeenth century.[174] There was some use of the playfield, but it seems probable that the English actors who played in the tolbooth in 1601, were the celebrated King's Men led by Laurence Fletcher on a thespian tour of Albion (with or without Shakespeare).[175] Cultural continuity to the end of the century was represented by Dr Patrick Blair (possibly from a line of Dr Patrick Blairs[176]) a Fellow of the Royal Society, who published his dissection of an elephant, deceased near Dundee, in their *Transactions*.[177] With 'several honourable and learned gentlemen', Blair planned to erect in Dundee a 'Public Hall. . . to use all means for the improvement of Natural History, to make a collection of curiosities [i.e. a museum] . . . and to establish a Physick Garden' in 1708.[178] The only hint as to where this Physick Garden might have been is that the sunny land lying to the north of the Overgate Port sloping down to the Scouringburn was known as Blair's Orchard.[179]

From the scanty evidence available, it appears that Dundee's lack of a university was compensated for by a vivid cultural life; and the emerging picture of David Wedderburn is of a very well educated, intelligent and cultured man. An excellent networker, astute trader, amateur poet, and versatile in the classics and in several European languages, both a purchaser and commissioner of art, Wedderburn could, as much as any prince, claim to be a renaissance man. Yet in his manner of living, his trading patterns, his focus upon kinship, and in his cultural interests, he was probably not exceptional amongst his fellow Dundee merchant venturers. What signals him out is the survival of his account book.

CONCLUSION

Rather than other Scots burghs, Dundee's nearest equivalent towns were the Baltic ports with which it traded, and its merchant venturers shared with them a reputation for independence and free thinking, a taste for enquiry and culture, and a fondness for conspicuous consumption. The seventy years following its reorganisation in the 1560s, when by all measures it was the second town of the realm, were probably Dundee's most prosperous decades, its port thronged with increasing numbers of vessels. When it came to the standing of the burgh, internecine difficulties could be put aside; as when, in 1620s, the burgesses set about replacing the Trinitarian almshouse on the western approaches with probably the largest Town's Hospital of that date in the country, equipping it with hall, chapel, dormitories and fine gardens.[180] Those difficulties, however, might have led the Baltic merchants to develop a fondness for retiring from the burgh, withdrawing to their nearby villas to relax; developing attitudes that led to their eighteenth century transformation into gentry. So when Daniel Defoe concluded that 'the inhabitants here appear like gentlemen, as well as men of business, and yet are real merchants too', in 1725,[181] they might have been well pleased.

ACKNOWLEDGEMENTS

I am grateful to the many people who have provided input into this research, but particularly Innes Duffus, Clara Young, Stuart Mee, Iain Flett and the Friends of the City Archives, David Kett, Lesley Lindsay, Stuart Walker, Neil Grieve, and Alan Macdonald.

NOTES

1 Spelling slightly modernised.
   Devoit Dundee doughtie and doubtit ay
   Ane seur to fois ane pleasor to thy prince
   Who neyer from god nor kyng declined away
   For churche and cuntreye soore suddartis in defence
   Thy policie puissance and prouidence
   Thy ships thy strengthis. What poet can furth skan
   Thy situation of such magnificence
   By nature wrought is figured lyik a man
   I say no more. Look, Albiones Ile all through
   Is none lyik the siff Lundone & Edinborough.
   Dundee City Archives (DCA), inscribed in the flyleaf of notary Alexander Wedderburn's protocol book 1589–92. I am grateful to Iain Flett for this.
2 For the dating, and the extent to which Pont was solitary or not, and how much reliability can be put upon his drawings, see C. McKean, 'Timothy Pont's Building Drawings' in I. Cunninghame (ed.), *The Nation Survey'd* (East Linton, 2001), pp. 119–120.
3 A. Maxwell, *History of Old Dundee* (Edinburgh, 1884), p. 262.

4 I. D. Whyte, 'Scottish and Irish urbanisation in the seventeenth and eighteenth centuries: a comparative perspective', in S. J. Connolly, R. A. Houston and R. J. Morris (eds.), *Conflict, Identity and Economic Development: Ireland and Scotland, 1600–1939* (Preston, 1995), p. 24.

5 See, for example, E. P. D. Torrie, *Medieval Dundee* (Dundee, 1990); C. A. Whatley, A. S. Smith, D. B. Swinfen, *The Life and Times of Dundee* (Edinburgh, 1993); A. M. Smith, *The Guildry of Dundee* (Dundee, 2005) and many of the nineteenth century histories. The converse is provided by the summary of recent archaeological evidence by D. Perry, *Dundee Rediscovered* (Perth, 2005).

6 D. Nicholas, *Urban Europe 1100–1700* (Basingstoke, 2003), particularly ch. 4.

7 A. C. Lamb, *Dundee, Its Quaint and Historic Buildings* (Dundee, 1895), p. xixa.

8 When the Bordeaux ships arrived in Dundee in the 1560s, her majesty's taster had first access to select for the royal table. A. Maxwell, *Old Dundee Prior to the Reformation* (Edinburgh, 1891), p. 314.

9 I. B. Cowan, and D. E. Easson, *Mediaeval Religious Houses in Scotland* (London, 1976), p. 126.

10 DCA, Town Council Minutes (TCM), 2 January 1603.

11 D. Hay (ed.), *The Letters of James V* (Edinburgh, 1954), p. 221.

12 Maxwell, *History of Old Dundee*, p. 571.

13 Ibid., p. 26.

14 J. Thomson, *The History of Dundee* (Dundee, 1847), p. 332; Maxwell, *Old Dundee Prior to the Reformation*, p. 386.

15 Maxwell, *Old Dundee Prior to the Reformation*, p. 384.

16 Maxwell, *History of Old Dundee*, p. 242.

17 These rights had to be reconfirmed periodically: see W. Hay (ed.) *Charters, Writs and Public Documents of Dundee* (Dundee, 1880), p. 228, and *The Municipal History of Dundee* (Dundee, 1878), p. 218.

18 A. J. Warden, *Burgh Laws of Dundee* (London, 1872), p. 534. Maxwell, *History of Old Dundee*, pp. 236–238.

19 '. . . my provisione which I gef him to keip in jugement in the tolbuith of the hill'. A. H. Millar (ed.), *Compt Buik of David Wedderburne*, (Edinburgh, 1898), p. 74.

20 H. Paton (ed.), *Accounts of the Masters of Works: Volume 1* (Edinburgh, 1957), p. 313; R. Edward, *The County of Angus 1678* (reprint Edinburgh, 1883), p. 24.

21 Maxwell, *History of Old Dundee*, pp. 240–241 and 64.

22 Ibid., p. 207.

23 Maxwell, *Old Dundee Prior to the Reformation*, p. 63.

24 All the donations were round up into the single gift on 14 Apr 1567. Maxwell, *History of Old Dundee*, pp. 125, 224.

25 It was later converted to tenements and then the Cholera Hospital in South Union Street.

26 It barely merits a mention in, for example, R. Fawcett, *Scottish Mediaeval Churches* (Stroud, 2002).

27 R. A. Mason, *Kingship and Common Weal* (East Linton, 1998), p. 60.

28 Maxwell, *Old Dundee Prior to the Reformation*, pp. 11, 41.

29 Ibid., ch. 2. Lamb, *Dundee, Its Quaint and Historic Buildings*, p. xxxiv. Lamb says date unknown anterior to 1525.

30 See C. McKean, 'The Wind-Protected City – European Urban Design' in P. Dennison (ed.), *Conservation and Change in Historic Towns* (York, 2000).

31 I am very grateful to Iain Flett and Dundee City Archives for this information.

32 Edward, *The County of Angus, 1678*, p. 30.

33 See for example, Maxwell, *History of Old Dundee*, p. 146; Torrie, *Medieval Dundee*, p. 27 and Lamb, *Dundee, Its Quaint and Historic Buildings*, p. xia. Rather than being located between the water conduit and the 'Cross Well' (crucis fontem), the tolbooth was placed between the conduit and the 'Market Cross' (crucem fori). I am grateful to Professor Archie Duncan, letter 1 April 2000, and Iain Flett for this translation.

34 Thomson, *Old Dundee*, p. 354.

35 TCM, 4 October 1560, 18 June 1567.

36 DCA, Book of Acts and Decrees of the Council, 2 December 1588, when Bailie William Man was appointed.

37 Maxwell *Old Dundee Prior to the Reformation*, p. 99, Maxwell, *History*, Appendix A.

38 H. M. Paton (ed.), *Accounts of the Masters of Works for Building and Repairing Royal Palaces and Castles. Vol. 1, 1529–1615* (Edinburgh, 1957), pp. 123, 124, 179–182, 262–287.

39 Warden, *Burgh Laws*, pp. 14, 21.

40 DCA Burgh Court Book, 7 October 1550.

41 Warden, *Burgh Laws*, pp. 114, 120.

42 TCM, 4 October 1560.

43 TCM, 10 January 1561.

44 Maxwell, *History of Old Dundee*, p. 145.

45 Ibid., p. 160.

46 In 1614, Andrew Wast was responsible for maintaining the building. Maxwell, *History of Old Dundee*, p. 405. The route was also known as the Shorehead to Spalding's Wynd.

47 Maxwell, *History of Old Dundee*, pp. 160–162, 473.

48 Lamb, *Old Dundee*, p. xxx.

49 Maxwell, *Old Dundee Prior to the Reformation*, p. 99.

50 J. Beveridge (ed.), *Register of the Privy Seal of Scotland Vol. IV (RSS)*, (Edinburgh, 1952), p. 138.

51 Maxwell, *Old Dundee Prior to the Reformation*, p. 391.

52 Maxwell, *History of Old Dundee*, p. 272.

53 Ibid., p. 404a.

54 Lamb, *Old Dundee*, p. 19.

55 Maxwell *History of Old Dundee*, Appendix A.

56 *RSS*, p. 132; Maxwell, *Old Dundee Prior to the Reformation*, p. 111.

57 Maxwell, *Old Dundee Prior to the Reformation*, p. 112.

58 Ibid., p. 115. The English-built fortress of Brackenrig on the eminence of Fort Hill was not wholly removed until 1816. Thomson, *The History of Dundee*, p. 49.

59 Maxwell, *Old Dundee Prior to the Reformation*, p. 119.

60 TCM, 3 January 1555. Repeated in 5 October 1556. Lamb, *Old Dundee*, p. 26: slates still required to repair damage caused by the English invasion. The prohibition against exporting slates to Leith remained in force until 1587. *Municipal History*, p. 44.

61 The conversion was by David Schang: DCA Burgh Court Book 13.10.1550. Maxwell, *Old Dundee Prior to the Reformation*, p. 223.

62 Maxwell, *Old Dundee Prior to the Reformation*, p. 304.

63 Ibid., p. 125.

64 Maxwell, *History of Old Dundee*, p. 211.

65 Maxwell, *Old Dundee Prior to the Reformation*, p. 129.

66 DCA, Burgh Court minutes, 12 November 1550.

67 The trial of the town's elite for collaborating with the English was held in a tolbooth in 1553, and later attributions of the name 'the old Tolbooth' to the tenement on the south-east corner of the Market Place indicates its location.

68 Edward, *Angus*, p. 29.

69 D. Calderwood, *The Historie of the Kirk of Scotland*, vol. 1 (Edinburgh, 1842), p. 142.

70 Maxwell, *Old Dundee Prior to the Reformation*, pp. 393ff. The principal people of the town were acquitted of breaking up the Friars preachers (Dominicans) and the Minorites (Greyfriars) on 31 Aug 1543. Cowan and Easson, *Religious Houses*, p. 126.

71 *RSS*, p. 2580. The Blackfriars: David Hill, James Methven, Laurence Johnston, John Kers, David Alexander, David Strathauchine, Patrick Johnston, David Roger, John Lyall. . . John Ferrear, webster, Archibald Garvie, John Hay, Andrew Watson, Thomas Wood, John Michell, webster, John Spence, Walter Lovell, John Kennel, Master Walter Spalding, James and David Rollock, Thos Strathauchine, James Blythman, Robert Strathauchine and son, John Hay, cutler, James Gibson Baxter, Robert Doig, £400 collectively or £50 each, cautioners include the Earl of Crawford, a cooper, walker etc. RPS 2580 15.3.53/4.

72 Warden, *Burgh Laws*, pp. 18–19, 40.

73 TCM, 7 January 1588.

74 Maxwell, *History of Old Dundee*, p. 165.

75 Maxwell, *Old Dundee Prior to the Reformation*, p. 182; Maxwell, *History of Old Dundee*, p. 336.

76 *Municipal History*, p. 40; TCM, 10 January 1561. This is distinct from Perry, *Dundee Rediscovered*, who places the building in the Howff itself. In fact, the presence of a large well and an ancient gable lying on the west side of Burial Wynd implies that the Greyfriars lay there.

77 TCM, 13 October 1601.

78 At 42 feet by 18.5 feet, St Clement's was never a large building, but one of Lawson's drawings implies that it was very finely constructed.

79 Maxwell, *Old Dundee Prior to the Reformation*, pp. 181–186; Lamb, *Old Dundee*, p. xixa.

80 Maxwell, *Old Dundee Prior to the Reformation*, pp. 185–186.

81 It was the length of seven cellars, and they were normally *c.* 20 feet wide.

82 TCM, 1588.

83 Warden, *Burgh Laws*, pp. 45–46.

84 This was something that needed redoing from time to time. In 1613, the windows of the Tolbooth had to be coloured again.

85 See C. McKean 'The Scottish *Hôtel de Ville* during the Renaissance' in K. Ottenheym and C. Mignot, *Bâtiments Publiques – le Gouvernement, la Justice, et l'Économie* (forthcoming).

86 Warden, *Burgh Laws*, p. 45. To build 'a sufficient prick of stone, fine ashlar work, well hewen, rising with eight square pains, like the old foundations of the work, the roof of the prick to be raised thirteen foot above the said table, eight lights or windows to be put in the body of the prick, in such parts and of such height as the Dean shall appoint. Under the window soles a moulded [string course] circuiting was to be placed. The whole prick well hewen. Under the roof thereof shall circuit the same with a timber table, and decore the work by putting on every tunzie looking toward the High Street ane knap with an fyall therupon. In the roof shall place eight little lights with fyalls upon ye headis therefore.'

87   Maxwell, *History of Old Dundee*, p. 54; Lamb, *Old Dundee*, p. xiib; TCM, 14 Oct
     1560.
88   Thomson, *History*, p. 330.
89   *Compt Buik of David Wedderburne*, p. 80; Lamb, *Old Dundee*, p. xixa.
90   This was a substantial building, measuring 21 ells by 14 ells (virtually 21 metres by 14
     metres).
91   TCM, 4 October 1566. Now Sugarhouse Wynd.
92   TCM, 4 October 1566.
93   *Municipal History*, pp. 243–244.
94   TCM, 2 October 1559.
95   It was completed by Adam Balmanno in 1589.
96   TCM, 18 December 1610.
97   I am grateful to Dr Susan Rennie for this.
98   Thomson, *History*, pp. 339, 343.
99   Warden *Burgh Laws*, pp. 46, 50.
100 Maxwell, *Old Dundee Prior to the Reformation*, p. 380.
101 Burgh Court Book 23 May 1551, and as recorded in Lamb's *Old Dundee* or in the
     drawings of Charles Lawson.
102 Lamb, *Old Dundee*, p. xxii.
103 Ibid., p. xlvi.
104 Thomson, *History*, p. 323.
105 Ibid., pp. 333, 347, 351.
106 Conference paper – 'Uwe Albrecht, Troisième Rencontre d'Architecture Européenne':
     Bâtiments Publiques, Utrecht, 2006.
107 TCM, 28 September 1648. George Hallyburton demurred at being appointed bailie
     because only Merchant Venturers, which he was not, were qualified. The Council
     refused to let him off the hook. (The spellings 'Hallyburton', 'Halyburton' and
     'Haliburton' are used promiscuously in original documents.)
108 Torrie, *Medieval Dundee*, p. 42, believes that this represented the entire body of
     burgesses. Smith, *Guildry*, p. 13, notes that this represented only those who attended a
     given meeting,
109 *Compt Buik of David Wedderburne*, p. 106.
110 TCM, 2 May 1605.
111 TCM, 12 February 1578.
112 Warden, *Burgh Laws*, p. 16.
113 Ibid., p. 120.
114 Ibid., p. 126.
115 Ibid., p. 41.
116 Ibid., pp. 129, 16 Mar 1590–1591.
117 Maxwell, *History of Old Dundee*, p. 46.
118 Warden, *Burgh Laws*, p. 132.
119 Ibid., p. 130.
120 Ibid., p. 102.
121 Smith, *Guildry*, pp. 113, 117–118.
122 Maxwell, *History*, p. 88.
123 Burgh Court books November 1550 – October 1551.
124 Lamb, *Old Dundee*, p. 13.
125 Heir lyes ane godly and vertwvs voman, Sarah Auchinleck, spovs to Abraham

Martine, Frenchman, Chirvrgeon-Barber, vho departit this lyf 25 Jvly, 1665, of her age 40. Heir also lyes ane honest man, Abraham Martine, Frenchman, chirvrgeon-Barber, lavfvl son of Abraham Martine, merchant, Bvrgis of the City of Metz in Loraine, vho departit this lyf 13 June, 1673, of his age 57.

126 See Smith, *Guildry.*
127 Warden, *Burgh Laws*, p. 256.
128 TCM, 7 Sep 1610. *Compt Buik of David Wedderburne*, p. 178.
129 Nicholas, *Urban Europe*, p. 79.
130 Lamb, *Old Dundee*, p. xli.
131 Ibid., p. xivii.
132 *Compt Buik of David Wedderburne*, p. 87.
133 *Black Book of Taymouth* (Edinburgh, 1855, reprint, n.d.), p. 336.
134 Maxwell, *Old Dundee Prior to the Reformation*, p. 173.
135 I am indebted to Innes Duffus for this: personal communication.
136 S. Mee, unpublished dissertation, 2006, Dundee University Archives.
137 National Archives of Scotland, GD/CM/1/2/1; Patrick Gray to Robert Clayhills of Baldovie
138 See C. McKean, 'Some Later Jacobean Villas in Scotland' in M. Airs and G. Tyack, (eds.), *The Renaissance Villa in Britain* (Lincoln, 2007).
139 TCM, 26 March 1605, 2 May 1605, 18 August 1606, etc.
140 He was forbidden to play the spring 'Tobacco or the Laird tint his gantlet' even in private houses. TCM, February 1604.
141 Maxwell, *History of Old Dundee*, p. 284.
142 'Dundee Shipping Papers', W. A. McNeill (ed.), *Scottish History Society Miscellany* x (Edinburgh, 1965).
143 *Compt Buik of David Wedderburne*, pp. 19, 145, 143.
144 Lamb, *Old Dundee*, p. 29.
145 *Compt Buik of David Wedderburne*, pp. 171, 84.
146 Ibid., pp. 93, 110.
147 Ibid., p. 112.
148 Ibid., pp. 68, 112, 181, 182.
149 Ibid., pp. 111, 182.
150 Ibid., p. 115.
151 Ibid., pp. 117, 102.
152 Hay (ed.) *Charters, Writs and Public Documents of Dundee*, p. 172.
153 Thomas Clayhills instructed to buy 'Enemy to Atheism'. *Compt Buik of David Wedderburne*, pp. 56, 168.
154 *Compt Buik of David Wedderburne*, p. 168.
155 I am grateful to Michael Bath for identifying this book amongst its rivals. He doubts the Combs since Wedderburn clearly loved books and the Combs was 'a small, unprepossessing scrappy little book'. Personal communication. A. H. Miller, editor of the Compte Book, concurred.
156 *Compt Buik of David Wedderburne*, p. 89.
157 Lamb, *Old Dundee*, pp. xiv, and also pp. xx, xxii, xxv, xxxvi, xxxvii, xlviii.
158 Ibid., p. xlvii.
159 Over 600 drawings by Charles Lawson, undertaken *c.* 1850–1880, have recently been discovered in the Wellgate Library. Many of them depict elaborate and sophisticated interiors.

160   *Compt Buik of David Wedderburne*, p. 184.
161   P. Davidson, 'Mute emblems and a lost room: Gardyne's House, Dundee' in
      A. Saunders and P. Davidson, (eds.), *Visual Words and Verbal Pictures* (Glasgow, 2005),
      pp. 51–68.
162   Edward, *Angus*, p. 30.
163   *Proceedings of the Society of Antiquaries of Scotland*, 8 January 1886.
164   Lamb, *Old Dundee*, p. xxxvi.
165   Maxwell, *Old Dundee Prior to the Reformation*, p. 369.
166   Edward, *Angus*, p. 33.
167   Transcribed from the Latin by Alexander Wedderburn, *Municipal History*, p. 54.
168   Calderwood, *The Historie of the Kirk of Scotland*, vol. 1, pp. 141–143.
169   Thomson, *History*, p. 384.
170   *Compt Buik of David Wedderburne*, pp. 33, 107.
171   Maxwell, *History of Old Dundee*, p. 314; Lamb, *Old Dundee*, p. 33.
172   Warden, *Burgh Laws*, p. 58.
173   Maxwell, *History*, pp. 336–338, 340.
174   *Municipal History*, p. 87.
175   I am indebted to Ian. S. Fraser for this.
176   A Dr Patrick Blair, burgess, lived in Whitehall Close in 1625. Lamb, *Old Dundee*,
      p. xxviii.
177   C. Dingwall, 'Dr Patrick Blair and Dundee's first Botanic Garden' (Unpublished
      research paper, Dundee, 1987).
178   P. Blair, letter 1708 quoted in Ibid.
179   Lamb, *Old Dundee*, p. xli.
180   Maxwell, *History of Old Dundee*, p. 230.
181   D. Defoe, *A Tour through the whole Island of Great Britain* (London, 1725).

(*Left*). The Choristers' House, Overgate. The Chorister's House lay on the south side of the Overgate against St Mary's precinct, and had an exceptionally finely painted interior. It probably derived its name from a connection with the Song School, of which the burgh was enormously proud. (Lawson)

(*Below*). Dundee from the river's edge. This drawing by David Small of how Dundee looked in the 1850s conveys an echo of the riparian nature of the port before the arrival of the enclosed docks and railways in the nineteenth century. (Dundee Museums)

A close off Tyndall's Wynd. Ancient fabric such as this, densely occupied and increasingly dilapidated would naturally have been regarded with distaste by English visitors such as Henry Skrine. (Small)

Dundee in its setting c. 1587. Drawn by Timothy Pont c. 1587 (the square towers on Claypotts Castle are not yet complete), this map depicts the port as dominated by the steeple of St Mary's church. The Wellgate, Seagate and Hilltown are perfectly clear, as is the busy harbour. Most significantly, Dundee is surrounded by an array of greater and lesser country houses or villas lying within half a day's ride, most of whose owners were involved with the life of Dundee in one way or another. (National Library of Scotland)

This elaborate plasterwork of Grecian mythology depicting a chariot drawn by lions stands testimony to the elaborate internal decoration of Dundee's apartments. Unfortunately the artist did not identify which one. (Lawson)

The Vault. This enclosed space lay on the principal axis of the port between the Hie Gait or market place and the harbour. In 1550, the tolbooth was relocated to the Vault's northern edge, and the grammar school and burgh Weighhouse added within it a few years later. (Lawson)

Dundee's 'narrows' entering the market place: top left, the 12 foot wide narrows of the Murraygate (from Lamb's *Dundee*); top right, the 12 foot wide narrows of the Overgate in the later nineteenth century (D.C. Thomson); above, the 6 foot wide narrows of the Seagate (Small).

Dundee from the east drawn *c.* 1678 by Capt John Slezer when he was given the freedom of the burgh. It was one of three drawings made by Slezer, although only two were published. The Seagate lies at the centre, with the Seagate Port facing towards the viewer. The sea laps up to the garden walls of the Seagate houses. The Cowgate, to the right, remains in ruins after damage during the civil war. The centre of town lies on the distant high ground, marked by the turret of the tolbooth and St Mary's tower. (*Theatrum Scotiae*)

Plan of Dundee 1776. William Crawford's plan of Dundee is the earliest credible map of the port, and was probably prepared to celebrate the opening of the Trades Hall in the High Street 1776 (the black square on the right-hand end of the High Street). The mediaeval plan remained largely unchanged. The market place lies at the centre, from which the four principal streets – the Overgate, Nethergate, Murraygate and Seagate – lead out through their respective 'narrows'. All closes leading down to the shore are curved. Fish Street and the newly renamed Butcher Row (formerly New Shore) line the western seafront. (Dundee University Archives)

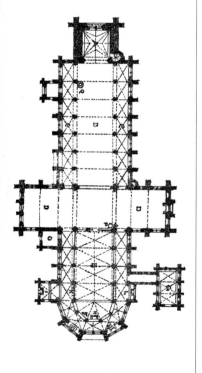

St Mary's church was the largest parish church in Scotland as may be seen from James Maclaren's plan. Its tower (section also by Maclaren) is the principal survivor of the medieval church. The crown steeple was destroyed in 1549 and never replaced.
(*History of Dundee*)

(*Left*). It was a Renaissance conceit to conceive of a town in human form, but as town clerk Alexander Wedderburn sketched in his protocol book, it was an apt way to describe Dundee. The right leg is named Seagate, the left Murraygate, the left arm Argylisgsait (the old name for Overgate) and the right arm Fleukergait (the old name for Nethergate). St Mary's lies upon the town's heart, and the fleshmarket upon its loins. (Dundee City Archives)

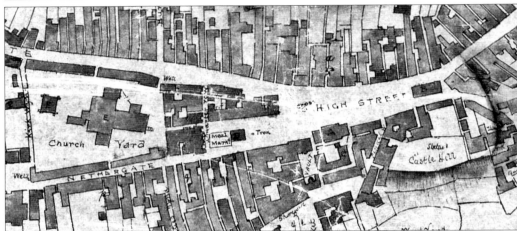

(*Above*). The burgh market place or Hie Gait. This weather-protected space was the focus of town life and contained the tolbooth, the fleshmarket, the meal market, and the market cross. Its enclosed form kept out the winds of the port, and ground level arcades provided shelter from the rain. (Crawford's map, 1776)

(*Right*). Fish Street lined the shore of Dundee prior to the construction of the New Shore in front of it in the sixteenth century. Striking blocks of tall apartments with projecting stair towers were constructed, probably as an investment, by Dundee's elite such as the Wedderburns and the Clayhills, who themselves preferred to live in the Overgate. (Dundee Central Library)

When the first packhouse was constructed *c.* 1560 (later invariably known as Provost Pierson's lodging after his apartment above) it possibly looked like this: characterized by a fine array of arcades at ground floor level and proud corner towers. (McKean)

When St Mary's was rebuilt after 1550, it was not rebuilt as a single kirk, and after the Reformation the nave was used for the burgh Song School. Burnt again by Montrose's troops in 1645, the site remained empty (save partially used for the grammar school) until 1791, when the Steeple Church was built there. This view shows St Mary's soon afterwards, indicating the extent to which it had become a number of separate buildings. (Small)

(*This page and opposite top*). Lady Warkstairs (probably originally the stairs of Our Lady's Wark) was rebuilt after English destruction in the early 1550s. There were two timber-gabled blocks of apartments reached by stairs at each side. Merchants' booths lay behind the stone arcades at ground floor, which were rediscovered only on demolition. Lawson provides some evidence of fine carved timberwork and elaborate plaster within.

(*Below*). Warkstairs under demolition.
(This page, Lawson; opposite page, Dundee University Archives)

The Weighhouse was a key public building in contemporary Europe, often converted from a handy church. Thus also in Dundee, when St Clement's chapel in the Vault was customised as the burgh weighhouse with floors and an external timber gallery inserted in the 1560s. (Lawson)

This view of the Market Place looking east in the later nineteenth century would, in spatial terms at least, have been quite familiar to David Wedderburn and his fellow merchant venturers. The principal differences would have been the removal of external stair towers and timber galleries from the dwellings, the filling in of the arcades, and the arrival of new buildings such as the 1733 Town House on the right in place of the 1560 tolbooth. (Small)

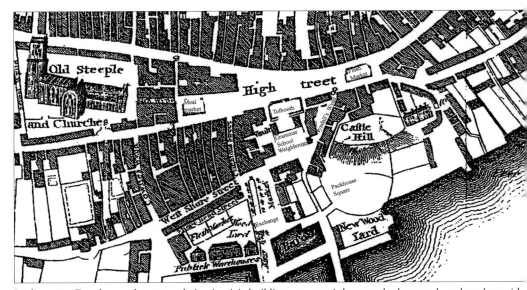

In the 1560s, Dundee set about re-ordering its civic buildings on an axis between harbour and market place with the Vault at its centre. This plan of the Vault in the mid eighteenth century indicates the location of the principal buildings. (McKean, based on 1793 plan)

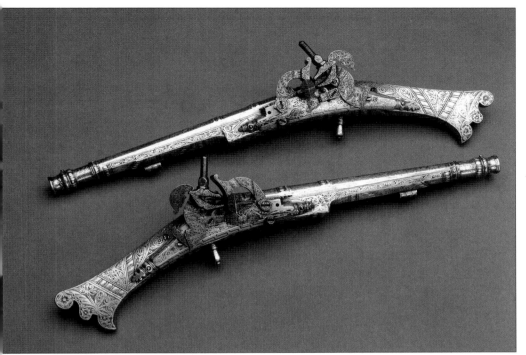

Dundee hammermen were celebrated for the fashion accessory of carefully wrought and elaborately carved guns and pistols, so fine indeed that David Wedderburn exported them to Europe. 'Black Duncan' Campbell of Glenorchy bought a beautiful firearm from Patrick Ramsay in 1595; whereas King Louis XIII of France added the elaborate brass pistols above, made by James Low in 1611, to his personal collection. (National Museums of Scotland)

Dundee
from St Rogues Chapel
from an old German print.

The villa of Wallace Craigie copied by Lawson from an unidentified 'German drawing' – probably one by Slezer. Lying on the immediate eastern boundary of the town, Wallace Craigie was a typical villa of the Baltic trader – undemonstrative, horizontal in proportion and embosomed in gardens. (Lawson)

(*Right*). David Wedderburn stamped his bundles of
cloth and parcels of fish with this seal.
(*The Wedderburn Book*, 1898)

(*Below*). David Hunter's Great Lodging lay at the north
end of a long close opening from the Overgate. Its fine
courtyard was lined on the east by an arcaded gallery,
but its principal, tall U-plan, big windowed façade
looked north-east over the Meadows. It was finely
panelled within, and had Hunter's monogram above
the fireplace. (Lawson)

This view of Dundee from the north, drawn by Capt John Slezer *c.* 1678 shows Dudhope Castle, seat of the Scrymgeours, hereditary constables of Dundee's castle, in the right foreground. On the left skyline the turrets of Dundee's splendid 1550 tolbooth proclaim the burgh's sturdy independence from them. (*Theatrum Scotiae*)

The Dundee Town Council Fine Box, for burgesses who failed to attend a Council meeting. The engraving reads: 'Love and Blesse the Provost, Baillies, and Counsell of Dundie'; and 'Fear God and Honour the King'. It was presented by James Scrymgeour, Provost, on 14 May 1602. (From *Charters, Writs and Public Documents* …)

(*Right*). The Arms of Dundee used as the frontispiece to the Dundee mariner John Marr's pioneering navigation book *Navigation in Coasting; or a seamans instructer*, published from Marr's Dundee dwelling in 1693.

(*Below*). The harbour sundial was commissioned and erected by the Guildry of Dundee in 1649–50 at a cost of £33 10s 8d – a significant sum for the Guildry only four years after the sack by the Marquess of Montrose, and perhaps a sign that the port was beginning to recover. (D.C. Thomson)

Prudentia & Candore.

Insignia Urbis TAODUN.

CHAPTER 2

Dundee and the Crown
c. 1550–1650

Alan MacDonald

Only Edinburgh was bigger and wealthier than Dundee in early modern Scotland. There were many reasons why it ought not to have been important, as Chapter 1 has shown, but it overcame its multiple handicaps by establishing itself as the premier port on the Firth of Tay,[1] eclipsing Perth and leading to a deep-seated hostility that arose between the two burghs, vestiges of which remain to this day. The vigour of Dundee's economy meant that it comfortably outperformed the next wealthiest burghs (Aberdeen, Perth and Glasgow), not losing ground to Glasgow until the later seventeenth century, when trade to the west was emerging as the key to mercantile wealth as Scotland entered the Atlantic world. So, what were the implications of Dundee's prosperity? Was it able to use its wealth and status to its advantage in its interactions with the Crown and the institutions of central government? Few studies of the interactions between European localities and central government have focused upon one town, unless that is a capital city.[2] However, the exceptional nature of a capital means that it tends only to be compared with another one.

The intention here is to examine a second-rank town and its fortunes in its interactions with national institutions of government, notably parliament – collectively termed 'the state' – through what it did, what influence it had, and how successful it was. Only parliament, Conventions of Estates, the Privy Council, the exchequer, the Court of Session and the king himself could reasonably be understood as the normal central organs of 'the state' at this time.[3] In common with most early modern states, Scotland had a national political assembly – parliament, also known as 'the three estates' or simply 'the Estates'.

However, alongside parliament, there were three other national representative assemblies. First, there existed a sub-parliamentary body called the Convention of the Estates. It could not make permanent law but could pass interim measures, including direct taxes which were always time-limited. Being easier and quicker to summon than parliament, which required forty days' notice, it was also very good for consultation on problems which arose unexpectedly. Next, there was the General Assembly of the Church, and finally, the Convention of Royal Burghs. Both the latter were national delegate assemblies with virtually exclusive and autonomous jurisdiction over a wide range of issues. That is not to say that they were, either in theory or practice, rivals to parliament or that they ever really challenged the authority of the national legislature.[4] They had specific remits and were effectively subordinate to parliament, in the sense that they were unable to override statute yet were sufficiently autonomous to make it difficult to think of them as part of the 'state'.

Dundee's economic strength meant that it played a prominent role in parliaments, Conventions of the Estates, Conventions of Burghs and general assemblies, for all of them included urban representatives. The commissioners from Dundee, in common with their counterparts from elsewhere, were always ready to act to ensure that the interests of their burgh were maintained, enhanced and defended. Any challenge to what a commissioner saw as the rights of his town would provoke a formal protest, recorded for posterity by a notary and entered into the records. Thus how Dundee figured on the national stage can tell us something important about it.

PARLIAMENT

Dundee's parliamentary pedigree dates back to 1357 when a sederunt of burghs at a General Council was first recorded,[5] with Mr John Somerville and Robert Kidd present (along with sixteen others) right at the beginning of urban Scotland's parliamentary story. Thereafter, a parliament without a commissioner from Dundee was virtually unknown and, before 1621, a parliament with only a single commissioner from Dundee was a rarity. Although only Edinburgh was permitted two votes, other burghs often sent more than one person to parliament; and Dundee's habit of sending multiple commissioners results in Dundee's entry in the constituency lists being the second longest after Edinburgh.[6] Sending multiple commissioners was closely related to the wealth of the burgh, for the next largest list is that of Aberdeen, the third wealthiest in early modern Scotland. Between 1540 and 1617 (after which multiple commissioners were no longer permitted), Dundee sent two commissioners at least twenty-one times, three at least seven times, four at least twice and once even five.

That Dundee was in a different league from most other burghs in the parliamentary context is demonstrated by comparison with the parliamentary attendance of the burghs of north-east Fife (Anstruther Easter, Anstruther Wester, Crail, Cupar, Kilrenny, Pittenweem and St Andrews). All but Cupar and St Andrews sent commissioners to parliament relatively infrequently; they rarely sent more than one and those commissioners were never selected to serve on the key committee – the lords of the articles – which received draft legislation and, in consultation with the full membership of parliament, prepared it for voting by the house on the final day of the session.[7] Commissioners from St Andrews often served on that committee and Cupar's commissioner served occasionally. Even Aberdeen (in 1592) and Perth (in 1612) were occasionally absent from the committee, even though they had commissioners at those parliaments. There is not a single instance when a commissioner from Dundee did *not* sit on the articles, putting it alongside only Edinburgh in being a permanent fixture on the committee.

That was undoubtedly a consequence of its standing among the parliamentary burghs. The wealthier ones played a leading role in the Convention of Burghs, driving the urban agenda both inside and outwith parliament; and between eight and ten would often be delegated by the convention to deal with a range of matters on behalf of the others, including negotiation with the Crown.[8] The regular election of a commissioner from Dundee as one of the lords of the articles should therefore come as no surprise: no other burghs' commissioners were as well-qualified to represent the interests of the urban estate as Edinburgh and Dundee. Whether it involved redistributing the tax burden among the burghs, drafting supplications to the king or numerous other issues, a commissioner from Dundee was normally included.[9] When the Convention of Burghs appointed a standing commission to deal with matters arising between conventions from the end of the sixteenth century, Dundee was always represented on it.[10] It was chosen as one of four burghs to attend the coronation of James VI as king of England in 1603 and was represented on the parliamentary commission of 1604 to negotiate closer union between Scotland and England.[11]

Another key indicator of Dundee's national rank can be found in the presence of its commissioners at Conventions of the Estates. Conventions of the Estates were akin to parliaments in some ways but differed in others. The most significant difference was that whereas parliaments met by a general summons of all those entitled to sit, the king could choose whom to summon to Conventions of Estates. Dundee was one of those who could not be ignored. Only Edinburgh has more commissioners recorded at Conventions of Estates than Dundee and, since the capital commonly sent two commissioners while Dundee usually sent only one, Dundee's commissioners were certainly summoned more often than the commissioners from any other burgh, standing well ahead of St Andrews, Perth and Glasgow – their nearest rivals.[12] Whatever was the case with the other estates (and a detailed study of Conventions of the Estates has yet to be carried out) if important decisions were to be made by a Convention of the Estates, the economically powerful burghs had to be present. Theoretically the king may have been free to call whoever he pleased, but his choice was constrained by the necessity to secure meaningful consent from a properly representative selection of the political classes. Had he ignored too many powerful nobles and burghs, the legitimacy of any decision would have been seriously undermined and almost certainly challenged by those who had been excluded. The king well understood that Dundee was of such importance that it had to be included whenever a Convention of the Estates was to meet.

DUNDEE'S REPRESENTATIVES

Much can be learned about a burgh by examining the nature of its representatives. The membership of Scotland's parliament, like that of England, attended partly by election and partly by right. Nobles, churchmen and officers of state sat by dint of their title or their job. Shire and burgh commissioners were elected, the former by the lairds of each county, the latter by the council which governed each burgh. The representatives of Scotland's towns were therefore delegates. Even more important, however, was that they all had to be merchants – all that is except for one of Edinburgh's commissioners who was the only craftsman in parliament. In the 1560s, the Crafts of Dundee had pushed for a comparable craft place in parliament, the spokesman for the Crafts alleging 'that use and wount wes of befoir that ane craftisman' was commissioned along with a merchant. Frustratingly, this is the first record in Dundee's council minutes of the election of commissioners to parliament, so it is impossible to test the veracity of this assertion, but it was made in vain.[13] Dundee, like almost every parliamentary burgh, was controlled by its merchants, even though they would not have consti-tuted as many as one in ten of the adult male population. A small elite group within the merchant class dominated the burgh council through an electoral system whereby every year a certain proportion of the council demitted office and was replaced by co-option. So the parlia-mentary commissioners from Dundee represented the interests of a small, wealthy group within burgh society rather than those of the burgh as a whole – although they would have regarded the two as synonymous. What was understood by 'Dundee' would have depended very much upon whom one asked.

Dundee produced some exceptionally experienced parliamentarians. Between 1560 and 1581, Mr James Haliburton was elected to parliaments and Conventions of Estates ten times; Patrick Lyon fourteen times between 1587 and 1602; Mr Alexander Wedderburn thirteen times between 1585 and 1621; William Auchinleck nine times between 1600 and 1617, and Robert Fletcher, Robert Davidson and Alexander Wedderburn (grandson of his namesake) seven times each. A number of others were elected on two or more occasions and very few were elected only once. This again marks out Dundee as a major player in the counsels of the realm since in smaller burghs, by contrast, more than three quarters of all parliamentary commissioners were elected only once or twice, and none more than seven times.[14] Wealthy towns were much more likely to prioritise parliamentary experience, while the poorer ones were less committed to parliamentary participation, probably because they were much less able to exercise influence. Dundee liked to ensure that it sent safe pairs of hands with knowledge and experience of the workings of parliament. The wealth of the town also meant that it was easier for Dundonian commissioners to develop parliamentary experience since sending multiple commissioners was something which was beyond the means of more than half of the burghs. It allowed those with experience to pass on their knowledge to a less experienced colleague who might take on the mantle at a later date. It also meant that the influential burghs were much more able to retain and enhance their influence.

Dundee exhibited a striking tendency not to elect its provost (with one notable exception), often selecting its clerk as its parliamentary commissioner. It preferred to elect its lesser magistrates (bailies, deans of gild and treasurers) and its clerks, the people who actually ran the burgh on a week-to-week basis, as parliamentary commissioners. The provost, by contrast, was elected on only sixteen occasions between 1540 and 1651, and James Haliburton, provost for over thirty years from the 1550s to the 1580s, accounted for ten of those.[15] There are various possible explanations for this, principal among them being the fact that he was well-connected at court, but his evident commitment to the burgh and his close relationship with its ruling merchant elite were significant factors too. Indeed, so committed was he to urban affairs that he was once actually elected as Dundee's commissioner to a Convention of Burghs. He was not permitted to sit because he was not a merchant, but the council of Dundee staunchly defended having sent him.[16] It is therefore just as likely that he was sent as commissioner because of his abilities, his connections and his growing parliamentary experience as his office – and this fits with patterns observed for other burghs.[17]

It was very unusual, however, for at least one of the bailies not to appear in a commission. The burgh's bailies were its working magistrates, the most active members of the town's government because they presided over the burgh court, having exclusive jurisdiction over all crimes committed in the burgh. With the prominence of the Wedderburn family in the wider affairs of Dundee, frequent election of the burgh clerk (an office that became the preserve of the family in this period) was not surprising. Three Alexander Wedderburns, all graduates of the University of St Andrews and all lawyers,[18] were commissioned to represent the burgh a total of sixteen times between 1585 and 1660. Although they had close kinship connections with Dundee's merchant elite, they were not themselves merchants. Given that the Convention of Royal Burghs forbade all but genuine merchants from being chosen as parliamentary commissioners, that the Wedderburn lawyers were able to represent Dundee in parliament says something about the status of the burgh at the national level. Few others would have been able to get away with such a breach of the rules.

Ordinary councillors were often elected to parliament too, either as a colleague to a more senior commissioner, or because they were experienced parliamentarians in their own right. Magistrates normally served for only one year at a time but they always continued as councillors in the year following their magistracy, after which they might be restored to their former office. Patrick Lyon, with fourteen appearances in parliaments and Conventions of the Estates, was frequently a bailie, but it was likely that he would be chosen to attend parliament anyway even in years when he was not. Experience rather than office-holding was more significant when it came to choosing a commissioner.

James Haliburton and Sir James Scrymgeour of Dudhope, two of Dundee's provosts who did represent the burgh in parliament, provide a striking contrast in their relationships with the burgh and in their parliamentary activities on its behalf. Haliburton, the younger son of the laird of Pitcur (indeed he was the tutor of Pitcur because of his role as guardian of his nephew, the young laird, during the latter's minority), was elected provost for an almost unbroken stint of thirty-three years. Even though he came from a landed family, he clearly had an active commitment to the burgh,[19] and remained active on its behalf, frequently representing it in parliaments (six times) and Conventions of the Estates (four times) even when prominent in national affairs. An ally of James Stewart, the Earl of Moray, he fell from royal favour in 1565 along with his noble patron, and was briefly replaced as provost when Queen Mary imposed the Earl of Crawford on the town. Haliburton quickly recovered his position, however, and during the minority of James VI he served for more than ten years on the Privy Council, probably as a result of his connections with Moray, the king's uncle and the first regent after Mary's forced abdication in 1567. It was a rarity and therefore an asset for any burgh, to have such a well-connected provost with access to the corridors of power. It was also unusual for a burgh to elect a laird to parliament who was not also an active merchant but, as with the Wedderburns, Dundee was able to bend the rules. It was even fined by the Convention of Burghs for sending him as a commissioner to a convention which was meeting immediately before parliament in 1579.[20] When Haliburton died in 1589, the burgh honoured their late provost by paying for his funeral and constructing an ornate tomb in the parish church.[21]

The Scrymgeours of Dudhope (the hereditary constables of

Dundee), whose seat lay at the very boundary of the burgh, are a surprising rarity amongst those chosen as Dundee's parliamentary commissioners. On only eight occasions was anyone bearing the surname Scrymgeour elected to represent the town at a meeting of the Estates. Four of those are accounted for by the relatively minor Alexander Scrymgeour (apparently not a close relative of the family of Dudhope) between 1579 and 1586. Scrymgeour lairds were elected in 1543, 1544, 1569 and 1600, but only two of those four were provosts and only two were Scrymgeours of Dudhope – one sitting in 1543, the other in 1600. Previous generations of scholars would have explained this in the context of the impotence of the Scottish parliament, in contrast to England, where ambitious gentry sought urban seats because of the importance and strength of Westminster. Recent reassessments indicate that Scottish burghs retained more firm control over their representatives, particularly because of the power of the Convention of Burghs in ensuring that urban parliamentary commissioners had a genuine commitment to the burghs that they represented. Virtually all of the lairds who represented burghs were active in the lives of the burghs for which they sat. Sir James Scrymgeour of Dudhope, although provost in all but five years between 1587 and 1609, was chosen to represent Dundee at parliament only once, even though he was an active parliamentarian with more attendances to his name than Haliburton, representing the county of Angus at ten meetings of the Estates during his provostship.[22] He evidently considered himself to be a laird, first and foremost, for even when he was not elected as one of the shire commissioners for Angus, he did not use his position as provost to get into parliament. The exception was in 1600 when he sat for Dundee – but it is not clear why.

If his position as provost had actually given him authority within the burgh, he would surely have used it to gain an easy route into parliament by bypassing the inconvenience of an open election by the lairds of the shire. Indeed, had he possessed such influence over what might be understood as his client burgh, he need never have bothered with the troublesome route of election as a shire commissioner. That he did this raises significant issues in relation to the nature of urban parliamentary representation in Scotland and the relationship between towns and their neighbouring landowners. Perhaps Scrymgeour may have been reluctant to sit for the burgh because his status as hereditary constable of Dundee implied that being a member of the estate of burgesses was beneath his dignity. Perhaps he might have found his freedom to act restricted since burgh commissioners had to follow the agreed policy of the burgess estate.[23] The tight grip which the burghs collectively kept on the behaviour of individual urban commissioners in parliament would have made it difficult for a laird whose interests did not lie in trade to act as freely as he might want. This had not been a problem for Haliburton but it appears to have been for Scrymgeour. Moreover, by the later sixteenth century the Convention of Burghs was strictly enforcing the requirement that burgh commissioners had to be 'merchantis and traffiquaris, haifand thair remanyng and dwelling within burgh, and beris burdene with the nychtbouris and inhabitantis thairof'.[24] This increased attention to the residential qualifications of commissioners was beginning to become evident towards the end of Haliburton's parliamentary career, and by the time that Scrymgeour was provost, it was much more prominent. Scrymgeour was neither a merchant, nor lived in the burgh, and neither contributed to its upkeep nor paid a share of its taxes.

Scrymgeour never represented Dundee at the Convention of Burghs, because those commissioners to the Convention of Burghs who were also lairds were active merchants as well.[25] By contrast, Scrymgeour was a landed outsider provost who did not have an active role in urban affairs, and clearly did not think of himself as urban in the way that Sir James Haliburton and the landed provosts of many other burghs across Scotland did. He held the office of provost as an honorific title and, perhaps, as an agent of the Crown in the troubled period in the burgh's history on either side of 1600.[26] Most of the time, the council saw no reason to elect him as a commissioner to parliament, choosing genuine merchants instead. Dundee would never have considered sending Scrymgeour to a Convention of Burghs, nor would Scrymgeour have considered attending.

Scrymgeour's parliamentary attendance and other aspects of his behaviour were not only typical of outsider landed provosts but epitomised the relationship between Dundee and its hereditary constable. Historians have tended to assume that most burghs – whether Aberdeen and the Gordons of Huntly, Perth and the Ruthvens of Gowrie, Burntisland and the Melvilles of Murdocairnie or Dundee and the Scrymgeours of Dudhope – were in the pockets of greater or lesser members of the nobility; but the more research that is carried out, the less the proposition stands up.[27] What evidence there is suggests that burghs frequently squabbled with their powerful landed neighbours; lairds tended not to use their influence over their neighbouring burghs to gain access to parliament for themselves or their family members; and being a landed provost who was not an active merchant was an honorific position.

Scrymgeour very rarely participated in council business, and his name almost never appears on the sederunts of council meetings.[28] He was hereditary constable not of the burgh itself, but of its ancient and long-vanished royal castle – and the office conferred certain personal rights in the burgh. However, by seeking to assert those rights, he interfered with the burgh administration, and that created tension. Maxwell in his *History of Old Dundee* relates a number of instances of his overbearing behaviour. The main dispute related to the nature of his jurisdiction as constable and dated from the fourteenth century.[29] After an incident in 1580, the Privy Council recognised that, on four days on either side of Dundee's August fair, as well as on the day of the fair itself, he had the right to deal with all crimes and disputes within the burgh.[30] He had sought to assert such rights at other times; but in a decisive victory for the burgh, the burgh court had exclusive jurisdiction for all but nine days in the year. After 1580, relations between the burgh and the constable settled down. His becoming provost in 1587 may even have been part of the reconciliation.

Although it was complicated in this case by his hereditary position, having Scrymgeour as provost was fairly typical of the relationship between landed proprietors and neighbouring burghs. For most of the year, that position was honorific. His neglect of the office of provost, in terms of attendance at council meetings and the fact that he represented the burgh in parliament only once supports this. Perhaps Dundee made him their provost to flatter him in the sure knowledge that it would not involve having to put up with him in the tedious business of running the town. This contrasts markedly with Haliburton, diligent in his service as provost and in parliamentary affairs, happily serving the burgh there on numerous occasions – with no thought of adding to his family's influence in parliament by attending as a burgh commissioner: the Haliburtons of Pitcur were conspicuous by their absence from the Estates. In exercising his office of hereditary constable, Scrymgeour was not using his office of provost to assert his authority over the burgh, so much as interfering *as a landed outsider*.

A MATTER OF PRECEDENCE

There was more to parliament than securing favourable laws or blocking unfavourable ones. Parliament, as the embodiment of the nation, virtually represented by the Estates, was the foremost public stage on which an individual or a corporation had their status affirmed. Early modern elites were acutely conscious of precedence and would go to great lengths to ensure that their place in the pecking order was acknowledged.[31]

The most acrimonious and longest-running urban dispute over parliamentary precedence – between Dundee and Perth – began in December 1567 when burgesses of the two burghs were 'striving for the neerest place to the Tolbuith'. The issue was 'that long lasting debait betuix the tounes of Perth and Dundie anent the 2d place of precedincey amongest the burrowes'[32] and the Privy Council was displeased that a 'tumult happynnit upoun the gait of Edinburgh betuix the nychtbouris [of Dundee] and the inhabitantis of Sanctjohnnestoun [Perth] in the tyme of the . . . parliament'. The regent for the infant James VI, James Stewart, Earl of Moray, intervened in an attempt to reconcile the towns, perhaps because he was a patron of James Haliburton, provost of Dundee.[33] This dispute, which according to one Victorian historian of Perth, 'raged with ludicrous vehemence on the part of the Dundonians',[34] had its origins in the fourteenth century, when Dundee overtook Perth as the richest burgh on the Tay.[35] In 1402, it fought off Perth's attempts to assert rights over the whole firth and proceeded to demand exactions from Perth, whose liberties stretched to Invergowrie, within 5 miles of Dundee. To carry goods to and from Perth's docks, smaller boats had to ply between Perth and Dundee, so cargoes had to be trans-shipped at Dundee, where harbour and anchorage fees were demanded.[36] The rivalry intensified again in the sixteenth century as Dundee's share of urban taxation grew at Perth's expense.[37]

The dispute erupted again when parliament met at Edinburgh in 1579, and the Convention of Burghs was ordered to decide the question of priority between Perth, Dundee and Stirling 'according to the auncientie of the saidis burrowis;' and was also to rank the other burghs, 'swa that perpetuall ordour may be establischit'.[38] At the Convention of Burghs, the commissioners from Dundee and Perth agreed that their 'contentioun' should be submitted to arbitrators chosen by the convention. Dundee and Perth were each to choose three merchants to meet at the church of Rait (between the two burghs) and choose an 'overisman' with a casting vote. To ensure that this crucial individual was chosen fairly, each burgh would name five burgesses of other burghs, both lists would be put into a hat (literally) on one piece of paper along with a blank piece. If Perth's representative chose the paper with the names, Dundee would choose from Perth's nominees and vice versa and the panel of seven would settle the question once and for all.[39]

It is easy to imagine the exasperation at the next Convention of Burghs in July 1580 when it transpired that the meeting at Rait had not even taken place. It was ruled that Dundee and Perth should bring 'thair allegeances, defenssis and ressonis' and their 'titillis, writis and documentis' to another convention at Edinburgh in April 1581.[40] In the following April, there was 'lang debaitt and controversie' between Perth and Dundee. Their written arguments were 'hard, red and at lenth avysitlie considerit', and remitted to the king and Privy Council because the dispute was 'swa debaitabill and intricate'.[41] The Privy Council would have none of it, insisting that the burghs give judgement as parliament had commanded. So, threatened with horning (outlawry) 'the maist pairt' of the Convention gave Perth 'the priority . . . before the burch of Dundie' until the next parliament or Convention of the Estates, or until a judgement was made by the king and Privy Council. The commissioners of Dundee 'alluterly dissentit' as did others, asserting that this ruling should 'preiuge nocht thair burghis in the places quhilk thai merite as mair ancient nor the burchis contendant'.[42]

Dundee would not let the matter lie. In November 1581, it petitioned parliament, alleging that Perth's claim to second place was recent, and that Dundee was older, paid more tax and was governed exclusively by merchants, while Perth had an even split of merchants and craftsmen on its council. Parliament handed the decision back to the burghs to resolve 'but [i.e. without] fordar delay'.[43] The next Convention of Burghs, at Perth in June 1582, judged in favour of Perth and another, immediately preceding parliament in October, followed suit.[44] The Guildry Book of Perth giving a full account of events, recorded the lengths to which its Dean of Guild, Henry Adamson, had gone. He rode to Edinburgh to raise a letter on the act of parliament to charge the Convention of Burghs to resolve the dispute. He secured the signatures of the treasurer, William Ruthven, Earl of Gowrie and patron of Perth, and the abbot of Dunfermline, Robert Pitcairn. He then rode to Stirling for the king's signature, returning to Edinburgh to obtain the signet. The Convention therefore 'declarit the burgh of Perth to haif the first place afoir Dondy . . . in all tym to cum'. Dundee sought redress at parliament in October but the Estates remitted the case straight back to the burghs, ordering them to make a final decision on this and 'the haill remanent burowis without delay'. The royal letter made it clear that the burghs should 'considder onlye . . . the maist . . . ancient burgh', clearly indicating the expected outcome in noting 'the ancie[n]tie and antiquitie of our said burgh of Perth'. The Convention of Burghs duly obliged.[45]

In 1582, Gowrie's support had been worth having, but by 1584 the political tables had turned. A coup headed by Gowrie in August 1582 had led to the captivity of the king but a counter-coup in July 1583 overthrew Gowrie's regime. He was arrested, ironically at Dundee while trying to flee the country and was executed for treason. Dundee's reward was 'second place in voting in parliament nixt [to] Edinburgh' in May 1584, in spite of Perth's protest. A royal letter then charged the Convention of Burghs 'to rank and crave [Dundee's] voitt befoir . . . Perth'.[46] In July 1587, Perth insisted on the judgements of 1581 and 1582, declaring that a 'previe letter, purchest of his Majestie' (Dundee's of 1584) could not overturn a judgement carried out on the order of parliament.[47] In exasperation, the burghs tried to remit the decision to Edinburgh, on the logical basis that its rank was the only one beyond dispute, but its commissioner 'disassentit to thatt burding'.[48] At the next parliament, Dundee again tried to obtain a decision but parliament remitted it to the Court of Session.[49] Nobody wanted to take responsibility.

In 1594, Perth was back in royal favour and the king ordered the Earl Marischal to place it second after Edinburgh in accordance with the acts of the Convention of Burghs, presumably referring to the decisions of 1581 and 1582.[50] Although this sounded like a final judgement, Dundee would not acquiesce and, seven years later, the dispute was no closer to resolution; if anything, relations between Perth and Dundee were deteriorating because a new royal charter to Perth ostensibly rescinded Dundee's rights over navigation on the Tay.[51] In February 1601, the king's messenger came to the cross of Dundee to proclaim royal letters, raised before the Court of Session by Perth, but the bailies of Dundee organised a crowd to heckle him, 'caling him knaif, lowne, and deboschit swingeour [i.e. scoundrel], casting of snaw ballis at him, and interrupting him in proclaimeing of the saidis letters, and . . . schoutting and hoying of him with loud cryis throw the gait as gif he haid bene a theif or malefactour'. Dundee closed ranks and the poor messenger 'failed in his proof', no Dundonians being willing to bear witness in his favour.[52]

On 1 July 1601, Perth's commissioners at the Convention of Burghs at St Andrews informed their council that the convention intended to resolve the dispute and that Dundee was agreeable. They evidently believed that speed was of the essence and asked the council to 'heist ane heir on the secund of this moneth althocht he suld ryd the haill nycht'. The council gave its commissioners full power to act but insisted that no writs dating from before their new charter of 1600 should be considered.[53] On 3 July, Perth's commissioners at Edinburgh obtained a suspension of the process before the Court of Session on the grounds that the Convention of Burghs was to 'submit the saidis matteris . . . to the amicabill decisioun of certane uther burrowis'. The commissioners from Dundee and Perth agreed 'to submit thair actiouns presentle depending in the law, and all utheris thair grudgeis and controvereis' to a special Convention of Burghs at Edinburgh. It duly met but, when it was resolved that the most important task was 'to tak away all grudge of the prioritie', Perth perversely 'refuissit to submit except that particular . . . war left furth' because they had not been commissioned to discuss it, insisting that the judgement of 1582 should stand.

The case was postponed yet again until the general Convention in 1602.[54] However, by that time, the process before the Court of Session had reached an advanced stage. The council of Perth authorised its commissioners at Edinburgh to borrow whatever sums were necessary for their case, while Dundee borrowed 5,000 merks (£3,333 6s 8d) 'in the defense of certane wrangous actionis and persuittis intendit aganes thame be the toune of Perth'.[55] On 30 December 1602, the Court of Session, sitting with King James VI, gave their final judgement.[56] Perth's submission began with its strongest suit:

the gryt antiquitie, gud and pleasant cituatioun of the said burgh, of auld theresidence of your hienes progenitouris with thair princeis, bairnes, and fameleis, and quhair parliamentis, publict conventiounes, generall counsellis and assembleis of the esteattis of the realme wer hauldin.

It went on to say that its new charter of 1600 exempted its merchants from any exactions that might harm their trade, protesting that the rights obtained by Dundee over parts of the Firth of Tay were invalid because they had already been granted to Perth. Dundee's response cited various crown grants from the thirteenth century onwards which had given it jurisdiction in 'all pairtis foiranent the sherefdome of Foirfair' along with the right to insist that all ships entering the Tay had to 'break bulk' at Dundee. Furthermore, it provided reasons why it should have 'the first place [after Edinburgh] in all parliamentis, assembleis, counsallis and conventiounes'. The first was that Dundee was 'mair ancient', having existed before Perth's claim to foundation by William the Lion (1165–1214).

William had indeed granted Perth its oldest extant charter, but other sources demonstrate foundation by David I (1124–1153) in the 1120s and Dundee could not match that.[57] The second stated that, Dundee 'beiris the double of the chairgis of Perth in the subsideis of the realme, in the quhilk respect Edinburgh is preferrit to the rest of the burrowis'. Such an argument is not found anywhere else in the context of urban precedence, nor is it one that was used by nobles in their claims for precedence. If accepted, priority would have been established simply by referring to the most recent tax roll, a solution which would have led to interminable arguments involving numerous burghs and a change in the order of the parliamentary procession every few years. The third asserted that 'Dundie is mair civilie governit', a reference to Dundee's two craft councillors compared to the even division of merchants and craftsmen on Perth's council. This point would have made Edinburgh less 'civilie governit' than Dundee, for the capital's council of eighteen included six craftsmen and, like Perth, one of its four bailies was a craftsman. This was an argument which could not be entertained.[58] Finally, Dundee claimed that it had had priority in parliament before the burghs' judgement of 1582. It pointed out that the Convention had met at Perth in that year and that judgement had been obtained with the help of 'mony sinister moyenis usit be umquhile William erle of Gowrie'. This was clearly aimed at the king who would not easily forget his captivity in 1582–83 and would still have an alleged attempt on his life by Gowrie's sons at Perth in August 1600 fresh in his mind.

Yet his generous charter to Perth in 1600 was evidence enough that, for James, there was nothing to forgive. The judgement favoured Perth: it would have liberty of the Tay in Perthshire, on both sides of the water, while Dundee would have the same liberty in Forfarshire but would not have the right to levy tolls on Perth's ships except to pay for the upkeep of the 'tines in the watter mowthe of Tay' placed by Dundee to guide shipping into the safe channels of the firth. Finally:

> As to the first place and rank acclamit be ather of the saidis burrowis of Dundie and Perth in parliamentis, generall conventiounes, counsellis of the esteattis of this realme and assembleis of burrowis, Our said soverane lord findis and decernis that the said burght of Perth and thair commissioneris sall have the plaice befoir the said burght of Dundie and thair commissioneris in all the foirsaidis publict meittingis, And the said burgessis of Dundie thair saidis successouris and commissioneris sall mak na impedimentis to thame thairin in na tyme cuming.

No reasons were rehearsed, but the judgement in favour of Perth was just, for it had been founded before Dundee, and antiquity was the most important criterion for determining rank. For Perth and Dundee, and for the other burghs which added their own assertions for a better place in the ceremonials of parliament, this was an important matter since the pride of their burghs was at stake.

Dundee's assertion that it was 'mair civillie governit' than Perth because of the minimal craft presence on its council was to suffer another blow not long after this. A controversy arose in 1604 when the Crafts, in an attempt to secure more than two places on the council, staged a coup.[59] Apparently under the leadership of Mr Robert Howie, one of the town's ministers, the Crafts rose up in arms and, with a force of over 300 and with the support of some merchants made an independent election of the new council, packing it with craft deacons. The dispute was so serious that the Privy Council intervened, the ringleaders were imprisoned in Stirling, Dumbarton and Blackness Castles and all those involved were barred from public office for life. The issue was complicated by the fact that the provost, Sir James Scrymgeour of Dudhope, was using James VI to maintain his position as chief magistrate against the will of a majority of the council. It would appear that some merchants had joined with the two craft councillors to try to exclude Scrymgeour, while the rest of the merchants were willing to ally with him to counter the influence of the Crafts and the burgh's hot-headed, socially radical minister Robert Howie who had championed their cause. The dispute was resolved with a compromise which firmly favoured the merchants. The craftsmen had sought to double their representation from two to four councillors but were permitted only three and only for a trial period.[60] Soon afterwards, parliament passed an act banning those who were not merchant burgesses from holding urban office, and one historian has suggested that this resulted from events in Dundee which might never have arisen had there not been an outsider as provost.[61]

ACHIEVEMENT OF LEGISLATION

The five burghs which dominated parliament's legislative output in favour of individual towns between 1550 and 1651 were Edinburgh, Dundee, Aberdeen, Glasgow and Perth. Edinburgh accounted for nearly half of those burghs' acts. Remarkably, given its wealth and standing, Dundee had the fewest – only twelve, compared to thirteen for Glasgow, fourteen for Perth, twenty for Aberdeen and forty-eight for Edinburgh.[62] Only two of Dundee's acts were obtained before 1639. How can this be squared with Dundee's regular attendance at parliament and its consistent sending of relatively large delegations of skilled commissioners?

Obtaining legislation was not the only thing to be gained from parliamentary attendance. Burghs were intensely proud of their standing and large, expensively-furnished commissions helped to make that manifest. In 1567, Dundee's parliamentary commissioners even brought an ensign-bearer with them (for he was involved in a brawl on the High Street, so severe that the matter came before the Privy Council).[63] A high degree of mercantile solidarity was the crucial driving force behind regular parliamentary attendance by the commissioners of burghs, and this was fostered and maintained by the Convention of Burghs. Burghs that could afford to send their commissioners regularly did so as much to ensure that the collective voice of merchants was clearly heard as to promote their own individual interests. Although the estate of burgesses was the single biggest estate, it could be outvoted by the others (dominated by the landed classes) and therefore needed to maximise its presence to have any hope of securing favourable legislation.

Regularity of representation was also important to ensure that a town's rights and privileges were safeguarded, sometimes by obtaining an

act of parliament, sometimes by blocking unfavourable legislation put
forward by a rival. Even though Dundee rarely obtained an act of
parliament in its favour, the fact that its commissioners always served on
the key parliamentary committees meant that they would be able to
exercise influence in parliament, and in the Convention of Burghs,
where the interests of the merchants of the whole of Scotland were artic-
ulated and framed into legislative proposals. So Dundee must have had
a hand in many of the acts collectively promoted in parliament by the
whole burgess estate.

Yet none of this actually explains why Dundee sought, or at least
obtained, so few acts before 1633 and so many thereafter, especially
because the sorts of acts which it obtained were common to all burghs
(confirming its crown charter in 1601 and, in the 1640s, obtaining relief
from taxation because of the problems arising from war).[64] Perhaps
Dundee's comparative security and confidence in its privileges and
properties before the 1640s meant that it felt less of a need to seek
protective legislation. That is borne out by the fact that the first act of
parliament in its favour, obtained in 1594, ratified an acknowledgement
by the Crown that Dundee had repaid a loan of £20,000 plus £8,000
interest which it had been compelled by the Crown to take out in 1590.[65]
Even as late as 1644, Dundee managed to raise over £6,000 in a few days
to finance the army of the Covenant as it passed through the burgh, and
its commissioner confidently approached parliament in July seeking a
guarantee that that sum, along with other monies owed by the state,
would be reimbursed out of excise duties due from the burgh. Until
1644, therefore, the parliamentary record gives the impression of a
wealthy and secure burgh. Its new crown charters of 1601 and 1641 were
confirmed by parliament in 1606 and 1641 and its commissioners were
appointed to numerous parliamentary commissions on issues ranging
from coinage, weights and measures, the law relating to rape, to union
negotiations with England after 1603.[66]

Dundee firmly supported the Covenanters, pouring tens of thousands
of pounds into the war effort from 1639 onwards. But, as the 1640s wore
on with no end to the fighting in sight, so the financial burden became
increasingly onerous. Although the acts secured by Dundee were similar
to others, they do suggest that the civil wars had a particularly severe
impact on it. The first blow occurred in April 1645, when the royalist
army of James Graham, Marquis of Montrose, performed a lightning

raid on the burgh. In its immediate aftermath, Dundee's parliamentary commissioner managed to secure an act recognising 'the prejudices and sufferings' of the burgh and promising 'ane speciall caire and consideratione of the same for redress theirof'.[67] This was the best he could get in the circumstances, for the Covenanting regime was reeling from a fifth defeat at the hands of Montrose, at Alford in Aberdeenshire on 2 July. Parliament met at Stirling less than a week later for only four days with its mind on more immediate military matters.[68] In September, Montrose's rising was crushed at Philiphaugh and the Covenanting regime had regrouped sufficiently to hold another parliament in November. Dundee's commissioner again submitted a petition which revealed its now parlous state as a result of Montrose's attack in which many had been killed and much property destroyed, 'quhairby that town whiche was ane of the cheife of this kingdome is fearfullie defaced'. The burgh was unable to pay its taxes or provide recruits for the army, and a government commission appointed to enquire into the extent of the burgh's losses had not yet reported. Unless they received help, the petition groaned, 'we ar readie to sink under the weight of these intollerable burdingis and to perish from the comoune wealth'.[69]

In January 1646 the committee for bills and supplications reported that the state owed Dundee £26,500 of borrowed money and £31,000 for quartering troops there, that Dundee's losses as a result of Montrose's attack were £162,000 and that the burgh had spent £35,000 in building new fortifications: a total of over £250,000. An immediate payment of £20,000 was recommended to help the destitute inhabitants of the town and in February the committee for moneys was ordered to make payment.[70] It was less than one tenth of what Dundee needed but it was something, and on 16 February, Alexander Wedderburn, the burgh's returning commissioner received the thanks of the burgh council for 'his extraordinar paynes' on their behalf.[71]

The ubiquitous hyperbole of petitions to parliament counsels caution in assessing the severity of Dundee's plight, yet comparison with the losses of other burghs does suggest that it must be taken seriously. In 1649, Lanark sought 'some effectuall meanes wherthrew [it] . . . may be preserved from utter destructioune'. Its petition claimed that the burgh's total losses as a result of military attacks, money lent to the state and that owed for quartering soldiers amounted to less than £20,000.[72] Dundee's losses in 1645 were more than twelve times as much as Lanark's in 1649.

It is not clear how much money, if any, ever actually reached Dundee. Not much, it would seem: in January 1649, the burgh's commissioner to parliament was instructed to seek help for 'the supplicantis of the brunt [i.e. burnt] land' and that 'the act maid at St Andrews [in January 1646] be presentit for thair furtherance', for they had not been paid.[73] By 1649, not only were the burgh and its inhabitants owed a great deal of money by the state, but Dundee was falling behind in its monthly payments of 'maintenance' (a tax to support the army) and plague had arrived to add to its woes (see Chapter 3).[74]

Whatever happened in 1651, the burgh was already in a pitiful state by the time it was stormed by the English army under General Monck.[75] Although Dundee remained the second wealthiest burgh in Scotland as far as its share of national taxation was concerned, it had begun to decline significantly by 1649 when it was assessed to pay only 7% of the total (compared to nearly 11% before the wars). This was significantly more of a decline than its nearest rival, Aberdeen, which had suffered at least as badly from military incursions during the wars of the 1640s but was possibly recovering by the later 1640s.[76] Dundee may not have lost its second place among taxpaying burghs until 1670, but it was already falling fast in 1649 and that decline continued. By contrast, Aberdeen, which pushed Dundee into fourth place in 1670 suffered a less severe decline and recovered slightly after the Restoration, while Glasgow, which took second place in 1670 was already paying an increased share by 1649 and continued to grow relative to the others.[77]

Dundee's pleas to parliament in the 1640s indicate that success in securing acts of parliament in one's favour did not necessarily indicate power and prosperity. However, the fact that it was the larger, wealthier burghs which were able to secure acts, whether they bolstered privileges or were intended to extricate the burgh from dire straits, suggests that size mattered when it came to securing legislation. Whether prospering or in difficulty, a burgh's status was mirrored in its success in obtaining acts.

CONCLUSION

Dundee's interactions with central institutions serve to highlight the burgh's national standing. In numerous different contexts, only Edinburgh had a more prominent role which reflected Dundee's economic power as the second wealthiest burgh before the later seventeenth century. Perth was older and was given precedence in parliament as a result, yet those who controlled Dundee could go home to lick their wounds, content in the knowledge that, however irksome it might be to have to give way to Perth in public ceremonial, they were wealthier, and Perth was never going to mount an economic challenge. What is clear is that, whilst more goods were being imported and exported through Dundee than through any port other than Leith, whenever the views of Scotland's burghs were sought, Dundee could not be denied a place.

NOTES

1 For further discussion of Dundee's prosperity as a seaport, see C. McKean and C. Swan with M. Archibald, 'Maritime Dundee and its Harbour, c. 1755–1820', ch. 11 in this volume.

2 See, B. Kümin and A. Würgler, 'Petitions, *Gravamina* and the Early Modern State: Local Influence on Central Legislation in England and Germany (Hesse)', in *Parliaments, Estates and Representation (PER)*, 17 (1997), pp. 39–60; P. Sanz, 'The Cities in the Aragonese Cortes in the Medieval and Early Modern Periods', in *PER*, 14 (1994), pp. 95–108; R. Tittler, 'Elizabethan Towns and the "Points of Contact": Parliament', *Parliamentary History*, 8 (1989), pp. 275–288; D. M. Dean, 'Public or Private? London, Leather and Legislation in Elizabethan England', *Historical Journal*, 31 (1988), pp. 525–548; E. P. Dennison and M. Lynch, 'Crown, Capital, and Metropolis. Edinburgh and Canongate: The Rise of a Capital and an Urban Court', *Journal of Urban History*, 32 (2005), pp. 22–43. For Scottish towns and the state, see M. Lynch, 'The Crown and the Burghs, 1500–1625', in M. Lynch (ed.), *The Early Modern Town in Scotland* (London, 1987), pp. 55–80; A. R. MacDonald, ' "Tedious to rehers"? Parliament and Locality in Scotland c. 1500–1651: the Burghs of North-East Fife', in *PER*, 20 (2000), pp. 31–58. There is only one general history of the Scottish parliament, another on the Convention of Burghs and one more on the burgess estate: R. S. Rait, *The Parliaments of Scotland* (Glasgow, 1924); T. Pagan, *The Convention of the Royal Burghs of Scotland* (Glasgow, 1926); J. D. Mackie and G. S. Pryde, *The Estate of the Burgesses in the Scots Parliament* (St Andrews, 1923).

3 The most prolific writer on the early modern Scottish 'state' is Julian Goodare, see esp. his *State and Society in Early Modern Scotland* (Oxford, 1999), passim (see p. 215 for the role of the burghs).

4 J. Goodare, 'The Scottish Parliament and its Early Modern "Rivals" ' in *PER*, 24 (2004), pp. 147–72; Rait, *The Parliaments of Scotland*, pp. 9–19; E. E. MacQueen, 'The General Assembly of the Kirk as a Rival of Parliament' (St Andrews PhD, 1927).

5 M. Young, *The Parliaments of Scotland: Burgh and Shire Commissioners*, 2 vols. (Edinburgh, 1992–93), vol. 1, p. 396; vol. 2, p. 651. Somerville was the only university graduate to represent a burgh at this meeting.

6 Young, *The Parliaments of Scotland*, vol. 2, Appendix 2, Constituency Lists, pp. 765–788. These figures carry the caveat 'at least' because of the incomplete nature

of local and national records: for many parliaments there is no surviving sederunt (attendance list), burgh records tend to have gaps and they do not always record who was commissioned to attend parliament.

7 For the operation of this committee, see A. R. MacDonald, 'Deliberative Processes in Parliament, *c.* 1567–1639: multicameralism and the Lords of the Articles', in *Scottish Historical Review*, 81 (2002), pp. 23–51.

8 A. R. MacDonald, *The Burghs and Parliament in Scotland c. 1550–1651* (Aldershot, 2007), ch. 3.

9 J. D. Marwick and T. Hunter (eds.), *Records of the Convention of the Royal Burghs of Scotland* (*RCRBS*), vol. 1, pp. 67–68, 166–167, 179; vol. 2, p. 14.

10 *RCRBS*, vol. 2, pp. 15, 32, 58.

11 *RCRBS*, vol. 2, p. 163; T. Thomson and C. Innes (eds.), *The Acts of the Parliaments of Scotland* (*APS*) (Edinburgh, 1814–75), vol. 4, pp. 263–264.

12 See Young, *The Parliaments of Scotland*, passim: Dundee has 34 commissioners recorded, Edinburgh 55, St Andrews 21, Perth 20, Stirling 18, Glasgow 16, Aberdeen and Ayr 15.

13 Dundee City Archives (DCA), Council Minutes vol. 1, 1553–1588, pp. 76–77; A. Maxwell, *History of Old Dundee Narrated out of the Town Council Register with Additions from Contemporary Annals* (Edinburgh, 1884), pp. 184–186.

14 MacDonald, 'Parliament and locality', pp. 45–50.

15 MacDonald, *The Burghs and Parliament*, ch. 2.

16 *RCRBS*, vol. 1, p. 80; I. E. F. Flett, 'The Conflict of the Reformation and Democracy in the Geneva of Scotland 1443–1610: An introduction to edited texts of documents relating to the burgh of Dundee' (St Andrews MPhil, 1981), p. 106.

17 MacDonald, *The Burghs and Parliament*, ch. 2; Young, *Parliaments of Scotland*, passim.

18 Young, *The Parliaments of Scotland*, pp. 722–724.

19 Maxwell, *The History of Old Dundee*, pp. 189–198.

20 *RCRBS*, vol. 1, p. 80.

21 DCA, Dundee Treasurer's Accounts vol. 1, 1586–1606, account for 1588–89; Maxwell, *History of Old Dundee*, p. 198.

22 Young, *The Parliaments of Scotland*, II, pp. 621–622.

23 MacDonald, *The Burghs and Parliament*, chs. 2 and 3.

24 *RCRBS*, vol. 1, pp. 25–26.

25 See J. D. Marwick, *Index to the Records of the Convention of the Royal Burghs of Scotland* (Edinburgh, 1890).

26 Flett, 'The Conflict of the Reformation and Democracy'.

27 M. Verschuur, 'Merchants and Craftsmen in Sixteenth-Century Perth', in Lynch (ed.), *The Early Modern Town in Scotland*, pp. 36–53, at 39; D. Stevenson, *The Scottish Revolution 1637–1644: The Triumph of the Covenanters* (Newton Abbot, 1973), p. 27. But see Lynch, 'The Crown and the Burghs', p. 56 where the assumption is questioned.

28 DCA, Council Minutes vols. 2 and 3, passim.

29 Maxwell, *History of Old Dundee*, pp. 19–21, 347ff.

30 J. H. Burton et al. (eds.), *Register of the Privy Council of Scotland* (*DCA*), first series (Edinburgh, 1877–98), vol. 3, pp. 303–304.

31 For a general discussion of the issues see MacDonald, *The Burghs and Parliament*, ch. 7.

32 Balfour, *Works*, vol. 1, p. 242.

33 *RPC*, first series, vol. 1, pp. 604–605; Calderwood, *History*, vol. 2, p. 338; Birrel, 'Diary', p. 13.

34 O. Ranum, 'Courtesy, absolutism and the French state', *Journal of Modern History*, 52 (1980), p. 430; R. S. Fittis, *The Perthshire Antiquarian Miscellany* (Perth, 1875), p. 358.

35 P. G. B. McNeill and H. L. MacQueen (eds.), *Atlas of Scottish History to 1707* (Edinburgh, 1996), pp. 250–260.

36 Detailed accounts of the trade disputes can be found in Fittis, *Perthshire Antiquarian Miscellany*, pp. 355–364; Maxwell, *The History of Old Dundee*, pp. 114–122; E. P. D. Torrie, *Medieval Dundee: A Town and its People*, (Dundee, 1990), p. 33.

37 McNeill and MacQueen, *Atlas of Scottish History*, p. 310; M. Lynch, 'Continuity and Change in Urban Society, 1500–1700', in R. A. Houston and I. D. Whyte (eds.), *Scottish Society, 1500–1800* (Cambridge, 1989), pp. 85–117, at 115.

38 *APS*, vol. 3, p. 174.

39 Ibid., pp. 84–85.

40 Ibid., pp. 107–108.

41 Ibid., p. 114.

42 Ibid., pp. 118–119.

43 *APS*, vol. 3, pp. 232–233.

44 The record of this Convention of Burghs is incomplete but the act is preserved in Perth: Perth and Kinross Council Archives (PKCA), Court Books and Court Minute Books, B59/12/1, fol. 83 r – v; *RCRBS*, vol. 1, 126–138; M. L. Stavert (ed.), *The Perth Guildry Book, 1452–1601* (Edinburgh, 1993), pp. 327–328.

45 Stavert, *The Perth Guildry Book*, pp. 328–329; PKCA, 'Letteris for Perth for the superioritie of place Perth aganis Dundie', 16 June 1582, B59/26/1/9/2; PKCA, Act of Convention of Burghs, 1582, B59/26/1/9/7/1; R. Renwick (ed.), *Charters and other Documents relating to the Royal Burgh of Stirling AD 1124–1705* (Glasgow, 1884), no. 48, Act of Parliament 11 November 1579.

46 *APS*, vol. 3, p. 291; *RCRBS*, vol. 1, pp. 175, 186–187, 195–196.

47 Ibid., pp. 230–231.

48 Ibid., pp. 232–233.

49 *APS*, vol. 3, p. 448.

50 PKCA, James VI to the Earl Marischal, 30 May 1594, B59/26/1/9/1.

51 Fittis, *Perthshire Antiquarian Miscellany*, p. 368.

52 *RPC*, first series, vol. 6, pp. 253–254, 265.

53 PKCA, Register of Acts of the Council, 1601–1602, B59/16/1, fols. 4 r – 5 r.

54 National Archives of Scotland (NAS), Court of Session, Register of Acts and Decreets, Gibson's Office, CS7/195, fols. 89 v – 92 v; *RCRBS*, vol. 2, pp. 111, 116.

55 PKCA, Register of Acts of the Council, 1601–1602, B59/16/1, fol. 42 r; DCA, Town Council Minute Book, vol. 2, p. 118; Maxwell, *The History of Old Dundee*, p. 121.

56 NAS, Court of Session, Register of Acts and Decreets, Gibson's Office, CS7/201, fols. 387 r – 393 r; DCA, Charters and Writs, 'Decreet by King James VI and the Lords of Council deciding the dispute between the towns of Perth and Dundee respecting their privileges on the Tay and the precedence', CC1/79.

57 G. S. Pryde, *The Burghs of Scotland: A Critical List* (Oxford, 1965), p. 4.

58 M. Lynch, *Edinburgh and the Reformation* (Edinburgh, 1981), pp. 49–51, 63, Appendix i; Verschuur, 'Merchants and craftsmen', p. 38.

59 For details see Maxwell, *History of Old Dundee*, pp. 353–368; Flett, 'The Conflict of the Reformation', ch. 6.

60   Ibid.; DCA, Dundee Council Minutes, vol. 3, fols. 26 r – 29 v, 40 r – 41 r, 59 r.

61   *APS*, vol. 4, pp. 435–436; Lynch, 'The Crown and the Burghs', pp. 64–65.

62   MacDonald, *The Burghs and Parliament*, ch. 4; *APS*, vols. 2–6, passim.

63   *RPC*, vol. 1, pp. 604–605.

64   *APS*, vol. 4, p. 304; vol. 5, p. 457; vol. 6 part 1, pp. 138–139, 434, 519–521, 579, 804; vol. 6 part 2, pp. 206, 312, 338.

65   *APS*, vol. 4, pp. 86–87; *RPC*, vol. 5, p. 149.

66   *APS*, vol. 3, pp. 214–215, vol. 4, pp. 263–264, 585–589.

67   *APS*, vol. 6 part 1, p. 434.

68   D. Stevenson, *Revolution and Counter Revolution, 1644–1651*, revised edn (Edinburgh, 2003), pp. 24–35.

69   *APS*, vol. 6 part 1, pp. 519–521.

70   *APS*, vol. 6 part 1, pp. 519–521, 579.

71   DCA, Council Minutes vol. 4, 1613–1653, fol. 192 r.

72   R. Renwick (ed.), *Extracts from the Records of the Royal Burgh of Lanark* (Glasgow, 1893), pp. 36–38.

73   DCA, Council Minutes vol. 4, 1613–1653, fol. 216 v.

74   *APS*, vol. 6 part 2, pp. 206, 312, 338.

75   J. Robertson, 'The Storming of Dundee, 1651', in *History Scotland*, May/June 2003, pp. 23–27 argues that the 'legend' of the devastation of Dundee by Monck is exaggerated.

76   Its share fell only from 8 to just under 7%. *RCRBS*, vol. 2, p. 10, vol. 3, pp. 332–3; G. DesBrisay, ' "The civill warrs did overrun all": Aberdeen 1630–1690', in E. P. Dennison, D. Ditchburn and M. Lynch (eds.), *Aberdeen Before 1800: A New History* (East Linton, 2002), pp. 238–266.

77   *RCRBS*, vol. 4, pp. 622–623.

CHAPTER 3

Battered but Unbowed – Dundee during the Seventeenth Century

Karen J. Cullen, Christopher A. Whatley and Mary Young

The seventeenth century was probably the most challenging in all of Dundee's long history. The period of the Anglo-Scottish regal union under King James VI (and I of England) began promisingly for Dundee and Scotland generally, and there was little intimation of the disasters that were to befall this cultured, prosperous and bustling port town. From its sheltered harbour and strategic location at the mouth of the River Tay, its merchants accessed the trade routes of the North Sea, described as second only to Leith 'for number of goode schippis and skilfull and able marinaris' in 1609.[1] When the king visited the burgh in 1617, the inhabitants of the town raised without difficulty the 3,000 merks needed for a royal reception befitting the status of Scotland's second town.[2]

Scotland's principal exports were primary products such as hides and skins, fish, wool, grain in good years, some coal, and live cattle; and substantial quantities of linen, woollens and salt were beginning to be manufactured. The first two were aimed at the lower end of the market. The rise in production and sales of Scottish marine salt from the 1570s had largely been owing to the interruption of supply of the preferred 'Bay' salt into northern Europe – to which consumers would turn again once the conflict between Spain and the Netherlands was over. Early on, Dundee and its region had established a foothold in manufacturing: 'narrow blew clayth', 'hemp clayth' and 'lyning', sent mainly to the Baltic.[3] The town imported almost as many dyestuffs as the rest of Scotland put together, while rising imports of hemp and lint (or flax), underlined the growing importance of textiles for the town (a similar transformation also taking place at and around Montrose, Dundee's coastal neighbour to the north).[4] Woad was imported from Bordeaux and Spain along with wine; red madder came from Flanders.[5]

The last decades of the sixteenth century were prosperous for Dundee and its shipping trade. Shipping lists for the fifteen months between August 1588 and November 1589, recorded the arrival of seventy-six vessels[6] whose cargoes provide an insight into the nature of the burgh's trade and also what was being consumed both in the town and the region it served. Thirty brought wood from Norway, and the large quantity of timber coming into Dundee testifies to the amount of building work being carried out (see Chapter 1). Commodities such as copper vessels and iron were imported from Stockholm; and soap, lead and glass from Danzig. There was also a sizeable trade in luxury goods largely paid for with the sale of animal skins: sheep and lamb skins, cow hides, goat and hare skins. Six vessels brought wine from Bordeaux and another from Spain, and fine cloth, soft furs for linings, glass and ceramics came from Holland and London.[7] However, the low value of Scotland's exports traded against the more expensive products bought in from abroad, left an imbalance that put a serious and long-term drain on the country's economy. Moreover, Scotland had neither the economic muscle to safeguard her interests nor a navy to protect her shipping. In the difficult and tumultuous years of the seventeenth century, after Dundee had survived plague, famine, storm, sack and hostile occupation, the degree to which the burgh relied on North Sea trade made her vulnerable and she suffered badly – more than any other of Scotland's large towns.

There are indications, however, that Dundee's decline relative to some other Scottish towns – Edinburgh and Glasgow – was a continuation of a trend begun in the later sixteenth century. In the 1550s and 1560s, Dundee contributed roughly 12.5% of the country's royal burghs tax. Thereafter, the percentage fell steadily – to 10.8% between 1591 and 1612, falling thereafter to only 4% by the late seventeenth century (see Figure 3.1), even though the town continued to hold second place behind Edinburgh until well into the 1660s.[8]

The town suffered a serious outbreak of bubonic plague in the 1590s, and the pestilence swept again through eastern Scotland in the first decade of the seventeenth century.[9] (See Chapter 5.) Throughout 1604 and 1605 the town council continued to receive reports of the disease

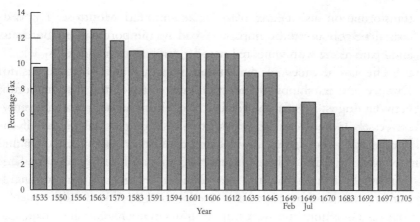

FIGURE 3.1
Percentage of burgh tax paid by Dundee, selected years 1535–1705[10]

ravaging St Andrews, Leith and Edinburgh. Goods and strangers were prevented from entering the burgh and boats from Fife were stopped from entering the harbour. In May 1605, townspeople were forbidden to trade with or even visit St Andrews. Thomas Mayne was banished for transporting goods from plague-afflicted St Andrews, which he falsely claimed to have brought from Leuchars. In December, two merchants were fined £20 for trying to sell cloth in St Andrews.[11] The first note in the council minutes of the plague's presence in the burgh was recorded in October 1606,[12] the rate of infection increasing over the next year. John Bell, one of the cleansers, was charged with negligence in dealing with the goods of the sick, which resulted in the spread of infection and the death of a number of townspeople.[13] The pace of the pestilence waxed and waned; strongest in the summer and autumn months while dying out over the winter. The scale of the infection was such that significant numbers of the townspeople, including members of the council, fled, and neighbours were forbidden under pain of death from visiting friends 'in a suspected state'. The magistrates who remained struggled to maintain order. A guard was appointed to protect the interests of the inhabitants, and a tax raised to help support the poor.[14] Although the crisis abated in February 1609, the council had to set yet another tax to pay the debts accrued in protecting the town and caring for the sick and poor during the previous two years.[15]

The plague was a disaster both in terms of lives lost and also for the town's economy. Food became scarce as country farmers stayed away, and work dried up as urban employers fled to the countryside. Markets closed and trade ceased. Plague tended to target households; whole families could be wiped out while others remained unscathed. No record survives of the number who died in Dundee in this outbreak, but a study of epidemics in English towns in this period suggest death rates of between 25 and 30% of their populations, although it might have been lower in the burgh, given Dundee's reputation for good health. Of the individuals infected, only half died; but those who recovered remained seriously ill for up to twenty-two weeks.[16] The high numbers of ill and poor in need of support increased the drain on the town's resources.

A further natural disaster befell the town in the 1620s, when Scotland suffered its worst subsistence crisis of the century. In most years, the rich arable acres of Forfarshire and the Carse of Gowrie produced a healthy surplus of cereals. Dundee's status as a royal burgh and market centre, its medieval trading privileges over a sizeable swathe of the surrounding sheriffdom of Forfar, large population and coastal location, combined to make the burgh the most important commercial centre in the region, not least for the grain trade – in terms of distribution, local consumption and exports. In 1621, however, the first of three consecutive years of harvest failure occurred, and not even Dundee's fertile hinterland could spare the town's inhabitants from the threat of starvation. A bad harvest might bring dearth, but failure year on year brought famine which gripped the area. Mr James Guthrie, the minister of the kirk of Kinnell in Angus, recorded the catastrophe in his diary:

> . . . for that haill summer tyd [of 1621] the weather was most unseasonabil, the harvest tyed was such lyk, so that be reason of the continual rain neither was their any eilding wind in many places nor the corns reapit. Ye hail harvest through the weather continued most inconstant and unseasonable and by reason of the continual rain there was gryt inundations of waters quhairby gryt hurt was done both by carying away of corns that were in valleys and haughes and by demolishing of hail houses and bridges. In the moneth of September the bridge of St Johnstoun [Perth] was born doun with spaitt of water to the gryt hurt of that citie. The winter in showing gryt scairsitie of victual . . . all prices waxed higher and higher but in the summer tyd their was

such scairsage that many sterved almaist for famine and if victual had not beiin brought from forraign Cuntreyes their was no appirance bot of extream famine. The year following their was not gryt store of corns; quhairapon throughout the hail summer their was gryt scaircitie and dearth in the hail land and numbers dying from day to day be famine. The winter theirefter was sore and long for their was no plewing or sawing almaist til the . . . midst of Marche 1624 . . . [17]

Although the town council minutes are silent and no church records survive, the severity of the crisis becomes evident from the shipping records which show that as early as 1622, over half of the vessels arriving at the port brought grain, and about one fifth brought famine relief in the following year. There is little further record of the importation of grain to Dundee in the next seventy years until the great famine of the 1690s.

Although the burgh had been able to weather these storms, trading patterns were changing, and shifting ever more towards the Atlantic. Glasgow was growing fast in wealth, size and importance, and east coast trade with the Low Countries was becoming increasingly concentrated on Leith and Edinburgh.[18] From early in the seventeenth century, Dundee's council had lamented the smallness of the town's revenue, but from the late 1630s, a series of man-made disasters befell the burgh to wreak further havoc upon its already strained economy.

Charles I's imposition of the 1637 prayer book on Scotland provoked the signing of the national covenant in defence of the Kirk in 1638, the dispatch of an expeditionary force to Scotland in 1639, followed by a series of wars and subsequent guerrilla risings, which would effectively not cease until 1655. As early as 1641, the town council was complaining that the burgh's income was insufficient to meet all of its new expenses such as quartering troops, fortifications, supplying fighting men and furnishing them with supplies.[19] Then the Marquis of Montrose, with a band of 'Irish rebelles', attacked and sacked the town in 1644 with 'the slaughter of many' and a destruction of property, which included the burning of the nave of St Mary's. The town council was obliged to pay compensation to 'a great number [of] poore people who had thair landis brunt at the assaulting be the crewel & bloodie rebellis'[20] assessed at £162,221. The proportion of Dundee's burgh stent roll was reduced by 36%.[21]

To compensate those who had their houses burnt or suffered related damages during the attack by Montrose, the national committee of estates recommended that a voluntary contribution be gathered throughout the country. In April 1647 further relief was offered through an act of parliament which allocated £2,000 to Dundee to help with the costs incurred in quartering troops, and to pay for the losses experienced by the townspeople – and also towards maintaining the poor.[22] Yet in December 1648, the council recorded concern at the continuing difficulties the town was facing, due to 'the great and extraordinary debt accrued' during the civil wars.[23]

A feared re-visitation of plague hampered the burgh's attempts at recovery. River trade with Fife was curtailed in September 1645, and the death of two children with 'blew spottis upon thair corpses' in October of the following year, sparked fear that the contagion had again reached Dundee. However, the measures taken by the council were so effective that evidence of plague in the town did not appear until August 1648, when a footman from Aberdeen died from the disease, with outbreaks of infection continuing into the next year. In 1647, presumably to avert the danger of a local food shortage, the town council attempted to stop grain exports from the port, but the Privy Council refused to permit such actions – by no means the last time that 'national' interests would seem to be in conflict with the needs of the wage-dependent portion of the urban population.[24]

When plague finally reached Dundee in autumn 1648, its effects were severe: from 'the twenty-twa day of August to the end of November, the merchant's booths were closed up, and no mercats were keiped, nor fleishes bocht'.[25] It ravaged the population until March of the following year. The impact of the disease was marked, for as much as 20% of Scotland's urban population was wiped out between 1644 and 1649.[26] Perhaps in view of the heavy tax burdens and financial difficulties already faced by the inhabitants, the council requested only a voluntary contribution to support the town's straitened coffers, rather than the demand for payment as in the earlier outbreak.[27]

Over the next two and a half years the burgh continued to borrow heavily. Increased taxes were laid upon the inhabitants to pay its expenses in light of the 'meanes and smallness of thair comone good'. Additional money had to be borrowed to meet the interest payments on existing loans.[28] In 1651, the treasurer's accounts show that the extraordinary discharges alone exceeded the town's income. 'Great soumes of money' were owed to the town's debtors and in May 1652 the council borrowed a further 14,000 merks.[29] Contemporaries described the 'decay of traid & merchandise' as exacerbating the burgh's difficulties. Even though there were occasional very good years, Figure 3.2 indicates that the trough of the second half of the 1640s was part of a longer downward trend.

In the light of the severe damage suffered in the attack by Montrose, the effects of the plague and the on-going costs of the war to the town in terms of money, commerce and lives, it says much for the spirit that existed in Dundee that the council and inhabitants stood against the formidable English army led by General Monck in August 1651. Their resistance however was quickly overcome and the burgh suffered heavily for its defiance. Although recent research indicates that the traditions of a long siege, no quarter being given, a massacre of one third of the inhabitants and the sinking of 50 ships full of booty as they sailed from the harbour are far from the mark,[30] contemporary reports about the extent of the injury inflicted on Dundee and its population at this time vary widely. One contemporary described townspeople 'stripped even to the sark' with losses estimated at £200,000.[31]

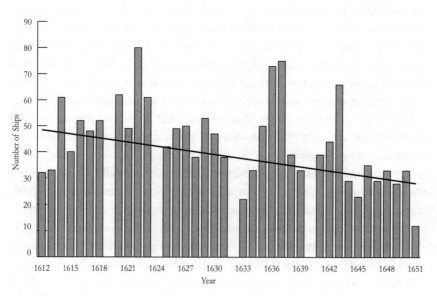

FIGURE 3.2
Number of ships importing goods to Dundee harbour, 1612–1651[32]

Occupation by the English followed. There is no surviving record of any incoming shipping 1652–54, which may either be the result of the damage by Cromwellian forces at Dundee and several of the Fife ports (Kirkcaldy may have lost ninety-four vessels between 1644 and 1660), and Ayr,[33] or because Dundee vessels had been commandeered by the English. It seems likely that Cromwell's war against the Dutch, which prevented trade between Scotland and one of her most important commercial partners, created additional problems for the town, and the town council lamented the dearth of both men and trade in 1654.[34] The burgh and the surrounding area were still suffering in the aftermath of war and defeat some two years later; the countryside was thick with displaced and desperate people.[35]

Seriously hampered by the restrictive English navigation Acts of 1651 and 1660, Dundee's trade was slow to recover, and the second Dutch War between 1665 and 1667 was a further setback. A great storm and tempest in the Tay in October 1668 virtually skinned the burgh's shore, breaching the sea walls from west to east and obliterating the harbour and bulwark, sinking all the ships within with the loss of their goods.[36] As was customary in exceptional circumstances, the town appealed to other burghs through the convention for financial support, and the losses incurred during the siege and capture of Dundee by Monck were used as an inducement to generosity. The town was granted the proceeds of yet another voluntary contribution.[37] It must have been speedily remedied, since Rev. Robert Edward could write in 1678: 'the harbour, by great labour and expense, has been rendered a very safe and agreeable station for vessels; and from this circumstance, the town has become the chief emporium not only of Angus but of Perthshire'.[38] However, the cost of these repairs had incurred considerable debt, £20,333 of which was still being carried forward in 1691.[39]

In spite of all this, in the first years after the wars, Dundee remained the second town in Scotland in terms of the proportion of revenue paid, albeit much reduced,[40] a role which it would lose by the 1670s – overtaken by both Aberdeen and rapidly-rising Glasgow. According to the burgh tax roll in that year, Dundee paid only 6.1% – against 33.3% by Edinburgh, 12.0% by Glasgow and 7.0% by Aberdeen.[41]

The economic difficulties faced by the burgh in the second half of the seventeenth century are reflected in a dramatic fall in the burgh's population after 1639, when it is estimated to have been in the region of

12,000.[42] Information from 1645 suggests a slight fall to 11,200, which could reflect losses sustained as a result of the attack by the Marquis of Montrose.[43] No further data from which calculations can be made is available until the beginning of the 1690s, when estimates using hearth tax records indicate a population at that time of only 8,250 – almost a third below the pre-war figure.[44] In the early modern period, the maintenance and any increase in the population of Scottish towns relied to a large degree on inward migration from the surrounding countryside or further afield. The principal draw for these migrants was the employment generated by a prospering economy – something much wanting in Dundee in these years.

An increase in economic activity in the rural areas around the burgh at this time had both positive and negative aspects. There was an expansion in cereal production and investment by a number of landowners in their country houses and estates as well as in agricultural improvements. There was also a very significant increase in the quantity of linen manufactured by small tenants in the countryside. This appears to have been fuelled by the 1680s arrival at the Perth markets of merchants from the north of England and the south and west of Scotland, seeking to purchase linen for transport overland by pack train.[45] The opening up of such overland routes is yet another manifestation of the diversification and changing pattern of trade that eroded the base on which Dundee's prosperity had been built a century earlier.

Competition with the burgh's trade also came from the countryside in the form of the proliferation and growth of burghs of barony. Charters erecting these burghs granted the basic right to buy and sell goods within their bounds, to hold markets and fairs, to have craftsmen and burgesses and to have the right to elect bailies and other officers. They lacked only the privilege of foreign trade.[46] By fostering a great deal of local commercial traffic, the burghs of barony diverted business from the old established royal burghs. The Convention of Royal Burghs took a protectionist stance and in 1691:

> . . . resolved no longer to suffer the rights of royal burghs to be abused and encroached upon by there owne burgesses, whoe be joining stocks with un-freemen inhabitants in the burghs or regalities and baronies and other unfree places bothe in point of trade and shipping.[47]

Royal burghs from across the country complained of loss of trade and an inability to meet their heavy public burdens. Substantial numbers of their inhabitants were being driven out of the burghs and into country areas where taxes and restrictions were less. In a plea for a reduction in their proportion of burgh taxes, Fortrose listed the lack of trade, the quartering of soldiers, an absence of Common Good and the level of public burdens as causing 'above tuentie families . . . this last terme' to desert the town.[48] In the failing burgh of Anstruther Wester even some 'of the ablest persones' had removed themselves to be free of the 'heavie impositions'.[49] Large burghs were affected along with the small. At Stirling, in spite of the town council reducing the cost of entry to burgess-ship by half, the commissioners reported that lack of trade resulted in 'many of the houses being waiste for want of Inhabitants'.[50] Perth town council complained of similar problems in 1700, but more particularly lamented the 'decay' in the trade of local produce and principally the effects of the French ban on fish imports which had been 'a most considerable part of the Common good and stock of the burgh'.[51] The merchants of Dumfries complained of the:

> . . . Incroachments by these unfree trades and the laws prohibiting the importation of cloath silks and other commodities from England Which was the trade that formerly supported this burgh. All traffiq is so universally extinguished and dead in this place that we are altogether incapacitate to sustain the heavy burden and bear that proportion of the Burrows [burgh's] taxt roll . . . Severall of our number . . . have withdrawn . . . Others living [in] this place are going to dwell in the countrey.[52]

Dundee's response to the increasing competition from the burghs of barony and the growth in trade occurring beyond the town's jurisdiction was of necessity pragmatic. In the 'Register containing the state and Condition of every burgh within the Kingdome of Scotland in the year 1692', the town admitted to trading links with at least fifteen such unfree towns and villages.[53]

There was a distinction between the burgh's own wealth, which was severely squeezed in the wars and continued to drain away through the second half of the seventeenth century, and that of a substantial number of its merchant burgesses. The size and quality of town houses belonging to Dundee merchants dating from this period indicate some considerable private wealth at a time when the fortunes of the burgh itself were at very low ebb. The drawings contained in Lamb's *Dundee* show a town boasting substantial buildings, predominantly of later seventeenth century appearance, many with the then relatively new large sash windows, possibly pioneered in Holland.[54] Robert Edward was vastly impressed by Dundee's architecture in 1678, writing: 'the citizens here (whose houses resemble palaces) are so eminent in regard to their skill and industry in business, that they have got more rivals than equals in the kingdom'.[55] One such 'palace' was the laird of Strathmartine's splendid new lodging in the Vault, behind the Town House.[56] With its elegant 'dutch' gables, projecting octagonal staircase, smart inner court, and elaborate wainscoting and plasterwork within, it was distinctly more fashionably cosmopolitan than anything contemporary in Edinburgh or Aberdeen. Drawings by Charles Lawson, a Dundee printer and lithographer, carried out before many of the buildings were taken down to make way for the city improvements of the nineteenth century, show rich and lavish interior decoration.[57]

The economic growth in Dundee's hinterland was due in no small part to the activity of its merchant-manufacturers, and the relationships between them and regional landowners. Links were social, economic and, in many cases, familial. Rural estates generated trade and contributed to the commerce of the burgh in their production of grain, linen, woollens and basic items such as shoes. The households of the lairds were significant consumers of imported luxury goods, as well as of wood, iron, lead, glass and the numerous materials needed for the building work and improvements that were being carried out on a significant number of estates throughout the district.[58] In their turn, Dundee merchants and burgesses were involved in the economy of the surrounding countryside far beyond their role as traders. Their commercial ethos and expertise had a direct impact on the economic health and development of the town's hinterland. Families of some notable Dundee burgesses were themselves directly engaged in agricultural production as farmers, and it was not unusual for sons of tenant farmers to become apprenticed to merchants. Many of the agricultural improvements carried out on the country estates near Dundee were at the instance of estate owners who had strong trading links with the burgh. The prominent Dundee merchant Henry Crawford, for instance, who purchased the estate of Monorgan, was later credited as one of the pioneers of using lime as manure in the district.[59] The estate of Mylnefield, founded by Alexander Mylne a provost and bailie of Dundee, was one of the first in the district to have a significant proportion of its land enclosed. Some of these enclosures are depicted to the east of Longforgan on John Adair's 1683 map of the area.[60]

Merchants granted loans and allowed considerable credit to landowners at a time when specie was in very short supply and many families within the landed elite were burdened with large and long-standing debts. When, for instance, William Ogilvie, possessor of the estate of Murie in the parish of Errol died in 1669, his executors were Patrick Yeaman and George Brown, both merchant burgesses of Dundee. They were also among his chief creditors, Yeaman holding a bond of £3,000 and Brown one for 5,000 merks. Yeaman was eventually to purchase the whole of the Murie estate.[61]

Examples of Dundee's merchant burgesses investing in estates are numerous. The estates were for the most part on good, fertile ground situated little more than an hour's ride from their places of business in Dundee. These estates elevated their owners to the very significant and elite status of landowner. One such was Alexander Forrester, who held the feus of the small estates of Knapp and Millhill in Longforgan parish in the Carse of Gowrie. Forrester acted as agent for the Earl of Strathmore when the Earl exported grain to the Low Countries, holding a commission to buy materials for the refurbishment of Glamis Castle.[62] Another was Alexander Duncan, a provost of Dundee who not only held the estate of Lundie in the Angus parish of the same name, but also the small estates of Seaside, Auchmuir and Gourdiehill in the parish of Errol in the Carse of Gowrie. These latter were farmed by a nephew, the family having been tenant farmers in the Carse of Gowrie from at least the fifteenth century.

Entrepreneurial members of Dundee's merchant community responded to the changes in Scotland's economy by stepping outside the constraints imposed by the traditional practices that governed the trade of the royal burghs, taking full advantage of such new commercial opportunities that were arising. In the longer term, they played a crucial role in bringing Dundee through its darkest days. Their acquisition of land and progressive relationships with the traditional landed elite also did much to foster a more modern society. This vigorous mercantile class was to prove capable of exploiting the emerging markets and technical advances of the eighteenth century to the full.[63]

However, the pursuit of their own interests by numbers of Dundee's merchants without doubt served to further undermine the economic wellbeing of the burgh at a time when it was under severe pressure. From medieval times the merchant guildry dominated the governance of the burgh and its economy. Accusations by the Nine Trades suggest that there was both negligence and misconduct by those holding office in the town council towards the end of the seventeenth century. The seriousness of the situation is revealed in a formal complaint lodged by the Nine Trades in 1698 in regard to the 'malmanagement' of the burgh's finances. There is accusation that the town's money had been applied by particular persons to their private use, that the provost, James Fletcher, was continuing in office longer than legally allowed, and that the bailies had concurred with him in the destruction and dilapidation of the town's Common Good. A list of ten grievances included the lack of an audit, which fostered the widely held belief that the town was 'Drowned in Debt' with a consequent loss to its credit; that there was no account of what had happened to the rents of the barony of the Hilltown and the lands of Logie; that a reduction by the Convention of Royal Burghs in the cess levied on the town had not been passed on to the inhabitants; that there was need to know what had become of the money taken by Bailie Yeaman to Edinburgh to pay off one of the town's creditors; that there was forestalling and profiteering by retailers of meal to the great prejudice of the inhabitants of the town; that there was failure to make timely repairs to the bulwarks of the harbour and also that the practice of issuing free burgess tickets should cease.[64] No response to this exhaustive list of allegations appears in the council minutes, and there is little evidence of any change of course.

If the heart of seventeenth century Dundee was its trade, then shipping was its life blood. From the low point of the mid 1650s, there was evidently some recovery during the second half of the century. However, the shipping figures reveal that there was great disparity across this period (see Figure 3.2). The 1650s, early 1660s and 1670s were disastrous. In 1656, Thomas Tucker recorded only ten vessels of significant tonnage registered to the port.[65] Few vessels were of a size that would allow for long voyages beyond the North Sea, and foreign trade sank into absolute and relative decline – compared to Glasgow and Ayr for example where transatlantic trade was expanding rapidly. Instead, Dundee's merchants concentrated their attention on coastal trade, their traditional partners in Norway and the Baltic, and on the commodities produced in the town's hinterland. Wood was still by far the largest foreign import, with 24.6% of all vessels between 1638 and 1680 carrying timber as the main cargo, overwhelmingly from Norwegian ports, followed by iron from Sweden and salt from France (trailing far behind at 8.5% and 7.3% of the total respectively – see Figure 3.3). Salt imported from Rochelle in western France was used to preserve herring from Orkney, Shetland and the Hebrides before it was traded on, and forty-eight vessels carried salt into the port between 1638 and 1680.[66]

Whereas the shipping lists for the earlier part of the seventeenth century focused primarily on international trade, the full extent of coastal trade, which in terms of number of vessels greatly overshadowed foreign, becomes possible to analyse from the 1690s. As direct trade with France declined and sources of Scottish-produced marine salt became more readily available, Dundee's imports of salt from the Fife ports where salt was manufactured increased substantially. Between 1696 and 1699 a total of sixty-two vessels brought salt from Scottish ports (Table 3.1). In the second half of the seventeenth century, the main item shipped in from the Lothian, Stirling and Fife ports, however, was coal, imported in greater quantities than any other item. In 1710, it constituted 79% of all cargoes entering Dundee.[67]

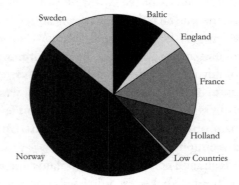

FIGURE 3.3
Vessels importing goods to Dundee, 1638–1680: Countries of departure.

TABLE 3.1: Numbers of vessels off-loading goods at Dundee, 1696–1699[68]

Country of departure	Number of ships
Baltic	3
England	15
France	4
Holland	15
Norway	30
Scotland	427
Spain	1
Sweden	4

Although a gap in the records from 1681 to late 1694 makes it difficult to reach firm conclusions about the state of Dundee shipping in those years, a contemporary was able to describe the town's trade, both landward and overseas, as 'very great' by 1685,[69] and recovery appears to have been under way by the early 1690s. Indeed, Customs sources indicate that in the first half of the 1680s foreign trade had recovered to a significant degree, with an average of twenty-five ships per year between 1680 and 1686.[70] In 1692 twenty-one vessels were registered in the town and a further nine – to the value of £65,000 – were registered as lost or stranded.[71] The largest, freighted at 200 tons, belonged to Alexander Wedderburn (who had recently lost a valuable £5,000 ship with a Bordeaux loading). Nevertheless, entries in the shipping lists from 1695 reached levels not seen since the 1640s.[72]

From 1695, when the shipping lists recorded imports from both domestic and foreign ports, to 1700, around thirty vessels imported goods into Dundee from abroad, accounting for 23.8% of all ships entering the port.[73] But this expansion of shipping, heralding increased economic prospects for the burgh, was to be short-lived, for the burgh suffered its share of difficulties in Scotland's last national famine that took place between 1695 and 1700.

Grain shortages and spiralling prices became apparent in the east of Scotland after the failed harvest of 1695, although early signs of an impending disaster were to be seen in Dundee's western bread basket – the Carse of Gowrie – over the preceding two years, when crop yields had already begun to fall. As in the 1620s, despite the quantity of grain produced locally, victual had to be brought in to Dundee from abroad to supply the inhabitants.[74] The effects of harvest failure upon grain prices can be seen in Figure 3.4.[75] The Candlemas fiar for crop year 1695 (i.e. October 1695 to September 1696), set in February 1696 after the harvest was gathered, marked the beginning of a run of four years of high prices.

As prices rose, urban wage-earners and small tenants, including part-time flax spinners and linen weavers in the countryside, struggled to obtain sufficient to survive, and by early 1697 the poor were described as being, 'both numerous and through scarcity likely to starve'.[76] The position of both rural spinners and handloom weavers, both in Dundee and the surrounding counties of Fife, Forfar and Perth, deteriorated further in 1698 when England, the main market for Scottish linen, imposed an additional tariff on linen cloth from Scotland. The mercantilist policies adopted by other states in Europe were making it increasingly difficult for the Scots to sell what were usually commonplace goods, abroad.[77] Cloth lay in Scotland unsold; in the years immediately preceding the Union in 1707, the value of imported linen, muslin and cottons was greater than that of exports of Scots-made linen.

Although individuals went hungry, it was epidemic disease combined with serious malnutrition that caused most famine-related deaths. With rising mortality, a fall in birth rates, and outward migration, the population nationally dropped by as much as 15%.[78] The only useable

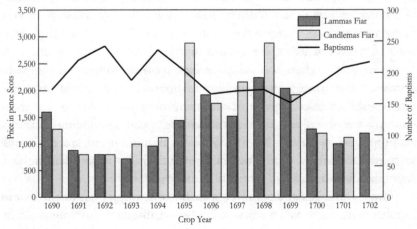

FIGURE 3.4
Forfarshire oatmeal fiars and baptisms in Dundee, crop years 1690–1702[79]

demographic data relating to Dundee's population during the crisis are the records of baptisms (see Figure 3.4). Since records of births were not generally kept until the nineteenth century, baptisms have been used instead to give an impression of the impact of famine upon the birth rate. There was a clear reduction in the number of baptisms between crop years 1696 and 1699, which, allowing for a nine month reaction period, coincided with the higher grain prices between crop years 1695 and 1699. Many women of child bearing age must have been unable to reproduce, or deliberately avoided pregnancy, owing to the dire financial difficulties they and their households faced as a result of high food prices.[80] As prices returned to normal levels with the harvest of 1700, the birth rate began to recover, and the population slowly began to grow again.

Despite rising prices, an influx of rural poor into the town and heightened mortality levels, Dundee coped relatively well during the famine as compared with some of the other large east coast burghs like Aberdeen, Montrose and Edinburgh, that is, until 1699 when serious famine-related problems became evident. In April, the town council was forced to take the unusual step of intervening in the grain market as a buyer, to ensure that grain was available for sale in the town 'in regard of the growing necessity of the poor in this place'. This move had been largely motivated by a riot in March when a mob boarded a ship loaded with grain for export owned by the Marquis of Douglas (now proprietor of Dudhope) and attempted to unload it. It was 'the want of meall in weekly mercats' that 'ocasioned the people to rise'; and the town's magistrates had bravely 'ventured their lives among the mob' to bring an end to the violence.[81]

The town council, however, was unable to control all movement of grain out of Dundee. Roderick Mackenzie of Prestonhall was initially prevented from transporting meal, malt and oats from part of his estate in Forfarshire to his home in Midlothian, through the port of Dundee. Nevertheless, upon petition to the Privy Council and on the grounds that the grain was designed for his or his family's use, Mackenzie was permitted to carry on with the warning that 'he should not be troubled or robbed within the said town of Dundee';[82] all of which undermined the town council's attempts to ensure that the burgh's inhabitants were supplied with meal. Whereas merchants were able to make large windfall profits from selling grain at extraordinarily high prices, there was little incentive for them to supply Dundee's inhabitants. The latter were priced out of the market, inducing the town council to request the Sheriff of Forfarshire to 'see Dundee markets also well provided as that of Forfar', which was evidently better supplied.[83]

While sections of the town's population faced starvation, some merchants and local landlords profited from grain sales at high prices, and the Nine Trades were complaining about this in the early summer of 1698. By the spring and summer of 1699, no relief could be obtained, even by importing grain from overseas. Henry Crawford declared in April that year that 'I doe not think we have victuall heir to maintain the countrie till jullie'.[84] His prediction proved accurate. On the 8th of that month he wrote that even those with money could not purchase grain, whilst admitting privately to a fellow merchant to the hoarding and the forestalling of grain himself.[85]

The town's controlled grain market collapsed. Other than a grant of the vacant minister's stipend for the relief of the poor, no special provision appears to have been made for such individuals, and there is no evidence that the town conformed to parliament's instruction to provide support for those in distress.[86] Although that was not unusual, it was probably an indication of Dundee's burden of debt that the authorities had been unable to provide the kind of financial support for the town's population that they had done in the plague years of the early seventeenth century. Intimations of difficult times can be inferred from the attempts by the burgh's trades to restrict the number of new entrants.[87]

The famine of the late 1690s, coming on top of the increasingly hostile economic environment, exacerbated the town's financial difficulties. Payments from the burgh's Guildry to support their poor or elderly brethren and their dependents – widows for instance – had risen steeply after 1693–94, and were three times higher in 1701–02. For several years thereafter it appears that the pension fund was empty.[88] Losses were incurred too by the numerous Dundee investors in the Company of Scotland's stunningly ambitious but ultimately ill-fated venture at Darien in Central America (see Chapter 4). By 1692 Dundee's debts had already reached £38,253 Scots, and the indications are that by 1701 the figure had grown to £73,500 Scots. In recognition of the town's 'low condition', a portion of the salaries of the burgh's writing master and music master were paid by the Guildry. In 1703 and again in 1704, Dundee petitioned the Convention of Royal Burghs, representing its 'sad decay of trade' (see Chapter 4).

Some of the evidence of signs of recovery comes ironically in the form of complaints from Dundee's long-standing rival, Perth. Doubling the irony was the fact that Dundee's revival owed much to the efforts of George Yeaman, a provost of Dundee and MP for the Perth cluster of burghs (which included Dundee from 1707), to improve regulations relating to the manufacture of linen.[89] In 1696, as part of the town's determination to breathe life into its ailing economy, Dundee's Guildry had taken steps to attract new blood by slashing the former entry fee of £60 Scots down to £12 Scots, and reduced the period of apprenticeship from five years to three; the success of this and other measures have been noted already.[90] To prise from Perth its place as the premier cloth market in east central Scotland, local taxes on linen cloth (the petty Customs) sold in Dundee were cut to a minimum, and following Yeaman's lobbying in London, the town council appointed a stampmaster in 1712 to inspect linen cloth brought to Dundee's market for sale.[91] He also managed to secure a fund to maintain the burgh's harbour. Benefits were not long in coming. In 1713 the former tacksman of the Tay bridge at Perth, Thomas Craigdaillie, explained that his inability to pay what he owed to Perth town council for his lease was due to the drop in traffic – and revenue – owing to 'the Country people who used to resort to this burgh with their cloth . . . going all to Dundie'. His successors made a similar complaint, observing how the centre of gravity in the linen trade was shifting from Perthshire towards Dundee (and Coupar Angus) 'by reason that they [producers of brown and bleached linen] payed but little or no custome . . . at these places'. Linen merchants were buying up cloth even near Perth itself to sell in Dundee.[92] By 1719 victory (for Dundee) was virtually complete, with the burgesses and inhabitants of Perth conceding that the bulk of the business that they had formerly enjoyed at their burgh's midsummer fair – the biggest for linen in Scotland – had gone to Dundee and its satellite towns.[93]

But Dundee's recovery was neither inevitable, nor easy to achieve. Its neighbours to the north, Arbroath and Montrose, had their share of enterprising merchants and merchant-manufacturers who vied with Dundee's to capture the rising market for coarse linen in what was a highly competitive international market. There was still concern in and around Dundee in 1726 that some merchants were buying cloth from hawkers and others before it was checked for quality and width, and stamped; in some cases too, cloth was still being bleached with 'lime pidgeons dung or other hurtful stuff', thereby damaging the town's reputation.[94]

In 1716, takings from Dundee's petty Customs – a useful measure of local economic activity – were still below their 1700 level, for the boom in foreign shipping of the early 1690s had not lasted. Most extraordinary charges on the council concerned shipping and the loss of a number of Dundee vessels. Robert Rankine's ship, the *Concord*, lost with its cargo, was valued at £20,000; some six years later he lost another to the value of £15,000 Scots.

The report does list twenty-one ships belonging to Dundee but only two of at least 100 tons. The remainder were smaller vessels, most weighing 60 tons or less and valued from £20 to £150 Scots each. It was often difficult to compete with the larger ships freighted by most of Scotland's European competitors, although a survey compiled in 1707 shows that Dundee was not atypical. An average Scottish ship weighed 67 tons, while over half of the nation's 215-strong registered fleet weighed in at less than 50.[95] Between 1705 and 1710 just over ninety vessels out of a total of 716 which arrived at Dundee came from a non-Scottish port, constituting only 12.8% of arrivals, attributed to changing duty levels imposed following the Union of 1707. By 1710 cargoes from Scandinavia and the Baltic, previously so vital to the town's economy, dropped to only 1% of the total imports.[96] When visiting in the 1720s, Daniel Defoe found that although Dundee continued to have good trade with Holland, Norway, Danzig, Köenigsberg and Riga, there was now 'a very good and large correspondence with England'. He made no mention of southern European links.[97]

On the other hand, a comparison of shipping registered in 1707 and 1712 reveals more than a doubling of the numbers at Dundee, and an increase in tonnage from 1,315 to 2,922,[98] although there are doubts about the accuracy of the figures. Another count conducted for the Admiralty in 1709 gives a tonnage total of 1,104, and twenty-three vessels (as opposed to twenty-five registered in 1707), but since fifty-seven vessels were registered at Dundee in 1712, there is no question that the trend was upwards. The 1709 evidence is sufficiently detailed that we know not only the names of the ships and barques and smaller boats at Dundee, but also their masters' identities and the sizes of their crews. Dundee had eleven 'ships': three over 100 tons (which were also armed), six barques and another six small 'boats', each of which was crewed by one man in addition usually to a master and perhaps a boy. The burgh's merchant vessels were manned by crews ranging from eighteen down to four, with the barques getting by with crews of two or three along with their skippers, and in some a mate and an unspecified number of boys. In total around 144 masters and crew (excluding boys), as well as eight carpenters, appear to have been required to sail Dundee's merchant fleet, although of these only the masters and perhaps only a third of the others belonged to the burgh itself.[99] (See Chapter 11 for a comparison with a century later.)

Seaborne trade was only one indicator of economic health. The immediate impact of the Union of 1707 on the Scottish economy generally was mixed – as it was in Dundee. Timber imports, which had already been in decline before 1707, fell sharply afterwards, owing to English restrictions. On the other hand, imports of goods from England increased, as reflected by the increase in shipping. More serious was the virtual block on the export of wool and woollen cloth from Dundee to the Netherlands and elsewhere; even more damaging were the duties imposed on Scots-made linen.[100] In a survey of Scotland's circumstances in 1730, Sir John Clerk observed that Scottish merchants were driving a 'prejudicial' trade, not only by importing luxury goods but also commodities that were 'harmful to our [Scottish] manufactures and especially to the poor'.[101]

In winter 1719–20, Dundee and the other coastal burghs of Angus were the locus of serious food rioting, due to a combination of grain shortages during a particularly cold spell of weather, Union-related dislocation, and uncertainty – about the future of one of the mainstays of the local economy: flax spinning and linen weaving.[102] To protect the burgh from further harm, if not to secure its future development, Dundee was in the vanguard of the flood of protests that were presented at Westminster in 1719 about actual and proposed legislation – which it was feared would be gravely damaging to the Scottish linen industry. On top of new burdensome excise duties on linen exports in 1711, and a new tax on printed cloth in 1715, English woollen and silk manufacturers had begun to lobby hard for a prohibition on printed or dyed textiles either from abroad or home-produced, but such was the strength of Scottish (and Irish) opposition – allied to fears of further economic privation in Scotland and consequent political disaffection – that British-made linen was exempted from what became the Calico Act of 1721.[103] Similarly, hard campaigning had been necessary in 1709 when Dundee, as well as other east coast towns, was threatened by the prospect of higher coal prices – which would have transpired had not a tax concession on coastwise movements of coal within the estuarial limits of the Forth, agreed at the time of the Union, been extended. Yeaman, again, was in the front line.[104]

The burgh's magistrates, merchants and some of the neighbouring landowners – men like the Earl of Strathmore who also had interests in linen – had been ahead of the establishment of the Board of Trustees for Manufactures in 1727 in setting up stamp offices to ensure that linen cloth brought to market was of the requisite length and quality.[105] The stage was being set for the burgh's emergence as the leading player within the community of coarse linen producers and distributors in eastern Scotland (see Chapter 6). Thus behind the real challenges that Union brought, there were grounds for cautious optimism, not least the free access Scottish linen cloth would have to England and the plantations, and protection from the royal navy of merchant vessels on the high seas.

Even so, there was a long way to go. Dundee's shipping tonnage in 1759 was less than it had been in 1712.[106] Although the port did manage to break into the lucrative tobacco trade, Dundee only ever managed to capture around 4% of the Scottish total. Further assistance from Westminster was required if Scottish manufacturing was to grow and provide relief for Scotland's large army of the underemployed – potential recruits to the anti-Hanoverian Jacobite cause.[107] It was not until the 1730s that linen output began to grow more rapidly, and even by mid century the position of the industry as the east of Scotland's 'staple', was far from secure.

NOTES

1 Letter from the Council to his Majesty, reporting on the necessity and importance of repairing the harbour of Ayr. D. Masson (ed.), *Register of the Privy Council of Scotland Vol. VIII 1607–1610* (Edinburgh, 1887), p. 555.

2 A. Maxwell, *The History of Old Dundee Narrated out of the Town Council Register* (Dundee, 1884), pp. 400–402. One merk was equal to 13s 4d (Scots); £12 (Scots) was equal to £1 (sterling). All money mentioned in this chapter is in Scots unless otherwise stated.

3 E. P. D. Torrie, *Medieval Dundee: A Town and its People* (Dundee, 1990), p. 36.

4 S. G. E. Lythe, 'The Origin and Development of Dundee: a Study in Historical

Geography', *Scottish Geographical Magazine*, vol. 54 (1938); T. Riis, 'The Baltic Trade of Montrose in the Sixteenth & Seventeenth Centuries: from the Danish Sound Toll Registers', in G. Jackson and S. G. E. Lythe (eds.), *The Port of Montrose* (Tayport and New York, 1993), pp. 102–114.

5   A. H. Millar, (ed.), *The Compt Buik of David Wedderburne, Merchant of Dundee* (Edinburgh, 1898), pp. 219–220.

6   Ibid., pp. 215–228.

7   See for instance National Archives of Scotland (NAS), E72/7/9, Dundee Entry book: Imports and exports (1681–1682).

8   Dundee's percentage of burgh tax was temporarily knocked out of second place by both Glasgow (at 8.45%) and Aberdeen (at 6.96%) in February 1649. This position was reversed only five months later when a new assessment in July 1649 re-established Dundee's position behind Edinburgh.

9   T. C. Smout, *A History of the Scottish People, 1560–1830* (London, 1987), pp. 152–153.

10   M. Lynch, 'Continuity and Change in Urban society, 1500–1700' in R. A. Houston and I. D. Whyte (eds.), *Scottish Society 1500–1800* (Cambridge, 1989), p. 115.

11   DCA, Dundee Town Council Minute Book (TCM), vol. 3, 1597–1613, 18 October 1603, 29 May 1604, 7 May 1605, 27 May 1605, 6 August 1605 and 31 December 1605.

12   Ibid., 6 October 1606. Scott, however, believed that the town was visited with plague for a period of four years between the autumn of 1605 and 1609. A. M. Scott, *Discovering Dundee: The Story of a City* (Edinburgh, 1989), p. 22.

13   TCM, vol. 3, 1597–1613, 17 September 1607.

14   Ibid., 28 June 1608 and 25 October 1608 and 'Act for the better government of the burgh of Dundee now visited with the plague, 5 July 1608', D. Masson (ed.), *Register of the Privy Council of Scotland Vol. VIII 1607–1610* (Edinburgh, 1887), p. 123.

15   TCM, vol. 3, 1597–1613, 11 February 1609 and 7 March 1609.

16   P. Slack, *The Impact of Plague in Tudor and Stuart England* (Oxford, 1990), pp. 174–177.

17   Dundee University Archives (DUA), BRMS 3/DC46, *Mr James Guthrie's Diary*, pp. 81–83.

18   M. Lynch, 'Introduction: Scottish Towns 1500–1700', in M. Lynch (ed.), *The Early Modern Town in Scotland* (London, 1987), p. 11.

19   A. H. Millar, *The First History of Dundee 1776* (Dundee, 1923), p. 121.

20   TCM, vol. 4, 1613–53, 22 August 1648.

21   Maxwell, *History of Old Dundee*, p. 496. Dundee's proportion of the stent was changed to £6 17s 4d per £100 (Scots). DCA, Dundee Town Council Minute Book, vol. 4, 1613–53, 15 July 1646.

22   However, by 9 January 1649 this compensation appears not to have yet been paid. Ibid.

23   TCM, 20 December 1648.

24   A. J. Warden, *Angus or Forfarshire, the Land and People Descriptive and Historical, Vol. 5* (Dundee, 1885), p. 268.

25   A. Warden, *The History of Old Dundee* (Dundee, 1884), p. 508.

26   M. Flinn (ed.), *Scottish Population History from the Seventeenth Century to the 1930s* (Cambridge, 1977), pp. 146–147.

27   TCM, vol. 4, 1613–53, 30 September 1645, 19 October 1646, 22 August 1648 and 11 October 1648.

28 The town council borrowed 3,000 merks to pay annual rents. Ibid., 19 August 1648 and 21 November 1648.

29 Ibid., 31 May and 28 June 1652.

30 The siege lasted overnight, quarter was given, the harbour could not take fifty ships at a time, and the deaths of Dundonians might have reached into the low hundreds at most. See J. Robertson, 'The Storming of Dundee, 1651', in *History Scotland* (May/June 2003), pp. 23–27.

31 As quoted in Lynch, 'Introduction', p. 7.

32 DCA, Dundee Register of Ships 1612–1681. Gaps in the lists occurred in: 1619, 1624, 1632, 1633 and 1640. A figure of zero has been returned for these years, where there were no records for the year, or the year was estimated to have been incompletely recorded.

33 DCA, Dundee Register of Ships 1694–1700; E. J. Graham, *A Maritime History of Scotland, 1650–1780* (East Linton, 2002), pp. 136–140.

34 A. J. Warden, *Burgh Laws of Dundee* (London, 1872), p. 139.

35 Warden, *The History of Old Dundee*, p. 132; Perth and Kinross Council Archives (PKCA), MS100/20/1099 (1656).

36 W. Hay (ed.), *Charters, Writs, and Public Documents of the Royal Burgh of Dundee, the Hospital and Johnston's Bequest: 1292–1880* (Dundee, 1880), p. 94.

37 Act of Parliament, in favour of the Burgh of Dundee, for a Voluntary Contribution, in respect of the loss incurred at the Storming of the Town and destruction of the Walls, dated 23 December, 1669, Hay (ed.), *Charters, Writs, and Public Documents*, pp. 94–95.

38 R. Edward, *The County of Angus 1678* (reprint Edinburgh, 1883), p. 30.

39 Report on the Condition of the Burgh of Dundee, 1692, in J. D. Marwick (ed.) *Extracts of the Convention of the Royal Burghs of Scotland, 1677–1711* (Edinburgh, 1880), p. 573.

40 J. D. Marwick, (ed.), *Extracts from the Convention of the Royal Burghs of Scotland, 1615–1676* (Edinburgh, 1878), p. 585.

41 M. Lynch, 'Continuity and Change in Urban Society, 1500–1700', in R. A. Houston and I. D. Whyte, (eds.), *Scottish Society 1500–1800* (Cambridge, 1989), pp. 115–117.

42 I. D. Whyte, 'Scottish and Irish Urbanisation in the Seventeenth and Eighteenth centuries: a comparative perspective', in S. J. Connolly, R. A. Houston and R. J. Morris (eds.), *Conflict, Identity and Economic Development: Ireland and Scotland, 1600–1939* (Preston, 1995), p. 24.

43 C. A. Whatley, D. B. Swinfen and A. M. Smith, *Life and Times of Dundee* (Edinburgh, 1993), p. 19.

44 Whyte, 'Scottish and Irish urbanisation', p. 24.

45 M. Young, 'Rural Society in Scotland from the Restoration to the Union: Challenge and Response in the Carse of Gowrie, circa 1660–1707' (Unpublished PhD, University of Dundee, 2004), pp. 256–302.

46 I. D. Whyte, *Scotland Before the Industrial Revolution* (Harlow, 1995), p. 59.

47 Marwick, (ed.), *Extracts from the Records of the Convention of the Royal Burghs of Scotland, 1677–1711*, p. 133.

48 Edinburgh City Archives (ECA), SL 30/216 – Petition by the Burgh of Elgine, 1697.

49 ECA SL 30/223 Petition, Burgh of Anstruther Wester, July 1705.

50 ECA SL 30/223 Accompt of the State and condition of the Burgh of Striline, 1700.

51 PKCA, B59/34/12, Address by the Burgh of Perth to the Parliament, 1700.

52 ECA SL 30/223 Petition by the Merchants of Dumfries, 4 July 1704.

53 *Miscellany of the Scottish Burgh Records Society* (Edinburgh, 1881), p. 75, quoted in T. M. Devine, 'The Merchant Class of the Larger Scottish Towns in the Seventeenth and Early Eighteenth Centuries', in G. Gordon and B. Dicks, (eds.), *Scottish Urban History* (Aberdeen, 1983), p. 94.

54 A. C. Lamb, *Dundee, its Quaint and Historic Buildings* (Dundee, 1895), passim.

55 T. Edward, *A Description of the County of Angus in the year 1678* (Dundee, 1883), p. 30.

56 Lamb, *Dundee*, section xx.

57 Dundee Central Library, Charles Lawson Collection.

58 C. Wemyss, 'Some Aspects of Scottish Country House Construction in the Post Restoration Period; Patrick Smyth and the Building of Methven Castle, 1678–1681' (MPhil Dissertation, University of Dundee, 2002), passim; Young, 'Rural Society', pp. 256–280.

59 DUA, MS15/218/4(1); National Register of Archives (NRA(S)) 885, Papers of the Earl of Strathmore, vol. 273 and 198/2/33 (1691). J. Donaldson, *General View of the Agriculture of the Carse of Gowrie* (London, 1794), p. 12.

60 J. Adair, *The Mappe of Straithern, Stormont & Cars of Gourie* (1683).

61 NAS, CC20/4/13; PKAC, Hunter of Glencarse, 97/2.

62 NRA(S) 885, 30/1/3 (6).

63 Devine, 'The Merchant Class', p. 94.

64 Records of the Nine Trades of Dundee, 2 May 1698. The authors wish to thank Innes A. Duffus, Archivist to the Nine Incorporated Trades of Dundee, for supplying this information.

65 Extract from: The Report by Thomas Tucker upon the Settlement of the Revenues of Excise and Customs in Scotland 1565 as presented to Sir Walter Scott, President, and other members of the Bannatyne Club, in F. Wilkins, *The Smuggling Story of Two Firths: Montrose to Dunbar* (Worcestershire, 1993), Appendix.

66 DCA, Dundee Register of Ships 1612–1681.

67 S. J. Monaghan, 'The Dundee Shipping Lists as a Record of the Impact of the Union upon the Dundee Shipping Industry, 1705 to 1710' (Unpublished MA dissertation, University of Dundee, 1988), pp. 10–12.

68 DCA, Dundee Register of Ships 1694–1700.

69 Ochterlony's Account of the Shire of Forfar, 1684–5, in Warden, *Angus or Forfarshire*, p. 260.

70 T. C. Smout, *Scottish Trade on the Eve of the Union* (Edinburgh and London, 1963), pp. 286–287.

71 Marwick, *Extracts from the Records of the Convention of the Royal Burghs of Scotland, 1677–1711*, pp. 572–573.

72 State and Condition of the Town of Dundee, 1692, Hay (ed.), *Charters, Writs, and Public Documents*, p. 258. DCA, Dundee Register of Ships 1694–1700. Gaps in the shipping registers in 1652–1653, 1656, 1665–1670, 1674 and 1681–1693 make it impossible to determine what levels were during these years – particularly important for the last thirteen year gap.

73 DCA, Dundee Register of Ships 1694–1700.

74 In September 1696, for example, grain from Hull, 'Yeremonts' and London was imported to Dundee; ibid.

75 It demonstrates the movement of oatmeal fiars prices, set biannually at the fiars court in Forfar in February (Candlemas) and August (Lammas).

76 DCA, CH2/103/2, Dundee Presbytery Minutes 1691–1700, 29 July 1696 and 3 March 1697.

77 C. A. Whatley, 'Taking Stock: Scotland at the End of the Seventeenth Century', in T. C. Smout (ed.), *Anglo-Scottish Relations from 1603 to 1900* (Oxford, 2005), pp. 112–113; Smout, *Scottish Trade*, pp. 233–234.

78 Flinn, *Scottish Population History*, p. 181.

79 NAS, E20/60/8, Extract of the Fiars of the year 1689 to the year 1703, Forfarshyre; and General Register Office for Scotland (GROS), OPR 282/3, Dundee Baptisms 1682–1722.

80 For further discussion see, E. Le Roy Ladurie, 'Famine amenorrhea (Seventeenth–Twentieth Centuries)', in R. Forster and O. Ranum (eds.), *Biology of Man in History: selections from the Annales, économies, sociétés, civilisations*, trans. E. Forster and P. M. Ranum (Baltimore, 1975), p. 164.

81 The riot is first discussed in the minutes on 29 March 1699, but it is possible that it actually occurred some days earlier as an entry of that date records that Bailie Duncan had already discussed the situation with the King's Advocate in Edinburgh. DCA, TCM, vol. 6 1669–1707, 29 March 1699 and 19 April 1699.

82 R. Chambers, *Domestic Annals of Scotland Vol. 3* (Edinburgh, 1874), p. 211.

83 Ibid., 29 March 1699.

84 NAS, RH15/101/5, Letter from Henry Crawford to Mr Alexander Pyper, Dundee 1 April 1699.

85 NAS, RH15/101/5, Letter from Henry Crawford to [Alexander Pyper], Dundee 8 July 1699.

86 DCA, CH2/103/2, Dundee Presbytery Minutes 1691–1700, 29 July 1696 and 3 March 1697, and TCM, vol. 6 1669–1707, 29 September 1698. Acts and proclamations of March 1698, September 1699 and October 1699. See, R. Mitchison, *The Old Poor Law in Scotland* (Edinburgh, 2000), pp. 36–38.

87 A. M. Smith, *The Nine Trades of Dundee* (Dundee, 1995), p. 23.

88 A. M. Smith, *The Guildry of Dundee: A History of the Merchant Guild of Dundee up to the 19th century* (Dundee, 2005), pp. 77–78.

89 E. Cruickshanks, S. Handley and D. W. Hayton (eds.), *The History of Parliament, The House of Commons, 1690–1715, v* (Cambridge, 2002), p. 954.

90 Devine, 'The Merchant Class', p. 94.

91 Smith, *Guildry*, p. 64.

92 PKCA, B59/26/4/1, Petitions, 1689–1739.

93 PKCA, B59/26/4/1, Petition of the Burgesses and Inhabitants of the Burgh of Perth, 1719.

94 PKCA, B59/24/8/4, Sederunt of the Committee of Freeholders of the Shire of Forfar, 10 November 1726.

94 Graham, *Maritime History*, p. 119; *Miscellany Scottish Burgh Records Society*, pp. 62–63; Smout, *Scottish Trade*, p. 51.

96 Monaghan, 'The Dundee Shipping Lists', pp. 26–31.

97 D. Defoe, *A Tour through Great Britain* New ed. (London, 1983) vol. III, p. 278.

98 Graham, *Maritime History*, p. 124.

99 ECA, SL 30/226, Lists of shipping, skippers and sailors in Scottish ports, 1709.

100 C. A. Whatley, 'Economic Causes and Consequences of the Union of 1707: A Survey', *Scottish Historical Review*, LXVIII, ii, 186 (October 1989), pp. 171–173.

101 Quoted in ibid., pp. 171–172.

102 C. A. Whatley, 'The Union of 1707, Integration and the Scottish Burghs: The Case of the 1720 Food Riots', *Scottish Historical Review*, LXXVIII, ii, 206 (October 1999), pp. 207–208.

103 A. J. Durie, *The Scottish Linen Industry in the Eighteenth Century* (Edinburgh, 1979), pp. 10–11; R. Harris, 'The Scots, the Westminster parliament, and the British state in the eighteenth century', in J. Hoppit (ed.), *Parliaments, Nations and Identities in Britain and Ireland, 1660–1850* (Manchester, 2003), pp. 127–128.

104 C. A. Whatley, 'Salt, Coal and the Union of 1707: A revision article', *Scottish Historical Review*, LXVI, i, 181 (April 1987), pp. 40–41.

105 PKCA, B59/24/8/4, Lord Gray to the provost of Perth anent Stamping of Linen etc., 15 December 1726; Durie, *Scottish Linen Industry*, pp. 47–48.

106 Graham, *Maritime History*, p. 238.

107 C. A. Whatley, *Scottish Society: Beyond Jacobitism towards Industrialisation* (Manchester, 2000), pp. 55–61.

CHAPTER 4
Dundee in the Nation
c. 1686–1746

Derek J. Patrick

Between *c.* 1686 and 1746, Scotland witnessed a series of events of funda-mental importance to the kingdom, beginning with the accession of a catholic monarch, James VII, in 1685. The Revolution of 1688–89 that saw him ousted and replaced by his son-in-law and daughter, William and Mary, was followed by the incorporating Union of 1707 which created the kingdom of Great Britain; and the period ended with the last of three significant Jacobite rebellions with the common goal of restoring the exiled Stuart monarchs. While the implications of these episodes have been examined at a national level, less is known about their impact in the localities or on individual burghs. Focusing on the government of Dundee, this chapter examines how these events impacted on its economy, religion, loyalties and political allegiance, in order to better understand the burgh's place in the nation.

Between 1686 and 1716, membership of the burgh council followed the changing face of national politics. In the second session of his only Scots parliament, James VII made a concerted effort to repeal anti-catholic legislation to secure greater toleration for his co-religionists, and offered the Estates free trade with England as an incentive. This proposal was promptly rejected by a parliament overwhelmingly hostile to catholicism, one observer describing the representatives of the royal burghs as 'the brazen wall the Papists found hardest'.[1] So the king dissolved parliament and attempted to engineer a more compliant legis-lature by a systematic purge of Scotland's sixty-five royal burghs whose councils, besides the day-to-day administration of local affairs, were also responsible for choosing Members of Parliament.[2] In 1685–86, Dundee had been represented by its provost, an influential merchant called James Fletcher. Like his predecessor, Alexander Wedderburn of Kingennie, Fletcher was known to sympathise with the disenfranchised presbyterians and became an obvious target.[3] On 21 September 1686, the town council received a letter from the Chancellor, James Drummond, Earl of Perth, indicating that it was the king's intention to suspend annual burgh elections for an indefinite period,[4] and in early December Major General John Graham of Claverhouse, acting on behalf of the Privy Council, issued instructions that Fletcher and his council should be replaced.[5]

Dundee's new administration was headed by Alexander Rait who held office for approximately sixteen months until replaced by Claverhouse himself, who was installed by Colin Lindsay, Earl of Balcarres on 27 March 1688.[6] Considering the friction caused when King Charles II had chosen Graham as constable and first magistrate of Dundee four years earlier, it seems unlikely that this was a popular appointment. The council was resentful of the monarch's interference, drafting a protest that Claverhouse's new office should 'noewayes militat agt or be prejudiciall unto ye rights, liberties, & priviledges belonging & apperaining unto ye sd burgh of Dundie . . . that ye toune's rights, liberties & priviledges should stand firme, & in full force, strength'.[7] As a Privy Councillor and senior military officer, Claverhouse could not devote his full attention to burgh affairs, although he did preside at several council meetings, presumably while resident at Dudhope, his seat overlooking the town. His estates there had been erected into the barony of New Dundee in 1684.[8]

Rev. Robert Wodrow, author of *The History of the Sufferings of the Church of Scotland*, recorded Claverhouse's autocratic treatment of the burgh's presbyterian ministers who had been granted permission to preach as a condition of King James's second indulgence. Living up to his reputation as 'Bloody Clavers', nemesis of God's elect, he barred three ministers, Thomas Cobham, Alexander Auchmoutie and Alexander Orrock, from preaching in the burgh for various offences that ranged from Cobham's holding an unlicensed conventicle to Orrock's calling the king an idolater.[9] While Wodrow's account is not necessarily impartial, Claverhouse was clearly the king's man, and although tales of his high-handedness have almost certainly been exaggerated, he seems to have had no problem implementing the Restoration regime's more repressive policies. At odds with most of his contemporaries, who were increasingly alienated by James VII's catholicising initiatives, Graham remained loyal to his king, even after the Revolution.

By late September 1688, it was no secret that the king's son-in-law, William of Orange, was planning to invade Britain in order to secure protestantism, its established laws and liberties, and his wife, Mary's place in the succession – which had been put in doubt by the recent birth of a legitimate catholic heir.[10] In Dundee, the council made preparations to secure the town, issuing instructions on 4 October 1688 for establishing a guard in each quarter of the burgh – the Nethergate, Overgate, Murraygate and Seagate.[11] Burgh officials were authorised to seize all gunpowder in the town, and assemble its thirty-eight militiamen.

Claverhouse had no hand in the burgh's arrangements. He last appeared in council on 4 September, before he marched south with the Scottish regiments at the beginning of October. He arrived in London within days of Prince William's Dutch fleet landing at Brixham, near Torbay in Devon on 5 November. On 12 November, in return for his service and enduring loyalty to James VII, Graham was created Viscount of Dundee, but he could do nothing to influence a campaign that was progressively more hopeless. Neither James nor his commanders had much stomach for a fight, several having already defected to the Prince. So, despite the entreaties of Dundee, the king decided to flee, leaving for France on 23 December. A resident in London for most of that winter, Lord Dundee attended the several meetings of the Scots nobility and gentlemen, over one hundred of whom had arrived at Whitehall by the beginning of 1689 to discuss the preferred settlement of church and state. They decided to have William call a Convention of the Estates, and in order to negate any residual effect of King James's actions, the burgh franchise was extended to all protestant burgesses.

The result was an electorate that numbered in the hundreds, with over one thousand participating in the Edinburgh election alone.[12] This was some distance from the twenty or so officials who traditionally chose a burgh's MP (MPs in the case of Edinburgh).[13] The temporary influx of new voters contributed to an unprecedented number of contested elections in the burghs where King James's nominees clashed with the popular electorate. While there is no evidence of a disputed election in Dundee, it would be surprising if Claverhouse had made no attempt to win the burgh seat and establish a candidate sympathetic to King James. He was in the area, and had last appeared in council on 27 February 1689, the day before the town's election was held in the burgh's West Church. In a letter to his son on 2 March, John Hay, Marquis of Tweeddale, commented that since Dundee had chosen a presbyterian candidate, 'ther was a tumult lik to have bein, between them and ther provost the Viscount'.[14] James Fletcher, ousted in 1686, was chosen to represent the burgh in the forthcoming Convention of the Estates.[15] In the Convention, Fletcher signed both the act declaring it a lawful meeting, and the letter of congratulation to the Prince. He was also chosen as a member of several committees, and named as one of the Scots union commissioners in April 1689. These appointments were commensurate with his status as the representative of one of the kingdom's senior burghs.

The Convention was not long in addressing the problem of burgh government caused by James's meddling. The 'rights and priviledges of the Royal Boroughs . . . hindered in the free election of their Magistrates and Town Councils', was a subject raised by William in his Declaration for Scotland, and also appeared in both the Claim of Right (containing the strategic aims of the Scottish Revolution) and the articles of grievance drafted by the Estates.[16] It was decided that the successful poll elections that had helped secure a presbyterian majority in the Convention would also be the means of restoring the burgh councils, and Dundee was one of the first burghs instructed to elect a new council and magistrates. The act ordering the election reversed 'the great invasiones that have been made of late years, upon the priviledge of the royall Burrowes, particularly these of Dundee in the electione of their magistrats By recommendationes and nominationes made by the late King in ane arbitrary and Despotick way . . . so that the present magistrats and Councill of the said Brugh, are not ther true magistrats and Councill by them freely elected'.[17] All qualified burgesses were ordered to meet at 8 a.m. in the West Church on Thursday, 18 April and David Fotheringham of Powrie, appointed as an overseer by the Estates, was present to witness the re-election of several of those deposed in 1686 – including Fletcher who went on to serve as provost from 1689 to 1698.[18]

This was the second comprehensive shift in burgh politics in little over two years, and meant that a council well-disposed to the Revolution and presbyterian interest was now installed. Within a matter of weeks, it was taking steps to guarantee the security of the burgh, almost certainly in response to the actions of their erstwhile provost. For Claverhouse had withdrawn from the Convention and quit Edinburgh on 18 March, claiming, probably with some justification, that his life had been at risk, 'many people's being in arms without authority'.[19] When he failed to appear before the Estates and surrender his arms, he was declared a 'fugitive and rebell' on 30 March 1689. On 16 April, a few days after the Convention had offered the throne to William and Mary, Claverhouse raised his master's Royal Standard atop Dundee Law before riding north, signalling the start of the first Jacobite rebellion.[20] Returning to Dundee on the afternoon of 13 May in an attempt to enlist two companies of Sir Thomas Livingstone's Royal Dragoons (his old regiment) who were quartered in the town and apparently ready to defect, Claverhouse found the gates barred against him and the burgh occupied by regular soldiers and militia.[21] Local legend maintains that the Viscount, angered by his reception, had his men burn the suburb known as 'rotten row', now the Hilltown, but there is no corroborating evidence that this ever occurred (and it was part of his own barony of New Dundee anyway). Thus ended Claverhouse's direct association with Dundee. A chance musket ball ended his life at Killiecrankie some two months later.

By autumn, with Claverhouse dead and the remnants of his Highland army checked at Dunkeld, there was no longer any threat to Dundee. James VII had landed in Ireland in March 1689 where the war continued until hostilities were ended by the Treaty of Limerick in October 1691. In Dundee, the previous month, the council agreed that, as the country was 'more peaceable then it has been this long tyme bypast', the men who attended the burgh's guns should receive pay for only another week 'and the guns be drawen'.[22]

So Dundee had emerged from the Glorious Revolution relatively unscathed. But whereas the burgh's administration was restructured without much difficulty, church government would prove far more challenging. When episcopacy had been restored in May 1662, it had been resented by the presbyterian majority in the Lowlands, and subsequent religious discord dominated Scots politics for much of the period 1660–90.[23] The Revolution provided the opportunity for presbyterians, the greater part of King William's Scots supporters, to overturn the Restoration church settlement and restore the Kirk. News that James VII had fled to France was sufficient to spark a series of attacks on episcopalian ministers, who were turned out of their churches in almost every parish south of the Forth and Clyde.[24]

On 2 May 1689, the council wrote to their commissioner, James

Fletcher, instructing him to represent to the Convention of the Estates that the burgh's ministers had not read the proclamation ordering them to pray for William and Mary 'and yr not praying particularlie for them conforme yrto'.[25] Consequently, the Privy Council deprived the ministers of the second and third charges, Norrie and Rait, in 1689.[26] Whether they were forcibly removed in the manner of many of their colleagues, especially in the west and south-west where presbyterian mobs were charged with excessive brutality, is not entirely clear.[27] When merchant councillor John Smith entered a claim, on Tuesday, 7 January 1690, amounting to £54 17s 4d Scots, 'deburs ed be him for deposeing Mr Robert Raitt & Mr Robert Norie ministers',[28] there is no mention of what this not inconsiderable sum was spent on. The council refused Smith's request for recompense on the grounds that he had received no commission from the burgh to do whatever he had done. Henry Scrymgeour (minister of the first charge) continued to officiate until November 1690 when he chose to resign voluntarily for unspecified reasons. Following his resignation, all three charges in Dundee remained vacant for some months.[29]

Although presbyterian church government had been restored in June 1690, the Kirk could not supply every parish with a suitable minister. The shortage of qualified ministers being an obvious problem, the magistrates commissioned David Ogilvie, former schoolmaster at Kirriemuir, to continue preaching in the burgh 'dureing the counsells pleasure'.[30] After provost Fletcher petitioned the General Assembly regarding the 'vacancy in the ministry of the churches',[31] the Revs. John Spalding and William Mitchell were appointed as ministers of the South Church and St Paul's in 1691.[32] However, Dundee's first charge remained vacant for the best part of nine years until Samuel Johnstone was called from Southdean near Roxburgh, and appointed minister of St Mary's.[33]

In an attempt to compensate, episcopalian preachers were permitted to retain their otherwise vacant charges, provided they acknowledged King William and Queen Mary as legitimate sovereigns, and made no attempt to overthrow the government of the Kirk.[34] Episcopalians continued in possession of their churches across the kingdom but in far greater numbers in parishes above the River Tay, where their authority was strongest, and a large percentage of the region's landed gentlemen were sympathetic. In 1707, one hundred and sixty-five episcopal clergy in Scotland were still in possession of their churches and stipends,[35] and twenty years later Daniel Defoe highlighted the continuing religious divide in Scotland in his *Tour Through the Whole Island of Great Britain*, observing that in and around Angus 'there are far more of the episcopal perswasion than are to be found in the south; and the farther north, the more so'.[36]

With so many empty churches and the limited number of presbyterian ministers, the regular incursions of unqualified episcopalian clergymen into vacant kirks across Angus (and similarly afflicted regions) became an enduring problem at both the national and local level – not systematically addressed until after the failure of the 1715–16 Jacobite rising. After the two outed curates of Dundee, Norrie and Rait, had been obliged to leave their churches, they simply established a meeting house at Dudhope where they ministered to the burgh's sizeable episcopalian community.[37] On 27 April 1697, the Privy Council instructed the Sheriff of Angus, John Lyon, Earl of Strathmore, to close up the Dudhope meeting house 'made use of by non conforming ministers . . . and take care that the same be not made use of . . . at any time hereafter'.[38] This does not appear to have worked, for six years later, on 17 April 1703 Dundee received a letter from the Lord Advocate instructing the burgh magistrates to stop Norrie and Rait from preaching in meeting houses, 'in respect they are not qualified conforme to the act of Parliament . . . nor their sentence of deprivatione taken off'.[39]

Some efforts were made to examine these two persistent offenders, along with Messrs Ogilvie and Alexander Guthrie, another two curates also active in the area. Guthrie was interviewed and instructed to stop preaching within the burgh, before the council recommended that the bailies take legal action against the four. In April 1701, some twenty-eight parishes in the synod of Angus and Mearns were occupied by episcopal incumbents, twenty described as 'non jurant', having refused to recognise King William, only four qualified according to law, and the rest under process.[40] Presbyteries were asked to address the situation as best they could, dealing with ministers judged 'most opposite' to the government'; but matters were little different by October 1708, when a list of twenty-one further 'intruders and keepers of meeting houses' was drawn up, six resident in the presbytery of Dundee and Forfar. For Dundee, the situation was more acute than for most of its neighbours, and would become more pronounced once Queen Anne's reign came to a close and rebellion swept the land.

As was described in Chapter 3, the 1690s had been an extremely difficult decade for Dundee.[41] In 1692 a report compiled for the Convention of Royal Burghs described the 'state and condition' of each of its constituent members, so as to adjust the tax roll accurately, and demonstrate how competition from unfree burghs (burghs of barony and regality) had contributed to their overall decline.[42] That agenda casts some doubt on the accuracy of the data, since the burghs had a vested interest in showing themselves in the worst possible light. Moreover, the report was compiled during the Nine Years War which had had a negative impact on trade.[43] Dundee's income (generated by customs, its mills and various rents) was said to amount to £3,351 2s while its discharge was a staggering £7,564 5s 8d including £2,295 3s 8d of interest payable on £38,253 owed by the burgh, and an additional charge of £1,566 13s 4d for the ministers' stipends. The result was the large deficit of £4,212 3s 8d Scots. Over and above ordinary expenditure, Dundee's accumulative losses were calculated at £111,666 13s 4d, going back several years and including £20,000 spent during the magistrates' legal action against the Duke of Lauderdale.[44]

The council's attempts to secure the burgh in 1689–90 had cost a further £7,952 10s 3d with charges ranging from £939, 7s for firelocks and ammunition to £166 4s 2d spent on candles for the guard. Having considered 'the low condition of the burgh and the increasing of ther debts by reasone of the extraordinarie emergents', the brewers had offered a voluntary contribution of 10 shillings on each boll of malt in October 1691, 'for support of the burgh'.[45] While this was a welcome addition to the burgh's coffers, it was not sufficient. But Dundee was far from exceptional. Aberdeen's annual deficit exceeded £7,000, and 'haveing alreadie borrowed soe much that they can not have credit'.[46] Perth's was £1,038 13s 2d, Forfar's some £457 2s 8d, while Montrose covered its losses 'by taxting the burgessis and inhabitants'. What sets Dundee apart was the scale of its problem. However, at a meeting of the Convention of Royal Burghs in Dundee in July 1692, it was agreed that the tax roll should be altered and that the burghs of barony and regality should be liable for a tenth part of the burghs' regular taxes. Dundee was one of the beneficiaries in that its contribution was cut from the £5 Scots appointed in 1683 to £4 13s 4d.[47]

There were attempts to bolster burgh trade during the 1690s, as explained in Chapter 3. Dundee established a linen fair in 1695 to help compensate for the loss of most of its overseas trade, purchased the neighbouring barony of Hilltown in 1697, and on 31 August 1698 was granted an act of parliament for an annual fair on the first Tuesday of each June, 'for buying and selling all kinds of vendible Commodities'.[48] There was certainly capital in Dundee – although not necessarily in the hands of the burgh council. The hugely ambitious Company of Scotland Trading to Africa and the Indies, established in June 1695, was considered by a great many Scots to be the solution to the nation's economic problems.[49] Darien captured the imagination of the Scots who, envisaging a more prosperous nation and lucrative returns on their individual investments, hurried to subscribe.

Between March and May 1696 Dundonians, almost all categorised as merchants or burgh officials, subscribed at least £6,205 sterling to the company. John Scrymgeour (a future provost) made the largest single contribution, pledging £300 on 11 March 1696, whereas most Dundee subscriptions were of £100 sterling.[50] Taking into account local heritors such as David Duncan of Lundie and those whose subscriptions were made by Thomas Scott – a merchant deputised by many of his contemporaries – the total amount subscribed from in and around Dundee was approximately £9,000 sterling.[51] While only part of the subscription was ever paid up, the fact that so many in Dundee were keen to take advantage of what had promised to be a profitable and patriotic undertaking, shows that there were individuals in the burgh with ready access to capital or a reliable source of credit. Although most subscribers were merchants and former bailies of the burgh, they included John Watson, doctor, Archibald Arnot, apothecary, John Dick, writer, Thomas Abercrombie, shipmaster or skipper, and the Dundee Seamen's Box itself. In 1707, a portion of the capital was repaid from the Equivalent, the principal short-term financial benefit to Scots from the Union.[52]

A burgh's finances were not necessarily a reflection of the wealth of local merchants or its more affluent inhabitants for whereas Dundee's council was facing an unenviable task, some individuals were clearly prospering. Nonetheless, in June 1700, the Convention of Royal Burghs was informed that Dundee's annual obligations exceeded its income by £4,800 Scots – a marginal increase from 1692.[53] The town's trade was described as 'decayed' and 'their peir, harboure, Tolbuith and other publict works are become ruinous'.[54] In December, Fletcher unsuccessfully petitioned parliament for an imposition that would allow Dundee to repair the harbour, tackle its debt and 'other causes'. This helps explain why the council was unable to cover the expenses incurred by John Scrymgeour of Kirkton (provost 1700–02) who had been named as one of the Scots union commissioners in September 1702.[55] That December he was informed that 'the toune was not in such Circumstances as Edinburgh or Glasgow for refounding his debursements in goeing to Londone, else they assured him of as kindly treatment from the toune'.[56] Perhaps Scrymgeour anticipated this resolution, explaining why he stayed at York for three days and delayed the commissioners' meeting, in order 'to save himself the expense of travelling otherwayes then by the stage coach, which is the least expensive'.[57]

In 1703, Dundee petitioned the Convention of Royal Burghs, representing its 'sad decay of trade' and 'insupportable burding of debt',[58] estimated the following year at upwards of £120,000 Scots. Dundee's combined income was not sufficient to cover the annual interest on its debts – never mind its other burdens – falling short by £5,000 or £6,000.[59] So the capital debt owed by the burgh continued to grow. On 5 August 1703, the Convention approved the burgh's decision 'to sell the lands of Hiltoun and Loggie to the best advantage' and apply the proceeds to its debt, but made no amendments to the tax roll.[60] By 1706, Dundee's debt had risen to £122,487 – which, at 5.5% interest, required a yearly repayment of £6,736 16s. 4d.[61] At this point, the sale of various town lands, authorised to relieve the burgh of its crippling burden, realised £37,106 2s. 2d.[62]

Incorporating union (back on the political agenda in 1704–05) offered a possible solution with its promise of free trade with England and her 'Dominions and Plantations'. Dundee had become so heavily dependent on the shipment of linen cloth to London that she would have suffered had England implemented the 'Alien Act' and blocked Scots imports.[63] There is no record of any debate concerning union in Dundee, but it is doubtful that such a crucial matter passed without notice.[64] Union was a divisive issue, unpopular with most Scots, but MPs from the coastal burghs were more inclined to vote in its favour. For example, Montrose, similarly reliant on the export of linen to England, instructed its commissioner to be 'active and zealous' in his support of union, convinced of the 'many and great' advantages.[65] Dundee's MP, John Scrymgeour, voted for union in all but two of the recorded divisions. Whether this was done with the blessing of the burgh council is unknown, although no one appears to have complained. Scymgeour, a court whig, was likely to have voted for union with or without the magistrates' consent.

The burgh had been keen to secure the imposition on ale and beer ever since December 1700 when Scrymgeour and bailie John Duncan had been commissioned to solicit an act from the Estates; and the burgh minutes suggest that the council was more preoccupied with trying to secure this new source of income rather than discussing the details of union. After several abortive attempts, for the final sessions of William's parliament were chaotic and with no opportunity for 'privat bussiness'[66] the council, in September 1706, appointed Captain George Yeaman (one of the bailies), to assist Scrymgeour and the lairds of Lundie and Denhead, in persuading parliament to agree to a contribution of 'tuo pennies per pynt of all ale and beir brouen, vended and sold, within this burgh and barronie of the Hiltoune'. They were assured that should they make an arrangement with any 'stats men or any other persone who shall befriend the toune in procureing the said gift, The Councell binds and obleidges them and their successor to performe any such promises as shall be made, provydeing the toune obtaine the forsaid gift'.[67] This time the town was successful. Overcoming an unsuccessful counter petition offered by Dundee's brewers, the burgh's petition and draft of an act were introduced on 26 November and approved on 4 January 1707. It granted an imposition of 2 pence on each pint of ale or beer 'either brown or inbrought topt vended and sold within the said toun . . . and other liberties and suburbs', and was fixed to last twenty-four years.[68]

Its preamble underscores what contemporaries considered responsible for Dundee's decline.

OUR SOVEREIGN LADY the Queens Majestie with the advice and consent of the Estates of Parliament, takeing unto their serious consideration the great and unsupportable debts, extreame distress, manifest decay and imminent ruine of the Royall Burgh of Dundee, partly contracted and occasioned in the time of the troubles in King Charles the First his Reign, they being then obleidged by publict authoritie to fortifie the Toun upon their oun expenses, and partly by the sad callamity and loss the toun sustained in the year [one thousand six hundred] and fiftie one, throw its being stormed and taken in by the then

Usurper, wherby the said Burgh was pillag'd and plundered in a most lamentable manner, As also the vast damnages and losses the toun sustained by the beating doun of its harbour and necessar reparation whereof was exceeding expensive and burdensome, Moreover the great charges which the toun was at by the marching and countermarching of troups throw the Burgh about the time of the Revolution, with the universall decay of trade especially in that place . . . [69]

The act of parliament cost the burgh £3,548 16s 4d Scots. George Yeaman (provost 1706–08) borrowed an additional £3,000 sterling from the bank to offset expenditure. He was also obliged to issue a burgess ticket to William Ramsay, a local merchant, having struck a bargain with James Moir of Stoneywood, one of the MPs from Aberdeen, in the last session of parliament. Displaying an interesting example of seventeenth-century Scots politics in practice, Moir had offered to 'befriend ye toun [and] also to procure others', in return for Ramsay's ticket. The imposition on ale was no short-term fix, for it would take several years to clear the burgh's considerable debt which stood at £97,809 17s ½d in May 1707.[70] This was some £20,000 less than what was owed by the burgh in 1704.[71] However, the amount was still a problem, and the reason why the burgh officials elected in September 1706, refused to accept office until April 1707.[72] In January, Dundee's creditors had been cited before parliament to arrange protection for the magistrates and council.[73] It appears the future magistrates were only prepared to accept after receiving some further guarantee that they would not be held liable and prosecuted on account of Dundee's arrears.[74]

While closer union with England and access to colonial trade may have seemed an attractive prospect, in the short-term the Union had a detrimental impact on Dundee's economy.[75] The burgh's low-quality linen cloth and wool manufactures were exposed to greater competition and increased export duties.[76] Within months of the treaty's inauguration, the town's baxters were complaining that the price of wheat had risen to such a level that they were unable to bake bread at either the price or weight appointed by the council.[77] Likewise, the deacon of the waulkers claimed the trade was 'near ruined', though through no fault of the Union. The inhabitants of the burgh, particularly women, were encroaching on their liberties, 'taking in all sort of cloath and worsett and dying ye same'.[78] On 6 June 1710, commissioners from Edinburgh, Crail and St Andrews compiled a new report on the condition of Dundee for the Convention of Royal Burghs. In material terms it was no different from earlier assessments.[79] The visitors agreed that the recent imposition on ale was 'prudently managed and faithfully applied', but the town's revenue was exhausted by stipends and public charges. 'No fund [was] remaining for paying missive dues and making publict reparations, whereby the burgh yearly runns in arrears on that account in a considerable summe'. The harbour and tolbooth were said to be 'very much decayed and if not speedily repaired, will utterly go to ruine'. It was also the opinion of the assessors that the burgh's trade was in a 'very low condition' and was the reason why some of the town's buildings had fallen into disrepair, 'even in the most publict places of the town'.[80] This was not the image of an especially prosperous burgh.

But Dundee was not the only Scots town to experience hardship, and the benefits of union remained negligible across most of the country for almost half a century. The settlement was so disliked across so much of Scotland that a small French fleet with the Old Pretender on board appeared off the east coast in March 1708, in an attempt to exploit Scots' anti-union sentiment. The invasion was quickly abandoned – but not before the burgh council had commissioned officers in each of the four quarters 'in case of [the] necessity for putting ye inhabitants in armes', and searched the town for shot and gunpowder. Once the French had been dispersed, the council sent a congratulatory address to Queen Anne.

But the character of Dundee's council changed dramatically in the years after the Union. Episcopalians – many of whom harboured Jacobite sympathies – achieved a greater voice in Dundee, and for some years before the 1715 rising, appear to have secured a majority in council. One critic complained that having gained control of the burgh, they, 'in after elections of Magistrates, proceed[ed] without regard to the rules and constitution of the said brough, By which Illegal and arbitrary steps, they gott themselves continued in the administration'.[81] George Yeaman, who became provost in 1706 and was re-elected in 1710, was an episcopalian who did a great deal to further the cause of his contemporaries; one Jacobite commentator credited him with almost single-handedly ending the dominance of the Revolution interest in the council.[82] Greater liberties were granted to Scots episcopalians on account of

PLATE 1. (*Above*) Dundee harbour *c.* 1770. It is not known why and by whom this painting was made, and it lacks a portion on the left which depicted the packhouses. Since the spire of St Andrew's church is missing, it must predate 1772. Given the focus is not the town but shipping and the harbour itself, it was probably painted to celebrate the recently completed Smeaton and Adam works to the harbour, and the new level of the Shore. Note the pier with the sundial, the Packhouses on the left, the open-air merchants' exchange at the centre, and lying beyond the Castle Hill the 1766 Sugar House on the extreme right. (Dundee Museums)

PLATE 2. (*Left*) Dundee Market Place looking west, by George McGillivray, 1847. Essentially, this view was unchanged from that of 1781, save that the 8-foot-wide narrows of the Nethergate, on the left, had been widened. Note the Luckenbooths on the right, blocking a view of the Overgate, Lady Warkstairs just visible beside Samuel Bell's pedimented English Chapel (by now the Union Hall) which blocked the western prospect. It was still an urban place where people met to do business, and had not yet mutated into a trafficked street. (Dundee Museums)

PLATE 3. (*Left*) This view was taken from a similar vantage point to Slezer's view from the north in 1678. Dudhope Castle remains in the foreground, shown shorn of its medieval tower, but the principal change is the occupation of agricultural land first by industry and then by the university. The spires of the Roman Catholic Cathedral, on the site of the Town's Hospital, lie behind the Dental Hospital directly ahead. (McKean)

PLATE 4. Gray's Close, from the High Street north to the Meadowlands, as it passes through Gardyne's Land, now restored as a backpackers' hostel. This complex of merchants' apartments and booths contains a thirteenth-century well, and a fine *c.* 1710 panelled chamber. The building in the left, with the projecting circular staircase, has timbers dated to 1591. It was in this close that George Dempster's father set up business in the second decade of the eighteenth century. (McKean)

PLATE 5. The castle at Broughty (Brughtie) controlled the entrance into the Tay estuary and the shipping 'roads'. On the high ground behind, the English army constructed a state-of-the-art fort in 1549. The castle was damaged after being abandoned by the English army, and subsequently fell into ruin. It was recreated by Robert Rowand Anderson in the 1860s as a naval defence post. (McKean)

PLATE 6. Invergowrie House, now concealed beside the Ninewells Hospital complex, was the country villa of the Baltic merchant venturers, the Clayhills family, who refashioned it in the early seventeenth century. More or less typical of this type of house, it had been extended horizontally from a small tower, providing a smart first-floor apartment above cellars, with an unusual semi-circular back court (known as a 'round square'). It was baronialised in 1836. (McKean)

PLATE 7. (*Above left*) A typically elaborate tomb in the Howff graveyard, laid out in the late sixteenth century just to the north of the medieval burgh on the former Greyfriars' garden. (McKean)

PLATE 8. (*Above right*) St David's Close, formerly Scott's Close, from Yeaman Shore. Possibly the most extensive survival of the Maritime Quarter, three closes rise from the shore up to the parish church, enclosing courts, gardens and a variety of buildings which contain fabric dating back to the fifteenth century onwards. (McKean)

PLATE 9. (*Right*) Looking east from the site of the Nethergate port. The 'great street' of Dundee followed the raised beach, curving round toward the High Street before entering the Murraygate and exiting to Forfar up the Hilltown. Originally it was narrow, then broadened for the 'broad' of the Nethergate, then narrowed, broadening into the High Street, thereafter narrowing and broadening both in Murraygate and Wellgate. (McKean)

PLATE 10. Dudhope Castle, ancient paternal seat of the Scrymgeours, on a bluff above Dundee. The twin-towered gatehouse is probably mid sixteenth century. The original tower to the right was demolished in the eighteenth century. Dudhope was reformatted by craftsmen from Holyroodhouse in the later seventeenth century, and passed into the hands first of Graham of Claverhouse and then of the earl of Forfar before becoming a textile mill. It was restored in the late twentieth century for Abertay University. (McKean)

PLATE 11. Tay Square from the west showing David Neave's splendid 1818 terrace of houses lining the western fringe of the burgh. The pinnacle of St Mary's tower can be seen just behind. (McKean)

PLATE 12. (*Above*) Dundee from Magdalen Green, painted by George McGillivray *c.* 1840, just before the arrival of the railways ended the port's riparian aspect. (Dundee Museums)

PLATE 13. (*Right*) The Maritime Quarter looking east toward Castle Wynd. The merchants' exchange lay to the right just beyond the Pierson Packhouses. (Private collection)

PLATE 14. Harry Harwood's 1822 caricature of the rulers of Dundee, collectively titled 'The Executive'. He not only rendered their physiognomies suitably bovine, but ascribed them character traits according to their personalities – for example Patrick Anderson, Provost in 1818, in top hat with cane over his shoulder, is called 'the Previous Question'. (*The Nine Incorporated Trades*)

PLATE 15. (*Above*) View of St Mary's
Steeple in the 1850s showing the
quarrying away of the Windmill (or
Corbie Hill) that rose behind the
Overgate. To the left, School Wynd
has been broadened into Lindsay
Street; the structures on the right are
the rear end of Overgate closes.
(Dundee Museums)

PLATE 16. (*Right*) View over
Camperdown Dock to the city centre.
Note the Customs House and the
spire of St Paul's Cathedral. St Mary's
steeple can just be glimpsed in the left
distance. The Frigate *Unicorn* rides on
the immediate left. (McKean)

parliament's act of toleration in February 1712, and Yeaman, who had been returned as MP for the Perth burghs in 1710, had voted for it.[83] The Dundee council not only allowed the Revs. Norrie and Rait to erect a meeting house in the Seagate, but in 1713 permitted unqualified ministers to preach in the Cross Church – the north transept of the original St Mary's.[84]

This infuriated the local synod, who approached the magistrates on 21 October 1714 to ask that 'the keyes of the said Church be by them presently delivered . . . to the intent the forsaid Church or part of the Church may be duely supplied by Loyal ministers'.[85] The synod also observed that neither provost nor any burgh official had attended the previous day's thanksgiving service for the coronation of King George I. Dundee's magistrates were well known to prefer the episcopalian services in the Cross Kirk or in the burgh meeting house.[86] However, the council had addressed the king on his accession and, on 27 September 1714, ordered 'ane solemnity for the King's . . . happy arrival in Britain, by setting on a Bonfire at the Cross and at the Shoar, and that the Magistrats and Councell goe to the Cross and drink his Majestie's health and other loyall healths, with the discharging of cannon'.[87] Similar instructions were given to mark George's coronation with 'the great guns brought to the Cross and [fired] at each health', where the town's fencible men would assemble and discharge their weapons three times that afternoon.[88]

These displays of dubious loyalty did little to comfort the burgh's presbyterian citizens or deceive the government. Dundee was increasingly divided as witnessed by the council's complaint lodged with the Lord Advocate, Sir David Dalrymple of Hailes, in January 1715, that a mob had insulted them. Dalrymple was under the impression that this 'proceeded from a zeall which the body of the people have to the government and against the magistrates' who, in his opinion, were all disaffected.[89] Rumours of Jacobite activity had been circulating for months, and Queen Anne's death and George's succession had provided as opportune a moment as any. Throughout the summer of 1715, alarming reports of the council's behaviour began to arrive in Edinburgh. In June, Adam Cockburn of Ormiston, the Lord Justice Clerk, wrote that some magistrates had been accused of 'cursing the King and other marks of disaffection'.[90] John Oliphant, William Ramsay, Alexander Watson, William Lyon and Thomas Wilson were charged with drinking

James's health 'in a solemn manner' at the market cross on the Pretender's birthday on 10 June.[91] The offenders were convicted, fined and imprisoned, and declared incapable of holding further office. Oliphant, who was found guilty of 'bidding God damn King George's blood', was debarred 'for ever of bearing any office in Scotland', Watson and Wilson from officiating in Dundee, and Ramsay and Lyon excluded from the council for the next three years.[92]

The council's politics had become contrary to the sympathies of the majority of Dundee's citizens. One observer described the burgh's magistrates as 'open enemies to the Protestant succession, and I am afraid, continue so, tho they feign subjection'.[93] By the end of July, Cockburn was writing to James Graham, first Duke of Montrose, to represent the case of the 'well affected' people in Dundee, Perth and Aberdeen, who 'are altogether exposed to the furie of the Jacobites'.[94] Bailie James Yeaman, one of the few Dundee officials still inclined to the Hanoverian establishment, wrote to the Advocate on 9 August 1715, that 'we are like to be swallowed up if the government do not send forces speedily here'. He had asked that the burgh's gates should be secured and the arms and ammunition of those disaffected to the government seized, but the council – including Oliphant and his colleagues who, freed from prison, had the 'impudence . . . to take their place . . . and act as formerly' – had only gone so far as appoint guards.[95]

In truth there was little that the government could do. There were insufficient regular troops in Scotland to garrison the town, and John Erskine, Earl of Mar, was already on his way north to raise the Pretender's standard on 6 September 1715. Reports from the excise office in Dundee show he had bypassed the town on, or just before, 27 August. From Edinburgh, Cockburn resignedly wrote that the 'well affected people in Perth and Dundee are much to be pitied'.[96] Jacobite heritors, led by William Graham of Duntrune, entered the burgh around two o'clock on 16 September, having coordinated events with Bailie Rolstone and the council.[97] The Pretender was proclaimed at the cross before Duntrune produced a patent ennobling himself as Viscount Dundee. The Jacobites secured the town and several 'parties [were] detatch'd for taking possession of the magazine, fort, ports [and] castle of Brochly'.[98] James Yeaman, Thomas Wardroper and David Maxwell, loyalists who fled Dundee shortly before the arrival of Duntrune, reported that all who refused to acknowledge James VIII were seized and imprisoned. Their shops in the town had been looted and their families left in Dundee: 'what outrages may be committed on them we know not'.[99] When Duntrune's Jacobites arrived, there were several ships in the harbour carrying what Yeaman, Wardroper and Maxwell described as 'people's effects'. As the sailors attempted to reach the comparative safety of their ships, the Jacobites opened fire with 'sharp shott'. There were no reported casualties although one unfortunate shipmaster was apprehended.

Mar's rebellion made good progress. The Jacobites controlled almost all Scotland above the River Tay within weeks, had taken Dundee, Perth, Inverness and Aberdeen, and were collecting taxes in Fife. However, Mar was a limited commander, and following the inconclusive confrontation at Sheriffmuir on 13 November, the only set piece battle of the campaign, the Jacobites lost the initiative. The rebellion slowly petered out, but not before James Stuart had landed at Peterhead on 22 December to reclaim his father's throne. He formally entered Dundee on at 11.00 a.m. on 6 January 1716, accompanied by Mar, George Keith, Earl Marischal, and around three hundred armed gentlemen; James was enthusiastically received.[100] Events surrounding the Pretender's arrival are described in a deposition made by William Gibb, a maltman in Dundee, who offered information against Alexander Wedderburn, the town clerk, who was prominent in the rising:[101]

> [The] clerk of Dundie then came into the Councill house accompanying the Earls of Marr & Marshall & severall Rebellious Gentlemen when they were getting . . . burges tickets in the said Councill house . . . and that the saids noblemen and Gentlemen had non when they went into the Councill house but had tickets in their hatts when they came out . . . and yt the said Alexander Wedderburn went to the Cross of Dundie with the Rebells at one or other of their treasonable solemnities, and also went and mett the Pretender when comeing to Dundie and came in with him & his sword drawn in his hand, And also collected the Excise for the use of the Rebells . . . [102]

James is said to have spent the night in Stewart of Grandtully's town house at the head of the Seagate, its approximate location now marked by a small stone plaque. However, recent evidence suggests he may have slept in a chamber in the town's Hospital.[103] In any case, his stay was necessarily short. With John Campbell, Duke of Argyll's government forces advancing from the south, and his own army rapidly disintegrating, the Pretender made the decision to return to France, sailing from Montrose on 4 February.[104] Dundee and the surrounding burghs were retaken without resistance. The magistrates and councillors involved in the rising had wisely decided to flee before the arrival of Argyll, whose appearance was almost certainly welcomed by 'the Inhabitants . . . weel affected to his Majesties interest and are by far the Majority of the said toun'.[105] The Duke appointed a group of six individuals to 'take care of this city, and the affairs thereof, till such proper Magistrates can be appointed by lawful authority'.[106]

The matter was remitted to Sir James Stewart of Goodtrees, the king's solicitor, the Lord Advocate and Lord Justice Clerk, appointed to find a suitable means of resettling the magistrates of the several burghs in North Britain.[107] It was ordered that 'a popular Election be made by ye Burgesses and Inhabitants resident within and bearing a share of ye Common burdens of . . . Dundie'.[108] The result of the poll was similar to that held in April 1689. The burgh chose John Scrymgeour of Kirkton as its provost, James Yeaman, David Maxwell and Thomas Wardroper, who had been compelled to leave the burgh in September 1715, were named as three of the four bailies. The Revolution or presbyterian interest was back at the helm, restored by means of a popular vote for the second time in three decades.

Meeting for the first time on 26 April 1716, the new council spent the coming months dealing with the consequences of the rising. It was decided that 'in all time comeing, no Inhabitant of this burgh that was active and assistant in the late unnatural rebellion, or were frequent hearers of the Pretender prayed for under the title of King James the Eight, be ever capable to carry any publick office in this Burgh for the future'.[109] The council compiled a list of the burgh's rebels in February 1717 as Bailie Yeaman had become aware that a number of individuals 'deeply engaged' in the rising had returned to the town and were 'keeping their shops & following their Trades as formerly'. But there was no witch-hunt.[110] In general, Scots statesmen (with the exception of Adam Cockburn of Ormiston) were more interested in reconciliation than retribution. They favoured a moderate settlement, and Scots Whigs were not averse to helping Jacobite friends and neighbours secure their release from prison or retain their estates. There was no overriding call for vengeance in Scotland, for the landed classes were closely knit and Whigs, like their Jacobite counterparts, had found the immediate post-union years difficult. Consequently, in Dundee, Wedderburn was the only noted casualty, losing his several lucrative offices.[111] The Kirk, on the other hand, was less charitable. The provincial synod of Angus and Mearns had been unable to meet at Dundee in October 1715 due to Mar's 'Rebellious Insurrection'. Accordingly, at Montrose on 19 April 1716, it drafted an act 'anent Complyers in the late Rebellion', declaring that:

> Whosoever minister or Incumbent hath in the time of the late Rebellion, Read or Caus'd Read, or Actually Consented to the Reading in their Church, any paper Emitted by the late Earle of Mar or the Pretender, ane and either of them, or by any having their or Either of Their pretended Authoritie, for Levying men, for a ffast or Thanksgiving, Or Dischargeing praying for our Soveraign King George, and appointing prayers for the Pretender and his Accomplices . . . having been ffound (all Circumstances being duely considered) Guilty in any the said Cases, shall be Deem'd and judged censureable with deposition from the holy Ministery . . . [112]

This was followed by an address to the king giving thanks that the nation had been delivered from the brink of destruction and 'Redeemed from Popery and slavery'.[113]

The rebellion was the pretext for more rigorous action against episcopalian ministers and intruders, most of whom had supported the rising. By the end of May 1717, the order allowing episcopalians to worship in the Cross Kirk had been revoked, the church having been used as 'a nurserie and seminary to Jacobites'. Disaffection might remain a significant issue across Angus, but Dundee's municipal government had been successfully purged by the Hanoverian regime,[114] and the influence of the established Kirk slowly edged northwards. From James VII's attempts to pack the local administration in 1686 to the reassertion of the Scots presbyterian establishment in 1716, control of Dundee's council and the political sympathies of its officials had gone full circle.

The later seventeenth and early eighteenth centuries had been difficult for Dundee, and while the Union did not offer an immediate solution to the town's serious economic problems, the following decades saw gradual improvement. By the 1740s Dundee was established as Scotland's leading centre for the manufacture of coarse linens – an industry that saw the town grow in confidence, ambition and prosperity.[115] In the 1720s Daniel Defoe had described Dundee as 'one of the best trading towns in Scotland . . . exceedingly populous, full of stately houses, and large handsome streets', quite a contrast with the accounts of some ten or so years earlier.[116] However, the most obvious example of the burgh's increasing success was the new Town House, completed in 1735. The finest contemporary municipal building in Scotland, the Town House was designed by the nation's foremost architect, William Adam.[117] The old tolbooth, inspected by Adam in June 1730, was found to be 'in danger of falling down . . . nor is it capable of repair'.[118] Consequently, Adam was commissioned to prepare a plan for a new building, the cost estimated at £2,852 3s 1d sterling, although the final figure was said to be nearer £4,000.[119]

But, while the economic fortunes of the town changed, the politics of those in control remained constant. The Hanoverian interest, restored in 1716, still headed the administration, and was supported by the bulk of Dundee's inhabitants even when the town was occupied by the Jacobite forces of Prince Charles Edward Stuart for around four months in 1745.[120] Provost Alexander Duncan of Lundie was arrested and replaced by David Fotheringham, appointed governor of Dundee.[121] Public worship was stopped, and the rebels were subsequently charged with plundering and having caused considerable damage – not least to the tower bells, 'rung with great vehemence' to celebrate the arrival of reinforcements from France.[122] Despite the town's rather precarious position, the citizens of Dundee were less than cordial to the occupying forces.

While many lairds whose estates surrounded the burgh were sympathetic to the Stuart cause, and the rebels recruited a significant number of men for Ogilvie's regiment in Dundee, the residents in general opposed the rebellion – but had little option other than to tolerate the Jacobite intrusion.[123] Nonetheless, a Hanoverian mob rioted on 30 October 1745, forcing the Jacobite governor to temporarily flee the town.[124] Some 1,000 soldiers of Kinloch's regiment were garrisoned in the town following the riot in order to keep the peace.[125] News that the Jacobite army had been broken at Culloden on 16 April 1746 prompted wholesale celebration in Dundee. To mark the occasion, the council organised 'publick Illuminations' from eight to ten at night on 24 April, agreeing that William Augustus, Duke of Cumberland, victorious commander of the Hanoverian army, should be made an honorary burgess of Dundee. He was presented with an illuminated scroll, delivered in a gold box made in Edinburgh and costing the sizeable sum of £45 10s 6d sterling.[126]

In 1715–16, the loyalties of the town had been harder to gauge than in 1745–46. In the earlier rising, the burgh administration was monopolised by men who appeared to sympathise with the exiled Stuarts, a stance at odds with the majority of citizens. That was not so in 1745. Although Dundee was still home to a large number of episcopalians – a label invariably, although not always accurately, associated with Jacobitism – who worshiped at either of the two local meeting houses, the council reforms of 1716 had been successful. By the '45, the council and majority of residents remained well-affected to the established government despite the burgh's occupation by a large number of rebel troops.

The enduring influence of the episcopalian clergy in Dundee, and the close proximity of a large number of landed gentlemen whose allegiance was first and foremost to the House of Stuart, were not necessarily typical. But the burgh's general economic and political experiences between 1686 and 1746 were not out of line with those of most other Scottish burghs. Events of a national, even international significance such as James VII's religious innovations, the Revolution, Union and the Jacobite rebellions were all replicated at a local level, and played out in the politics of Dundee. Likewise, the keenly felt interrelated economic crises of this period were similarly detrimental to the town. Although the linen trade brought renewed prosperity to Dundee, the town's economy was showing no signs of real improvement by the turn of the century. While its residents did not lack ambition, the council's finances, in marked comparison with other Scottish royal burghs who found themselves in similar straits, were more or less broken by 1707.

A similar distinction can be perceived in the religious and political commitment of the town and its inhabitants. In most cases, Dundee's episcopalian community was tolerated, residents adopting a pragmatic approach to religious worship. Although the Church of Scotland sent various directives directing the closure of meeting houses the burgh council, lacking the means to resolve the matter, adopted a somewhat laissez faire approach to dissent; and in the years immediately preceding the 1715–16 rebellion, episcopalians even gained temporary control of the burgh administration. But the presbyterian interest held sway for most of the period until the '45 and beyond.

Faced by events often beyond its control, Dundee coped well with the trials and tribulations of what proved an especially difficult and ultimately crucial chapter in Scots history. Perhaps in response to the burgh's well-understood economic weakness, its council and citizens placed a higher priority upon the burgh's interest and economic well-being than on pursuing its citizens for political or evangelical reasons; and this priority was to serve it well as it redefined its national role in the late eighteenth century.

Acknowledgement. Thanks to Professors Christopher Whatley, Charles McKean and Bob Harris for commenting on an earlier draft of this chapter.

NOTES

1 D. J. Patrick, 'Restoration to Revolution: 1660–1690', in R. Harris and A. R. MacDonald (eds.), *Scotland: The Making and Unmaking of the Nation c. 1100–1707*, *Vol. 2* (Dundee, 2007), pp. 65–66.

2 James VII was not the first monarch to interfere with burgh government. In 1661 Charles II's Privy Council had been ordered to ensure that those chosen as magistrates and councillors were known for their loyalty.

3 J. A. Rollo, *Dundee Historical Fragments* (Dundee, 1911), p. 23.

4 Dundee City Archives (DCA), Town Council Minute Book (TCM), 21 September 1686.

5 Ibid., 2 December 1686.

6 On 4 October 1688 a letter from the Privy Council instructed the burgh to continue the magistrates and council 'during his majesties furder pleasur'.

7 A. M. Scott, *Bonnie Dundee* (Edinburgh, 2000), 39; Rollo, *Historical Fragments*, p. 23; C. S. Terry, *John Graham of Claverhouse, Viscount of Dundee 1684–1689* (London, 1905), p. 153.

8 Terry, *Graham of Claverhouse*, p. 228. Claverhouse attended council on eleven occasions between 29 March 1688 and 27 February 1689. He was also chosen, with John Graham, the burgh's assessor, to represent Dundee at the Convention of Royal Burghs in July 1688.

9 Ibid., pp. 228–230; H. Paton (ed.), *Register of the Privy Council of Scotland* (*RPCS*), vol. XIII (Edinburgh, 1932), p. 288. A list of presbyterian ministers preaching in Dundee between February and June 1688 was compiled for the Privy Council.

10 Patrick, 'Restoration to Revolution', pp. 66–67. On 28 September 1688 the Privy Council issued a proclamation announcing William's anticipated invasion.

11 On 29 November 1688 the town guard was limited to thirty men per night and discontinued on 20 December.

12 D. J. Patrick, 'Unconventional Procedure: Scottish Electoral Politics after the Revolution', in K. M. Brown and A. J. Mann (eds.), *The History of the Scottish Parliament 1567–1707, Vol. 2* (Edinburgh, 2005), pp. 218–219; Patrick, 'Restoration to Revolution', p. 69.

13 In Dundee the sett established that the magistrates and council would number twenty including the provost, four bailies, a treasurer and dean of guild.

14 National Library of Scotland (NLS), Yester MS 7026/149, John Hay, second Earl of Tweeddale to Lord Yester, Edinburgh, 2 March 1689.

15 Patrick, 'Unconventional Procedure', p. 218.

16 C. G. Maccrie, *Scotland's Part and Place in the Revolution of 1688* (Edinburgh, 1888), p. 217.

17 National Archives of Scotland (NAS), Acts of Parliament 1689–90, PA2/33, fol. 42.

18 It appears there were no council meetings from 27 February to 20 April 1689. Duncan of Lundie and Hay of Naughton were also named as overseers but only Powrie attended.

19 A. M. Scott (ed.), Letters of John Graham of Claverhouse', in *Miscellany of the Scottish History Society* (Edinburgh, 1990), p. 234.

20 M. G. H. Pittock, *The Myth of the Jacobite Clans* (Edinburgh, 1995), p. 43. There seems to be some confusion concerning the date Dundee raised the King's standard, Scott suggesting 14 April and Terry either 16–17 April.

21 Scott, *Bonnie Dundee*, pp. 137–139; Rollo, *Historical Fragments*, p. 23; Terry, *Graham of Claverhouse*, pp. 281–282.

22 TCM, 23 September 1689.

23 Patrick, 'Restoration to Revolution', pp. 56–67.

24 Ibid., p. 68; A. L. Drummond and J. Bulloch, *The Scottish Church 1688–1843* (Edinburgh, 1973), p. 7.

25 TCM, 2 May 1689.

26 Rait had succeeded his father as a minister in Dundee in 1682. He died in 1704. Norrie was deprived on 29 August 1689 and appointed a Bishop of the Non Jurant Church in 1724.

27 *An Account of the Present Persecution of the Church in Scotland in Several Letters* (London, 1690), p. 16.

28 TCM, 7 January 1690.

29 Rollo, *Historical Fragments*, p. 24. The first charge was not declared vacant until July 1694.

30 Ibid., 10 December 1689.

31 Ibid., p. 24.

32 John Spalding succeeded George Anderson as minister of the second charge. Anderson was admitted in November 1690 but moved to Logie in December that year. Spalding had been deprived in 1662 but was serving as minister of Kirkcudbright in 1689 before his move to Dundee on 6 August 1691. He died in 1699 and was replaced by John Dalgliesh, admitted on 27 August 1700. William Mitchell was minister at Leslie in 1688 and transferred to St Paul's on 20 May 1691.

33 I. McCraw, *The Kirks of Dundee Presbytery 1558–1999* (Dundee, 2000), p. 35.

34 Drummond and Bulloch, *Scottish Church*, p. 16. In 1692, after a meeting with represen-
    tatives of the episcopalian clergy in Holland, King William ordered that provided they
    acknowledge his title to the throne and subscribe the Westminster Confession, episco-
    palian ministers could keep their benefices and share in the government of the church.
35 E. Luscombe, *Across the Years, Episcopacy in Forfar 1560–2000* (Dundee, 2006), p. 10.
36 D. Defoe, *A Tour Through the Whole Island of Great Britain* (London, 1978).
37 W. C. Skinner, *The Barronie of Hilltowne of Dundee* (Dundee, 1927), p. 58. Dudhope
    Castle and Claverhouse's estates appear to have passed to Archibald Douglas, first Earl
    of Forfar, after the Revolution.
38 NAS, Register Privy Council 1696–99, PC 1/51, fol. 190.
39 TCM, 17 April 1703.
40 NAS, CH2/12/1, fols. 8–9. Within the presbyteries of Dundee, Meigle and Forfar, the
    parishes of Abernyte, Inchture and Rescobie were occupied by qualified episcopalian
    preachers; the ministers in Mains and Monifieth were under process; Monikie,
    Kinettles, Lintrathen, Kingoldrum, Forfar, Tannadice, Kellas and Dunnichen were all
    settled by uncertified intruders.
41 *RPCS*, vol. xiv (Edinburgh, 1933), p. 787. In early 1690 Dundee was owed
    £2,914 11s 11d by the army.
42 *Miscellany Scottish Burgh Records Society*, xxviii. The report was compiled between
    August 1691 and June 1692.
43 E. J. Graham, *A Maritime History of Scotland, 1650–1790* (East Linton, 2002), p. 57.
44 Rollo, *Historical Fragments*, p. 23. The dispute concerned Lauderdale's claim that as
    Constable of Dundee he was also patron of the South Church, a claim opposed by the
    council which had founded the second charge.
45 *Miscellany Scottish Burgh Records Society*, pp. 61–64.
46 Ibid., 66. In September 1691 Aberdeen's common good was calculated at £3,748 2s 2d.
    The burgh's yearly outgoings amounted to £11,578 4s 6d Scots. This included annual
    rent of £6,765 6s 6d – Aberdeen's borrowings standing at £112,755 9s. The accounts of
    other local burghs show a modest profit. Arbroath had a surplus of £333 9s 3d and
    Brechin £416 3s Scots.
47 Marwick, (ed.), *Extracts from the Records of the Convention of the Royal Burghs of
    Scotland, 1677–1711*, pp. 160–161.
48 C. A. Whatley, *Scots and the Union* (Edinburgh, 2006), p. 163; C. A. Whatley, D. B.
    Swinfen and A. M. Smith, *Life and Times of Dundee* (Edinburgh, 1995), p. 62; T.
    Thomson (ed.), *The Acts of the Parliaments of Scotland* (*APS*), vol. 10 (Edinburgh, 1823),
    p. 165. It was the opinion of Parliament that 'fairs and mercats in convenient places
    does greatly tend to the advantage and ease of His Majesties Leidges inhabiting the
    same and dwelling near therto and also to the advanceing the Trade of the Nation'.
49 It was hoped that colonial trade would see Scotland emulate her English and Dutch
    neighbours. The fact that Darien – the site on the Isthmus of Panama chosen for the
    Scots' settlement – was actually a Spanish possession was given little thought.
    Colonists were ill-prepared, under-provisioned, and at length forced to abandon the
    venture in 1700.
50 J. H. Burton (ed.), *The Darien Papers: Being a Selection of Original Letters and Official
    Documents relating to the Establishment of a colony at Darien by the Company of
    Scotland* (Bannatyne Club, 1849). The figures are based on subscription lists extracted
    from this volume. Only the subscriptions of those with some obvious connection to
    Dundee have been included.

51 The list includes several heritors, a medical doctor, three ministers, an army officer and Rachel Zeaman, widow of George Forrester of Knap. It is presumed that those using the burgh's deputy had some connection to Dundee.

52 *The Darien Papers*, pp. 389–390; A. M. Smith, *The Guildry of Dundee: A History of the Merchant Guild of Dundee up to the 19th century* (Dundee, 2005) pp. 58–59.

53 Edinburgh City Archives (ECA), Convention of Royal Burghs, SL 30/223, Report of the Commissioners Appoynted for visiting the Burgh of Dundee, 13 June 1700.

54 Ibid.

55 M. D. Young (ed.), *The Parliaments of Scotland, Burgh and Shire Commissioners, Vol. 2* (Edinburgh, 1993), p. 623.

56 TCM, 17 December 1702.

57 NAS, Ogilvie of Inverquharity MSS GD 205/32, Robert Bennet to William Bennet of Grubbet, Edinburgh, 5 November 1702.

58 ECA, SL 30/221, Petition for Dundie, 1703; ECA, SL 30/221, Petition for the Burgh of Dundee, 1704.

59 Ibid., Petition for the Burgh of Dundee, 1704; C. A. Whatley, *Scottish Society 1707–1830* (Manchester, 2000), p. 37. On 12 September 1706, Bailie Yeaman reported in council that, after considering income and expenditure, there was a shortfall of £6,522 17s 9d Scots.

60 *Extracts from the Records of the Convention of the Royal Burghs*, p. 349.

61 W. Hay (ed.), *Charters, Writs, and Public Documents of the Royal Burgh of Dundee, 1292-1880* (Dundee, 1880), 125.

62 Council minutes, 25 September 1706, in Hay (ed.), *Charters, Writs, and Public Documents*, p. 124.

63 Whatley, *Scots and the Union*, p. 304.

64 Historical Manuscripts Commission, *Report on the Manuscripts of the Earl of Mar and Kellie* (London, 1904), pp. 303–04

65 Whatley, *Scots and the Union*, p. 304; T. C. Smout, 'The Burgh of Montrose and the Union of 1707', *Scottish Historical Review*, 66 (1987), pp. 183–184.

66 TCM, 28 July 1702. Scrymgeour made another attempt to secure the act in 1702 but 'there was no private bussiness medled with or don'.

67 Ibid., 23 September 1706.

68 *APS*, vol. 9, p. 479.

69 Ibid., p. 479. The act specified that the imposition was purposely for the relief and support of the burgh and payment of its debts.

70 TCM, 13 May 1707.

71 Hay (ed.), *Charters, Writs and Public Documents of the Royal Burgh of Dundee, 1292–1880* (Dundee, 1880), p. 123. On 25 September 1706, the burgh's treasurer, James Guthrie, indicated that he had paid a part of the sum owed to Dundee's creditors from the proceeds generated by feuing the lands of Logie and Hilltown. This cleared over £30,000 Scots of the town's debt. The outstanding principal sum, 'due by bond', then stood at £4,254 12s 10d. The estate of Logie was afterwards sold to Alexander Wedderburn of Blackness for 17,500 merks.

72 TCM, 26 September 1706. The council refused to accept office on account 'of the great debt with which the toune is burdened at present and the hazard of their persons for the same'.

73 *APS*, vol. 9, p. 399.

74 TCM, 5 April 1707. The burgh's creditors granted a 'supercedere ay & while ye terme of Martimas [one thousand seven hundred] and eleven years'.

75 See Whatley, *Scots and the Union*, ch. 9.

76 Whatley, Swinfen and Smith, *Life and Times of Dundee*, p. 62; Whatley, *Scots and the Union*, p. 337. Linen was subject to Westminster-imposed duties on exports in 1711 and 1715.

77 Ibid., 24 February 1708. The burgh was still without the new 'English' weights on 31 March 1708.

78 Ibid., 29 April 1708. On 29 April 1708, Gilbert Auchinleck, a litster in the burgh, petitioned the council on account of the fact he was 'reduced to great straits and difficultie by reason of the losses he has sustained by severalls of his debitors their breaking and becoming insolvent'.

79 ECA, SL 30/223, Report of the State of the Towne of Dundie, 6 June 1710.

80 In April 1707 the council had ordered heritors 'or others concerned with ruinous houses within the toune, to repaire the samen and to putt them in such condition that neighbours and others passing through the streets & closes may be free of any hazard or danger'.

81 NAS, State Papers Scotland, RH 2/4/308, Case of the Toun of Dundie.

82 E. Cruickshanks, S. Handley and D. W. Hayton (eds.), *The House of Commons 1690–1715*, 5 vols. (Cambridge, 2002), vol. v pp. 953–955.

83 Ibid.

84 An episcopalian congregation appears to have been worshiping in the Seagate from 1704. The 1712 act did not authorise episcopalians 'to hold their assemblies for worship or use the liturgie of the Church of England in any Paroch Church'. There seems to be some confusion concerning the condition of the Cross Kirk. Rollo claimed it was run-down and unfit for worship. However, it appears that services were regularly held in the Church, the ministers of Dundee describing it in May 1717, as 'very usefull and necessary to the ministers and Inhabitants of this Burgh for yr Religious exercises upon week days & some times also upon Sabbath days & particularly for yr accom-modation upon occasion of the Celebration of the Lords supper'. By the 1745 Jacobite rebellion a second episcopalian meeting house had been erected in Yeaman Shore.

85 TCM, 21 October 1714.

86 NAS, CH 2/12/3, fol. 217, 226; NAS, Montrose MSS GD 220/5/453/13, Sir David Dalrymple of Hailes to James Graham, first duke of Montrose, Newhailes, 27 January 1715. The Lord Advocate reported that two episcopalian ministers, messrs Goldman and Cockburn, preached in the town's meeting house, but only the latter 'reads the prayers not omitting what concerns the King'. Consequently, each time Cockburn prayed for King George and the royal family 'the Magistrates sit down and are mute and that being over rise again and join in the litanie'.

87 TCM, 25 September 1714.

88 Ibid., 19 October 1714.

89 NAS, GD 220/5/453/13, Hailes to Montrose, Newhailes, 27 January 1715; Whatley, *Scots and the Union*, p. 351. The Lord Advocate believed that the magistrates, postmaster, neighbouring heritors and justices of the peace were 'very counterband'. His letter reveals a level of friction between the Jacobite officers and generally well-affected 'townsmen'.

90 NAS, GD 220/5/454/50, Adam Cockburn of Ormiston to James Graham, first duke of Montrose, Edinburgh, 9 June 1715; NAS, GD 220/5/475/6, Sir James Stewart of

Goodtrees to Montrose, Edinburgh, 9 July 1715; NAS, GD 220/5/472/24(A), John Stirling to Montrose, Edinburgh, 9 July 1715. One of the councillors under process for 'cursing the King' was expelled from the Convention of Royal Burghs in July 1715.

91 NAS, RH 2/4/308.

92 Ibid; D. Szechi, *1715 The Great Jacobite Rebellion* (New Haven and London, 2006), p. 112. Oliphant and his several colleagues were released from prison on 10 August 1715.

93 NAS, GD 220/5/455/4, [. . .] to [Ormiston], Aberdeen, 13 June 1715.

94 NAS, GD 220/5/455/38, Ormiston to Montrose, Edinburgh, 29 July 1715.

95 NAS, RH 2/4/303/28, James Yeaman to Hailes, Dundee, 9 August 1715; NAS, RH 2/4/308.

96 NAS, RH 2/4/303/87(A), Ormiston to [. . .], Edinburgh, 28 August 1715.

97 Szechi, *1715*, p. 112; NAS, GD 220/5/453/13, Hailes to Montrose, Newhailes, 27 January 1715; NAS, GD 220/5/455/4, [. . .] to [Ormiston], Aberdeen, 13 June 1715. The greatest part of the Angus gentry was Jacobite.

98 NAS, RH 2/4/303/70, David Maxwell, James Yeaman and Thomas Wardroper to Ormiston, Woodhaven, Fife, 16 September 1715.

99 Ibid.

100 J. Thomson and J. MacLaren, *The History of Dundee* (Dundee, 1874), p. 114; B. Lenman, *The Jacobite Risings in Britain 1689–1746* (Aberdeen, 1995), p. 138.

101 D. Dobson, *The Jacobites of Angus 1689–1746* (St Andrews, 1995), p. 47; A. Livingstone, C. W. H. Aikman and B. S. Hart, *No Quarter Given: The Muster Roll of Prince Charles Edward Stuart's Army, 1745–46* (Glasgow, 2001), p. 53. In addition to Burgh Clerk, Wedderburn was a Collector of Excise, Sheriff Depute and Sheriff Clerk of Forfarshire. He succeeded his cousin as baronet of Blackness sometime after 1716. His son, Sir John, a volunteer serving with Prince Charles's Lifeguards, was executed on 28 November 1746 for his part in the '45, one of seventeen rebels executed on Kennington Common, near London.

102 TCM, 9 August 1716. It would appear that the Jacobites appointed a new provost in Dundee, replacing Alexander Ballingall. Gibb's deposition mentions two burgess tickets subscribed 'be the therein designed Sir Alexander Watson, Provest'. This was probably the same Watson formerly charged with drinking the health of the Pretender at the market cross.

103 Thomson and MacLaren, *History of Dundee*, p. 114; N. Watson, *Dundee: A Short History* (Edinburgh, 2006), p. 81.

104 NAS, RH 2/4/309/90, John Leslie, ninth Earl of Rothes to [. . .], Edinburgh, 5 February 1716; Szechi, *1715*, p. 168.

105 NAS, RH 2/4/308.

106 Lenman, *Jacobite Risings*, p. 138; Rollo, *Historical Fragments*, p. 29; Thomson and MacLaren, *History of Dundee*, p. 116; Hay (ed.), *Charters, Writs and Public Documents*, p. 137. On 3 February 1716 the Duke of Argyll appointed John Scrymgeour, James Alison, David Maxwell, Alexander Preston, James Fairweather and Mungo Murray as interim administrators.

107 ECA, SL 30/227, Information to the Right Honourable Convention of Burrows anent the Caice of the Royall Burghs in the shire of Angus, 1716; NAS, RH 2/4/309/122, Goodtrees to [. . .], Edinburgh, 16 February 1716.

108 TCM, 10 March 1716; NAS, RH 2/4/308. The government considered a popular election as the only means of progress, 'seeing there cannot be found in the town such

a number of any former magistracy and Councill That were legally Constitute Befor
the Incroachments made by the said Disaffected party as will be sufficient to proceed
in a manner of such Consequence . . . Most of these former legally Constitute
Magistrats and Councillors being dead or removed from the place'.

109 Ibid., 25 September 1716. On 30 October 1716 the council ordered that the burgh
mark the birthday of the Prince of Wales. The 'whole inhabitants att half ane hour
after five a clock this night yt those who have windows to the street shall have full
Illuminations & those that have not to have Bonefires at yr Closs heads under ye
penalty of five pound Scots each'.

110 Ibid., 19 February 1717.

111 Szechi, *1715*, pp. 236–250; Hay (ed.), *Charters, Writs and Public Documents*,
pp. 140–141. In addition to Wedderburn, the master of the grammar school, Patrick
Lyon, was deposed on 1 May 1716, having 'joined a schismaticall meeting-house set up
in opposition to Church and State'.

112 NAS, CH 2/12/4, fols. 24–25. Presbyteries were also instructed to consider the actions
of schoolmasters. This was a particular grievance of the Synod. In April 1715 it had
represented to the General Assembly that the practise of magistrates choosing schoolmasters without the respective presbytery's consent was unacceptable.

113 Ibid., p. 34.

114 NAS, RH 2/4/311/20, Memorial Concerning the Present State of Angus and Mearns,
Brechin, 31 May 1716; NAS, RH, 2/4/312/219(B), Colonel Charles Hotham to
Lieutenant-General George Carpenter, Dundee, 18 October 1716. In October 1716,
Provost Scrymgeour informed Colonel Charles Hotham that 'he did not know three
men in the whole shire of Angus whose informations we might rely upon'. Similar
reform was attempted in other burghs occupied by Jacobite forces.

115 C. McKean, ''Not even the trivial grace of a straight line' – or why Dundee never
built a New Town', in L. Miskell, C. A. Whatley and R. Harris (eds.), *Victorian
Dundee: Image and Realities* (East Linton, 2000), p. 18.

116 Ibid.

117 Ibid.

118 Hay (ed.), *Charters, Writs and Public Documents*, pp. 146–147.

119 Ibid., pp. 148–149.

120 I. D. McIntosh, 'The East of Scotland Lodges during the Jacobite Uprising of 1745',
in *Year Book of the Grand Lodge of Ancient Free and Accepted Masons of Scotland*
(Edinburgh, 2007), pp. 55–56. The Jacobites entered Dundee on 4 September 1745
and left on 14 January 1746.

121 M. G. H. Pittock, *The Myth of the Jacobite Clans* (Edinburgh, 1995), p. 66; Watson,
Dundee, p. 83; C. Duffy, *The '45* (London, 2003), p. 354.

122 Rollo, *Historical Fragments*, pp. 33–34, 250; Duffy, *The '45*, p. 354. In order to mark the
arrival of troops and supplies at Montrose on 25 November 1745, the residents of
Dundee were instructed to illuminate their windows. The windows of those who
refused were broken, shot was fired into some houses and transgressors were subject to
a fine of £20 Scots.

123 Ibid.

124 Duffy, *The '45*, p. 354; Pittock, *Jacobite Clans*, p. 66.

125 Ibid.

126 Hay (ed.), *Charters, Writs and Public Documents*, p. 145.

CHAPTER 5

Life Outside the Medical Centre: Health and Sickness in Early Modern Dundee

Elizabeth Foyster

What seemed to be emerging in medicine and in society in general was a series of concentric circles, with the epicentre around Edinburgh. The inner circles contained most of the elements of change, while the outer circles, outer in all senses of the term, were not changing nearly so quickly and decisively.[1]

So concludes Helen M. Dingwall in her chapter on 'Medicine in Early-Modern Scotland'. It was Edinburgh that led the way in the provision of professionalised and institutionalised medical care. Change had begun as early as 1505, when a charter of incorporation for Edinburgh surgeons and barbers was issued, followed by the establishment of the Royal College of Physicians in 1681, the establishment of Edinburgh Medical School in 1726, and the opening of Edinburgh Infirmary in 1729. Other Scottish cities followed similar patterns of development; in 1656 Glasgow town council set up an Incorporation of Surgeons, Glasgow Medical School began in 1751, Aberdeen Infirmary was opened in 1742, and Glasgow Infirmary in 1794. But Dundee, even during the eighteenth century, remained outside this 'inner circle' of change. The Nine Trade Incorporations of Dundee did not include any medical practitioners. The nearest medical school to Dundee was in St Andrews, but its lack of a hospital meant that its students had no clinical training. Conflicts within Aberdeen University meant that a medical school was only firmly established in the early nineteenth century. Dundee's Infirmary was not founded until 1794.[2]

Faced with evidence like this, it is all too easy to believe that the sick in early modern Dundee faced little prospect of receiving quality medical treatment. Indeed, it has been concluded that in fifteenth- and sixteenth-century Dundee, 'provision for the care of the sick was so minimal as to be in effect non-existent'.[3] Certainly, prominent medics such as Sir Robert Sibbald, who was born in Edinburgh in 1641, lived in Dundee. But such was the importance of Edinburgh to the Scottish medical scene, even at this early date, that when Sibbald took steps to found the Royal College of Physicians, its home could be in none other than Edinburgh. Nevertheless, a network of physicians, surgeons, apothecaries and midwives was operating in Dundee by the eighteenth century – albeit the views of some contemporaries could be disparaging. It was said of Dundee doctors in 1746, for example, that they had 'worn large muffs, dangled gold-headed canes, hummed loud and looked wise: and according to the strength or weakness of their natural constitution, the patient survived or died'.[4]

This chapter supports a far more positive view of medicine in early modern Dundee. It argues that a lack of institutional provision did not mean that Dundee's authorities were unable to organise medical care for those in need. Furthermore, it shows that although Dundee was without its own centres of medical education and training, its population could resort to a range of medical opinions and resources. Indeed, it is precisely because of the absence of professional medical bodies and institutions, that Dundee offers so many opportunities for a social history of medicine. Instead of institutional, formal or official medical histories of the 'medical centre', Dundee provides the opportunity to examine in detail the informal, unofficial and 'amateur' aspects of medical care, and enables us to shift our focus away from the often 'male-centred' concerns of medical history. By looking at the medical encounters of ordinary Dundonians, we can begin to understand more about their standard of living, and open up a world that contained their greatest fears and anxieties as they faced illness and death.

The sources available to the historian suggest this direction of research, for with no medical incorporations nor medical school, there are no minutes or lists of attendees that could be used to track members or medical students. Medical societies, the focus points for education and social activities, produced their own minute books and publications, but Dundee's first medical society (the Phrenological Society) was not established until 1825.[5] Since newspapers published advertisements by individual practitioners and their organisations, they have been useful to medical historians, but regular editions of Dundee newspapers were issued only in the nineteenth century.[6] We are left with sources that contain medical information only incidentally. Dundee's General Session, for example, presided over by the key church ministers, has surviving minute books from 1682 which dealt with medical matters when judging on the administration of the poor law. The disciplining of those who offended its moral codes meant that the views of midwives in cases of pre-nuptial pregnancy, illegitimacy and suspected abortion or infanticide, could be crucial in determining guilt or innocence. Dundee's town council minutes contain some information about the limited measures that were taken by the authorities to prevent the spread of disease. The returns to Sir John Sinclair's queries that would form his *Statistical Account* (1791–99), give an overview of the state of the populations' health in Dundee and its surrounding countryside at the end of the period. Finally, the letters, account books and journals of some of Dundee's elite families provide a perspective on the interplay between 'professional' and self-administered medical care experienced by them, their servants and their employees.

MEDICAL PROVISION

Was Dundee perceived as a healthy or unhealthy place to live in the early modern period? In the view of the Rev. Robert Small, author of Dundee's entry in Sinclair's *First Statistical Account,* 'no part of the parish can be called unhealthy'. To Small, Dundee's natural position, with its high position on a ridge above the tidal River Tay, and its 'exposure' to fresh winds, meant that it had 'as healthy a situation . . . as, perhaps, any in the world'. The causes of ill-health, Small believed, were all man-made. It was 'the height of the houses, the narrowness of the tenements and of some streets, by which the people were too much crowded upon one another', which caused sickness. In these circumstances, Small recognised that it was children who were most vulnerable to illness. The minister of a rural Angus parish may well have been thinking of Dundee when he bemoaned, 'the sickly looks of many children, in large, crowded, ill situated or ill constructed towns', which he believed showed that 'the country is the preferable place for children'.[7] Since it was often young adults who came to Dundee in search of work, and who subsequently bore children, infant mortality probably had a significant effect upon the death totals for the town.[8]

Yet Dundee, like other early modern urban centres, continued to expand because migrants kept coming to the city. Ironically, given its mortality rates, one of Dundee's attractions was the opportunities it offered for medical care. Dundee's social elite, who lived on large estates outside the city, could still resort to the town's medical services when they became ill. Elizabeth Stanhope, Countess of Strathmore, made payments in March 1715 to a sicknurse for 'waiting on my three sons at Dundee when they had the small pox', and kept an account with a Mr Forister, an apothecary in Dundee.[9] By 1722–23 the favoured apothecary for Elizabeth and her children was Thomas Crichton, also based in Dundee, who received repeated orders from the family for a variety of medicines.[10] This patronage of Dundee's medical resources was of benefit to more than the elite themselves. A letter to Charles Wedderburn, dated 28 August 1822, from Dr John Malloch, Kirremuir, reveals that he had been treating the Wedderburn's cook for some time. As she had not responded to his remedies, the advice was that Charles should send the cook in a coach to Dundee, where 'medical gentlemen' would examine her.[11] By the 1820s, it was certainly the perception of those living in rural areas that they lacked the medical facilities that Dundee could offer. The Reverend John Gellaty, residing in Tealing parish, on the south side of the Sidlaw Hills above Dundee, believed that 'one of the greatest evils under which the country people labour is, the want of proper medical assistance'.[12] While they faced greater dangers from disease and premature mortality, Dundee's inhabitants could draw upon a greater number and range of medical practitioners than their rural neighbours. 'Towns were seen ambivalently as a source of strong remedies as well as strong diseases', and Dundee was no exception.[13]

Some of the earliest forms of medical care in Dundee are likely to have been offered by friars or monks. An estate on the outskirts of Arbroath was called 'Hospitalfield' in the eighteenth century, because this had been the site of a hospital for the sick from the Abbey of Arbroath.[14] On 20 July 1559, the friar Findlo Duncan was given compensation for the damage to his herb garden in Dundee's Blackfriars' kirkyard, and he was recorded as performing the offices of a surgeon the following year.[15] By the sixteenth century, an occupation based solely on medical knowledge was also a possibility. The records of the town council contain the names of thirty men practising as surgeons, barber-surgeons or physicians in sixteenth-century Dundee. These men were drawn from merchant and elite families, and whether because of their medical or commercial activities, many became burgesses.[16] Surgeons and apothecaries learned their skills via apprenticeship, while physicians were usually trained at university. Occasionally medical skills were passed down the generations from father to son, which was a custom that was also found in some Highland communities.[17]

Within the early modern period, at least two Dundee medics gained a reputation that extended well beyond the town. David Kinloch (1560–1617), matriculated at St Andrews in 1576, and subsequently studied medicine on the continent. He was reputed to have served the French royal family as a physician before an ill-fated journey to Spain led to him being tried by the Inquisition in Toledo. After six years imprisonment, Kinloch was released and returned to Scotland, where he was appointed physician to James VI in 1597. He lived in a house near Coutties Wynd in Dundee around 1600, and retired to lands around Aberbrothie where he died in 1617. A portrait of Kinloch, painted in 1614, now hangs at Ninewells Hospital in Dundee, and his gravestone is in the Howff.[18] A bizarre twist of fate contributed to the fame of another Dundee medic, the surgeon Patrick Blair (c. 1680–1728). The death of a travelling elephant on the road from Broughty Ferry to Dundee, presented Blair with the opportunity to conduct the first dissection of its kind, and he published the results of his research with the Royal Society of London in 1710. Such was the local public fascination with the elephant that Blair mounted an exhibition or 'cabinet of curiosities' in Dundee, dedicated to the study of natural history, and founded a physic garden for the study and collection of medicinal herbs. While Blair was elected a fellow of the Royal Society of London in 1712, and subsequently spent most of the rest of his life in England, his legacy for Dundee was the establishment of the town's first museum and botanical garden. By the start of the eighteenth century, as Blair expressed it in a letter, there were sufficient numbers of 'honourable and learned gentlemen' living 'in the neighbourhood' to fund such projects, but there also existed a confidence that an interest in botany, medicine and science in general extended beyond elite circles in the town.[19]

As with medical practice elsewhere, patients could expect the fee for their treatment to be agreed in advance of treatment, and could withhold payment if the treatment was unsuccessful. A test case came before the Dundee Burgh Court in February 1614, when Alexander Smyt from Overyeards demanded repayment from John Fordyce, surgeon, for failing to cure his wife's wounded arm. Far from getting better under the care of Fordyce, the condition of the woman's arm had become so serious that she and her husband had travelled to Edinburgh to see another surgeon. This surgeon declared that Fordyce had 'not rightly understood the said hurt', and so had administered the wrong treatment. Smyt demanded compensation for the costs incurred by the Edinburgh trip, as well as a refund of Fordyce's fee. But the bailies would grant neither, and their reason for absolving Fordyce was not given.[20] Nevertheless, this case study of the patient–practitioner relationship is revealing on two counts. First, it suggests a patient-driven hierarchy of medical treatment. Whereas those living in the rural areas of Angus could consider a medical consultation in Dundee as a 'step-up' from what was available to them in their immediate environs, Dundee inhabitants saw Edinburgh practitioners as offering a level of expertise that could be called upon when their own town's medics failed to deliver results. Second, it gives some insight into the position of Dundee's women in this medical world, a matter that will be discussed later. Although it was Smyt's wife who was the patient, the payment of her medical costs, the decision to seek a second opinion and the case for medical negligence, were all led by her husband.[21]

Outbreaks of plague in Dundee represented medical crises that the town authorities attempted to manage. Dundee was struck by plague in 1544, 1547, 1566, 1585, 1606–08 and finally in 1644–45, as outlined in Chapter 3. Powerless to save the lives of those it struck, the authorities nevertheless did all they could to prevent the spread of plague. Taking measures to stop those who might already be infected from entering the town was difficult when it meant disruption to trade, and necessitated the watch of the port and river, as well as incoming roads. On 18 October 1603, for example, both Nethergate and Cowgate were closed as a precaution against the plague, and on 29 May 1604 there was an order from the town council to prevent persons crossing the Tay, with the threat of death for anyone who broke this order.[22]

Once plague had arrived in the town, it was a matter of trying to limit the numbers of those it affected. The sick were separated and sent to lodges near the river, called 'the Sick men's Yards, lying under the town of Craigy'.[23] Traumatic and unpopular as this separation of individuals from their families may have been, this was action taken by other town authorities when faced with plague, and may well have saved lives. Clearly, the governors of Dundee were able to organise and enforce measures to try and protect the town's inhabitants from plague. It seems likely that this experience also helped the town cope better with other points of crisis in its early modern history. Famine was well known to weaken the poor's resistance to disease, and probably stretched the town's medical resources.[24] Dundee's surgeons, such as Robert Pypar, who in 1550 was trying to recover the costs of treating 'Riche Saidlar's head hurt by Englishmen', or James Neill, who was made a burgess in April 1615, 'for his services in curing the inhabitants of the burgh who were wounded in the service of the country', were kept busy.[25]

Dundee's town council also took more mundane steps to keep the town's inhabitants healthy. This could include orders to keep the streets clean, for example on 2 October 1559 the council directed that 'any person leaving filth in any area of the town to be put in the branks for twenty-four hours'. In October 1597 concerns about how the skinners were infecting the water supplies of Lindsay Street, led to orders for the trade to be carried out at the east end of Seagate. By the early eighteenth century, the protection of public health had become more organised, and men were paid and horses bought for the purpose of street cleaning[26] (see Chapter 6).

The sick poor could receive support under the poor law. A royal charter of 1391 or 1392 had granted a hospital or 'maison dieu' at the foot of South Tay Street for the sick, old or infirm. By the mid sixteenth century, this had become an almshouse where the poor could be admitted if they were 'aigit and decayit persons, being single, naither having bairns nor wyiff'. Even after the hospital was rebuilt in 1678, it continued to restrict access to male burgesses, and thus could only ever house a small proportion of the poor.[27] Poor law officials, however, could also help to meet the costs of medical care that was administered to patients in their homes, especially when illness or handicap was preventing an individual from earning a living. The Auchterhouse Session Minutes, for example, record the payment of a substantial sum for the medical expenses of one of their residents after his leg was amputated in June 1749, and in December 1778 they paid a Dr Mitchell direct for the medicines he had given to William Robertson. Similar payments were made to practitioners in Barry, Angus.[28] Jean Anderson's condition in June 1744 was so serious that she could not be treated locally, so the Sessions agreed to pay 10 shillings for her to visit the Infirmary in Edinburgh. Recovery at the Infirmary, of course, was not guaranteed, for in June 1788, the Dundee General Session agreed to pay the funeral expenses of a patient from Dundee who had died there.[29] Nevertheless, in recognition of the services that the Edinburgh Infirmary could offer Dundonians, (it was said that by March 1786, Dundee was 'daily' sending patients there), there was a series of financial donations from the town's churches and Trades to that institution.[30]

Yet there is limited evidence that the Kirk authorities were keeping a check on the activities of medical practitioners within Dundee. In September 1685, when two new barber-surgeons arrived in Dundee and set up in Murraygate and Seagate, the General Session ordered that their testimonials be verified.[31] Medical practitioners were not immune from punishment for the sexual offences that came under the Sessions' jurisdiction, and that is sometimes the only way that we learn of their existence. Hence in 1716–17 Alexander Crooks, an apothecary from Cupar, admitted fornication with a servant when he was visiting another apothecary, John Forrester, in Dundee's Seagate. Initially failing to appear before the Sessions 'having several patients under his hand', he successfully won the right to appear for shaming in church twice in one day, arguing that two separate visits to Dundee would risk the loss of his employment.[32] Recognition that a charge of sexual incontinence could tarnish reputation and jeopardise future business, especially with female patients, meant that some male practitioners did all they could to avoid such public shaming. Rather than appear himself before the General Session when accused of being the father of his servant's child in 1770, Dr William Reid sent letters. He admitted the fault, promised to support the mother and child, paid an extra two guineas to the poor 'besides the ordinary penalty', but resolutely refused to make any public appearances admitting to his offence. John Coulls (or Coutts), a surgeon, issued furious denials that he had made his female patient pregnant when he had treated her in 1784.[33] In a period when fears about the sexual impropriety of male medical practitioners were rising, and medics could be accused of supplying abortifacients to their mistresses to cover their tracks, the position of these men was highly vulnerable.[34]

Thus life outside the medical centre certainly did not mean freedom from medical controversy. Dundee was not immune from medical scandals that would shock the rest of the nation. In October 1722, finding that several surgeon apprentices were guilty of that 'barbarous and inhumane practice of taking up dead bodies out of their graves', the Dundee General Session appealed to the town's magistrates to take steps to 'stop such a vile practice in time coming'.[35] The fear that surgeons and their apprentices were grave-robbing in order to gain bodies for dissection led Edinburgh and Glasgow practitioners in the 1720s and 1740s to provide guarantees that they would stem the practice.[36] But in Dundee, the problem reoccurred: in May 1736, James Carstorphin was forced to give up his apprenticeship to Alexander Watson, surgeon apothecary in Dundee, because James had been discovered to be accessory to the raising of the body of a dead child out of its grave.[37] The issue would cause nation-wide alarm in 1828–29, when the Edinburgh anatomist, Dr Robert Knox, was accused of encouraging murder in his quest for bodies for dissection.[38]

Medical decisions could be considered invasive for the living as well as the dead. Inoculation against smallpox was available in Scotland from the early decades of the eighteenth century, but was widely resisted. It is easy to detect the frustration felt by those who encountered this opposition. 'It were to be wished', reported the minister of one Angus parish to Sinclair, 'that the lower classes could be prevailed upon to inoculate their children for the small-pox; but no arguments will persuade them to lay aside their absurd prejudices'. At no point in the early modern period was the clash between popular and elite ideas of medicine more evident. The popular belief that 'to inflict a disease' in small doses through inoculation 'is tempting providence', was held in Auchterhouse, and may hold clues about why it attracted so much suspicion. Although most ministers supported it, and doctors offered children free inoculation, evidence of refusal to be inoculated can be found in Dundee, as well as throughout Angus. Vaccination against smallpox was not compulsory in Scotland until 1863.[39]

A more welcome medical innovation was undoubtedly the establishment of the Dispensary in Dundee in 1782. Funded by voluntary contributions, and supported by the General Sessions, this gave medicines and advice to the poor – gratis or for a very small charge.[40] Scotland's first lunatic asylum, at nearby Montrose, was established a year earlier, and was soon taking patients from Dundee. The Kirk Session helped with meeting the costs of the poor insane at Montrose, as well as with fund raising for the institution.[41] Philanthropic activities of Dundee's middle class also supported the town's poor and sick as with the establishment in Dundee in 1797, for example, of the Society for the Relief of the Indigent Sick in the Town and Suburbs.[42]

Thus by the final decades of the century, the institutions and organised medical care that would be such an important feature of nineteenth-century support for the sick and needy, were firmly in place in Dundee. But for much of the early modern period, medicine and care for the sick was home-based, and the most immediate and long-term carers of the sick were neither professionals nor formally trained. They were either family and household members, or sick-nurses who were employed on a casual and informal basis – and the majority of these carers were women.

WOMEN AS MEDICAL PRACTITIONERS

Dundee women had a long established reputation for recognising the potential of cultivating herbs that could be used in medical cures. Alexander Maxwell noted that the town had 'some huckster wives, who had made a bad speculation in the purchase of growing herbs' in 1522.[43] A knowledge of the healing properties of plants was essential to the practice of early modern medicine, and was by no means confined to women, as evidenced by the friar's herb garden in Dundee in 1559, and Dr Patrick Blair's botanic garden at the end of the seventeenth century; and the surgeon John Coulls claimed that the reason why he was often seen visiting the house of a female patient, was because it had a garret 'where his herbs lay'.[44] But it was gentry women, with extensive gardens where they could grow herbs, who often had the most space and time to develop medical remedies. Fortunately, these elite women were literate and recorded their cures in recipe books. Three such books from the mid seventeenth to the mid eighteenth centuries, belonging to the Countesses of Strathmore, contain remedies for a diverse range of complaints, including plague, apoplexy, deafness, 'fits of the mother', migraine and melancholy.[45]

Able and willing to try home-made cures for the most to the least serious of illnesses, the Countesses of Strathmore were part of a network of gentry women who exchanged information about tried and tested medicines. Hence one list of recipes was under the heading 'these are my

Lady Northumberland's'.[46] These women also had access to medical publications. For example, a catalogue of books belonging to Helen, Countess Dowager of Strathmore in July 1699 included two volumes by the noted herbalist Nicholas Culpeper.[47] Researching and recording medical cures was deemed a suitable occupation for elite women when it could be presented as 'kitchen physic'. Listing cures for medical ailments amongst recipes for marmalade, pickles and perfume, the Strathmore women must have appeared to others to be simply building upon their 'natural' feminine qualities of care, nurture and healing. Very occasionally, these perceptions of the feminine role enabled women to gain a public voice in medical matters. It was a wealthy woman, Mrs Susan Carnegie, who first proposed in 1769 that a specialist institution for the insane should be built in Montrose.[48]

For Dundee women lower down the social scale, involvement in the care of sick family members was not an option. They were assumed to be the primary carers of the sick, and a second opinion from a medical 'expert' was probably only called upon if funds and the condition of the patient made it absolutely necessary. Sometimes the long-term burden this created for women was recognised. When Dundee's General Session agreed that John Taylor should be sent to Montrose Lunatic Hospital in February 1789, they arranged for over 14 shillings to be paid to his sister 'for the trouble she has had with him'.[49] If the mistress of a household was unwell, a female servant might assume the role of a sick-nurse. James Smith in November 1790, for example, admitted giving clothes to his servant, Margaret Miln, but said that these were to acknowledge that she had been 'careful of his wife in distress', as she lay dying, rather than as a sign that he was the father of Margaret's illegitimate child.[50] Other aspects of medical care could form part of a servant's routine duties. When her mistress was suffering from toothache, Grissell Finnie was sent to Dr Kinloch's to get something to allay the pain, but was rebuked by the Kirk authorities for 'wandering in the street' at sermon time on a Sunday in February 1723.[51] Elizabeth Wilson admitted having illicit sex in the back of a shop owned by Andrew Wilkie, druggist, where she had been sent to buy salts.[52]

Women were prevented from being apprentices of surgeons, and because no Scottish university allowed women to matriculate, they were excluded from the possibility of becoming physicians. But as midwives they could be medical practitioners. Very little is known about midwifery in early modern Scotland.[53] The situation in Scottish towns was different from that in England, where the Church scrutinised testimonial certificates, administered the oath taken by midwives, and issued licenses.[54] In Scotland there were efforts to licence midwives. Edinburgh town council, for example, passed an Act in 1694 that all midwives in the city should be licensed; but no register has survived, and it is possible that the act was never enforced.[55] The Faculty of Physicians and Surgeons in Glasgow, which began examinations or 'trials' for midwives only in 1740, was more successful than in Edinburgh, and its minute books list the names of women who were licensed after examination.[56] There is no evidence that women in Dundee had to obtain licenses to practise midwifery.

Although the Kirk does not seem to have been involved in the supervision of midwifery in the systematic way that licensing required, this did not preclude occasional intervention. The fear was that women from rural parishes migrated to towns to deliver their illegitimate children, with the intention of then abandoning the baby at the town's expense.[57] In sixteenth-century Glasgow, for example, the Presbytery examined one woman about her profession as a midwife, and on a separate occasion, issued orders to all midwives to discover the name of the father of a child before they helped with its delivery.[58] Edinburgh and Aberdeen sessions made all midwives sign a bond agreeing to report the names of any women they helped who were from outside their parishes. Dundee's authorities became involved in the regulation of midwifery only when it looked likely that malpractice was at issue. Investigations into the birth of an illegitimate child led the General Session to hear a report 'of this child having got harm in the birth' from the midwife, Isabell Tod. No proof could be found that Isabell had 'designedly done hurt to the child', but because 'people seemed to be possessed of the notion of her not being qualified for performing the office of a midwife', it was agreed that 'she should give over that business', and be rebuked for her conduct.[59]

Isabell's case gives us some insights into the practice of midwifery in early modern Dundee. The qualifications for a midwife playing the central role in the safe delivery of both mother and child seem to have amounted to experience and skill, rather than formal and documented training. Correspondence between Scottish gentry families suggests that they often chose midwives on the basis of personal recommendation, and it seems likely that lower down the social scale, midwives got business via word-of-mouth and previous experience, rather than by virtue of their learning.[60] But this is not to suggest that midwives were poorly educated. The Dundee evidence tends instead to support the findings of historians of provincial English midwives, that these were usually fairly prosperous, literate women, even though their skills were largely practical, with knowledge usually exchanged verbally. Hence the midwife Mrs Scoular submitted her evidence about one woman's medical condition to the Dundee General Session in 1768 in the form of a letter she had written, rather than appear personally.[61]

The first *Dundee Directory*, produced in 1782, listed six midwives – a significant number when we consider that the same *Directory* named only eight physicians, surgeons or druggists in the town.[62] Fourteen different midwives were named in the Dundee Session proceedings between June 1737 and June 1792, while others were mentioned but remained anonymous. Sometimes referred to as 'the Mamie', a midwife could build a local reputation. A place popularly known as the 'Mamysroom' is marked in the parish of Errol on James Stobie's 1783 map of the counties of Perth and Clackmannan. Since midwives usually travelled to the mother, it is possible that this had been where a well-regarded midwife lived, rather than the site of a delivery room.[63]

The main source of information about Dundee's midwives derives from their testimony as witnesses before the General Session which means that we do not learn about the practice of midwifery when pregnancy and births were legitimate or non-problematic. It is clear that their expertise allowed midwives to play an important role in the policing of women's bodies. When a baby was found in Logie, and Janet Crab was suspected to be the mother, two midwives inspected Janet and found that her breasts contained 'plenty of green milk', so confirming her guilt. Admission to the Kirk community could depend on a midwife's word. The Moderator would not baptise twins in January 1774, for example, until a midwife would testify that they had been born prematurely, and therefore legitimately.[64] Dundee midwives could refuse to deliver the babies of unmarried women until they had named the fathers,[65] and their presence at childbirth could be crucial in determining the mother's innocence if the baby subsequently died.

Infanticide had become a capital crime in 1690, and would remain so until 1809. If a mother had concealed her pregnancy, did not seek help from a midwife or other woman during the birth, and the baby was found dead, she was presumed guilty (forming the mainspring of the plot in Sir Walter Scott's novel *The Heart of Midlothian*.) Thus in 1683, it was because 'when she was brought to bed there was no woman with her', that it was 'presumed' the servant Marjorie Walker 'had intention to murder the child'.[66] As an offence carrying the death penalty, Dundee General Session had to pass on cases to be tried to the secular authorities.[67] But a measure of the general concern about this crime is shown by the copying of the 'Act against Murdering of Children' in the final pages of the third volume of Session minutes. When the bodies of two dead children were found by a grave digger near a burying place in June 1788, the Session ordered that the Act be read from all the town's pulpits.[68] For the single mother, the presence of a midwife was therefore an insurance against accusations of infanticide, if not premarital sex.

Dundee's female healers and midwives do not seem to have provoked the witchcraft allegations that they did elsewhere in Scotland.[69] Nor did midwives always cooperate with the authorities, given their own agendas and priority to protect mothers as well as themselves. Despite attempts to ensure that midwives reported illegitimate births, Edinburgh records show that not all midwives complied.[70] Dundee's midwives could also make short shrift of interference. When an official was sent by the Dundee Session to ask a midwife whether William Allison's wife had delivered a premature baby in April 1702, she answered brusquely 'that was none of her business go ask the parent'.[71] However, Margaret Darling's story of her delivery of Elizabeth Wedderburn's child in August 1740 – when she claimed that she had been so hurried away that she did not discover whether the baby was a boy or a girl, let alone if it was legitimate – seems highly improbable.[72] The role of midwife certainly seems to have given these women a confidence that was not easily shaken. These were medical practitioners, after all, who were privy to women's most intimate secrets and spaces. When the midwife Jean Maclean discovered that Catherine Macleod had been infected by venereal disease as well as made pregnant by her lover, John Kennadie, she confronted him. John admitted before several witnesses that he had sexual relations with Catherine, but he denied categorically ever having venereal disease. However, Jean was party to information to contradict John's story, since she knew that John had also infected his wife with the disease. As a midwife, Jean was fully aware of the complex and sometimes illicit sexual relationships between her neighbours, but she also had control over if and when to disclose that knowledge. Unashamed by Jean's revelation, John persisted with his denials, and even offered to 'show himself' for inspection by Jean. Jean's reply, 'you shall not show yourself to me for no man ever did so', may suggest that she was a spinster, and thus that maternal or even sexual experience was not a prerequisite to practise midwifery.[73]

Jean's story demonstrates that midwives served a far wider function in early modern towns than simply delivering babies. A week after Margaret Walls was raped by her master, John Brown, in July 1762, she visited Isabell Todd, a midwife, to ask her whether, 'in consequence of her being ravished, she might be with child'. Margaret showed Isabell a petticoat that she claimed had been cut by John in the course of the rape, and begged Isabell to go to John and get him to acknowledge what had happened. Margaret's primary concern seems to have been to get her master to support her and the child if she was pregnant (it turned out that she was not), rather than to have him punished for rape. As a midwife, Isabell acted as confidante, go-between, negotiator and eventually legal witness.[74]

The eighteenth century was a period of change in the practice of midwifery, and the rise of the man-midwife, and the formalisation of training for midwives has already been the subject of investigation.[75] Scotland certainly had its share of prominent man-midwives, although a number of them migrated to practice in London,[76] there are no references to man-midwives in Dundee's session records – albeit this is not conclusive proof of their absence. Notes in Dundee's archives taken from a series of obstetrical lectures, dating 1791–92, appear to have been made by a male student.[77] Certainly, Dundee's elite families were aware of the controversy surrounding man-midwifery. From the early nineteenth century, the Wedderburns had frequent medical consultations by letter with the influential Edinburgh physician James Gregory. Gregory vigorously opposed man-midwifery and the proposal to make the teaching of midwifery compulsory for male medical students at Edinburgh University. He published his views in a series of pamphlets, and his feuds with James Hamilton, professor of midwifery at Edinburgh University, and Alexander Hamilton, his father, resulted in legal cases for assault and defamation. Charles Wedderburn, meanwhile, kept abreast of events, receiving copies of pamphlets by Gregory, and correspondence that referred to the disputes.[78]

Gregory lost his battle with Hamilton over the teaching of midwifery, which became a compulsory component of the medical course at Edinburgh from 1830. There had been lectures on midwifery at Edinburgh University from at least the mid eighteenth century. In Aberdeen, Dr David Skene delivered a course of midwifery lectures during 1758,[79] and the *Glasgow Journal* contained two advertisements by surgeons who were offering women lectures in midwifery in October 1759 and March 1778.[80] Hamilton, however, gave extra-mural courses of lectures that women could attend, on completion of which each woman got a certificate 'of her being qualified to practice midwifery'.[81] Dundee's midwives were also invited to attend lectures by a surgeon, when the enterprising Mr Grant announced in an 1801 edition of the *Dundee Weekly Advertiser* that,

> as several women had approached him seeking instruction and that he, finding it inconvenient to his private practice to give the attention necessary to instruct them separately, proposed to establish a formal class for midwives.[82]

It seems, by then, that knowledge imparted formally and by men was regarded as superior to that which had for generations been exchanged between women through oral culture. Such was the kudos attached to male-directed learning, that midwives were forced to recognise that learning 'on the job' was no longer enough. In 1820 when Mrs Adam, a widow living in West Port, Dundee, decided to boost the family's income by working as a midwife, she advertised her services in the *Dundee, Perth and Cupar Advertiser*. What would bring her business, she thought, was the fact that she had recently attended Hamilton's lecture course in Edinburgh.[83] Although women were still practising midwifery in nineteenth-century Dundee, their occupation had mutated into a profession in ways that had been approved and controlled by men.

CONCLUSIONS

Medical care away from Scotland's medical centre, as experienced by those living in early modern Dundee, was largely administered at home and often by the patient themselves or other family members. Edinburgh could be perceived as offering a greater quality of medical resources and specialists, but Dundonians themselves were probably regarded as privileged by those living outside the town. Dundee's medical practitioners were certainly not always revered, and the eighteenth century controversies over grave-robbing and smallpox inoculation did not help to strengthen their status. Nevertheless, Dundee's authorities did take steps to ensure minimum standards of medical care (even if these appear to have been reactive rather than proactive), and medical crises such as plague were managed with some degree of efficiency.

The regulations for admission to the town's hospital reveal assumptions about who bore the responsibility for amateur health care. Women were excluded from being patients altogether, and old, single men were only admitted where they had no mother nor wife to tend to them. Even when married women became patients at home, the situation was managed by their husbands who bore the costs of their treatment. It is telling that in all the eighteenth and early nineteenth-century Wedderburn family correspondence with their physicians, for example, there is not a single letter from a female member of the family to her doctor. Although journals show that women from this family were literate, it was the male head of household who engaged medical practitioners, and described their ailments in the correspondence. As practitioners rather than patients, it was acceptable for elite women to explore herbal cures that might benefit their families as well as themselves, but by the end of the period, midwives who had hitherto earned their living from their medical knowledge were subject to greater supervision. This element of change was probably felt as acutely in Dundee as in the medical epicentre of Edinburgh.

Acknowledgements. I should like to thank Iain Flett and Richard Cullen for their expertise using the Dundee City Archives; Anne Cameron, Vivienne Dunstan, Alan Macdonald and Mary Young for references and advice; Murray Frame, Andy and Denise Jackson for their kind hospitality.

NOTES

1 H. M. Dingwall, *A History of Scottish Medicine: Themes and Influences* (Edinburgh, 2003), p. 105.

2 L. Walsh, ' "From the Grampians to the Firth of Forth": the development of the Dundee Royal Infirmary', in L. Miskell, C. A. Whatley and B. Harris (eds.), *Victorian Dundee: Image and Realities* (East Linton, 2000), pp. 96–103.

3 E. P. D. Torrie, *Medieval Dundee: A Town and its People* (Abertay Historical Society, 30) (1990), p. 88.

4 As cited in T. Ferguson, *The Dawn of Scottish Social Welfare* (London, 1948), p. 237.

5 J. Jenkinson, *Scottish Medical Societies 1731–1939: Their History and Records* (Edinburgh, 1993).

6 H. M. Dingwall, ' "To be insert in the *Mercury*": Medical Practitioners and the Press in Eighteenth-Century Edinburgh', *Social History of Medicine* 13, 1 (2000), pp. 23–44.

7 J. Sinclair (ed.), *The Statistical Account of Scotland 1791–1799*, vol. XIII: Angus (Wakefield, 1976), pp. 147–148, 340.

8 M. Flinn (ed.), *Scottish Population History from the 17th Century to the 1930s* (Cambridge, 1977), p. 238.

9 Dundee University Archives (DUA), Glamis, vol. 238, entries for 12 June 1714; 2 March 1715; and 21 May 1715; for ease of comprehension all spellings have been modernised.

10 DUA, Glamis, Bundles 49/7 and 50/5.

11 Dundee City Archives (DCA), Wedderburn of Pearsie (GD/We/SR 0131), Box 5, Bundle 14.

12 Sinclair (ed.), *Statistical Account*, p. 675.

13 P. Griffiths, J. Landers, M. Pelling and R. Tyson, 'Population and disease, estrangement and belonging 1540–1700', in P. Clark (ed.), *The Cambridge Urban History of Britain Vol. II: 1540–1840* (Cambridge, 2000), p. 222.

14 Sinclair (ed.), *Statistical Account*, p. 616.

15 A. Maxwell, *Old Dundee, Ecclesiastical, Burghal, and Social, Prior to the Reformation* (Dundee, 1891), p. 165.

16 R. C. Buist, 'Dundee Doctors in the Sixteenth Century', *Edinburgh Medical Journal*, vol.37 (January–June, 1930), pp. 293–302, 357–366; and *Roll of Eminent Burgesses of Dundee 1513–1886* (Dundee, 1887).

17 J. Bannerman, *The Beatons: A Medical Kindred in the Classical Gaelic Tradition* (Edinburgh, 1986).

18 K. G. Lowe, 'Dr David Kinloch: Mediciner to his Majestie, James VI', *Scottish Medical Journal*, 36, 3 (1991), pp. 87–89; and A. Yagüi-Beltrán and L. Adam, 'The imprisonment of David Kinloch, 1588–1594: an analysis of newly discovered documents in the archives of the Spanish Inquisition', *The Innes Review*, 53, 1 (2002), pp. 1–39.

19 C. Dingwall, 'Dr Patrick Blair and Dundee's First Botanic Garden' (unpublished paper); *Oxford Dictionary of National Biography*, entry for Blair, Patrick (*c.* 1680–1728).

20 Buist, 'Dundee doctors', pp. 362–363; and D. Hamilton, *The Healers: A History of Medicine in Scotland* (Edinburgh, 1981), pp. 32–33.

21 The absence of a married woman's rights as a patient was also found in England; see C. Crawford, 'Patients' Rights and the Law of Contract in Eighteenth-Century England', *Social History of Medicine*, 13, 3 (2000), pp. 381–410.

The New Shore (renamed Butcher Row in the mid eighteenth century) had been constructed probably in the middle sixteenth century. It had been refashioned and rebuilt (possibly two storeys lower to judge by the gables and chimneys) after the civil war attack in 1651. (Lawson)

General George Monck's letter 29 September 1657 ordering the demolition of Dundee's fortifications, since the soldiers presently quartered in the town were about to be drawn away. 'It may be inconvenient and dangerous for the town to have the Workes continue standing . . . soe they may not bee an Advantage to any Enemy to possesse the Towne'. (From *Charters, Writs and Public Documents . . .*)

(*Right*). Methodist Close, off the Overgate, drawn by Charles Lawson. It only became Methodist Close after the Methodists had established their first chapel in the hall of Hunter's Lodging at the top in mid century. Here was the dwelling of Fyshe Palmer. (1870 *Guide Book to Dundee*)

(*Below*). The Glasite Chapel. Dundee's thousand-strong Glasite congregation had their octagonal chapel cheek by jowl with the establishment's own Trades Kirk of St Andrew's. (Small)

22 DCA, Town Council Minutes, 18 October 1603, 29 May 1604; for later measures, see 3 February 1607, 30 September 1645, 7 October 1645, 4 November 1645; see also, Torrie, *Medieval Dundee*, pp. 87, 104–105.

23 A. Maxwell, *The History of Old Dundee, Narrated out of the Town Council Register, With Additions from Contemporary Annals* (Dundee, 1884), p. 375.

24 See K. Cullen, M. Young and C. Whatley, 'Battered but Unbowed: Dundee during the Seventeenth Century', ch. 3 in this volume.

25 Buist, 'Dundee doctors', p. 298; *Roll of Eminent Burgesses*, entry for 8 April 1615.

26 DCA, Town Council Minutes, 2 October 1559, 14 October 1718; and Maxwell, *History of Old Dundee*, pp. 100–103.

27 W. Hay (ed.), *Charters, Writs, and Public Documents of the Royal Burgh of Dundee* (Dundee, 1880), pp. 16–17; Maxwell, *History of Old Dundee*, pp. 223–232; and C. McKean and D. Walker, *Dundee: An Illustrated Introduction* (Edinburgh, 1984), pp. 10–11.

28 DCA, Auchterhouse Session Minutes, CH2/23/2, 4 June 1749, 12 December 1778; J. Lindsay, *The Scottish Poor Law: Its Operation in the North-East from 1745 to 1845* (Ilfracombe, 1975), pp. 31–34; and R. Mitchison, *The Old Poor Law in Scotland: The Experience of Poverty, 1574–1845* (Edinburgh, 2000), p. 225.

29 DCA, Auchterhouse Session Minutes, CH2/23/2, June 1744; DCA, Dundee General Session Minutes (CH2/1218)/6, 30 June 1788.

30 See, for example, DCA, CH2/1218/2, 13 April 1730; CH2/1218/6, 22 February 1786, 6 March 1786, 26 July 1786, and 9 August 1786. For a history of Edinburgh's Infirmary see, G. B. Risse, *Hospital Life in Enlightenment Scotland: Care and Teaching at the Royal Infirmary of Edinburgh* (Cambridge, 1986).

31 DCA, CH2/1218/1, 7 September 1685 and 14 September 1685.

32 DCA, CH2/1218/2, 10 September 1716; 17 September 1716; 18 March 1717; John Forrester was probably the same apothecary who was supplying the Countess of Strathmore with medicines, as discussed above.

33 DCA, CH2/1218/4, 8 October 1770, 12 October 1779; DCA, CH2/1218/6, 14 November 1785, 4 January 1786, 18 January 1786.

34 For context see, R. Porter, 'A touch of danger: The man-midwife as sexual predator', in G. S. Rousseau and R. Porter (eds.), *Sexual Underworlds of the Enlightenment* (Manchester, 1989), pp. 206–232, and M. Pelling, 'Compromised by gender: the role of the male medical practitioner in early modern England', in H. Marland and M. Pelling (eds.), *The Task of Healing: Medicine, Religion and Gender in England and the Netherlands 1450–1800* (Rotterdam, 1996), pp. 107–112; for an example of a Dundee surgeon who was accused of trying to abort his illegitimate child see, DCA, CH2/1218/1, 12 February 1683 and 5 March 1683.

35 DCA, CH2/1218/2, 22 October 1722.

36 H. Dingwall, *Physicians, Surgeons and Apothecaries: Medicine in Seventeenth-Century Edinburgh* (East Linton, 1995), pp. 77–78, and J. Geyer-Kordesch and F. Macdonald, *Physicians and Surgeons in Glasgow: The History of the Royal College of Physicians and Surgeons of Glasgow 1599–1858* (London, 1999), pp. 221–222.

36 National Archives of Scotland (NAS), GD7/2/505, and GD7/2/512.

38 T. Marshall, *Murdering to Dissect: Grave-Robbing, Frankenstein and the Anatomy Literature* (Manchester, 1995).

39 Sinclair (ed.), *Statistical Account*, pp. 50–51, 163, 210, 217, 344, 439–440, 493; Dingwall, *History of Scottish Medicine*, pp. 138–140.

40 For examples of Sessions support for the Dispensary see, DCA, CH2/1218/6, 17 July 1782, 16 July 1788, 30 July 1788 and 21 August 1788.

41 See, for example, DCA, CH2/1218/6, 17 November 1784, 21 September 1785, 11 July 1787, 1 August 1787 and 4 February 1789.

42 Mitchison, *Old Poor Law*, p. 129.

43 Maxwell, *Old Dundee*, p. 197.

44 DCA, CH2/1218/6, 14 November 1785.

45 DUA, Glamis, vol. 243 (the date given on the inside cover is 1666), and vols. 244–5 (dated 1692–1746).

46 DUA, Glamis, vol. 245; for context and comparisons see, L. Pollock, *With Faith and Physic: The Life of a Tudor Gentlewoman, Lady Grace Mildmay, 1552–1620* (London, 1993), and S. Nenadic, 'Experience and Expectations in the Transformation of the Highland Gentlewoman, 1680–1820', *Scottish Historical Review*, 80, 2 (2001), p. 204.

47 DUA, Glamis, vol. 243.

48 F. J. Rice, 'The Origins of an Organisation of Insanity in Scotland', *Scottish Economic and Social History*, 5 (1985), 45.

49 DCA, CH2/12/8/6, 4 February 1789.

50 DCA, CH2/12/8/6, 24 November 1790; for the role of sick-nurses see, E. C. Sanderson, *Women and Work in 18th-Century Edinburgh* (Basingstoke, 1996), pp. 47–49, and M. Pelling, *The Common Lot: Sickness, Medical Occupations and the Urban Poor in Early Modern England* (London, 1998), ch. 8.

51 DCA, CH2/1218/2, 18 February 1723.

52 DCA, CH2/1218/4, 16 December 1767.

53 Hence the value of A. Cameron, 'From Ritual to Regulation? The Development of Midwifery in Glasgow and the West of Scotland, c. 1740–1840', Unpublished PhD thesis, (University of Glasgow, 2003). For an oral history of Scottish midwifery see, L. Reid, *Scottish Midwives: Twentieth-Century Voices* (East Linton, 2000).

54 See, for example, D. Evenden, *The Midwives of Seventeenth-Century London* (Cambridge, 2000), especially ch. 1.

55 Sanderson, *Women and Work*, pp. 53, 55–66.

56 Geyer-Kordesch and Macdonald, *Physicians and Surgeons in Glasgow*, pp. 251–253.

57 L. Leneman and R. Mitchison, *Sin in the City: Sexuality and Social Control in Urban Scotland 1660–1780* (Edinburgh, 1998), pp. 50–51, 67–68.

58 A. Duncan, *Memorials of the Faculty of Physicians and Surgeons of Glasgow 1599–1850* (Glasgow, 1896), p. 19.

59 DCA, CH2/1218/5, 13 June 1781.

60 James, 17th Lord Forbes, Putachie, for example, recommended a Mrs Taylor, midwife, to Alexander, Duke of Gordon because she had delivered all six of their children safely, see Papers of the Gordon Family, NAS, GD44/43/35, Letter dated 30 January 1771.

61 D. Harley, 'Provincial midwives in England: Lancashire and Cheshire, 1660–1760', in H. Marland (ed.), *The Art of Midwifery: Early Modern Midwives in Europe* (London, 1993), pp. 27–48; DCA, CH2/1218/4, 16 August 1768.

62 *The Dundee Register of Merchants and Trades* (Dundee, 1782).

63 For an example of the use of the term 'mamie' see, DCA, CH2/1218/1, 30 March, 1702; J. Stobie, 'Map of the counties of Perth and Clackmannan' (London, 1783), held at the National Library of Scotland, Edinburgh. Two contemporary documents also refer to the 'Mamysroom': see St Andrews University Library, Hay of Leyes

Muniments, MS36220/77 (dated 1728), and MS36220/1843 (dated 1820, 1830).

64 DCA, CH2/1218/2, 22 June 1738; DCA, CH2/1218/4, 25 January 1774. For context see, Leneman and Mitchison, *Sin in the City*, ch. 4, and L. Gowing, *Common Bodies: Women, Touch and Power in Seventeenth-Century England* (London, 2003), chs. 1 and 5.

65 See, for example, DCA, CH2/1218/2, 19 June 1737; and DCA, CH2/1218/3, 6 May 1760.

66 DCA, CH2/1218/1, 12 February 1683; for context see, D. A. Symonds, *Weep Not For Me: Women, Ballads and Infanticide in Early Modern Scotland* (Pennsylvania, 1997).

67 See, for example, DCA, CH2/1218/1, 26 January 1711 and 25 January 1714; and DCA, CH2/1218/2, 13 August 1716.

68 DCA, CH2/1218/6, 30 June 1788.

69 See, for example, the *Survey of Scottish Witchcraft Database* at www.arts.ed.ac.uk/witches/

70 M. F. Graham, *The Uses of Reform: 'Godly Discipline' and Popular Behaviour in Scotland and Beyond, 1560–1610* (Leiden, 1996), p. 285.

71 DCA, CH2/1218/1, 6 April 1702.

72 DCA, CH2/ 1218/2, 14 August 1740.

73 DCA, CH2/1218/6, 13 June 1792, 29 June 1792 and 25 July 1792; other historians have noted the ability for single women to practice midwifery, see, for example, Harley, 'Provincial midwives', p. 34.

74 DCA, CH2/1218/3, 15 December 1762, 26 January 1763, 7 March 1763, 9 May 1763, 23 May 1763; some of the details of this case are reproduced in Leneman and Mitchison, *Sin in the City*, pp. 61–62.

75 See, for example, B. Ehrenreich and D. English, *Witches, Midwives and Nurses: A History of Women Healers* (New York, 1973), J. Donnison, *Midwives and Medical Men: A History of Inter-Professional Rivalries and Women's Rights* (London, 1977), and A. Wilson, *The Making of Man-Midwifery: Childbirth in England, 1660–1770* (Cambridge MA, 1995).

76 J. Willocks, 'Scottish man-midwives in eighteenth-century London', in D. A. Dow (ed.), *The Influence of Scottish Medicine: An Historical Assessment of its International Impact* (Carnforth, 1988), pp. 45–61.

77 DUA, BrMs 2/2/11 (1791–92).

78 DCA, GD/We/SR0131, Box 6, Bundle 15, letter no. 27 (dated 18 May 1809) and letter no. 29 (dated 20 May 1809).

79 Sanderson, *Women and Work*, p. 54.

80 Duncan, *Memorials of the Faculty of Physicians*, p. 134.

81 L. Rosner, *Medical Education in the Age of Improvement: Edinburgh Students and Apprentices 1760–1826* (Edinburgh, 1991), pp. 11, 59.

82 *Dundee Weekly Advertiser* (16 January 1801), p. 1.

83 *Dundee, Perth and Cupar Advertiser* (11 August 1820), p. 3.

CHAPTER 6

An Introduction
to Georgian Dundee

Bob Harris, Charles McKean,
and Christopher A. Whatley

What sort of a town was Georgian Dundee? Images of a populous, unruly, socially dysfunctional industrial city, with a townscape overwhelmed by chimneys belching out clouds of steam and dense smoke, exercise a tenacious hold on perceptions of the town's past. These images, however, were the product of the explosive industrial and population growth led by the buoyant jute industry of the middle and later decades of the nineteenth century, subsequently entrenched even more deeply by the grim experience of industrial decline and depression in the 1920s and '30s. Dundee before the advent of jute had by then, in the case of its Georgian architectural heritage quite literally so, been cleared away in the aggressive, unsentimental pursuit of salubriousness, modernity and improvement which began in the 1870s.

It would be perverse to ignore what was to come in the nineteenth century, for its backwards shadow was a lengthy one, and indeed is discernable as early as 1784, when the Rev. John Snodgrass's valedictory sermon warned his Overgate congregation of the difficulties of maintaining a vital religious faith in a populous town where relationships were fast becoming marked by anonymity.[1] Only four years later, in response to the challenges posed to the Church by the growth of the population, the town's ministers agreed to divide the parish into five districts.[2] By the end of the eighteenth century, some contemporary accounts of the town have much in common with those of half a century later. Distinctly unimpressed was English visitor Henry Skrine, reacting against a Dundee which, in Enlightenment terms, remained unmodernised:

We found it [Dundee], in spite of its beautiful situation, an irregular and unpleasant place, in which all the ill smells of the universe seemed contending for a superiority; while its inhabitants, unusually coarse both in their manners and figures, were strangely huddled together in every street, conveying an appearance of unbounded population greatly exceeding that of our most crowded English towns.[3]

Others, however, reached different verdicts, praising the town's relative size; the solidity, if not necessarily the modernity, of its architecture; the peaceful religious relations and temper of Dundonians; but above all the picture of industry and activity presented by the town and its population. As an Irish visitor in 1818 observed: 'Dundee is a very considerable Town built in the old style but the Houses are substantial as all in Scotland appear to be, several very fine ones in the suburbs on all sides of it very fine quays building and land taking in from the sea. The place seems busy and opulent.'[4] Some forty years earlier, the shipowner and writer on trade and economic affairs, David Loch, had assessed the town as being 'in a most flourishing and thriving state, a sober and industrious people; and above all, those of every persuasion live upon the most friendly and cordial terms'.[5]

If we were searching, however, for a turning point – the moment when nineteenth-century Dundee comes into clear relief – then the 1820s, when a surge of steam-powered mill development began to penetrate within the town's boundaries, may well be that watershed. In common with most places in Britain, the bulk of Dundee's early mills had been located outside the burgh boundary, explained by the absence of sufficient running water within the burgh's bounds. By the early 1760s, there appear to have been as many as sixteen mills on the three main burns over which Dundee had control – the Scouringburn, the Dighty and the much less reliable Dens, 'no other than a torrent' according to one witness – used not only by the waulkers and dyers (or litsters), but also by corn millers and, increasingly, for cleaning linen cloth. The number of mills on the Dighty, which ran beyond the north-east of the town but was part of the burgh's Common Good, reached 63 by the end of the century, 34 of which were less than 2 miles from the town.[6] It was, nevertheless, only after 1820 that the indices of economic activity, industrial output and expanding international trade soared to new heights.

It was also only in 1824 that a police act was passed for Dundee establishing a local police board, recognition that new ways of maintaining
order were required to match changing social conditions. This was
considerably later than, for example, Glasgow, and may well be
indicative of a town which remained surprisingly orderly and peaceable
for most of the previous half century – albeit that this calm was inter-
rupted on several occasions by outbursts of protest.[7] More difficult to
detect, as examined in Chapter 9, is any steady accumulation of concern
about public order, certainly before the end of the Napoleonic wars.

There are, thus, different ways of looking at the town and its development in the century or so before 1820. However, another important
perspective is to examine what was special and what was normal or
unsurprising about the development of a town, especially when viewed
against the background of national patterns of urbanisation in the
eighteenth century. This chapter follows that approach, exploring the
changing character of the town from three main angles: the development
of the local economy; its social structure; and the changing physical
development and appearance of the town. Subsequent chapters examine
other, complementary elements of the story.

ECONOMY

At the beginning of the eighteenth century Dundee was, in Scottish,
British and European population terms, a large town with a long history
of achievement. In Scotland, only Edinburgh and Glasgow were appre-
ciably larger, while Aberdeen was of similar size. Most Scottish urban
dwellers inhabited much smaller places, reflecting one of the distinctive
features of Scottish urbanisation in the eighteenth century, namely, the
continuing presence and vitality of smaller and medium sized towns,
alongside very strong growth in the largest urban centres.[8] Between 1690
and 1755, Dundee's population grew by 25%, to stand by the later date at
around 12,400.[9] Growth of this order in the first half of the century was
not unusual, Dundee's record being just exceeded by that of towns with
populations ranging between 2,000 and 5,000 (26%), and specifically, by
Aberdeen (27%) and Glasgow (75%), although it did better than the 18%
rise in the population of Edinburgh.[10]

What lay behind Dundee's early eighteenth-century population
growth is not entirely clear, although demographic recovery from the

grim late seventeenth century (see Chapters 3 and 4) may provide part of the answer. The experience of Scotland's towns in the decades immediately following the Union of 1707 was a mixed one economically, some stagnating and declining whilst others prospered.[11] By 1720, Dundee appears to have begun to reap some of the benefits of its efforts both to seize the mantle of linen capital of east-central Scotland from Perth (by, for instance, lowering Customs duties into the burgh), and to attract fresh mercantile endeavour to the town.[12] This, in addition to successful lobbying at national level on the part of the industry's champions like George Yeaman MP for Perth Burghs (which included Dundee), ensured that Dundee would be in a strong position to benefit when the industry (Scotland's equivalent to England's woollen industry) began to recover nationally. Credit should be paid also to the determination of Dundee's merchants and linen traders, supported by the freeholders of Angus (including the Earl of Strathmore and other leading landowners), to implement the quality control measures introduced by the Board of Trustees for the Improvement of Fisheries and Manufactures, established in 1727, and thus improve the quality of flax and linen sold from the burgh so that it could command a transatlantic market. The introduction of a Bounty on coarse linen exports in 1742, effectively a price-cutting measure which enabled Scottish producers to compete with continental producers, proved crucial. This boon to the industry was renewed, with interruptions, until the early nineteenth century.[13] Moreover, the Seven Years War created additional opportunities for the Scots, as linen production on the European mainland was slashed and the military and naval demand for cheap cloth burgeoned.[14]

The town's population almost doubled again between 1755 and 1801, reaching 27,000 by the later date. This pattern of growth was broadly in line with the other main towns in Angus – Brechin, Montrose, Forfar and Arbroath (as illustrated in Figure 6.1 below) – and indeed other coarse textile manufacturing districts in the east, primarily Fife and Perthshire. Such growth rates were exceeded in Scotland in this period only in Lanarkshire, Ayrshire and Renfrewshire where fine linens, cotton and silk dominated the textile trades, and mining and metal-working tended to be concentrated – along with the booming Clyde ports such as Greenock.[15] Renfrewshire's rate of increase was little short of phenomenal, the consequence of – and contributor to – profound economic and social change.[16] Paisley's population increased more than

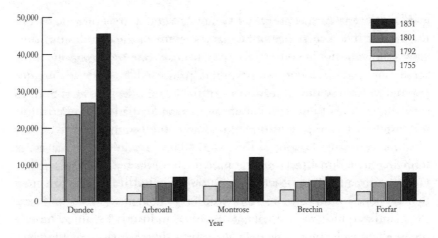

FIGURE 6.1: Population growth in the Angus burghs

fourfold between 1755 and 1801, and by 1821 it had left Dundee some way behind to seize third place in the urban league for a short while. The Renfrewshire town's later eighteenth century expansion depended heavily on large-scale rural in-migration from the surrounding counties, whereas, by contrast, there may have been some net out-migration from Dundee in the first two decades of the nineteenth century. Dundee's growth did continue, faster than most of its surrounding burghs,[17] but at a slower pace than in Paisley.

Dundee's eighteenth-century growth trajectory, then, was unexceptional, and part of a broader regional economic pattern that quickened markedly from the mid 1740s. Underpinning this was, above all, the rise of coarse linen manufacturing. Angus (then Forfarshire) became the main site of the Scottish coarse linen industry during the eighteenth and early nineteenth centuries. Already between November 1760 and 1761, 34% of linen, measured by yardage, and 23% by value, stamped in Scotland was produced in Angus. Of the other Scottish counties, only Fife, Perthshire and Lanarkshire produced anything like comparable quantities.[18] Sixty years later, its dominance was even more marked. By 1820, 62% of Scottish stamped linen as measured by yardage was manufactured there.[19]

Dundee and its merchants cast a long shadow not just over Angus, but over a textile-producing region which extended into the small Perthshire villages and hamlets – Longforgan, Inchture, Coupar Angus, and others – which lay to the west and north-west, as well as over the Tay to Fife to the south. Although there continued to be competition between Perth and Dundee, and merchant-manufacturers in the various burghs sought to differentiate their products in their search for market advantage, it is the interlinking of the fortunes of the region's burghs and smaller places which needs emphasising – particularly the circulation between them of entrepreneurial energy, commercial ability, labour and capital.[20] A regional economic identity took on a sharper definition from the 1790s, and the mutual and complementary interests of the region's urban leaders and landowners were reinforced with the establishment of the Forfarshire Chamber of Commerce in 1820. It was only in the thirty years from around 1840 that the industrial concentration within Dundee began seriously to undermine manufacturing in its neighbouring burghs.[21]

The salient question is how and why Dundee established its strategic position at the heart of this buoyant economic region in the eighteenth century. Its ascendancy was not inevitable; although lacking a comparable outlet to the sea, Perth represented a major source of competition. Nor had Dundee's businessmen any monopoly of the supply of low-cost, part-time labour in the countryside to whom they could distribute flax for spinning and webs to weave. Similarly, the slow and uneven move in the eighteenth century towards centralised workplaces – workshops, mills and factories with more or less full-time employees – was shared by most burghs. Nor did Dundee have any particular advantages with associated processes, like bleachfields, which after 1727 had spread rapidly throughout lowland Scotland with Board of Trustees' support, and were to be found in many places in Angus and Perthshire.[22]

The crucial factor was, in the words of the Rev. Robert Small, author of the *Statistical Account of Dundee*, 'the noble river on which it [Dundee] is situated', and Dundee's role as a port (see Chapter 11). With this came 'ready communication' not only with London, but also with the markets of 'the principal and most opulent countries of Europe'.[23] This had enabled generations of merchant dynasties to form long-established trading connections, bringing a concentration of mercantile expertise to the town. Sometimes ignored by those over-keen to focus upon nineteenth-century industrial Dundee, the earlier importance of the sea, shipping and of maritime commerce was symbolised in the prominent place seamen were accorded in the annual and later bi-annual ceremonial riding of the town's marches – immediately behind the magistrates and council and alongside the merchants, guild brethren and the like, and well in front of categories such as the 'Vassals in ye Hilltoun'.[24]

Through its port, Dundee gained access to the Baltic for raw materials (flax),[25] and it was favourably located to develop its east-coast coasting trade, to London, whence much Scottish linen was sent out to West Indies (see Chapter 11) – but which provided a substantial market for Scots' made cloth in its own right. This imperial market expanded rapidly from the mid century partly because of the strong performance of the Caribbean economy, but also because the Bounty payment on the export of coarse linens was increased in 1745.

The condition of the harbour presented a recurrent challenge to the town's ruling elite, as Chapter 11 examines, with merchants regularly complaining about the need for improvements and new handling capacity, a grievance which was to catalyse the beginning of the end for the unreformed system of burgh government in 1815.[26] Moreover, several important London merchant houses had strong connections with Dundee, and by the end of the eighteenth century there were wharves on the Thames dedicated to Dundee vessels (see Chapter 7). Dundee's strategic position was also reinforced by local transport and communications improvements, as well as inducements to import via Dundee offered to grocers in Forfar, Kirriemuir and other inland towns by the Dundee, Perth and London Shipping Company, for example.[27] From the 1790s, the pace of development of new turnpikes accelerated, cementing Dundee's role as the marketing centre for the widely-dispersed osnaburgs industry, although other regional port towns such as Arbroath and Montrose continued to import flax and to export cloth (and in the case of Montrose, yarn, thread and rope – and its speciality, sailcloth), mainly coastwise to London.[28] Carrier services centring on Dundee multiplied from the middle of the century. Inland towns such as Brechin, Forfar and Kirriemuir and manufacturing villages in Angus, Fife and Perthshire therefore came to be ever more firmly within Dundee's economic hinterland.

Dundee's merchants and merchant-manufacturers appear to have been notably industrious, as well as flexible (never mind frugal and sober, according to the Rev. Robert Small), responding quickly to new market opportunities.[29] Textiles loomed large, inevitably, with the focus being on 'osnaburgs' – a low-quality linen consciously copied from a hugely successful type of cloth identified with Osnabruck, in Hanover – in which Angus dominated. Other products were tried, not without success, and Loch was particularly impressed by attempts to develop a woollen manufactory in the early 1770s, in response to depressed conditions in the linen industry. He was probably influenced by his enthusiasm to see woollen manufacturing developed in place of linen which depended on erratic imports of raw materials. Canvas was a Dundee speciality by the end of the eighteenth century, of which over 700,000 yards were made in 1788–89. Although cotton was produced as well, this was to prove short-lived. More enduring was the manufacture of coloured threads – even if most of the hand-spinners resided outside Dundee, where wages were lower.[30] Most manufacturing in the town itself was based in small workshops or in the home, with handloom weavers clustered in particular areas of the town and particular streets. In the 1790s, the Seagate, Hilltown and Chapelshade housed between them 1,800 to 1,900 looms. Loch had counted 2,800 looms in the town in the 1770s. Most businesses were small in scale, as illustrated by figures for sail cloth manufacturers from 1804 (see Table 6.1 below), which flourished under the impact of wartime demand at the end of the eighteenth and first decade or so of the nineteenth century. The largest number of looms owned by any single business was 122, while the lowest was 10.

TABLE 6.1

Numbers of looms employed by sail cloth manufacturers, Dundee, 1804

No. of looms	No. of businesses
10–20	27
20–30	19
30–40	5
Above 40	8

Source: NLS, MS 642, fol. 66, certificate of number of sail cloth manufacturers and looms they employ in Dundee and its environs

Before the later eighteenth century, urban manufacturing tended to be focused on the production of finer goods often sensitive to changes in fashion, largely serving the needs of local consumers. By concentrating more production into the town, manufacturers could exercise greater control over the workforce in terms of achieving a more or less uniform quality of product, required quantity (part-time workers in the countryside worked irregularly, and could determine their own pace), and labour productivity. In what was a highly competitive industry, both within the region and internationally, costs had to be pared to the bone. Even though living standards and wages were lower in Scotland than England, production costs could still be higher.[31] An urban location not only reduced the difficulties associated with the collection and distribution of the finished product, but also often brought the closer proximity of a public bleachfield where standards would be higher than at the small, burn-side fields that proliferated in the country. Moreover, from as early as 1734, Dundee had its own bleachfield at Baldovie which used the harsher Irish method of bleaching, which was better suited to treating coarse linen than the Dutch method. Yarn would be purchased both from country hand-spinners who brought their wares to Dundee, and from the manufacturers of machine-spun yarn in mills close by.

Encouraged in part by heightened wartime demand for sail cloth, hammocks and cheap shirtings, some manufacturers experimented with steam engines to replace hand spinners, although with little success before 1820. Dundee textile manufacturers however, were the first to apply steam power to the calendaring process (a process of final polishing and flattening the cloth), a development in 1797 which enabled such work to be carried on in the town, rather than on the more distant bleachfields.[32] Dundee enjoyed easy import of coal from the Forthside collieries and from Tyneside at relatively low cost, albeit the most rapid increases in coal imports began to take place after 1815. Quantities of lime, a material vital for building work, were unloaded at the dedicated Lime Pier.[33] But alongside this preparedness to adopt new techniques, the decades-old ability of merchant-manufacturers to purchase their flax at the lowest price remained critical for success in spinning and weaving. It required close, accurate and up-to-date information about flax growing conditions and the likely state of the crop in Russia and the Baltic – as well as a great deal of good fortune.[34] Between 1789 and the start of the 1820s, there was more than a sevenfold increase in flax and hemp imports to Dundee, while the quantity of linen leaving the port between 1791 and 1817 tripled correspondingly.[35]

Several other manufactures of lesser volume and importance than textiles were based in and around the port: shipbuilding, sugar refining, glass making, tanning and shoemaking being significant local industries, although none of this was unique to Dundee. Much the same could be said of Montrose, or Perth – which was an important centre of textile manufacturing and shoemaking in the eighteenth century presided over by an enterprising, successful merchant body. Thus Dundee's pattern of activity and development was again broadly in line with other towns in the region, and indeed with other manufacturing regions in Scotland – apart from the newer, single-industry weaving or mining villages, or stark exceptions like the longer-established but rapidly transforming burgh of Paisley. The differences between towns within the region were principally ones of scale.[36]

Dundee was not Angus's county town – Forfar was that – and cannot be described as a leisure town (see Chapter 10), although it did develop a larger, more distinctive specialist retail and leisure economy from the end of the eighteenth century. It was home to several very successful professionals – doctors and lawyers – but the numbers of these were never very large.[37] Its markets and churches attracted traders and farmers from its rural environs. Nevertheless, and despite diversification into activities like whaling, sugar refining and brewing, the dominance of textiles to the Dundee economy by the final decades of the eighteenth century is clear. In 1792, all textiles generated around £176,000 to the town. Figures for earnings from other manufacturing activities are incomplete, but leather tanning was probably the most important, and its value was given at only £14,200.[38]

SOCIAL/OCCUPATIONAL STRUCTURE

Data on the social structure of Georgian Dundee is sparse and heavily weighted towards the end of the period, as with other Scottish towns. The basic picture, nevertheless, is fairly easily established. By at least the final third of the century weavers were very heavily represented among the male labouring classes. Of 741 men from Dundee parish recorded in militia records from 1801, nearly 44% were listed as weavers.[39] However, represented in the militia lists were 72 different occupations, significantly more than in other local towns and suggestive of a more diverse society.[40] Burgess admissions and the occupations of grooms as recorded in the Old Parish Registers (OPRs) confirm the general picture. The 287 new ordinary burgesses entered in the Dundee 'lockit book' between 1740 and 1760[41] were spread across 53 occupations, only a little over 20% being weavers – probably masters. Journeymen were not recorded in the weaver trade records, although apprentices were.[42] Of grooms resident in the parish whose occupations are listed in the OPRs between 1770 and 1780, weavers are around five times as numerous as the next largest category – shoemakers, while between 1795 and 1805, they are almost twice as numerous as the next largest category – soldiers. (The presence of so many soldiers and the absence of sailors was probably a temporary consequence of war – see Chapter 9.) The prominence of sea-related occupations underlines the significance of the port as a source of local employment. Other significant occupations represented between 1795 and 1805 were, in descending order, after sailors: shoemakers; wrights; merchants; labourers; flax-dressers; tailors; brewers; masons; shipmasters; manufacturers; and bakers.[43]

What this emphasises again is the importance of manufacturing to the town's economy and the livelihoods of its expanding population, but also the significance of a commercial and manufacturing sector comprising goods, clothing, food and drink and services aimed at domestic demand. Information drawn up for the 1811 national population census distinguishes 'families employed in trade, manufacturing and crafts', in recognition presumably of the continuing centrality of the household economy. It also shows the town's female population outnumbering the male by 16,673 to 12,943 in 1811: a sex ratio of 77.6, possibly indicative in a town where the number of servants was relatively low, and of substantial numbers of working women.[44] Some support for this is provided by a visitor's description in 1793 of the very plain dress of the town's female population, who were 'wrapped in coarse plaids'; there were few silk cloaks or bonnets.[45]

One further valuable source of information about social structure is town directories, although these are few in number, and again cover only the latter part of our period. Nor is the information within them readily comparable. The earliest Dundee directory was published in 1783 by the enterprising printer Thomas Colvill, while further separate directories appeared in 1818 and 1821, and the first national directory in which Dundee appeared was published in 1826, although it had been compiled in the previous year. Table 6.2, below, presents data drawn from the 1782, 1818, and 1826 directories. Montrose is included by way of comparison.

TABLE 6.2

Occupational structure as shown in town directories (percentages are of total number of individuals listed in each directory)

	Dundee (1782)	Dundee (1818)	Dundee (1825)	Montrose (1825)
Professionals[a]	32 (4.59%)	127 (10.1%)	139 (9.68%)	64 (10.6%)
Commerce[b]	229 (32.8%)	262 (20.8%)	291 (20.3%)	99 (16.4%)
Manufacturing/ crafts	298 (42.75%)	390 (30.9%)	387 (26.9%)	160 (26.4%)
Services (inc. retailing)	157 (22.5%)	345 (27.4%)	527 (36.7%)	241 (39.8%)
Luxury sector[c]	Data incomplete	144 (37)	127 (44)	90 (19)
Other			1	6
Res. Gentry	40 (excluding 6 in public admin)	Not separately identified[d]	91 (40 female)	35 (13 female)

Sources: *The Dundee Register of Merchants and Trades* (Dundee, 1782); *Dundee Directory* (Dundee, 1818); *Pigot and Co.'s Commercial Directory 1825–6*.

[a] Category comprises ministers of the Church; legal and medical professionals; teachers; those in public administration.

[b] Category comprises shipmasters; commercial agents; coal dealers; lime dealers; meal dealers; provision dealers; hardware dealers; furniture brokers; earthenware, china and glass dealers; tea dealers; yarn merchants; timber merchants; corn merchants; spirit dealers; flour millers; iron merchants; smallware dealers; as well as general merchants.

[c] Category includes confectioners; wine merchants; cabinet makers; milliners/mantua makers; drapers and haberdashers; silver and gold smiths; engravers; hairdressers and perfumers; toy shops; upholsterers; silk mercers; clock and watch makers; seedsmen; cutlers; coach builders; gunsmiths; china shops; musicians; portrait painters; music teachers; umbrella makers; chair makers; dancing masters; jewellers; book sellers; architects; instrument makers; dentists; opticians; language teachers; fencing masters; drawing masters; musical instrument makers. The number in brackets represents the total for cabinet makers, earthenware, china and glass dealers, and drapers and haberdashers combined. These figures almost certainly include individuals who dealt in necessities rather than luxuries, but the data allows no distinctions to be drawn here.

[d] 136 unclassified individuals listed, of whom 72 were women; 12 claimed or were given the designation 'esq'.

Directories represent a view from above and do not necessarily capture all or even most of a town's business and manufacturing classes. Despite their imperfections, however, the results confirm the centrality of commerce and manufacturing to the town's fortunes, and also the growing importance in the early nineteenth century of a diversifying services sector.

IMPROVEMENT

If, therefore, progress in manufacturing and marketing of well-made coarse linen and related products, allied to its maritime traditions and expertise, provided the key dynamic behind Dundee's growth and prosperity in the Georgian period, the town itself changed in various important ways, reflecting this buoyancy. Contemporaries tended to label this process 'improvement', and it was characterised by growing attention to amenity and pleasantness, the search for a more uniform, modern urban aesthetic, as well as a growing emphasis on the role of the town as a site and agent of civility, as well as efficiency and order. More directly, it involved, in the first place, removal of street obstructions and nuisances – such as the demolition of the town ports (or gates), the removal of the 'shambles' or slaughterhouse, and better control and collection of waste and filth. The widening of streets and wynds as necessary was also part of this strand. Next and more importantly, there was ornamentation: the adornment of the town by the construction of suitably imposing public buildings, greater regularity in private dwellings lining the main thoroughfares, and the laying out of recreational space – parades, walks and paths. Finally, there was the importation and imposition of a new geometrical urbanism exemplified principally in grid-iron and regular terraces and rows of identical suburban houses. This latter phase was different in kind, and may justifiably be characterised as 'modernisation' or the importation of a wholly novel urban form.[46] As we will see, whereas Dundee was in the forefront of the first two types of improvement – uniquely for a town of its importance – it remained steadfastly indifferent to the attractions of the last.

The first two aspects of improvement had their origins in the seventeenth century, but it was in the mid eighteenth century that the overall appearance of towns began to change markedly. In Dundee, significant improvement began in 1735 when, to ensure that the burgh's image lived up to the splendour of its new Town House, the Dean of Guild carried out a town inspection identifying all ruinous houses facing the public thoroughfares. Those that their owners refused to repair and re-occupy were compulsorily purchased and sold to others who would.[47] Three years later, probably following the same impulse, the masons decided to rebuild their Lodge on a prominent site in the Nethergate.[48]

The elimination of street obstructions began a little later, in 1755, more or less when other towns were doing so. Most of the town's ports were demolished, leaving only the Nethergate and Seagate Ports (removed in the 1780s and 1818 respectively) and the token Cowgate Port or Wishart Arch (which survives today).[49] The removal of the Mercat Cross followed in 1777.[50] Street lamps, purchased and sent from London, had first been erected in the town in winter 1752, and by 1768 there were 58 lamps shedding their light on the town's streets. Initially funded jointly by subscription and from the Common Good fund, by 1782 they had to be paid for by an assessment levied on rents. The sums spent on maintaining and lighting the lamps continued to increase so that something between £200 and £300 per annum was required by the early nineteenth century – although that still did not prevent some individuals from commenting adversely on the 'darkness' of the town.[51]

The paving of streets followed a meeting between the Guildry and some of the leading merchants of the town in 1767, which concluded that 'the whole streets in the town [were] in the utmost state of disrepair' and agreed to establish a committee for the purpose.[52] An annual sum of £100 was laid aside for paving, and nearly £1,000 additionally was borrowed for the purpose from George Dempster's Dundee Bank over the following two years.[53] When further street improvements were being contemplated in the 1790s, more money was spent on levelling and paving several streets at the heart of the burgh, including the Overgate and the Nethergate.[54] With better paved streets came renewed efforts to improve the cleanliness of the town through better scavenging. Dundee had been ahead of Edinburgh in banning slopping out of refuse from upper storeys into the street, and new police regulations were issued in 1770 to maintain the momentum. Three years later, scavengers were employed to clean and sweep the streets and to clear them of dung.[55] The final part of the cleansing of the High Street would be the removal of the Renaissance Shambles courtyard from the eastern end of the market place down to the New Shore, which was duly renamed Butcher Row: first mooted in 1763[56] it was achieved by 1775.

In terms of works to private property, the scale of deliberate ornamentation is more difficult to assess. The principal tenements fronting the High Street, Overgate, Nethergate, Seagate and Murraygate, that formed the civic setting for public buildings, were very old-fashioned. In the mid 1740s, they were mostly timber-fronted.[57] In 1725, to prevent 'ye hazard or damage by fire', the burgh had banned the use of clay, timber or plaster for chimneys[58] and, probably for the same reasons, most of the timber galleried facades had been scraped from the frontages of the principal thoroughfares by the later 1760s. Sasines record the incidence of modernisation or replacement of existing tenements to a greater regularity of building line.[59] So successful was this programme that barely a handful of timber galleried buildings facing the main streets made it into the nineteenth century.[60] The *First History of Dundee*, written probably by Alexander Nicoll in 1775,[61] observed that 'Murraygate street may be said to be almost new built from end to end, with Stately stone buildings that make a goodly Appearance.'[62] A visitor of the early 1790s noted, in similar vein, 'Though the town is not regular, it is full of good houses; and the more modern ones very neat'.[63]

Dundee's elite were ambitious for their burgh's ornamentation. It had begun with the erection of its splendid baroque Town House, designed with a significant hint toward the Netherlands by Scotland's leading architect William Adam. Completed in 1735, it provided facilities for the law (the courts with prisons in the attics), and the town: one of its principal chambers (often used for concerts and theatres) was for the Guildry and another for St David's Masonic Lodge. Premises for the Town Guard and shops were below. The Town House set the standard and remained Dundee's principal icon well into the early nineteenth century.[64] Once the town had relocated the Shambles to the Shore in 1776, the site at the eastern end of the High Street was purchased by the Nine Trades to develop as commercial premises, investing the profits they had made from the feuing of their lands around St Andrew's Street. The latter street had been opened both to provide a vista up to the newly constructed St Andrew's church (which they themselves had funded jointly with the Guildry),[65] and to improve access to the harbour. Having permission to construct a hall above their new shops with a pavilion roof, the Trades asked the council if, instead, they could erect a pediment – a

'Tympany on the West Gavel Wall, which would greatly ornament the building and beautify the street'.[66] Seven years later, when the Episcopalian presence in Dundee was about to be symbolised by a new chapel opposite, the council required that it 'raise an elegant front toward the High Street'. This was duly done.[67]

The central decades of the eighteenth century were, therefore, a crucial period in Dundee's improvement, ornamentation and civic embellishment. It was also at about this time that the town's wright Samuel Bell became titled 'Town's Architect', which itself was a sign of the town's urban ambition – for no other Scots burgh had such an appointment at that time, although Edinburgh had had one earlier. Bell was not retained on a fee basis: it was expected that any major civic commission would fall to him – as proved the case. In addition to St Andrew's church, the Trades Hall, and Episcopalian chapel, he designed Trinity House for the Seamen's Fraternity on the Shore in 1790, the Steeple Church on the site of St Mary's nave in 1791, and the Theatre Royal in Castle Street in 1809–10. The only public project to elude Bell was the Infirmary, located outside the town's centre on the Forebank slopes, which was designed by John Paterson, Robert Adam's former chief assistant.

Bell was also responsible for the laying out of any new streets which the council decided were needed. The feuing by the Trades of their lands south of the Cowgate, and the opening of St Andrew's Street in 1775,[68] was followed by the opening of Crichton Street in 1783. The latter had its origins in a suggestion made by George Dempster, following completion of the Trades Hall, that the poor communication between market place and harbour be remedied by a new street, and six years later work began.[69] Bell appears to have feued it as apartments rather than houses, and the lack of an urban design strategy is apparent from the fact that it was originally proposed to be 30 feet wide (three times the width of Couttie's Wynd), but was eventually narrowed to 25, and remained curved, like the wynd it replaced.

Eleven years later, Bell prepared a feuing plan for Tay Street, at the junction of the new turnpikes to Perth and to Coupar Angus. This imposing 40-foot wide street lined by decent, two-storeyed, slated, ashlar-fronted terraced houses was altogether grander; but there proved to be little market for such houses in Dundee. Most stances remained unbuilt; the few that were sold were built as apartments. Much the same

would occur in the contemporary Castle Street. As an efficient communication between market and harbour, the insufficiency of Crichton
Street had become almost immediately apparent; so when a plan for a
Tontine hotel (inspired by the Glasgow Tontine hotel), adjacent to the
Trades Hall was aborted in 1794 (perhaps because it coincided with a
trade depression and economic downturn caused by the outbreak of war
against revolutionary France[70]), the opportunity was taken to drive a
new street to the harbour through its site. This became Castle Street, for
which Bell planned the same kind of terraced houses as he had envisaged
for Tay Street.[71] However, Dundee's elite remained content in their
modernised apartments, and so the Castle Street plots remained empty
for almost two decades more.

Bell prospered in the final decades of the eighteenth century, the
beneficiary of growing streams of prosperity and demand for building.
He designed villas for the elite – the smartest being Provost Riddoch's
house in the Nethergate with its gently curving windows and side
pavilions in the manner of Glasgow's Tobacco Lords. He remodelled the
Morgan Tower opposite when Perth Road was switched from its north
side to its south, so that the provost might have a well-paved, well-lit
access to his house. Most of the villas that had begun to adorn the
southern slopes of the Blackness estate just west of the town, such as the
row of four known as 'Whiteleys', were probably by his hand – built for,
inter alia, the Baltic merchants, ('Riga Bob' Jobson returned from the
Baltic and James Johnston from St Petersburg), a variety of gentry, and
for the burgh's most prominent minister, Dr Robert Small. Bell died a
rich man. At his death in 1813, he left a movable estate valued at over
£4,000,[72] well up to that of Dundee's most prosperous merchants. It
included a substantial part of Gardyne's Land which he left in trust to his
son, who was incapable.[73] His career shows that Dundee's elite had both
the wealth and discrimination to make a post such as Town's Architect
prosperous.

His successor was David Neave, who was appointed in 1811 and held
the post until 1833 when he retired for ill health. Like Bell, Neave would
be responsible for most of the town's principal buildings as well as laying
out new streets, such as Park Place (1811),[74] Union Street (1824), Queen
Street – along the new turnpike road to Forfar (1825), and feuing several
abortive speculative housing developments on the higher Forebank
slopes. It was Neave who completed Tay Street (1818–20) for Riddoch, in

which he himself lived and had made elegant.[75] His particular specialism was the individual villa or groups of them, and a number down Roseangle, but his most extensive development of classical villas in Park Place was vitiated by the construction of a sugar house at the top end.[76] He was also responsible for an even larger number of smaller houses lining the western stretches of the turnpike road to Perth (identifiable from their distinctive fan-lights).

Unlike Bell, however, a number of the town's key public buildings in this second phase of ornamentation eluded Neave. William Stark, regarded at the time as Scotland's pre-eminent architect and specialist in lunatic asylums, was commissioned to design Dundee's lunatic asylum beyond the far north-eastern reaches of the burgh (completed 1819).[77] As with the Infirmary, the choice of Stark was a powerful statement of Dundee's determination to appoint the most expert. However, the subscribers to the 1828 Exchange Coffee House on the Shore selected George Smith, an assistant of William Burn then working in the town, rather than Neave, and their building was accordingly distinctly more rigorous. Both the Bridewell (1829) and the Seminaries (1829–33), at the centre of the Meadowlands to the north were designed by another of Burn's ex-assistants, George Angus. Indeed, Neave's only major public building was Dundee's new Assembly Rooms funded by the Thistle Operative Lodge of Masons in 1826 – the starkly neo-classical Thistle Hall at the centre of the west side of Union Street. There was no other publicly-funded building going on, the burgh's resources being drawn instead to the enormous harbour constructions then under way. Neave, who relinquished the post of Town's Architect to James Black in 1833, was also a relatively wealthy man when he died in 1841. Although his moveable goods were valued at only £1,826 (still a very sizeable sum), he was receiving rents from twenty-nine properties.[78]

Dundee's investment in public building and improvement impressed many visitors like Robert Heron, who observed of Dundee in the 1790s that, 'the houses in general are neat; and some public buildings have lately been erected that are noted by strangers as elegant'.[79] More gushing was Alexander Brown, who described the appearance of the Trades Hall and Town House as 'very magnificent', while of St Andrew's church he noted that it had a 'degree of elegance with respect to design which is not often to be met with'.[80] Nevertheless, records of the inhabited house tax in the later eighteenth century seem to indicate that in general Dundee houses remained quite modest in scale and pretension. Most Dundee housing liable for the tax fell within the lowest category of rentable values, as can be seen from Table 6.3.

TABLE 6.3
Inhabited house tax, royal burghs, 1786–87 [rentable values have been rounded down to nearest whole numbers]

Burgh	Number of houses	£5–20 rentable value	£20–40 rentable value	More than £40 rentable value	Total rentable value	% less than £20	% between £20 and 40
Aberdeen	672	5742	876	330	6948	82.64	12.61
Arbroath	74	506			506	100	
Ayr	139	1028	225	40	1293	79.51	17.40
Cupar	42	274			274	100	
Dundee	**380**	**3095**	**203**	**54**	**3352**	**92.33**	**6.06**
Edinburgh	2640	19730	11759	6550	38039	51.87	30.91
Lanark	17	100			100	100	
Montrose	169	1465	222		1687	86.84	13.16

These figures reinforce the impression created by Charles Lawson's drawings[81] that the town's elites were content to remain in their apartments in the maritime quarter and in the principal thoroughfares of the town, continuously re-modelling and refashioning them with the smartest of panelling, plasterwork and Adam fireplaces. What they may also indicate is a propertied elite concerned to accumulate money, not spend it.[82]

What did this all this activity add up to? In many ways, in pursuit of improvement, the council and citizens of Dundee were at or close to the forefront of a national process of urban renewal and change which gathered speed from the central decades of the eighteenth century. This has been traced for the main Angus burghs,[83] and the chronology of change is illustrated in Table 6.5. A similar record of improvement in towns as diverse and geographically disparate as Dunblane, Kilsyth,

TABLE 6.4
Inhabited house tax, royal burghs 1786–87, number of taxed houses per 1000
population [populations based on 1801 census], selected burghs only

Ayr	46.33
Banff	36.01
Edinburgh	32.59
Montrose	32.54
Stirling	30.65
Inverness	30.15
Dumfries	28.04
Haddington	27.74
Glasgow	25.77
Inverary	25.40
Aberdeen	24.89
Elgin	22.95
St Andrews	20.08
Jedburgh	17.5
Kirkwall	15.00
Linlithgow	14.46
Dundee	**14.07**

Source: NAS, E326/3/63, inhabited house tax, royal burghs, 1786–87

TABLE 6.5
Improvement in the main Angus burghs

	Montrose	Forfar	Arbroath	Dundee
Lighting	1760s	1793	1817?	1751–52
Paving	1760s	1800s	1814–15	1768
Shambles moved	1769	1789	1806	1768–75
Town House	Early 1760s, extended and refurbished 1819–20	1788	1808	1734

Kilmarnock, Ayr, Irvine, Beith, Paisley and Coupar Angus was noted in a diary written at the end of the century by a serjeant in the Royal Perthshire militia.[84]

On the other hand, progress was often sporadic and opportunistic, reflecting in part the influence of financial constraints. The funding of most civic buildings depended on private rather than public investment. The costs of St Andrew's church were originally intended to be split three ways between council, trades incorporations and the Kirk Session, before the council reneged on its agreement. Even initial funding for street lighting had to be raised by subscription. It is possible, moreover, to reach a rather negative judgement of the role at least of the council, which certainly showed no evidence of the strategic urban thinking exemplified in Edinburgh and Glasgow, and soon Aberdeen. And for all the progress that was achieved, much remained unreformed or unimproved. In his *Statistical Account*, even the town-proud Rev. Dr Robert Small criticised the 'uncommonly' narrow lanes and streets, crowded housing with little amenity, and lamented the absence of 'public walks and open spaces' which had now become virtually inaccessible. In 1804, a commentator not ill disposed towards the town observed the lack of advantage having been taken of the burgh's 'declivious' position in relation to the cleanliness of the streets, and the 'wealthy magnificence' of the High Street.[85] Small's further concern that even the newly-built suburbs were insufficiently planned 'without the least regard to health, elegance or cleanliness'[86] appears directed more at the industrial suburbs of Scouringburn and Dens than at the desultory villas along Perth Road, one of which he inhabited. Small was troubled by the insufficiency of the burial ground for the poor, but more by the 'almost total want of public institutions' – in particular a grammar school and a 'tolerable' public library.

Such mixed verdicts were, in fact, commonplace when it came to assessing conditions in most towns in the later Georgian era; and one of the problems in making assessments is the lack of any real criteria by which to make such a judgement. What should be the comparator? Tolerance of dirt and discomfort was decreasing, and the very process of improvement created its own new set of expectations about the civility, efficiency and cleanliness of urban society. It may have been this which is principally reflected in much contemporary comment. What is clear is that Dundee had improved itself almost as far as it could. On the other hand, the failure to conceive of an overall urban plan, so that its new public buildings might have the expected axial settings required to give them stature, was part of a wider failure to see the merit of *modernising*. In the end perhaps, this was not so much a failure as a reflection of the limited demand for individual houses, as indicated by the fate of the Tay and Castle Street projects, which may, in turn, explain the lack of impetus to lay out the town-owned lands to the north as a grid-iron suburb of houses in the approved manner. That such an iconic symbol of Georgian modernity and sophistication was not constructed, however, would come to damage the burgh's reputation ever afterwards.

A DIFFERENT TOWN?

By the later eighteenth century, Dundee and its population were changing increasingly rapidly. There was a clear sense that, like much of the rest of lowland Scotland, much had already changed by 1800. A striking expression of this was 'Philetas' comparative sketch of Dundee in 1746 and 1799 published in the latter year.[87] Modelled on the Edinburgh bookseller William Creech's anatomy of the changed manners of Edinburgh, and emulating Creech's dyspepsic, morally conservative tone, 'Philetas' presented a picture of a town and population transformed, a process led by its 'respectable, well educated, and wealthy' merchants who had undermined the 'feudal' order which had still exerted influence in the 1740s. Indicators of change were everywhere. Shops of various kinds were now to be found 'in every street and corner'; food was more plentiful and various, supplied by market gardens situated around the edge of the town. The harbour had been greatly extended, while the town was stretching outwards.

By the end of the eighteenth century, older loyalties and systems of governance were under increasing strain as a result of this quickening pace of change. Symptoms of the re-shaping of society included a thickening web of new clubs and forms of association (Sunday schools, missionary societies, philosophical clubs, subscription libraries, subscription coffee room), recurrent legal disputes over trading by non-burgesses, arguments between the town council, the incorporated trades and the Kirk Session. All this, it is true, was part of the normal jostling for influence and periodic resistance to oligarchical tendencies in urban government which had been endemic throughout the early modern period. However, arguments in defence of monopolies and privileges were becoming harder to sustain in the face of economic progress and a rising current of opinion hostile to such things.

The previously strong grip of the Kirk was also loosening. From the 1780s, there were growing incidents of defiance of the authority of the Kirk Session by those called to appear before it to answer charges of immorality.[88] The burgh authority was less ready to support the Kirk Session in its moral charge; or at least ceded this role to other, voluntary institutions, notably but not solely, to Sunday schools. In the mid eighteenth century, Dundee's population had been characterised by its Calvinist orthodoxy, and sections of it had participated enthusiastically in the evangelical revival of the early 1740s.[89] As in other large towns, religious pluralism had taken a strong hold by the end of the century, with congregations of Methodists, Bereans, Glassites, and Unitarians, as well as Seceders of various kinds. Older rituals of belonging, of community and conformity– for example, the celebration of the king's birthday and the annual procession of the incorporated trades – continued; but their meaning and significance altered as new social divisions established themselves. Alongside these older rituals, new ones developed – masonic marches on St John's Day, processions of friendly societies, and demonstrations of groups of working people. Despite the town council's determination to hold the periodic slow and highly structured perambulations of the marches (boundaries) of the town every two years from 1709 to guard against unwanted encroachments by neighbouring landlords, tenant farmers and cottars, these manifestations of urban solidarity diminished in significance. The collective sense of burgh identity was fraying, necessitating greater effort to mobilise.[90]

It is possible to portray this transformation in terms of growing social polarisation caused by commercialisation and the rise of manufacturing. Yet change in this period is not reducible to such a neat formula. Before 1800 at least, handloom weavers could do very well, as 'Philetas' noted in 1799. There are examples in the sasines of Dundee weavers owning property in the late eighteenth century, although for most it was a case of full-time work as waged employees with unstable earnings, removed from any foothold on or link with the land. From the 1800s, moreover, earnings tended to fall; and while numbers of new entrants to the weaver trade were reasonably buoyant until around 1820, thereafter they fell off sharply, a further indication of the occupation's loss of status.[91] Nor did generally positive conditions apply throughout the ranks of the working classes. By the end of the century, desperate – hungry – elements amongst the labouring poor in Dundee had the capacity to create fear in the surrounding countryside. During the winter of 1800, with grain hard to obtain in the town's market, it was rumoured that 'the Dundee People' were to be out, a scare that coincided with incidences of effigy-burning and fire-raising in the Carse of Gowrie.[92] In the town itself, a diverse band of people – tradesmen and shopkeepers, as well as master weavers – stood between the merchant elite and the ranks of the labouring classes.

The transforming impulses within Scottish urban society were complex, encompassing cultural liberalisation, evangelical revival, infusions of wealth from empire, as well as the growing power, wealth and confidence of the middling elite. Political developments in the final years of the century, notably the impact of war with Revolutionary France and the fight against domestic radicalism, also created new contexts for continuing landed involvement in the burgh. By the early nineteenth century, Dundee stood on the cusp of a new era, but it remained nonetheless a very different town from that of fifty years later.

NOTES

1 John Snodgrass, *The Means of Preserving the Life and Power of Religion in a Time of general Corruption. A Valedictory Sermon to the Inhabitants of Dundee* (Dundee, 1781), esp. pp. 10–11.

2 Dundee City Archives (DCA), Town Council Minute Book (TCM), 15 September. 1788.

3 Henry Skrine, *Three Successive Tours in the North of England, and Great Part of Scotland, Interspersed with Descriptions of the Scenes they Presented, and Occasional Observations on the State of Society* (London, 1795), p. 108.

4 National Library of Scotland (NLS), MS 2795, travel journal of unidentified Irish visitor, 1818, fol. 30 r.

5 David Loch, *A Tour through most of the Trading Towns and Villages of Scotland: Containing notes and Observations Concerning Trade and Manufacturers* (Edinburgh, 1778), p. 27. For similar comment, see also John Lettice, *Letters on a Tour through various parts of Scotland for the year 1792* (London, 1794), pp. 439–441.

6 NLS, MS 604, fol. 66.

7 The establishment of a police board in Glasgow occurred in 1800; Greenock (1801); Port Glasgow (1803); Edinburgh (1805); Leith, Paisley (1806); Inverness, Gorbals (1808); Kilmarnock (1810); Perth, Dumfries (1811); Calton (1819); Peterhead (1820); Aidrie (1821).

8   As emphasised by Ian Whyte in I. D. Whyte, 'Urbanisation', in T. M. Devine and
    J. R. Young (eds.), *Eighteenth-Century Scotland: New Perspectives* (East Linton, 1999),
    esp. p. 188.

9   Whyte, 'Urbanisation', p. 181.

10 Ibid., p. 181.

11 For some background, see C. A. Whatley, *Scottish Society, 1707–1830: Beyond Jacobitism,
    towards Industrialisation* (Manchester, 2000), ch. 2.

12 Perth and Kinross Council Archives (PKCA), Perth Burgh Records, Petitions,
    B 59/26/4/1, Petition of David Henry, late tacksman of the custom on the bridge of
    Tay port, 1709; Petition of Thomas Craigdallie, late tacksman of the port of Tay, 1713;
    Petition of the tacksmen of the four ports, 1714.

13 A. J. Durie, *The Scottish Linen Industry in the Eighteenth Century* (Edinburgh, 1979),
    pp. 143–157.

14 Bob Harris, 'The Scots, the Westminster Parliament, and the British State in the
    eighteenth century', in J. Hoppit (ed.), *Parliaments, Nations and Identities in Britain
    and Ireland, 1660–1850* (Manchester, 2003), pp. 127–131; Whatley, *Scottish Society*,
    pp. 61–64; PKCA, Perth Burgh Records, B59/24/8/4, Sederunt of the Freeholders of
    the Shire of Forfar Att Dundee the tenth day of November [1726]. On the impact of
    the Board of Trustees, see Durie, *The Scottish Linen Industry*, ch. 4, and pp. 162–165.

15 A. Slaven, *The Development of the West of Scotland, 1750–1960* (London, 1975),
    pp. 135–147.

16 R. E. Tyson, 'Demographic Change', in Devine and Young (eds.), *Eighteenth Century
    Scotland*, p. 196.

17 M. Flinn (et al), *Scottish Population History from the Seventeenth Century to the 1930s*
    (Cambridge, 1977), p. 466.

18 NLS, Saltoun Papers, MS 17567, Accompts of Linen Cloth Stamped in Scotland from
    1 November 1727.

19 Durie, *The Scottish Linen Industry*, p. 25.

20 See relevant comment in Christopher A. Whatley, *Onwards from Osnaburgs:
    The Rise and Progress of a Scottish Textile Company, Don & Low of Forfar 1792–1992*
    (Edinburgh, 1992).

21 See Whatley, *Onwards from Osnaburgs*, which explains how one Forfar-based textile
    firm survived and prospered alongside mid Victorian Dundee's industrial growth.

22 J. Shaw, *Water Power in Scotland, 1550–1870* (Edinburgh, 1984),
    pp. 231–233.

23 *The Statistical Account of Scotland, Vol. XIII, Angus* (Wakefield, 1976 ed.), p. 190.

24 TCM, vol. 8, 1704–1715, 21 June 1709.

25 G. Jackson and K. Kinnear, *The Trade and Shipping of Dundee, 1780–1850*
    (Dundee, 1991), p. 6.

26 Significant measures to improve and/or enlarge the harbour were undertaken in 1743,
    1768, 1770, 1780–2, 1789, and 1804. For the battle over the harbour in the 1810s, see
    Louise Miskell, 'From conflict to co-operation: urban improvement and the case of
    Dundee, 1790–1850', *Urban History*, 29 (2002), pp. 359–361.

27 Jackson and Kinnear, *Trade*, pp. 32–33.

28 C. A. Whatley, 'From Handcraft to Factory: the Growth and Development of
    Industry in Montrose, *c.* 1707–1837', in G. Jackson and S. G. E. Lythe (eds.),
    The Port of Montrose: A History of its Harbour, Trade and Shipping (New York and
    Tayport, 1993), pp. 256–276.

29 See David Loch's judgement on this in his *Tour*, p. 27; *Statistical Account, Angus*, p. 191.

30 *Statistical Account, Angus*, pp. 164–165.

31 Whatley, *Scottish Society*, pp. 79–95, 124–141.

32 C. A. Whatley, D. Swinfen and A. M. Smith, *The Life and Times of Dundee* (Edinburgh, 1993), pp. 65–68; Shaw, *Water Power*, pp. 226, 247.

33 Kinnear and Jackson, *Trade*, p. 26.

34 Whatley, Swinfen and Smith, *Life and Times*, p. 64.

35 Jackson and Kinnear, *Trade*, pp. 6, 29–30.

36 See Bob Harris, 'Towns, Improvement and Cultural Change in Georgian Scotland: the Evidence of the Angus Burghs, *c.* 1760–1820', *Urban History*, 33 (2006), pp. 195–212.

37 See ch. 10, below.

38 *Statistical Account, Angus*, pp. 165–167.

39 NAS, SC47/72/3, 'schoolmaster returns of militia names for year 1801'. These lists only covered men between the ages of 18 and 30.

40 Twenty-six occupations were recorded for Forfar; 36 for Brechin; 44 for Arbroath; and 57 for Montrose (NAS, SC 47/72/3).

41 DCA, Lockit Book, 1740–60.

42 A. M. Smith, *The Nine Trades of Dundee* (Dundee, 1995), p. 161.

43 Old Parish Registers (OPR), 282/12, 13.

44 NAS, SC47/71/4, demographic and occupational profile of Dundee, 1811.

45 Edinburgh Central Library (ECL), DA 1861.789, Andrew Armstrong's Journal, 1789–1793.

46 See C. McKean, 'Improvement and Modernisation in everyday Enlightenment Scotland' in Foyster and Whatley (eds.), *Everyday Life in Scotland Vol. 2, 1600–1800* (Edinburgh, 2009)

47 DCA, Guildry Sederunt 9 May 1735. We are grateful to Innes Duffus for this and other Guildry references.

48 Ibid., 3 January 1738.

49 Dundee: gates removed by 1770 except Cowgate; removal of Nethergate (1810) and Seagate (1817) narrows; widening of Fish Street; straightening of Overgate; opening of Crichton Street; plans, not realised, for removing narrows of Murraygate. For contemporary comment on failure to realise ambitions to widen the Murraygate, see *Dundee, Perth and Cupar Advertiser*, 27 December 1811; 3 January 1812.

50 Lamb, *Old Dundee* (Dundee, 1895), p. xxiv.

51 TCM, entries for 14 October, 11 November 1751; 31 August, 13 November 1752. From 1773, care of the public lamps and lighting was contracted out; previously it had been the responsibility of the Treasurer. For criticisms of lighting, see *Dundee, Perth and Cupar Advertiser*, 16, 30 October 1812; 22 January, 10 April, 30 October 1818; 22 January 1819; 18 February 1820.

52 A. J. Warden, *Burgh Laws of Dundee* (London, 1872), p. 195.

53 TCM, entries for 16 January, 5 April, 18 November 1768; 25 March, 11 May, 21 August, 6 November 1769; 8 February, 10 June, 10 September 1770. Sums borrowed amounted to £500 in 1769 and £449 in the following year.

54 DCA, Dundee Burgh Treasurer's Account Book, 1778–1815, entries for 1788–89; 1791–92; 1792–93; 1793–94; 1799–1800. See also J. M. Beats, *Reminiscences of Dundee* (Dundee, 1882), p. 30.

55   TCM, entry for 24 May 1770; 28 September 1773.

56   TCM, entry for 1 June 1763. We are grateful to Shona Stewart for this reference.

57   *The Dundee Magazine and Journal of the Times* (Dundee, 1799), pp. 181–188, 361–370. In fact, he said they were timber built, but that was a misconception: due to Scotland's timber shortage, entirely timber urban buildings were extraordinarily rare.

58   DCA, Guildry Sederunt entry for 13 October 1725.

59   Dundee Burgh Register of Sasines, held in Dundee Archives and Records Centre for before 1809 and the National Archives in Edinburgh for the period from 1809. Relevant references are too numerous to list separately here.

60   They included the Baltic merchants' Timber Land, in the Overgate, a gentry town house at the head of where Union Street is now (Beats, *Reminiscences*, p. 15) and Lady Warkstairs.

61   A. H. Millar (ed.), *The First History of Dundee* (Dundee, 1923).

62   Ibid., p. 179.

63   Lettice, *Tour*, p. 439.

64   See e.g. Alexander Campbell, *Journey from Edinburgh* (2 vols., London, 1802), vol. 1, p. 388; *The Traveller's Guide through Scotland and its Islands* (2 vols., 7th edn, Edinburgh, 1818), vol. 11, pp. 95–96.

65   Warden, *Burgh Laws*, p. 286.

66   *Charters and Documents relating to the Burgh of Dundee* (Dundee, 1880), p. 179.

67   TCM, entry for 1 May 1783. We are grateful to Shona Stewart for this.

68   Warden, *Burgh Laws*, p. 289.

69   TCM, entry for 1 October 1777, 6 October 1777, and 29 January 1781.

70   TCM, entry for 22 February 1794. A key figure behind plans was the inn keeper, William Gordon, and his proposals, launched in 1789, appear to have won considerable support in the town. For this, see *Edinburgh Advertiser*, 27 November 1792; NAS, GD 151/11/16, William Gordon to Robert Graham of Fintry, 28 October 1789; as above, 20 November 1792. In 1793, the Committee purchased land for the new inn. In January 1795 Council bought this land from them to enable the opening of a new street to the shore, which became Castle Street. In 1794, Gordon noted that 'this place [ie. Dundee] has stood in want of a good House as an Inn, for an Age past'. He also noted that he had had to pay high rents for his premises and that bad roads had diminished his business (GD 151/11/16, William Gordon to Robert Graham of Fintry, 25 November 1794). See also GD 151/11/35, William Scott to Graham of Fintry, 6 December 1793; same to same, 12 December 1793; same to same, 14 February 1793; 4 March 1794.

71   McKean, 'Not even the trivial grace of a straight line' in L. Miskell, B. Harris and C. A. Whatley (eds.), *Victorian Dundee – Image and Realities* (East Linton, 1999), pp. 26–27.

72   NAS, CC3/5/3, pp. 35–39, inventory of Samuel Bell, architect in Dundee, 1813.

73   DCA Burgh Register of Deeds vol. 46, fol. 139, Disposition by Samuel Bell, 26 March 1810.

74   TCM, entry for 25 February 1813.

75   DCA Land Tax Register, 1826–30, entries 67–71. We are grateful to Marilyn Healey for finding this.

76   Ibid., p. 34.

77   McKean, 'Not even the trivial grace of a straight line', pp. 15–37. In 1805, a subscription was also started for a new building for the Exchange Coffee Room, but it

was not until after our period that such a building was constructed (*Dundee, Perth and Cupar Advertiser*, 7 June 1805).

78 NAS, SC 45/31/5.

79 Robert Heron, *Scotland Delineated, or a Geographical Description of Every Shire in Scotland, including the Northern and Western Isles* (2nd edn, Edinburgh, 1799, report. Edinburgh, 1975), p. 128. See also Campbell, *Journey from Edinburgh*, vol. 1, p. 388.

80 NLS, MS 3294–5, Alexander Brown, 'Journey in Scotland with sketches of some Picturesque Ruins in that Interesting Country in Two Volumes', vol. 1, p. 71.

81 Charles Lawson, Collection of drawings and sketches *c.* 1855 – *c.* 1875, Local History, Dundee Central Library.

82 See Bob Harris, 'Towns, improvement and cultural change in Georgian Scotland: the evidence of the Angus Burghs, *c.* 1760–1820', *Urban History*, 33 (2006), p. 199.

83 Harris, 'Towns, improvement and cultural change', esp. pp. 199–202.

84 PKCA, MS 14/16/3, diary written by Thomas Murie of Perth, serjeant of Royal Perthshire Militia, 1798–1801.

85 *History of the Town of Dundee* (Dundee, 1804), p. 115.

86 *Statistical Account, Angus*, pp. 191–192.

87 *The Dundee Magazine and Journal of the Times* (Dundee, 1799), pp. 181–188, 361–370.

88 See Leah Leneman and Rosalind Mitchison, *Sin and the City: Sexuality and Social Control in Urban Scotland 1660–1780* (Edinburgh, 1998). From the 1790s, a growing number of 'delinquents' summoned before the Kirk Sessions were failing to appear.

89 On this, see John Gillies, *Historical Collections Relating to Remarkable Periods of the Success of the Gospel and Eminent Instruments Employed in Providing it*, 2 vols. (Glasgow, 1754), vol. II, pp. 356, 358, 399; *A Select Collection of Letters of the Late Rev. George Whitefield*, 3 vols. (London, 1772), vol. I, pp. 314, 324, 328, 339, 358, 411.

90 TCM, vol. 8, 1704–1715, 7, 18, 21 June 1709; for a wider study, see K. R. Bogle, *Scotland's Common Ridings* (Stroud, 2004).

91 Smith, *Nine Trades*, p. 167; N. Murray, 'The Regional Structure of Textile Employment in Scotland in the Nineteenth Century: East of Scotland Hand Loom Weavers in the 1830s', in A. J. G. Cummings and T. M. Devine (eds.), *Industry, Business and Society in Scotland Since 1700* (Edinburgh, 1994), pp. 226–233.

92 PKCA, MSS 100, Rossie Papers, Bundle 36, Robert Cranston to Lord Kinnaird, 8 February 1800.

CHAPTER 7

Dundee, London and the Empire in Asia

Andrew Mackillop

Dundee's eighteenth century has been portrayed as an ambiguous and ambivalent era, best characterised by slow if definite development; but the question of the burgh's interaction with the empire has generally been overlooked in that analysis. The high road from Dundee to the empire was not so much across the Atlantic, as was the case in Glasgow, as down the North Sea coasting routes to London. Once established in the imperial metropolis, Dundonian commercial and maritime interests joined Angus gentry in exploiting the vast new empire of the East India Company to a degree that has not hitherto been appreciated.

'INDUSTRIOUS' DUNDEE AND ITS HINTERLAND

To view the century or so after 1707 as a linear path leading inexorably towards Dundee's nineteenth-century factory economy downplays its earlier patterns of productivity, commerce and finance; and what needs to be done is to examine how far post-union Dundee might have been the regional centre of what economic historians now term an 'industrious revolution'.[1] Households in an 'industrious revolution' – where most forms of manufacturing still took place – expanded both their production and their disposable income, and subsistence in rural communities was replaced by a discernable engagement with the market.[2] Between the 1740s and 1770s, textile output trebled, and Dundee emerged as the undisputed centre of Scottish linen production, largely as a result of cottage-based, handloom manufacturing.[3] This quickening of linen production in Dundee's rural hinterlands of Perthshire and Angus closely fits the description of an 'industrious revolution'.[4] Both county and burgh were far less separate in this 'industrious' economy than was later to become the case in the era of mechanised factory production. The countryside shaped the urban economy, while the town acted as a collection and distribution centre for rural products.

So there were overlapping and reciprocal economic relationships between Dundee and Angus where the county, port and the other smaller burghs were all part of a single 'industrious' regional zone; and central to the area's economic success was the destination of Dundee's exported products. Dundee's fleet was overwhelmingly geared towards the coasting and tramping trade down the east coast (see Chapter 11). Yet the apparently mundane nature of this trade disguises the fact that it tied Dundee directly to the imperial metropolis, and the central position of London as the market for Dundonian and Angus products and produce was already being appreciated by the 1720s. Indeed, it had probably been a major export destination for decades earlier.[5] While Glasgow's trade was connected to the economically dynamic but politically marginal North American colonies, Dundee's commerce linked it straight into the mercantile and political heart of the empire.

The empire into which Dundonian entrepreneurs found their way has been re-interpreted as an alliance between the modernising social and economic power of the aristocracy and gentry on the one hand, and London-based financial elites on the other; and the theory of 'gentlemanly capitalism' has emerged to explain the specific nature of this important alliance. The landed classes believed in economic dynamism but political conservatism, and this delicate and potentially contradictory combination of agendas drew them into imperial activities as they sought acceptable income substitutes for those family members unable to inherit estates. The gentlemanly capitalists came to view the empire as the arena that offered honourable forms of service and *rentier* income.[6] The idea of gentlemanly capitalism places considerable emphasis on office-holding and the patronage networks which were required to secure imperial employment. The scramble for well-paid, honourable forms of occupation in the formal institutions of the empire – the army, navy and the East India Company – was as significant a feature of pre-industrial imperialism as the importing and re-exporting of colonial produce.

For the aristocracy, gentry and their clients, patronage politics was an alternative form of economics. Wealth and income were generated through a combination of official state service and private enterprise. In this understanding of imperialism, the social classes normally associated with rural affairs, agricultural improvement and unreformed politics join the tobacco lords and cotton barons as the prime instigators and beneficiaries of empire. It is important to note that this gentlemanly capitalist thesis does not view laird and merchant as existing in a hostile or competitive relationship. The old and new social orders buttressed each other, blurring the lines between the urban world of the mercantile and the rural order of the shire.[7]

The notion of gentlemanly capitalism, however, has not been without its critics.[8] Much of its supporting evidence relates to the nineteenth century rather than the eighteenth, whereas it was in the earlier period that the landed class held the reins of economic and political power far more completely and securely. Another criticism is that the thesis has concentrated to an excessive degree upon London and the South-East of England,[9] while it was often in regions of the United Kingdom, such as Scotland, that the aristocracy and gentry retained an impressive range of political, economic and social powers over their localities and estates.[10] It is the contention of this chapter that throughout most of the eighteenth century, Dundee and Angus can be perceived not only as a zone of 'industrious' revolution but also one of 'gentlemanly capitalism'.

John Drummond of Quarrell illustrates the entangled and complementary nature of political, economic, landed and urban power. The scion of middle-ranking Perthshire gentry, he became a merchant in Amsterdam and later in London during the 1690s and early 1700s.[11] Drummond's success was such that he went on to serve as the MP for the Perthshire burghs – which included Dundee – between 1727 and 1742.[12] His social standing had already come full circle when in 1722 he purchased an estate in Stirlingshire. From there he combined estate improvements with mercantile endeavour, such as shipping coal to London.[13] He also exemplified how Dundee's commercial elites and those of its rural hinterland intersected with London's economy. From as early as 1709 he was organising large-scale shipments of meal and barley from Dundee to the capital.[14]

Drummond was not exceptional. Indeed one of the most intriguing aspects of eighteenth-century Dundee is just how consistently the burgh was represented at Westminster by individuals who could be described as 'gentlemanly capitalists'. George Dempster of Dunnichen, the son of a Dundee burgess-merchant, traversed the boundary between commerce and landed and political power by becoming an estate owner, industrialist, agricultural improver, banker and provost. A well-respected MP, he represented Dundee (as part of the Perth burghs) from 1761 to 1790.[15] After a highly successful commercial career in Bombay, and having served as MP for Angus from 1791 to 1796, David Scott, the son of Robert Scott of Dunninald, represented Dundee between 1796 and 1805.[16]

Taken together, the notions of an 'industrious revolution' and the 'gentlemanly capitalist' provide a way of challenging the orthodoxy that eighteenth-century Dundee failed to engage fully with the empire. If participation in imperialism could be shaped by the political and social influence of the landed class, as well as by mercantile endeavour, then east-central Scotland did not lag significantly behind regions like Glasgow and its hinterland. As Angus landed families increasingly exploited linen production, they became directly or indirectly embroiled in the complexities of London's markets, prices, finances and overseas trade.

Once he became the burgh's MP, Drummond's interest in the town's exports had become political as much as commercial. In common with many Scottish MPs, he promoted linen as the country's premier manufacturing export, and actively encouraged its distribution in London.[17] In 1727 Drummond reported to landowners that Dundee and Montrose 'browns' sold badly in the capital, and that more political pressure was required to boost sales. This agenda was assisted by the establishment of a 'Scotch-Holland' warehouse at Charing Cross which specialised in the sale of linen in the London market.[18] As early as 1701, Drummond had used his connections in the City to facilitate marine insurance for London-Scots merchants venturing into the slave trade. By 1724 he was a director of the Royal African Company and in a position to encourage the use of Scottish linen on slaving voyages. Meanwhile, his kinsman, the banker Andrew Drummond of Charing Cross, extended credit for the purchasing of cargoes for London ships heading to the Gambia.[19] It has been calculated that as early as the 1750s, 10% of London's Africa merchants were expatriates from north of the border.[20]

As Scottish involvement in the London-based slave trade increased, so too did the potential export market for cheap Dundee and Angus cloth. Given the large volume of textiles sent from the burgh to the metropolis, there can be little doubt that 'industrious' Dundee and its hinterland were directly involved in the empire's most lucrative branch of transatlantic commerce.

By the 1760s and 1770s, Dundonians and individuals from Angus were running a number of well-established trading concerns in London. Among these were John Fotheringham's merchant house and the interlocking business interests of George, James and David Webster.[21] John and David Wedderburn, the brothers of Robert, laird of Pearsie near Kirriemuir, ran a large and successful West Indian merchant house. The extent of their shipping and trading concerns was such that the revolutionary war in America cost them between £2,000 and £3,000.[22] The Websters and Wedderburns eventually combined to form a commercial venture of considerable size, whose trading liabilities alone totalled £400,000 by 1801.[23] Another prominent merchant with links to the region was William Read of Greenwich, a kinsman of the Reads of Logie, near Dundee. These merchants maintained close reciprocal links with their home town and region, though not always to positive effect. The collapse of John Fotheringham's merchant house in 1773 was a case in point: although only one of a spate of London-Scots bankruptcies, it brought 'great distress' to Dundee in particular.[24]

Notwithstanding such disasters, the influence of London-based merchants could be immensely beneficial to their relatives and friends back home. They offered credit and patronage to kinsmen and to local associates arriving in the capital; the Wedderburns, for example, made their nephew, David, an apprentice before he went on to establish his own apothecary business.[25] As the sons of a Dundee merchant, it is hardly surprising that the Webster brothers acted as agents, financiers and trustees for other Dundonians in London and further afield in the empire. Continuing links with their place of origin ranged from lobbying on behalf of kinsmen and relations to organising credit on the London money markets. In January 1782 the Websters negotiated a £10,000 loan for George Dempster who, in turn, used his estate of Dunnichen as landed security.[26] This intersection of Angus landed property and City of London finance is a perfect illustration of how gentlemanly capitalism bound the region to the metropolis.

LONDON AND THE EAST INDIA COMPANY:
THE GATEWAY TO ASIA

With so much of their maritime, commercial and financial energy centred upon the capital, Dundee and Angus were ideally placed to exploit the one hemisphere of Britain's global empire that was accessible only through London. While any Scottish merchant could participate in the Atlantic system after 1707, the East Indies were the sole monopoly of the London-based 'United English East India Company' (hereafter EIC).[27] The distinctive nature of the east central Scottish economy facilitated links between Dundee, Angus and the EIC in a number of ways. As early as 1732, barley from the Angus estates of Andrew Fletcher, Lord Milton was used to provision EIC ships.[28] However, while the Company's fleet of East-Indiamen was impressive in terms of tonnage and capital investment, its victualling requirements were never large enough to constitute a sustainable point of entry for Angus interests into the East Indies trade.

Textiles constituted the obvious link between Dundee 'industrious' economy and the EIC. For most of the eighteenth century, the Company's economic life-blood consisted of imported Asian fabrics, especially South Asian calicos.[29] The need for expertise in textile production, bleaching, dyeing, and quality control meant that London cloth merchants, mercers, and wholesalers played an important part in the corporation's activities.[30] These entrepreneurs were also increasingly aware of the mass import of Dundee and Angus linen, and a common interest in textiles provided a bridge into the world of the EIC. As in so many other aspects of Scottish activity in London, John Drummond was an early leader. He was elected a director of the EIC in 1722, serving intermittently until 1734.[31] In 1730 he ensured coarse Scottish textiles were incorporated into the Company's annual quota of cloth exports by combining English broad cloth with Scottish linen; it was then dyed in a manner designed to be more appealing to consumers in India.[32]

The most important link between Dundee and the metropolis came in the form of human migration. Ships from Dundee entered and left London every year, carrying with them sailors from the burgh and the surrounding smaller ports.[33] It is difficult to exaggerate the significance of this human mobility. The Probate Court of Canterbury, the recognised legal channel for those working abroad wishing to register their testaments in Britain, contains the wills of 33 individuals from Dundee and Angus between 1690 and 1750. That 25 wills belonged to mariners (including 12 individuals in the Royal Navy) is a clear indication of the significance of shipping in defining the nature of contact between London and east central Scotland.[34] Between 1750 and 1800, a further 78 persons from Angus and Dundee registered their wills; 41 were either in the Royal Navy or merchant marine.[35] As the number of sailors from Dundee and the other county burghs moving in and out of London increased, so too did the likelihood that they would drift into the metropolis's various imperial trades.

Such occupational mobility intensified during the first half of the eighteenth century. As personnel entered London's merchant marine labour market, the EIC inevitably attracted seamen to its service. By 1740 the Company's fleet was manned by around 4,500 men. The number of ordinary seamen from Dundee employed in the East Indies trade requires further research, but, over the course of the century, the figure must have been considerable.[36] Not surprisingly, ship's officers are better documented, not least because their higher skill levels enabled them to maximise trading opportunities in Asia. Upon arrival in the East Indies, it was common practice for ordinary seamen and merchant officers to leave the Company's service and become 'country traders', which involved operating beneath the EIC's monopoly and conducting commerce between ports in Asia.[37] Though less prestigious than the Company's merchant marine, a number of Dundonians took this route. By the mid 1730s, Alexander Wedderburn and Anne Ogilvie from Dundee had several kinsman and sons in the East Indies country trade, sailing from ports as diverse as Calcutta and Mocha.[38]

Piecemeal involvement in the maritime aspects of the East Indies trade had remained the defining characteristic of Dundee's limited contact with the Company in the decades immediately following the union. After 1757, however, the EIC's position in South Asia was transformed. Having securing de facto political control over the Nawabs (princes) of the Carnatic (Arcot) and Bengal in 1752 and 1757 respectively, the Company rapidly evolved from a mercantile entity into a major military and territorial power in India.[39] The result was an explosion in Company employment, ranging from the lucrative civil service, to cadetships in the armies of Bengal, Madras and Bombay and a large number of surgeons' posts. Given that the corporation continued to be dominated by well-entrenched mercantile and financial dynasties from the City of London who were determined to retain control over the most profitable sectors of the trade, infiltrating the EIC was never a simple or easy proposition.[40]

However, Dundee's economic links to the metropolis helped London-based Dundee and Angus mariners access the EIC, and several of the gentlemanly capitalists who represented the burgh – John Drummond, George Dempster and David Scott – had close links to the Company's headquarters at Leadenhall Street. All three served as EIC directors: Drummond during the 1720s and 1730s; Dempster in 1769 and 1772; and Scott from 1789 until his death in 1805. Drummond's long-term impact lay in facilitating his clients' slow but steady penetration of the EIC's shipping and mercantile activities in the 1720s and 1730s.[41] Dempster's prestige at East India Company House arose from his reputation among the corporation's shareholders rather than a result of his short tenure as a director. Throughout the 1760s and 1770s he was one of the leading figures in the factional infighting that characterised Leadenhall politics.[42] He organised stockholder votes to support or challenge the directors on the powers granted to Clive in Bengal in 1764, the precise nature of negotiations between the Company and the government in 1767, and the dividend rate in 1771.[43] Dempster was also recognised as one of the few MPs who actually understood the complex minutiae of constitutional and financial relations between the EIC and the Crown. His reputation was such that he commanded the respect of MPs and directors alike. David Scott's career differed from Dempster's, but mirrored that of John Drummond. He made his money and reputation in Bombay from 1763 to 1786 before returning to Britain and establishing himself in London. By the early 1790s he was a close political ally of Dundas in Scottish electoral politics and a key adviser on the government's management of the EIC. Given Scott's commercial expertise and the status of his political allies, it is hardly surprising that he became deputy-chair and then chairman of the Company in the later 1790s.[44]

These major figures in the eighteenth-century history of the EIC each represented the Perth burghs and, in Scott's case, the county of Angus, as MPs. Moreover, they did so for a combined total of fifty-nine years.[45] For nearly two-thirds of the century after 1707, therefore, Dundee's electoral politics intersected with that of the EIC at the highest level. No other constituency region in pre-reformed Scotland had comparable close and persistent links with the institution that regulated commerce and government in the eastern half of Britain's empire. The burgh's lack of a strong mercantile profile in the Atlantic might have been compensated for by strong political influence in the Asian sector of the empire. One area where patronage proved particularly difficult to secure was in the Company's civil service. Only 16 individuals from Dundee and Angus were appointed between 1750 and 1813, the year the EIC finally lost its monopoly of trade to India. This figure constitutes 5% of all Scots appointed to the Company's civil service in this period, and is only slightly below the burgh and county's per capita share of Scotland's population.[46] The close correlation between the two sets of figures challenge the assumption that Dundee and Angus were conspicuous by their absence from the eighteenth-century empire. Whereas neither burgh nor county acquired a disproportionate share of EIC civil service patronage, the region did manage to secure a percentage of posts broadly in line with its population.

Table 7.1 reveals that the high status and remunerative Company jobs remained largely the preserve of the landed elites. The county's landowners heavily out-performed Dundee's mercantile and other middling sorts in the scramble for office, as scions of established families such as the Lyons of Glamis, Hunters of Burnside and the Grahams of Fintry secured some of the most sought after posts in the empire.[47] London-Scots merchants also looked after their own. The Webster brothers provided social and financial credit to Walter Ogilvy of Clova, while John Kerr did the same for his nephews Mungo and John Dick, the sons of a Dundee merchant. With several thousand pounds in EIC stock, the Websters were, like Dempster, influential in the Company's court of shareholders, and used this clout on behalf of their kinsman Charles Wedderburn, securing him letters of introduction to senior Company officials at Calcutta.[48]

Sixteen individuals might not seem especially impressive, yet the total must be understood in relation to the small quota of civil servants appointed each year by the Company directors. Too prestigious and competitive ever to offer an easily accessible form of imperial employment, the civil service's annual recruitment never exceeded 100; indeed only 473 were appointed throughout the 1790s.[49]

The EIC's military constituted an alternative means of exploiting

TABLE 7.1

Dundee/Angus personnel in the EIC's civil service, 1750–1813[50]

Area	Social origin	Parishes	Patrons
Dundee (3)	Merchant 2	–	London–Scots 2
	Landed gentry 1	–	David Scott 1
Angus (13)	Aristocracy 1	Montrose 5	London–Scots 3
	Landed gentry 6	Glamis 1	Immediate family 3
	Merchant 1	Dunnichen 1	George Dempster 2
	Clergy 1	Cortachy 1	David Scott 5
	Legal 1	Forfar 1	
	Unknown 1	Monfeith 1	
		Kinnell 1	
		Lethnot 1	

expansion in Asia, since it offered a respectable and potentially profitable career to a much wider range of social backgrounds. From the mid to late 1740s, the Company's three armies grew rapidly, employing 3,440 officers by 1805,[51] and Scots provided a disproportionate percentage of this military elite: in 1772 they comprised 31% of all commissioned personnel of the army of Bengal.[52]

Although Table 7.2 shows that participation in the military broadly mirrored patterns in the civil service, there were some significant differences. The Company's armies proved a popular career precisely because they held out to scions of the middling and artisan orders a realistic chance of social advancement. The merchant-burgesses of Dundee, Forfar, Brechin and Montrose were well represented, but the accessibility of EIC military patronage went further: Robert Webster, Alexander Ferrier and Charles Binny, who all acquired officer's commissions in the 1790s and early 1800s, were the sons of tenant farmers.[53]

These figures underestimate overall levels of regional involvement in the military since – prior to the 1780s – officers and cadets departing to the East were invariably listed as 'English', 'Scottish', 'Irish' or 'Welsh', and it was only after 1789 that extant EIC records include an officer's county or parish origins.[55] It is clear that the benefits of a military career in Asia were well understood long before the Company's records confirm the presence of officers from the region. Robert and Thomas Fletcher of

TABLE 7.2
Dundee/Angus officers in the Bengal army, *c.* 1750–1813[54]

Area	Social origin	Parish	Ranks
Dundee (5)	Merchant 3 Clergy 1 Legal 1	–	Lt. 2 Cadet 3
Angus (34)	Aristocracy 1 Landed gentry 7 Burgess-merchants 8 Clergy 5 Tenant Farmer 3 Medical 1 Artisan 1 Unknown 10	Montrose 9 Forfar 4 Brechin 3 Kinettles 3 Kirriemuir 2 Benvie 2 Kingoldrum 2 Others 9	Maj. General 1 Colonel 1 Lt.-Col. 3 Capt. 6 Lt. 14 Ensign 2 Cadet 7

Ballinshoe near Kirriemuir joined the army of Madras in 1757 and 1763 respectively. Both had highly profitable if controversial careers: Robert was promoted to commander in chief of the Madras army in the mid 1770s, while Thomas was a senior officer in a division of the same army which was destroyed at the Battle of Pollilur in 1780.[56] Neither brother survived their time in Asia: Robert died at sea in 1777 after being deported by the governor of Madras; Thomas perished in 1782 as a prisoner of the Sultan of Mysore.[57]

The Fletchers prove that the region's elite was taking up military employment in Asia from the earliest phase of EIC expansion. Moreover, the majority of the 39 officers shown in Table 7.2 joined the Bengal army between the mid 1790s and 1813 indicating that by the later decades of the eighteenth century, Dundee and Angus gentry were engaging with the EIC's military machine in considerable numbers. Additionally, records show that between 1791 and 1807 at least 32 individuals from Angus (including 11 from Dundee) became officers in the armies of Madras and Bombay.[58] Given that at least 70 officers can be confirmed for the period between the early 1790s and early 1810s, it is reasonable to suppose that at least 100 Angus personnel served as commissioned officers in the EIC's military between the Battle of Plassey (in 1757) and 1813.

A number of families sent several sons to India, one after the other. John Dick dispatched his two sons into the civil service in 1766 and 1770, and so far as the military was concerned, examples such as the Fletcher brothers are too numerous to list exhaustively. The departure of his eldest son John to Bengal in 1764 persuaded the laird of Pearsie to allow his second son, Charles, a military surgeon, to follow him in 1769.[59] Although it is hardly surprising that landed families relied on military employment, merchants and other middling elites also followed suit.[60] Two sons of Robert Maver, a Dundee lawyer, joined the armies of Bengal and Madras in 1805 and 1808. Robert Jobson, a scion of a key Dundonian merchant and banking dynasty, benefited from the patronage of both David Scott and Henry Dundas. As regional and national political managers, the latter were under constant pressure to meet rising material and social aspirations and this crucial political task could be facilitated through the use of Indian patronage.[61] What has not been fully appreciated is the extent to which merchant families, such as the Jobsons, could do extremely well out of the process. In the seven years after 1802, three of Robert's sons acquired commissions in the army of Madras. The creation of a familial co-operative enabled the Jobsons to pool their capital resources, cut living costs, and act as trustworthy attorneys for each other's legal and financial affairs.[62] The combination of imperial patronage and kin cohesion as an insurance mechanism against death or mishap in Asia was a highly effective strategy for exploiting the eastern empire.

There were two other sectors of the EIC which Dundonians and individuals from Angus could hope to exploit. By the 1790s the Company was a major employer of medical personnel, a human resource that Scotland was producing in ever larger quantities. Few other parts of the EIC contained as many Scots. Among the influx of Scottish surgeons, personnel from Dundee and Angus were already to be found in Company service by the early 1730s.[63] John Allardice from Brechin and John Matthewson, son of a Dundee merchant, became Company surgeons in 1769 and 1771, while John and Alexander Duncan combined private trading with their medical duties at Canton during the 1780s and 1790s.[64] By the end of the century Scots were over-represented within the Company's medical infrastructure. The sons of Dundee's chief Customs officer, Robert Hunter, and Episcopal minister, the Reverend Alexander Duncan, became assistant surgeons in the 1800s, while Helenus Scott, son of the minister of Auchtergaven, was president of the Bombay

Medical Board from 1806 to 1810.[65] Between 1805 and 1813 one in eight of the 125 Scottish surgeons appointed to the Company's settlements in Asia came from Angus (inclusive of Dundee).[66] This remarkably high per capita percentage shows that neither burgh nor county were in any way affected adversely by the lack of a university.

The EIC's merchant marine had provided an avenue of contact with the East Indies since the early decades of the century. And this link continued as the burgh's sailors transferred from the coasting trade into the far more lucrative, if extremely hazardous, Europe to Asia routes. The profits to be made as a senior officer or commander of an East Indiaman merchant ship were legendary. When Captain Robert Haldane, son of the laird of Gleneagles, returned home to Scotland in the mid 1750s, it was widely believed he had made £70,000 on a single voyage.[67] He had done no such thing of course, but the exaggeration surrounding his career is an accurate reflection of how the East Indies trade was viewed within Scottish society. In this fevered climate, it was only natural that sailors and merchant officers from Dundee should seek service with the EIC. The irony is that by the end of the century, the burgh's relatively low commercial and maritime profile in the Atlantic trades, and its reliance on London, resulted in a distinctive pattern of Dundonian involvement in the EIC's merchant marine. Table 7.3 summarises the social origin and careers of men from Dundee who became East-Indiamen commanders.

As was the case with the civil servants, these small numbers are

TABLE 7.3
Dundee's East-Indiamen commanders[68]

Name	Social origin	Ship	Period in command
John Ramsay	Artisan	*Union*	1750–1751
James Haldane	Landed gentry	*Melville Castle*	1793–1794
James Haliburton	Merchant	*Glatton*	1805–1813
William Maxwell	Merchant	*Calcutta*	1797–1808
Charles Raitt	Merchant	*Earl Spencer*	1750–1751
Robert Rankine	Landed gentry	*Union*	1810–1813

deceptive. It was extraordinarily difficult to obtain command of an East Indiaman. Being in charge of one of the Company's ships meant joining an exclusive commercial cartel, membership of which enabled captains to become merchant entrepreneurs with highly privileged access to the otherwise closed system of British trade between Europe and Asia. The value of an East-Indiaman captaincy reflected the extent of these economic privileges. By the 1780s commanders could sell their post for anything between £4,000 and £7,000.[69]

Although such sums help put the number of Dundonians serving as East Indiaman commanders into perspective, an equally telling comparison would be with Glasgow. Despite the latter's customary association with aggressive involvement in the British Empire, only one Glaswegian captained an East-Indiaman between the 1790s and 1810s.[70] Indeed, Dundee supplied more East Indiaman commanders per capita than any other major Scottish port (see Chapter 11 for more on Dundee as a port).

THE IMPACT OF THE EAST INDIES CONNECTION

The EIC's commercial and territorial empire was not an easy career option. The climate and climate-related diseases killed approximately 50% to 60% of all Britons who ventured to the East Indies.[71] The Company's main 'presidency' settlements were around 11,000 miles from Europe by sea, which meant that secure communication with associates in Britain was hard to sustain. The nature of life (and death) in the East forced the adoption of a number of social and networking practices. Trustworthy partners both in India and in London were vital if an individual's private business or EIC career was to blossom. Given such high mortality rates and personnel turnover, networks based on local or regional loyalties became more rather than less important.[72] The search for reliable business partners, creditors and executors meant that Dundonians in the East more often than not associated together, transplanting their local and regional allegiances to the other side of the world, as indeed they had done centuries earlier (see Chapter 1). Such unofficial connections were truly global in scope and enabled both Dundee and Angus to tap into the empire in Asia, notwithstanding the EIC's official monopoly.

The creation of hybrid local-imperial networks would begin even before an individual departed for Asia. London was central to the process, being the pivot around which allegiances and loyalties generated at home could be relocated to the East. David Scott and George Dempster's political leverage at East India Company House has already been noted in relation to the civil servants. Military careers likewise benefited from the burgh's unusually long run of MPs enjoying influence at Leadenhall Street. Dempster lobbied hard to secure promotion for Robert Fletcher in 1766 and the appointment of George Binny from Forfar as a surgeon at Madras in 1773. A year earlier he acted as security for his cousin, George Willison, who departed to India as a portrait painter.[73]

Whereas such acts of patronage might be dismissed as the routine graft and nepotism that typified Scotland's pre-reformed political culture, they constituted the first step in a complex and multi-layered networking that eventually spanned between Dundee and India. In 1776 George Bruce left Dundee for London, and there obtained a cadetship in the Madras army; but his career strategy in India depended on the protection of the high-ranking Fletcher brothers. News of Sir Robert's death came, therefore, as a nasty surprise. Writing from the Cape of Good Hope in April 1777, Bruce noted in his diary that, 'Nothing could have shocked me more than this piece of news, as my whole dependence was on Sir Robert as I have been long connected with all his nearest relatives in Scotland.'[74]

Burgh and county affiliations formed in Scotland could be central to career and material prospects in Asia, and the associations of individuals from Dundee and Angus confirm that Bruce was not alone in his thinking. Having benefited from the patronage of Sir Robert Fletcher and another high-ranking EIC officer, Major Robert Kyd of Drumgeith, Charles Wedderburn of Pearsie was in turn expected to support kinsmen arriving in Asia. In 1774 his father, writing from Dundee, informed him of the departure to India of a relative from the town, Thomas Fraser. He added: 'If it is in your power to be of service to the young gentleman I shall expect it from the connection he is in to you by your cousin'.[75] The nature of Wedderburn's contacts in India is testimony to the utility and durability of local networks of trust. Besides his two patrons, Wedderburn kept in touch with his kinsman, John Scrymgeour while trading in Indian cloth with the EIC civil servant George Guthrie, son of the laird of Craigie. Wedderburn's textile supplier was a Madras 'free' merchant, David Young, whose family were from Kirriemuir and Dundee.[76] These arrangements reveal networks based on Angus affiliations which spanned the South Asian subcontinent, and generated webs of business and financial interdependence.

A prominent example of the success wrought by commercial practice founded on such associations was that of the Binnys of Madras. No less than five sons of John Binny, a bailie in Forfar, sojourned to southern India between the late 1760s and 1790s. A key element in their early success was their links to George Paterson. The son of a weaver-burgess in the Wellgate, Paterson had a staggeringly successful career, making him one of Scotland's richest nabobs and an example of the social mobility made possible by empire. Through Dempster's political influence, Paterson obtained the post of private secretary to Sir John Lindsay of Evelix, who had been appointed to a senior naval command in the East in 1769. By virtue of Lindsay's status, Paterson became an intimate political and financial adviser to the Nawab of the Carnatic, one of the EIC's client princes in southern India.[77] Paterson in turn provided an opening for the Binnys, who serviced the Nawab's shipping and banking needs in Madras. Charles Binny acted as his private secretary in the town; meanwhile his brother Thomas commanded the Nawab's merchant shipping while employing another brother, Alexander, as purser.[78] His brothers' activities prompted John Binny to move to Madras in the mid 1790s, where he opened an agency house specialising in the consignment of cargoes and bills of exchange to Europe. By 1800 John's stock in Binny & Co., which was by then one of the largest private merchant houses in Madras, exceeded £16,000.[79]

One of the key functions of imperial-regional networks was the return to Britain of wealth acquired in the East. Nowhere is this more the case than in the networks of legal trusteeship operating in the EIC's main settlements. From the 1780s to early 1800s, Charles and John Binny acted as executors for Captain George Campbell from Coul, surgeon Alexander Anderson from Balmossie and James Dickson from Brechin, a ship's captain in the country trade.[80] Similar patterns of legalistic mutual reliance were evident in Bombay. Helenus Scott was an executor for several sojourners from Angus, including fellow surgeon James Small from Bervy and Bombay's governor, Jonathan Duncan, from Wardhouse near Montrose.[81] Hidden beneath and between the formal structures of the EIC throughout British Asia, lay a culture of highly localised affiliation and mutual support that facilitated the return home of sojourners and their fortunes.

It was common practice to reinforce these bonds of local trusteeship in South Asia by remitting monies to London merchant houses with close links to Dundee and Angus. The London connection, so vital to the outward movement of sojourners, was equally important when it came to returning home. David and James Webster specialised in handling monies and property sent back from Asia, and among their clients was George Paterson, who in 1773 and 1774 remitted £44,787 via navy bills and bonds of exchange on Canton.[82] The scale of the East Indian fortunes sent back from London to Dundee and Angus provides convincing evidence of the burgh and its hinterland's commitment to Britain's empire in Asia. The sums involved were considerable and reveal how East Indian wealth percolated into localities not normally associated with the empire.

Large sums also poured into the Dundee region through the purchase and modernisation of landed property. Besides the estates shown in Table 7.4, a further fifteen properties were acquired between 1780 and 1813, either through purchase or inheritance by individuals returning from the East Indies.[84] Alexander and John Duncan, the entrepreneurial surgeons working out of Canton, bought the estates of Allanbank, Parkhill and Rosemount near Montrose in the late 1780s and early 1790s. Small estates on the outskirts of Dundee were popular with returnees such as Major Walter Philip, Daniel Mackenzie and Captains Hugh Lyon and Robert Rankine, because they bestowed status while allowing easy access to the town's social and civic amenities.[85] Estate purchase was the most tangible expression of a successfully completed imperial career, but it was not the only way in which returning personnel invested their fortunes. Large amounts of capital remitted back from Asia were lent on landed securities across the shire between 1780 and 1813: sasine records confirm that £60,189 was offered as mortgages on Angus estates by individuals still in Asia or recently back from the East.[86]

By the later decades of the century large swathes of the county's landed order were sustained either by direct involvement in EIC service or by virtue of substantial injections of imperial credit. During the 1770s the estate of Pearsie was improved and enclosed through the arrival of monies from Bengal equivalent to three times the annual rent.[87] The growing influence of imperial finance in the rural 'industrious' economy

of Angus inevitably affected Dundee's prosperity and rate of development. Solvency and credit worthiness among the gentry drove forward
the linen economy of which Dundee was the regional hub. Monies left
to Dempster by Sir Robert Fletcher helped underwrite the creation in
1788 of his textile village of Letham, the manufactures of which were then
exported from Dundee.[88] Fortunes in the shire, in other words, corre-
lated to increased prosperity for the burgh.

Capital made in Asia percolated into Dundee through a wide variety
of channels. Over £16,000 in East Indies monies can be traced directly
to the burgh between 1774 and 1814, equivalent to 42% of the £38,600
raised by pier dues between 1764 and 1814, thus representing a substantial
income stream for the town.[89] Alongside the spectacular nabob fortunes
of the Fletchers or David Carnegie were other examples of success, and
women were notable beneficiaries in the wills of EIC officials, either as
mothers, widows or siblings. Agnes Tweeddale, the widow of the EIC
official John Cumming, was able to build up a textile exporting business
in Arbroath. When she died in 1812 she was described as a 'merchant of
Arbroath' with extensive links to local weavers and capital totalling
£530.[90] It was more usual, however, for women to benefit from imperial
profits in the form of annuities. Though the retired EIC surgeon Thomas
Morgan died at Haddington in 1815, his will reveals that he had strong
Dundee connections, where his two sisters and one of his executors
resided. Morgan was an extremely wealthy man, with a fortune in excess
of £17,400 in Britain, and a further £24,000 in stock in Calcutta. By a
clause in his will, both his sisters were to be provided for. In the case of
Colonel Alexander Read it is possible to quantify the amount he left to
relatives in Dundee. Though he had chosen to settle in London, Read
acknowledged 'my friends who have claims to my consideration derived
from kindred or family connections'. In 1803 he left £50 to a distant
female relative in the burgh and the substantial sum of £1,000 to his
cousin, 'Mrs Anderson of Dundee'. The widow of EIC surgeon John
Allardice, who lived in the town during the 1800s, had an estimated
fortune of £700. Upon their return home in the 1790s and 1800s,
Captain Patrick Scott and Doctor Helenus Scott resided in Dundee,
living as gentlemen on the interest arising from their loans to local gentry
and aristocracy.[91]

One of the key social consequences of the link with Asia was that
retired officers, widows, and annuitants supplemented the number and

resources of the burgh's middle class. One of the defining economic developments of later eighteenth-century Dundee was the emergence of a dynamic financial sector; and it is unsurprising that George Dempster was to the fore given his immersion in the financial affairs of the EIC, and of the money markets of the metropolis. It had given him an awareness of the importance of credit and shareholding in economic improvement. What has not been appreciated is the role of returnees in depositing their disposable capital into the burgh's emerging financial sector. When Colonel John Crow returned home from Bengal he not only purchased the estate of Amelia Bank just outside the burgh, but also opened an account worth £2,761 with the Dundee Bank. In the 1790s Captain Hugh Lyon invested £783 in the bank and the Dundee Assurance Company.[92]

It has been calculated that the average working capital of the new Scottish provincial banking companies was £50,000 by the turn of the 1800s. Viewed in this way, the significance of the sums coming back from Asia, especially capital lent on landed securities, can be properly appreciated. Another comparison with the figures in Table 7.4 is Reverend Robert Small's calculation that Dundee's paper credit in the mid 1790s stood at £160,000.[93] Both these examples suggest that, while certainly not as important as agriculture or textiles, East Indian profits were a major hidden element in the region's economy.

One final example illustrates how the East Indies connection both facilitated the burgh's modernisation and sustained its civic fabric. In January 1774 the retired East-Indiaman commander John Ramsay died.[94] His will was a complex expression of his sense of professional pride, loyalty to his native burgh, and a determination to provide for the moral and educational needs of the town's poor. Part of his estate included £160 in Dundee Bank bonds, which he asked be kept as part of a £900 annuity to his widow, the daughter of Dundee's provost, George Ramsay. He gave £300 to the Kirk Session on the express understanding that the interest be used to educate two poor boys (with the surname of Ramsay) from the burgh. The scale of this gift is best understood by noting that the town's annual poor relief fund in the 1790s was only £828. Ramsay's endowment was clearly a substantial boon to the Kirk Session. Another £240 was set side for retired brewers and merchant seamen; the burgh's ministers were given £5 each, with the remainder used to establish a fund for a burgh poor house.[95]

TABLE 7.4

East Indian fortunes in Dundee and Angus, 1774–1814.[83]

Individual	Amount	Estate*/Locality
David Carnegie	£47,000	Inverkeilor
Brigadier-General Robert Fletcher	£26,000	Ballinshoe*
Major Thomas Fletcher	£22,000	Readie-Lindertis*
Jonathan Duncan	£9,375	Abroath
Captain Charles Wedderburn	£9,347	Pearsie*
Captain Hugh Lyon	£5,000	Dundee
Captain David Read	£5,000	Drumgeith*
Commander John Ramsay	£4,400	Dundee
Surgeon Samuel Guise	£3,674	Montrose
David Young	£3,120	Dundee
Captain George Campbell	£1,000	Coul
Colonel Alexander Read	£1,050	Logie
Various	£4,306	Angus
Various	£3,860	Dundee
Dundee Total	*£16,380*	
Shire Total	*£128,752*	
Total	*£145,132*	

CONCLUSION

John Ramsay personified the pattern of contact between Dundee and the East Indies. The second mate on an East-Indiaman by 1732, and commander of the *Anson* by 1750, he exemplified how the burgh's coasting trade to London provided a springboard into the EIC's merchant marine. Dundee's interaction with London offers an alternative model for understanding post-union Scotland's development within the empire. If Glasgow and Greenock thrived on a mercantile system of colonial imports and re-exports, Dundee reveals the way in which an 'industrious' regional metropolis could use a combination of political, social and economic tactics to access the empire. Moreover, the links with London steered Dundonian and Angus networks into the

Eastern rather than Western hemisphere of British imperialism.

The first of these formative connections was patronage politics. In the era of the 'gentlemanly capitalist', politics proved a potent economic lever. Dundee's low profile in the transatlantic trade was never likely to prove fatal to the town's modernisation given its position as part of an electoral region with remarkably persistent links to the EIC. In Dempster and Scott, the town had MPs ranked among the most powerful East Indian politicians of the second half of the eighteenth century. Through their influence, Dundee was arguably an 'imperial' burgh by the 1760s, and certainly so by the 1790s. Both burgh and county acquired a respectable percentage of lucrative and sought after EIC civil service employment. When it came to surgeons and senior merchant marine commanders, the region punched well above its weight.

The role of political patrons was reinforced by the willingness of Dundee and Angus entrepreneurs in London to lobby on behalf of their kinsmen and associates. The London merchant houses of the Wedderburns, Fotheringhams, Reads and Webster proved to be an invaluable means of infiltrating the EIC. Their ability to deliver imperial opportunities means that any systematic assessment of Dundee's post-union history must include the London axis.

Once people from Angus and Dundee had travelled half way round the world to India and China, they tended to stick together – as they had always done (see Chapter 1). The commercial, financial and legal networks forged by such regional associations are clearly evident in the EIC's records. One consequence of these networks was a flow of capital from the East Indies back into the town and county that has neither been acknowledged nor explored. Although eighteenth-century Dundee's imperial wealth did not rival that of the Glasgow Tobacco Lords, the sums remained substantial: the county gentry, for example, being benefi- ciaries of the empire in the East to the tune of many tens of thousands of pounds. Wealth from Asia sustained a buoyant local land market and helped to promote the development of estate improvement and of activ- ities related to the textile industry. Nabobs added their wealth to the burgh's emerging financial sector while continuing to support the estab- lished educational and poor relief mechanisms. In their conspicuous rural and urban paternalism, the returnees presaged their later equiva- lents, the jute barons. Indeed the extent of Dundee's early links with Asia suggests that the burgh's nineteenth century role as 'Juteopolis' was less

an unprecedented new age of empire so much as a logical evolution from
its eighteenth-century phase of 'industrious' and 'gentlemanly' imperialism.

NOTES

1   D. C. Coleman, ' 'Proto-industrialisation': A Concept too Many', *The Economic
    History Review*, New Series, 36 (1983), pp. 438–448; R. Houston and K. D. M Snell,
    'Proto-industrialisation? Cottage Industry, Social Change, and Industrial Revolution',
    The Historical Journal, 27 (1984), pp. 476–478, 488–492.

2   Jan de Vries, 'The Industrial and the Industrious Revolution', *The Journal of Economic
    History*, 54 (1994), pp. 249–257. For application of the concept on a global scale see,
    C. A. Bayly, *The Birth of the Modern World, 1780–1814* (Oxford, 2004), pp. 51–64.

3   A. Durie, *The Scottish Linen Industry in the Eighteenth Century* (Edinburgh, 1979),
    pp. 27 and 65.

4   T. M. Devine, *The Transformation of Rural Scotland: Social Change and the Agrarian
    Economy, 1660–1815* (Edinburgh, 1994), pp. 19–45.

5   Christopher Whatley, *The Industrial Revolution in Scotland* (Cambridge, 1997),
    pp. 40–41; G. Jackson and K. Kinnear, *The Trade and Shipping of Dundee*, (Dundee,
    1991), p. 23; National Library of Scotland (NLS), Fletcher of Saltoun, MS 16530, fol.
    58; MS 16536, fol. 50.

6   P. J. Cain and A. G. Hopkins, 'Gentlemanly Capitalism and British Expansion
    Overseas, 1: The Old Colonial System, 1688–1850', *Economic History Review*, 2nd
    Series, 39 (1986), pp. 502–507.

7   P. J. Cain and A. G. Hopkins, *British Imperialism: Innovation and Expansion,
    1688–1914* (London, 1993), pp. 58–62, 66–71.

8   R. E. Dumett, 'Exploring the Cain/Hopkins Paradigm. Issues for debate; critique, and
    topics for new research', in Cain and Hopkins (ed.), *Gentlemanly Capitalism and
    British Imperialism: The New Debate on Empire* (London, 1999), pp. 5–11.

9   A. Porter, ' "Gentlemanly Capitalism" and Empire: The British Experience since 1750',
    Journal of Imperial and Commonwealth History, 18 (1990), pp. 266 and 272.

10 L. Soltow, 'Inequality of Wealth in Land in Scotland in the Eighteenth Century',
    Scottish Economic and Social History, 10 (1990), pp. 39–40, 55; Christopher Whatley,
    Scottish Society, 1707–1830 (Manchester, 2000), p. 154; F. O' Gorman, 'Ordering the
    Political World: the pattern of politics in eighteenth-century Britain (1660–1832)', in
    D. Donald and F. O' Gorman (eds.), *Ordering the World in the Eighteenth Century*
    (Basingstoke, 2006), pp. 88–89.

11 R. Hatton, 'John Drummond in the War of the Spanish Succession: merchant turned
    diplomatic agent', in R. Hatton and M. S. Anderson (eds.), *Studies in Diplomatic
    History: Essays in Memory of David Bayne Horn* (London, 1970), pp. 73–76.

12 Huntington Library (HL), Stowe Collection ST57/30, pp. 130 and 193–194; R.
    Sedgewick (ed.), *The House of Commons, 1715–1754*, 2 vols. (London, 1970), vol. 1,
    pp. 402–403.

13 National Archives of Scotland (NAS), Abercairney Muniments, GD24/1/464 D/31–2,
    37; GD 24/1/784, 'Airth, 1726', 'Account betwixt James Drummond of Blair
    Drummond and John Drummond of Quarrell, crop 1729'.

14 NAS, Abercairney Muniments, GD 24/3/249/1.

15 J. Ferguson (ed.), *The Letters of George Dempster to Sir Adam Fergusson, 1756–1813* (London, 1934), pp. 1–4; L. Namier and J. Brooke (eds.), *The House of Commons, 1754–1790*, 3 vols. (London, 1964), vol. II, pp. 313–317; Whatley, *Scottish Society*, p. 192.

16 R. G. Thorne (ed.), *The House of Commons, 1790–1820*, 5 vols. (London, 1986), vol. II, pp. 613–615.

17 Durie, *The Scottish Linen Industry*, pp. 52–54; R. Harris, 'The Scots, the Westminster Parliament and the British State in the eighteenth century', in J. Hoppit (ed.), *Parliaments, Nations and Identities in Britain and Ireland, 1660–1860* (Manchester, 2003), pp. 125–128; NAS, Clerk of Penicuik, GD18/5368; Abercairney Muniments, GD24/3/319/3.

18 NLS, Fletcher of Saltoun, MS 16538, fols. 172–173; MS 16536, fol. 50; *Scots Magazine*, 4 (London, 1742), p. 323.

19 NAS, Abercairney Muniments, GD24/1/464 C/9, 15–16; HL, Stowe Collection, ST 57/27, p. 185; ST57/24, pp. 79–80.

20 D. Hancock, 'Scots in the Slave Trade', in N. C. Landsman (ed.), *Nation and Province in the First British Empire: Scotland and the Americas, 1600–1800* (London, 2001), p. 63.

21 *The London directory for the year 1778. Containing an alphabetical list of the names and places of abode of the merchants and principal traders* (London, 1778) p. 174; Dundee City Archives (DCA), Wedderburn of Pearsie, Box 7/25/5: Pearsie, 5 January 1771.

22 DCA, Wedderburn of Pearsie, GD 131/25: Dundee, 8 April 1771, Robert Wedderburn to Charles Wedderburn; Balmure, 27 February 1778, E. Graham to Charles Wedderburn.

23 A. Wedderburn, *The Wedderburn Book* (Printed Privately, 1898), I, p. 442.

24 DCA, Wedderburn of Pearsie, Box 7/25/10: Dundee, 4 January 1773.

25 DCA, Wedderburn of Pearsie, Box 7/25/7: Pearsie, 16 July 1772.

26 NAS, Scrymgeour-Wedderburn Muniments, GD 137/1147; Register of Seisins, [Forfar], (126). David Webster's will reveals the extent of his transactions as agent and trustee for families and individuals in Angus. See, The National Archive, Kew (TNA), PROB 11/1161, pp. 382–386.

27 P. Lawson, *The East India Company: A History* (London, 1993), pp. 55–56.

28 NLS, Fletcher of Saltoun, MS 16549, fols. 143–144.

29 W. J. Barber, *British Economic Thought and India, 1600–1858* (Oxford, 1975), p. 68; K. N. Chaudhuri, *The Trading World of Asia and the English East India Company, 1660–1760* (Cambridge, 1978), pp. 13, 64, 97.

30 H. V. Bowen, *The Business of Empire: The East India Company and Imperial Britain, 1756–1833* (Cambridge, 2006), p. 248; Chaudhuri, *Trading World of Asia*, pp. 220–230.

31 For a ground-breaking study of Drummond and Scotland's early contacts with the English East India Company, see G.K. McGilvary, *East India Patronage and the British State: The Scottish Elite and Politics in the Eighteenth Century* (London, 2008), passim.

32 NLS, Erskine Murray Papers, MS 5073, fol. 158.

33 For examples of Dundee shipping in London, see J. Barclay, *The Voyages and Travels of James Barclay, containing many surprising adventures, and interesting narratives* (London, 1777), p. 6; R. Baldwin, *Baldwin's New Complete Guide to all persons who have any trade or concern with the City of London, and parts adjacent* (London, 1768), p. 182.

34 TNA, PROB 11/424–775 (vols. covering 1690 to 1750).

35 TNA, PROB 11/776–1315 (vols. covering 1750 to 1798).

36 For examples of Dundonian seamen, see Oriental and India Office Collections, British Library (OIOC), L/MIL/9/85, p. 68; TNA, PROB/11/611, p. 38.

37 P. J. Marshall, *East Indian Fortunes* (Oxford, 1976), pp. 54–59, 101–110; P. J. Marshall, 'Private British Trade in the Indian Ocean before 1800', in A. Das Gupta and M. N. Pearson (eds.), *India and the Indian Ocean 1500–1800* (Calcutta, 1987), pp. 276–297.

38 NAS, Abercairney Muniments, GD24/1/464 C/189, 208–209, 238; GD24/3/388.

39 H. V. Bowen, *Revenue and Reform: The Indian Problem in British Politics, 1757–1773* (Cambridge, 1991), pp. 5–15; P. J. Marshall, *The Making and Unmaking of Empire: Britain, India and America, c. 1750–1783* (Oxford, 2005), pp. 119–157.

40 J. G. Parker, 'Scottish Enterprise in India, 1750–1914', in R. A. Cage (ed.), *The Scots Abroad: Labour, Capital, Enterprise, 1750–1914* (London, 1985), p. 192; C. H. Philips, *The East India Company, 1784–1834* (Manchester, 1961), pp. 1–4.

41 G. K. McGilvray, 'Post-Union Scotland and the India Connection: Patronage and Political Management', *Cencrastus*, 37 (1990), pp. 30–33; A. Mackillop, 'Accessing Empire: Scotland, Europe, Britain, and the Asia Trade', *Itinerario*, 29 (2005), pp. 19–23.

42 L. Sutherland, *The East India Company in Eighteenth Century Politics* (Oxford, 1962), pp. 56 and 155; H. V. Bowen, ' "The Little Parliament": The General Court of the East India Company, 1750–1784', *The Historical Journal*, 34 (1991), pp. 865–866.

43 OIOC, B/80, p. 85; B/83, p. 33; B/87, pp. 294–296.

44   M. Fry, *The Dundas Despotism* (Edinburgh, 1992), p. 195; NAS, Melville Castle Papers, GD51/3/3/3–106.

45 J. G. Parker, 'The Directors of the East India Company, 1754–1790', PhD thesis, University of Edinburgh, 1977, I, pp. 82–4; II, pp. 241–242.

46 For Dundee and Angus's population see, D. J. Withrington and I. R. Grant (eds.), *The Statistical Account of Scotland* (Wakefield, 1983), I, xliv–xlv.

47 OIOC, B/75, pp. 470 and 483; O/1/1, No. 12; J/1/15, pp. 188–191.

48 OIOC, O/1/1, No. 12; J/1/6, pp. 443–446; B/82, pp. 255–256 and 289; J/1/8, pp. 192a–196; B/87, p. 30; DCA, Wedderburn of Pearsie, GD 131/30: London, 24 June 1778.

49 OIOC, J/1/13–17.

50 OIOC, J/1/1–28; O/1/1/12; D. 1087: 'David Scott's Patronage Book', pp. 3–13.

51 G. J. Bryant, 'The East India Company and its Army, 1600–1778', PhD, King's College, 1975, pp. 328–30; HL, Stowe-Grenville STG Box 198 (14), 'General State of the Company's Army in India, 1 January 1805'.

52 G. J. Bryant, 'Scots in India in the Eighteenth Century', *Scottish Historical Review*, LXIV (1985), p. 23–24; T. M. Devine, 'Scottish Elites and the Indian Empire, 1700–1815', in T. C. Smout (ed.), *Anglo-Scottish Relations from 1603–1900* (Oxford, 2005), p. 214; Michael Fry, *The Scottish Empire* (East Linton, 2001), p. 84.

53 V. C. P. Hodson, *List of the Officers of the Bengal Army, 1758–1834*, (London, 1927), I, p. 143; II, p. 176; IV, p. 420; OIOC, L/MIL/9/126/329; L/MIL/9/128/181.

54 Hodson, *List of the Officers of the Bengal Army*, vols. I–IV (London, 1927), passim; OIOC, L/MIL/9/107–112.

55 OIOC, L/MIL/9/89–90, 'Military Embarkations, 1775–1784'; L/MIL/10/131, 'Muster Roll of the Army of Bengal, November 1772'.

56 OIOC, B/79, p. 246; Grant and Withrington, *Statistical Account of Scotland*, vol. XIII, p. 190.

57 A. Buddle, P. Rohatgi and I.G Brown, *The Tiger and the Thistle: Tipu Sultan and the Scots in India* (Edinburgh, 1999), pp. 15–16; DCA, Wedderburn of Pearsie, Box 7/25/21: Pearsie, 6 December 1778.

58 Information from the EIC's 'early cadet papers'. See, OIOC, L/MIL/9/107–112 [1789–1802]

59 Hodson, *List of the Officers of the Bengal Army*, IV, pp. 420 and 422; DCA, Wedderburn of Pearsie, Box 7/25/1: Dundee, 31 December 1767.

60 P. E. Razzell, 'Social Origins of Officers in the Indian and British Home Army: 1758–1962', *The British Journal of Sociology*, (1963), pp. 249–251; P. J. Corfield, *Power and the Professions in Britain, 1700–1850* (London, 1995), p. 191; S. Nenadic, 'The Impact of the Military Profession on Highland Gentry Families, *c.* 1730–1830', *Scottish Historical Review*, 85 (2006), pp. 75–83, 94–99.

61 Philips, *East India Company*, pp. 15–16; R. M. Sunter, *Patronage and Politics in Scotland, 1707–1832* (Edinburgh, 1986), pp. 9, 13–15; D. J. Brown, 'The Government of Scotland under Henry Dundas and William Pitt', *History*, 83 (1998), p. 272.

62 OIOC, L/MIL/9/111/131; L/MIL/9/112/115; L/MIL/116/271.

63 TNA, PROB 11/721, pp. 220–221.

64 TNA, PROB 11/1163, p. 138, NAS, CC8/8/123, pp. 377–80; OIOC, B/85, p. 263; B/86, p. 292; B/91, p. 309. Centre for South Asian Studies, Cambridge (CSAS), Duncan Papers, 'Alexander Duncan's Ledger and Letter Book, 1787–1796'.

65 OIOC, L/MIL/9/358, pp. 50–53; L/MIL/9/364, p. 21–23. For Scott's career see, H. C. G. Matthew and B. Harrison (eds.), *Oxford Dictionary of National Biography*, 46 (Oxford, 2004), p. 388.

66 OIOC, L/MIL/9/360–65, 'Surgeon's Certificates, 1805–1813'.

67 J. A. L. Haldane (ed.), *The Haldanes of Gleneagles* (Edinburgh, 1929), pp. 293–296.

68 A. Farrington, *A Biographical Index of East India Company Maritime Service Officers, 1600–1834* (London, 1999), passim.

69 Philips, *The East India Company*, pp. 80–81.

70 Farrington, *Biographical Index*, p. 884.

71 Marshall, *East Indian Fortunes*, pp. 218–219.

72 For the importance of local loyalties and networks in the British East see, A. Mackillop, 'Europeans, Britons, and Scots: Scottish Sojourning Networks and Identities in Asia, *c.* 1700–1815', in A. McCarthy (ed.), *A Global Clan: Scottish Migrant Networks and Identities since the Eighteenth Century* (London, 2006), pp. 19–47.

73 OIOC, B/81, p. 357; B/86, p. 242; B/88, pp. 365 and 559; B/89, p. 573.

74 Tamil Nadu State Archives, Mayor's Court Records, Private Miscellaneous xii (c): 'Diary of George Bruce, 9 November 1776 to 18 September 1777'. I am grateful to Professor Huw Bowen of the University of Swansea for generously providing extracts from this important source.

75 DCA, Wedderburn of Pearsie, Box 7/25/7: Pearsie, 16 July 1772; Box 7/25/11: Dundee, 10 April 1774; Box 7/25/21: Pearsie, 6 December 1778; Box 7/25/12: Dundee, 20 January 1774.

76 DCA, Wedderburn of Pearsie, Box 7/8: Lincoln's Inn, 16 August 1813; Box 21/(9): 'Memorandum Book of Charles Wedderburn, 1775'; OIOC, J/1/16, pp. 224–229. Young arrived in Madras in 1764, see OIOC, O/5/30, fols. 210–213.

77 P. Nightingale, *Fortune and Integrity: A Study of Moral Attitudes in the Indian Diary of George Paterson, 1769–1774* (Oxford, 1985), pp. 1–32.

78 OIOC, O/5/31, fols. 1–16; B/89, p. 573.

79 Anon, *The House of Binny* (Madras, 1969), pp. 5–12.
80 OIOC, LAG/34/19/187 [1784], pp. 133–134, [1787], p. 160; LAG/34/29/205, p. 23; TNA, PROB 11/1444, p. 118–119.
81 OIOC, LAG/34/29/342, pp. 49–51; PROB 11/1534, pp. 118–119.
82 OIOC, B/89, p. 231; B/91, p. 132; Nightingale, *Fortune and Integrity*, p. 167.
83 This information is drawn from five-year samples of wills registered in Calcutta, Madras and Bombay, and from surveys of the Probate Court of Canterbury and the Scottish Sheriff Courts. OIOC, LAG/34/29/185–205; TNA, PROB 11/771–1534; NAS, CC3/4/32; CC3/5/2 and 6; CC8/8/105, 123, 129, 133; CC20/4/30; SC70/1/17.
84 NAS, Register of Seisins (Forfar), [1–3991]; DCA, Wedderburn of Pearsie, Box 7/25/7: Pearsie, 16 July 1772; Box 7/25/11: Dundee, 10 April 1774; Box 7/15/2: Liff, 12 March 1813; GD 131/25, Kinghorn, 18 March 1778.
85 CSAS, Duncan Papers, No 31, pp. 1–60; NAS, Register of Seisins (Forfar), [866], [1880], [6616], [6944].
86 This information is drawn from NAS, Register of Seisins (Forfar), [1–7184].
87 DCA, Wedderburn of Pearsie, Box 7/20/29, 42, 44; Box 7/25/11, 14, 17.
88 For Fletcher's will see, TNA, PROB 11/1034, pp. 43–45; Withrington and Grant, *The Statistical Account of Scotland*, xiii, p. 201.
89 William Kenefick, 'The Growth and Development of the Port of Dundee in the Nineteenth and early Twentieth Centuries' in L. Miskell, C. A. Whatley and Bob Harris (eds.), *Victorian Dundee: image and reality* (East Linton, 2000), p. 40.
90 NAS, CC20/4/30, pp. 560–564.
91 For Morgan and Read's wills see, NAS, SC70/1/17, pp. 419–27; OIOC, L/AG/34/29/205, pp. 33–63; TNA, PROB 11/1661, pp. 58–9; NAS, Register of Seisins (Fife), [8914]; Register of Seisins (Forfar), [1880], [6616].
92 NAS, CC3/5/5, pp. 294–300; CC/4/32, pp. 5835–5850.
93 C. H. Lee, 'The Establishment of the Financial Network', in T. M. Devine, C. H. Lee and G. C. Peden (eds.), *The Transformation of Scotland: The Economy since 1700* (Edinburgh, 2005), p. 109.
94 For Ramsay's career see, Farrington, *A Biographical Index*, p. 649.
95 NAS, CC/3/3/12, pp. 72–86.

CHAPTER 8

How Radical a Town? Dundee and the French Revolution

Bob Harris

During the 1790s, Dundee gained a lasting reputation for political disaffection and disorder. The Tree of Liberty riots of November 1792 were cited by ministers and their supporters in late 1792 as evidence of insurrectionary ambitions amongst the radical movement inspired by the French Revolution. This led, in an attempt to puncture the alarmist rhetoric of Pitt the Younger and his supporters, to the following mocking rejoinder from Thomas Erskine at a meeting at the end of December of the London-based Friends of the Liberty of the Press:

> *There was an old woman who liv'd at Dundee,*
> *And out of her backside there grew a Plum tree.*[1]

In Parliament, opposition Whig MP and friend of the radicals, Colonel Norman Macleod, talked of the ministry's 'insurrection at Dundee' as being in reality no more than 'an assemblage of a few boys, the eldest of whom did not exceed 16, to play at the game of Planting the Tree of Liberty'.[2]

But a child's game is not how most chose to see the disturbances. The 1793 trial of Thomas Fyshe Palmer for sedition once again put the town under the national spotlight for radical activity. In February 1794, Robert Dundas, the Lord Advocate, writing to his uncle, Henry Dundas about current plans to create domestic forces to maintain internal order in Britain, warned:

> Set the example in London & we shall immediately do the

business here [i.e. in Scotland] which I have no doubt will produce similar associations through the larger towns – only take care who are to be your lord lieutenants & sheriffs. Particularly Perth and Dundee.[3]

Fear of the Dundee 'mob' was evidently a major factor deterring farmers in Perthshire and the Carse of Gowrie from joining internal defence forces companies in 1794. George Paterson of Castle Huntly, whose estate lay a few miles to the south-west of the town, wrote in early September: 'Folk are loyal but lacking in military spirit to oppose invaders. They are in great fear of the Dundee mobs'.[4] In the later 1790s, the shadowy insurrectionary group linked to the United Irishmen, the United Scotsmen, had a presence in the town largely through the person of George Mealmaker. Transported for treason in 1798, and portrayed by some historians as the United Scotsmen's principal ideologue for his authorship of *The Moral and Political Catechism of Man, or a Dialogue between a Citizen of the World and an Inhabitant of Britain*, Mealmaker was a weaver from the Seagate, as his father had been.[5]

Local historians, of the nineteenth century and later, have tended to rehearse this reputation for political disloyalty and disorder largely uncritically, focusing particularly on the Tree of Liberty riots.[6] Yet the evidence on which such judgements have been made is often very slight, that is, if any evidence is produced at all. Who were the Dundee radicals of the 1790s, apart from Fyshe Palmer and Mealmaker? How many of them were there? Equally, scant attention has been paid to the strong evidence of loyalism and support for the political status quo amongst Dundee's citizenry in this decade. If we are to understand more fully the various and competing currents of opinion in the town in this decade, this loyal opinion needs to be brought into clearer focus.

In an effort to construct a more balanced picture, therefore, this chapter traces the rise and subsequent trajectories of both loyalist and radical politics in Dundee, and seeks to help fill, in a very modest way, a significant gap in the broader history of Scottish politics during the 1790s. Most work to date has been written from a national perspective, and detailed local or regional studies comparable to those which have existed for many years on English and Irish towns and regions are lacking for Scotland.[7] Admittedly, there are some significant obstacles, particularly looming gaps in the evidence. The Scottish authorities' attention with respect to radicalism was directed very firmly towards Edinburgh, centre of Scottish government and administration. 'J.B.', the principal informer on the radicals employed by the Lord Advocate, Robert Dundas – whose identity remains a mystery to this day – was based in Edinburgh. Robert Watt who was briefly in the pay of Dundas in late 1792 and early 1793, certainly claimed detailed knowledge of Dundee, as well as of Perth where he had been an apprentice, and of Glasgow; but in his capacity as an informer he seems to have travelled outside the capital on only two occasions.[8]

In late 1792, Robert Graham of Fintry, the Scottish Commissioner of the Excise who resided near Dundee, appears to have organised his own network of spies in the town in response to the Tree of Liberty rioting, but if any reports were written at all, none survive.[9] In late 1793, a man called Drummond was spying on local radical meetings, but we only know about this from one surviving report sent by a local revenue officer to Graham of Fintry, and even this referred to the likelihood that Drummond would soon be found out.[10] For the later 1790s and the United Scotsmen, the position is even worse. Of the sporadic reports from informers on the United Scotsmen that survive, none refer to Dundee.[11] There remains only the material collected or produced in the course of George Mealmaker's trial in 1798, which is not especially illuminating.[12]

Nor was there much in the way of a local press to shed light on responses to the events of the 1790s. Besides Edinburgh and Glasgow, only Aberdeen, Dumfries and Kelso boasted newspapers before the 1800s. Dundee did produce two relatively short-lived magazines – *The Dundee Repository of Political and Miscellaneous Information* (1793–94) and *The Dundee Magazine and Journal of the Times* (1799–1801) – both the creation of printer Thomas Colvill. These contained, however, strictly limited amounts of information on local affairs, and in the case of the earlier periodical hardly any at all. Occasionally, Dundee-based groups placed notices in the Edinburgh and Glasgow press and in the English press, and that is all that survives to alert us to their existence.

With regard to loyalism, the story is in most respects the same. Very few muster rolls of Scottish volunteer companies survive before 1803, when volunteer companies were re-formed (they had been stood down in 1801) to combat the invasion threat from Napoleonic France. However, there is some information about membership in the 1801 militia lists for Forfarshire, at least for the period after 1797 when the volunteer body was expanded significantly. Local archives contain little information relevant to either loyalism or radicalism, apart from the council minute books and treasurer's accounts, which from the 1720s and '30s comprised an increasingly bland and sparse record of official business.

Conclusions about the state of opinion in Dundee in the 1790s must, therefore, be tentative ones. There is much that remains hidden from view about the politics of this period, both at the national and local level; and it is doubtful whether much new evidence remains to be uncovered which will change this.

THE RISE AND FALL OF RADICALISM c. 1792–1795

The first radical society to be formed in Dundee in the 1790s was the Society of the Friends of the Constitution, established in mid September 1792.[13] A further society, called the Friends of Liberty, emerged probably in the spring of 1793. This second society was the one of which both Fyshe Palmer and Mealmaker were members.

About the precise origins of either society, little is known. The leading Perth radical society, the Perth Friends of the People, dated from mid August 1792[14], and given the close links between the towns, this may have influenced the timing of the emergence of the Friends of the Constitution. Between October and December 1792, however, radical societies sprang up across lowland Scotland, stimulated by an explosive conjunction of domestic and international conditions. The latter included the widespread dissemination of cheap editions of Thomas Paine's *Rights of Man* from the summer of 1792, and a fierce interest in the fate of the French Revolution then imperilled by attack from within and without.[15] Regionally, radical societies or groups emerged in the same period in Montrose, St Cyrus, Arbroath, Forfar and Kirriemuir.[16] There were also almost certainly pockets of radicals present within weaving villages and other manufacturing settlements in Angus and Perthshire.[17]

The better-known Scottish radical societies of the early 1790s represented cross-class alliances between wealthier merchants, manufacturers, dissenting ministers, tradesmen and artisans, especially weavers.[18] Dundee appears in this to have been no different, and a list of the chief reformers in Dundee compiled in late 1792 included five individuals described as 'rich'.[19] Their presence reflected in part the existence of several reformist currents which waxed and waned from the early 1780s, notably relating to burgh reform, but also the existence of deepening party divisions in Scottish politics from the period of the War of American Independence.[20] In the years immediately preceding 1792, a group of opposition Whigs had been active in the town and had greeted the early phases of the French Revolution with enthusiasm. Their number included the Rev. Robert Small, Dr Robert Stewart, and George Dempster of Dunnichen. Stewart, a successful surgeon, was, together with Small, the moving force behind the foundation of the Dundee Dispensary in 1782.[21] (See Chapter 5).

In 1790, the Dundee Whig club, of which Dempster was president, and Stewart and Small leading members, distinguished itself as one of only two Scottish bodies to send a congratulatory address to the French National Assembly.[22] (The other address came from the Aberdeen burgh reformers.) The club met on 14 July 1791 to mark the anniversary of the fall of the Bastille and toasts given included: 'May all Despotisms soon meet with the fate of French despotism'; 'Rights of Man, and an equal representation to the people'; as well as ones calling for the abolition of the slave trade and repeal of the Test Act.[23] However, by late 1792, many of these propertied opposition Whigs were not prepared to continue to support parliamentary reform, convinced that the conditions for such a campaign were no longer appropriate. Dempster refused the invitation to become president of the Friends of the Constitution, and by December 1792 was advising the authorities about how best to combat Paine's views.[24] Although identified as amongst the chief reformers in late 1792, and their reputation as reformers persisted,[25] there is no evidence that either Small or Stewart joined either of the radical societies. Nonetheless, on the ground of their being among the only 'three Democrates', the two of them were expelled from the Dundee Club, a body whose membership spanned the town's elites and neighbouring landowners, along with a Dr Willison (presumably Dr John Willison, a physician), in March 1793.[26]

No lists survive detailing membership of either society. As elsewhere in Britain, weavers and tradesmen and other artisans comprised the bulk of the rank and file. Known Dundee radicals included a watchmaker, several weavers, and other lesser tradesmen or artisans – a journeyman hairdresser, a staymaker and a stocking maker.[27] If anything, the Friends of Liberty appear to have a membership which was even more heavily slanted towards this sector of the local population than the Friends of the Constitution. The Dundee lower orders had demonstrated unequivocally their political awareness in 1777 in a demonstration against changes to the Corn Laws introduced into Parliament, when a large crowd had burnt the proposed bill in the market place.[28] The anti-patronage campaign of the early 1780s and anti-slave trade agitations from 1787 may also have fed support for reform in Dundee among lesser tradesmen and artisans. Yet more striking is the role of dissenting ministers within the radical ranks in Dundee. Fyshe Palmer, the Unitarian, is only the best known of these owing to his trial in 1793 and transportation. Others included James McEwan, an antiburgher minister who was a delegate to the second general convention of Scottish radicals held in Edinburgh between 30 April and 3 May 1793; James Donaldson, the Berean minister and a former shoemaker; and Neil Douglas, the relief minister.

Douglas is perhaps the most interesting of the three. A member of the Friends of the Constitution, he was one of their delegates to the third general convention of Scottish radicals held in the Scottish capital in the autumn of 1793, and Mealmaker was an elder of his church. In November 1793, Douglas sent William Skirving, the secretary of the Edinburgh Friends of the People, copies of his *Thoughts on Modern Politics*, the proceeds from the sale of which were to go to friends of the radical convention.[29] He was one of several dissenting ministers who regarded parliamentary reform as part of a wider programme of moral renewal. To this end, in 1792, he republished as an appendix to one his poems James Burgh's famous jeremiad from 1746, *Britain's Remembrancer, or the Danger Not Over*, a call to moral regeneration from a crisis of an earlier era.[30] Consistent too with this outlook, his formidable energy and commitment were being invested not in any lingering hopes for political reform but in the missionary movement which was launched north of the border in 1796.[31] At least one conservative suspected the missionary societies of being born of the same roots as the radical societies;[32] and the involvement of men such as Douglas helps to explain such views.

The role in this period of the dissenting ministry in radicalism in Dundee, and in Tayside in general, was unusual in a Scottish context in the degree of their influence. Why this should have been so is hard to say.

Dundee in the eighteenth century was a fertile environment for dissent, something which partly reflects the strength of support locally for the popular, evangelical wing of the Church of Scotland. In 1766, the town had unsuccessfully called John Witherspoon to one of the parish charges, a move resisted by his congregation in Paisley. (Witherspoon departed for North America and Princeton two years later.) In the first half of the century, the leading minister in the town had been John Willison, minister of the South Church between 1716 and 1750. Recently described as 'probably the most commonly read religious writer' in Scotland in the eighteenth century,[33] Willison was also the most notable early opponent of Moderatism in the Church of Scotland. He fought battles both with the Episcopalians and the Glasites, and was an advocate of rehabilitation of the Seceders. Another prolific clerical author and evangelical to make his mark locally was John Snodgrass. The foundation of the Glasite Church in Dundee drew on a rigid orthodox Presbyterian current of religious opinion. One contemporary remarked that in 1790, Dundonians filled five very large churches every Sunday, explaining this in terms of the town council foregoing its rights as patrons in favour of election of ministers.[34] The correlation, however, between religious dissent and political radicalism was not a simple one, and by no means all dissenting churches or congregations were supporters of the radical cause.[35] In 1794, the provost of Perth was looking for ways of allowing Glasites in his town to enrol as peace officers without their taking the requisite oath.[36] David Sangster, minister of the Relief Church in Perth, was denounced by a member of his congregation for preaching in favour of the French Revolution and against the war in 1794.[37] Unitarian influence in Scotland was very geographically confined in the 1790s and very recently implanted.[38] Neil Douglas, the radical relief minister, only arrived in Dundee from Cupar, Fife in December 1792.

The strength of support in Dundee for radicalism in late 1792 should not be exaggerated. The spy Robert Watt was told in October 1792 by the convenor of the Dundee Friends of the Constitution, William Bissett, a founder, that there were 40 in the society, although it had only just been formed at that point.[39] During the trial of Fyshe Palmer almost a year later (in September 1793), one witness stated that in July of that year, the Friends of Liberty had had a membership of around 30, although this may have been a deliberate underestimate.[40] These are small numbers, and their impact is diminished further by the fact that several individuals were apparently members of both Dundee radical societies.[41] Based on the fact that the Dundee Friends of the Constitution could afford to send only two men to the first general convention of Scottish radicals in early December – Perth, by contrast, sent nine – a membership of not more than 300 has been suggested.[42] Against these modest figures, however, must be set the fact that the radicals were able to call on sufficient numbers to enable them to take over a loyalist meeting in the town chaired by David Jobson in Dundee's West Church in December.[43] A total of 2,500 were said to be present at it, which one report claimed made it the largest meeting yet to have been held in the town.[44] At the meeting the radicals managed to have a pro-reform clause inserted into the loyal resolutions.

Surprisingly perhaps, given their reputation historically, the unfolding picture of limited support for the radical cause is further supported by the Tree of Liberty riots – as those in authority were keen to point out privately in correspondence with officials in Edinburgh in their aftermath.[45] The immediate catalyst for the disturbances had been news of Dumouriez's occupation of Brussels as the French Revolutionary armies pushed back the Austrian and Prussian forces which had threatened Paris, and thus the Revolution, earlier that summer. Several different strands of protest were interwoven within them, however, including worsening economic conditions during the autumn. Most notably, partly due to very wet weather, prices for coal rose sharply, leading burgh authorities, including Dundee, to take concerted action from September to supply coal at more reasonable rates.[46] Meal prices also showed some upwards movement owing to the bad weather during the harvest.

A ship bearing grain from Berwick was lying in the harbour but, owing to the Corn Act of 1791, could not be unloaded, which several contemporary accounts identified as the source of local tension. Following a deputation from some citizens calling for the grain to be disembarked, Provost Alexander Riddoch gained a dispensation from the Customs to unload it.[47] Opposition to excisemen was another significant aspect of the protest, although this hostility may have been stirred up by local brewers. An even more persistent feature, however, was the attachment of a section of the local population to the political symbol of the tree of liberty. As Riddoch later contended, they had taken 'a fancy of a Tree of Liberty'.[48]

This fancy had been provoked initially by the news of Dumouriez's entry into Brussels.[49] A tree of liberty, decorated by a lantern and a label bearing the words 'Liberty and Equality, no sinecures', was erected at the site of the old market cross at the very heart of the burgh. What led to disturbances was the decision by some young men, apparently under the influence of drink, to pull it down that same evening; and the following day, a Saturday, an advertisement appeared avowing an intention to avenge the insult by burning the young men in effigy on Tuesday evening. On the Monday, in the meantime, Riddoch received the deputation about the ship in the harbour unable to unload its cargo of grain. On Tuesday, the tree of liberty was re-erected, and a crowd bearing effigies of the young men formed behind a man carrying a flaming tar barrel, which marched through the streets crying liberty and equality. It attacked the house of the father of one of the men in the Hawkhill, and the houses of several excise officers. Later in the evening, the town bells were set ringing, although, on the personal intervention of Riddoch, this soon stopped. Throughout the night, a bonfire burnt, and the centre-piece of these revels was a tree of liberty. On the Wednesday, a meeting of inhabitants held to consider means to suppress the disturbances resolved to support the magistrates. That same evening, the tree was removed by Riddoch. On Friday, however, a crowd broke into the shrubbery of a townsman and seized one of his best trees which they planted at the centre of the market place, lit up with candles, and decorated with apples. On Sunday that town officers pulled it down, and two troops of dragoons entered Dundee to restore order on Monday.

The operation of the corn laws and hostility to excises and excisemen appear to have been contributory factors in the disturbances.[50] It was Customs officers who had initially refused to allow the ship in the harbour to unload its cargo of meal and the ship had remained in the harbour, unloaded, for sixteen days; and another target of the crowd on the Tuesday night, briefly, had been the Custom House.[51] Local excise officials were clearly profoundly troubled by the violence towards their property, one writing to Robert Dundas that the threats against the excisemen were so intense that 'there will soon be an end of charging the Duties of Excise in Dundee'.[52] James Mitchell alleged that the brewers were behind much of the hostility to the excisemen,[53] since methods of assessing beer had been changed only a few years previously, and had proved much more effective. The brewers had in response raised their prices.[54] Mitchell reported that they had also felt the 'Rod of Justice' for obstructing officers and committing frauds. There has also been growing opposition in recent years amongst the brewers in Scotland to local imposts on ale.[55] Finally, the Dundee labouring classes were certainly capable of protesting about meal prices and the availability of meal, as they had demonstrated earlier in the century (in 1720, 1773 and 1778) and were to do so again in August 1795, when the crowd seized meal from a ship in the harbour.[56] Meal prices were not notably high in late 1792, however, and there is no evidence that concern about the availability of grain was a particularly pressing matter.

Rather, it was politics that had brought sections of the Dundee populace into conflict with the authorities. The tree of liberty was a universally understood symbol of the cause of freedom and international republicanism.[57] Its erection in the market place was a signal affirmation of popular enthusiasm for the French Revolution and the causes it had become associated with; and it was the destruction of the tree that triggered the week of disturbances. On Tuesday night, the crowd had paraded a second tree of liberty around the town before fixing it to the front of the town house. Since the town house was the most prominent building of the town, fixing the symbol of French liberty to its door was a calculated provocation. A further tree was erected in the market place on Friday, and it is significant that Riddoch waited two days before ordering its removal.

One other aspect to the disturbances suggests political motivation. On the Tuesday night, the crowd had attacked the lodgings of one Lieutenant John Fyffe, who may have been selected for his public hostility to Fyshe Palmer. He had refused to play whist at the same table, and had threatened to break every bone in Palmer's body if he mentioned the subject of reform in his presence.[58] Being Graham of Fintry's man in the town, he was the authorities' eyes and ears during and following the disturbances. Fyffe himself was convinced the source of the disturbances was the 'inclinations & actions of a certain description of men to delude the unwary & ignorant into a belief of imaginary grievances' – the reformers, in other words. He also lamented the influence of 'scoundrels' from Forfar and Kirriemuir.[59]

Only a few hundred were involved in the disturbances, and the local authorities took succour from this fact. When the town's bells had been rung on Tuesday night, the usual signal for a celebration or gathering, few had responded; indeed many seem to have slipped away, leaving a core of two or three hundred on the streets. As Riddoch was keen to point out to Dundas after the trouble had subsided, this was from a population of around 23,000.[60] Following the riots, several Dundonians wrote letters to the press seeking to downplay their significance and asserting the fundamental loyalty of the town.[61] Many were evidently conscious of the reputation that the town had gained for being a radical haunt, so in subsequent months and years concerted steps were taken to efface this perception.

The authorities discovered not a jot of evidence that members of any radical society had been behind the rioting. Indeed, reaction to the disturbances by the Friends of the Constitution simply confirms the fundamentally moderate, peaceful nature of local reform ambitions in this period. They rushed to issue resolutions condemning the protests, testifying to their willingness to support local authority in maintaining peace and order.[62] Coincidentally, the Society was in communication with the Earl of Buchan about its existence and purpose.[63] They had almost certainly written to Buchan as a high profile Scottish member of the Whig Association of the Friends of the People, an aristocratic, moderate reform body formed in April 1792 with which the Scottish Friends of the People sought a close affiliation in late 1792. Radicals from Montrose spoke of the need for patience as well as 'steady, active resolution'.[64]

The optimism felt by Scottish radicals in late 1792 was to prove fleeting, and it seems very likely that numbers of radicals, or at least those attending radical meetings and supporting societies in Dundee, failed to grow from late 1792, and fell thereafter. This was part of a national pattern, and reflected the onset of demoralisation caused by the failure of Grey's reform motion of May 1793, and even more the impact of official repression and loyalist activity. During the spring and early summer of 1793, the radicals' decline may well have been masked by the attempts of some of the societies to exploit anti-war sentiment and economic downturn – consequent on Britain's entry into the war against Revolutionary France – to draw further support to the reform cause. On 2 January, the Dundee Friends of the Constitution issued a new set of resolutions, which including a condemnation of the war, which were reprinted in the *Edinburgh Gazetteer*.[65] The main charge against Fyshe Palmer was his role in the production and circulation of an address to their 'fellow citizens' drawn up and issued by the Dundee Friends of the People in July, denouncing what was described as 'this barbarous and calamitous war'.[66] However, the trial, conviction, and sentencing of Fyshe Palmer to seven years transportation in September 1793 almost certainly disrupted and intimidated radicals in Dundee. Whereas anger at the sentences of Thomas Muir and Palmer in Edinburgh and several other places galvanised what appears to have been a deflated cause, this appears not to have occurred in Dundee, although further public resolutions were issued by the Friends of the Constitution in June and October.[67]

Initially, Dundee radicals sent only one delegate – the Rev. James Donaldson – to the third general convention of Scottish radicals, and only prompting from William Skirving, the secretary of the Edinburgh Friends of the People, led them to send the Rev. Neil Douglas as well.[68] On 19 November 1793, it was reported that a meeting of radicals in the town had been called but so poorly attended that it was adjourned for a few days, and that hardly anybody had attended the reconvened gathering. The same informant observed: 'the People here much soured particularly as money is wanted – There are no persons of any respectability that now attend their meetings'.[69] There appears to have been some local concern about Skirving's plans for union with the English radicals, although this was probably less because of opposition to such an alliance, but because of the language Skirving was prone to use.[70] George Mealmaker and James Donaldson did attend the British convention as delegates from Dundee. (The British convention was in reality the reconvened third general convention which, with delegates from the London Corresponding Society, the Society for Constitutional Information and the Sheffield Society for Constitutional Information, turned itself into the British Convention.) Yet this attendance does not seem to have reflected any change in radicalism's condition in the town. By this stage, what radical gatherings did take place were in private and involved few.

Dundee radicalism was, therefore, already faltering before its end as an open movement was signalled by the suppression of the British convention in early December 1793, and the subsequent sedition trials in Edinburgh. There followed a confusing period when radicals in several places in Scotland, but probably not Dundee, sought to put into operation plans for an emergency British convention of radicals.[71] Several radicals from nearby Perth were also involved in the plan for a rising in

Edinburgh directed by the former government spy Robert Watt. In Dundee, seditious papers were allegedly distributed amongst Scots Fencibles, as part of the same plot.[72] Whatever the reality behind the talk and plotting, it reflected a deep vein of anger amongst radicals, an anger which probably reflected a sense of political impotence in the face of repression. In the crackdown which followed the accidental uncovering of the Watt Plot, George Mealmaker was arrested in Arbroath, where he had fled along with the Perth radical Robert Sands to the refuge of the home of Sands' father, but encountered a loyal mob with whom they fought, the ostensible reason for their arrest.[73]

Following the revelations of the Watt plot, and Watt's execution by hanging and drawing in Edinburgh in October 1794, Scottish radicals kept a very low profile. When the London Corresponding Society wrote to Scottish radical societies later in the same year calling for money to help fund the legal defence of leading English radicals, there was no response. The redoubtable Montrose inn keeper and informer, Susan Bean, was writing in the early summer of 1794 that the republicans were 'very busy', but in a 'private way'. In early July she wrote: 'I am sorry our Republicans have of late got much to say of the success of their friends the French they are very happy by appearance but afraid to say much'.[74] In 1795–96, partly under the impact of food shortages in England, the London Corresponding Society revived and sought renewed links with other radical societies.[75] These efforts elicited several responses from Dundee, which revealed a thoroughly cowed movement that lacked strategic direction. As Mealmaker wrote to the London Society on 3 September 1795:

> The late arbitrary proceedings of the enemies of liberty operated in so terrifying a manner on the Scots Patriots in general, that for a time their spirits sunk beneath the standard of mediocrity; in consequence of which their efforts became languid, and the sacred flame which had been kindled in their breasts almost extinguished.

Almost extinguished but not quite, because despite the 'formidable conspiracy . . . ranged against the cause of Truth, its principles are silently gaining ground, and a spirit of enquiry is manifest among all description of people . . .'[76] On 21 November, in a second letter, Mealmaker also urged the London Corresponding Society to make its publications cheaper so that they might fall within the reach of the purses of the 'labouring class of citizens'.[77]

Nor do food shortages in 1795–96 appear to have aided the radical cause. While one former radical or probable radical was involved in the riots at Dundee in August 1795, and there are hints of his having sought to politicise the protest, riots in general lacked political content.[78]

Open, constitutional radicalism made, therefore, only an evanescent appearance, and even at its height in late 1792 attracted but modest numbers. One explanation for this might be found in the reactions and activities of those who opposed, or who came to oppose, the radical cause in the 1790s.

THE RISE OF LOYALISM

From the summer of 1792, there was a marked polarisation of political opinion in Scotland. As the antiquarian John Pinkerton commented in 1794 in a letter to the Earl of Buchan, what people were then faced with was a 'choice of extremes'. On the one side was the government 'with its super-added abuses', and on the other 'the chance of mob tyranny'.[79] Most propertied individuals in and around Dundee appear to have opted squarely for the former.

The political rioting in Dundee, as well as several other places in Scotland in November 1792, served only to deepen this process. While there was no proof that members of the radical societies were involved directly in the protests, and the radicals moved quickly to distance themselves from them, such gestures had little or no apparent effect. To those already transfixed by the actions of the Paris mob in late 1792 – when the so-called September massacres in France fascinated and horrified the British press in equal measure – it seemed that Scotland, and Dundee, was menaced by its own Jacobin mob. The disturbances were concrete proof of the dangers of stirring up ambitions for reform amongst the lower orders. Those supporters of the status quo who took a more sanguine view of the radical threat recognised the benefits of the riots. As Douglas of Brigton wrote once they had died down: 'The mob at Dundee was nothing but a few hundreds of the miscreants of the Town & in place of doing harm they have in my opinion done a great service to the community by frightening a better sort of mob who kept within doors but who have now taken the alarm at being burned.'[80] The riots simply served to expose the large gap which existed between moderates within the reform movement and those less cautiously minded.

So the protests had the effect of polarising opinion even further, and of lending new urgency to the local task of defeating the radical threat and, as part of this, mobilising the forces of loyalism. There was also a desire to wipe away the stain of disloyalty created by the protests of late 1792. In Dundee, as in several other places, there was a special local motivation for highly visible public demonstrations of loyalty in the winter of 1792–93.

The initial steps taken to demonstrate this loyalty were far from successful. Public meetings in late 1792 were susceptible to being taken over by radicals, as had occurred in Dundee in December. Dissatisfaction with the content of the resolutions passed at this meeting appears to have led a group of the town's elite and neighbouring landowners, meeting as the Dundee Club, to organise a further testimony of loyalty at the beginning of the following February. Unlike the resolutions of December, this was signed individually.[81] Then, a few days later, the 'inhabitants of the town and neighbourhood' (in reality many of the most prosperous merchants and several professionals and officers of the Crown) subscribed a separate set of resolutions.[82] Both sets of resolutions were inserted in the Edinburgh and Glasgow press.

The Dundee Club took the more practical step to combat radicalism by raising a fund to pay for the dissemination of loyalist pamphlets and literature although similar propaganda appears to have been already circulating in Tayside. Perth was one of several Scottish towns to receive large volumes of loyalist pamphlets from London through the Post Office in late 1792; the other places were Edinburgh, Glasgow, Paisley and Greenock.[83] John Fyffe, who was later rewarded for his efforts (undisclosed) in the town at that time, wrote on 26 November 1792:

> The Avidity with which the last pamphlets have been read by the Farmers & Middle class of People, gives me reason to hope that short ones would have a good effect on the lower orders, if they were to be got which has never been the case as yet.[84]

Some weeks later, Douglas of Brigton was distributing such pamphlets at his own expense. Seeking to draw the attention of weavers to the benefits they derived from the government bounty paid on the export of linen, a statement making this case was drawn up and widely circulated;[85] and from sometime in early 1793, stamp offices were being used to disseminate loyal propaganda following an intervention by Graham of Fintry.[86] By March of the same year, George Dempster could report to Fintry: 'Every thing is quiet around us here and I think the diffusion of sound Political Pamphlets, among the People begins to operate considerably on their opinions.'[87]

Loyalism took various forms. Dundee town council issued loyal addresses on repeated occasions, starting with one in June 1792 prompted by the May Royal Proclamation against seditious writings.[88] In December 1792, the baker trade of Dundee issued their own loyal resolutions.[89] In March 1793, members of the coffee house in Dundee voted unanimously to stop a subscription to the *Edinburgh Gazetteer* on account of its radicalism.[90] William Brown, a Dundee bookseller, wrote several populist loyalist tracts which he sent to Edinburgh to Robert Dundas, who forwarded them to the Edinburgh loyal association, which had them printed. In 1794, Brown, who had also been the editor of *The Dundee Repository* and no doubt responsible for its pronounced loyalist stance, moved to Edinburgh where he became editor of the *Edinburgh Herald* and several subsequent loyalist papers.[91] The Rev. Dr Blinshall, who stood out locally as a loyal minister of the Church, was created a King's Chaplain in 1795 in recognition of his loyalty.[92]

Bounties were raised to aid recruitment to military forces. The town council funded such bounties on more than one occasion and they were also raised by private subscription.[93] They also demonstrated conspicuous support for recruitment to regiments stationed in the town, and, according to one report, 10,000 spectators gathered to watch a review of the second battalion of the 4th Fencibles in June 1794. A dinner with the officers of the regiment followed in the evening for local and neighbouring elites.[94] Several subscriptions were taken in support of families of those killed in the war effort or to fund clothing for troops wintering in Flanders. National initiatives organised from Edinburgh and fully publicised in the Edinburgh press, they attracted support from burghs throughout lowland Scotland, including Dundee.[95]

Towns were also sites of loyal spectacle and celebrations, annually on the king's birthday, and on the arrival of news of military victories in the war against Revolutionary France, and at military reviews. These events were carefully organised and publicised to emphasise the enthusiastic loyalty of the local citizenry. One report claimed that the 'rejoicings' on the king's birthday on 4 June 1794 were 'probably never exceeded, if equalled on any similar occasion'. The Revolution Club, formed in 1744 to celebrate the anniversary of William III's birthday (5 November), took a central role in these celebrations, as it had in 1793. At its meeting on 5 November 1793, under the chairmanship of the loyalist minister Dr James Blinshall,[96] it had expunged Thomas Fyshe Palmer from its list of members. Admiral Howe's naval victory over the French North Atlantic fleet – 'The Glorious First of June' – was enthusiastically greeted in early June 1794.[97] The celebrations which marked Duncan's victory at the Battle of Camperdown in 1797 appear to have been particularly elaborate, fittingly as Duncan was gentry, from the Duncans of Lundie, a long-established family of Dundee burgesses.[98] There is scant evidence that radicals managed to subvert these occasions.[99]

Defensive patriotism more accurately describes these phenomena, and by the later 1790s the war offered further opportunities for displays of it. In response to an invasion threat from revolutionary France in 1794, volunteer forces were enrolled as part of a wider plan to maintain internal stability and to provide for domestic defence. Volunteer infantry companies were formed in Dundee and several neighbouring towns.[100] In January 1797, in the aftermath of the abortive French invasion of Ireland, the local volunteers offered 'unanimously' to assume military duties in the town in the event of regular forces then stationed there being called away, emulating an initiative taken by the Royal Edinburgh and Royal Glasgow volunteers.[101] In 1797–98, there was a further major expansion in volunteering, provoked by the new invasion threat, and in March 1797, Dundee Council offered to raise a further 300 men for the defence of the town and county.[102] New volunteer companies were formed. In 1798, Pitt also introduced the voluntary subscription as a new means of raising money to finance the war effort, which again elicited a strong, positive local response.[103]

The salient question, however, is how broadly-based socially and how tenacious this spirit of loyalism was. There is, however, a marked paucity of evidence, for example, regarding the social composition of the volunteer forces before the later 1790s. Weavers, shoemakers and other artisans became volunteers in nearby Montrose, as early as 1794–95,[104] before the social composition of volunteering broadened three years later. Dundee may, of course, have been different, but there is some data for the later 1790s in the militia list for Dundee drawn up in 1801, which identified volunteers who were exempt from militia service.[105] 266 of the 741 Dundee men in this list had either '1R' or '2R' against their names, most likely a reference to the two battalions of volunteers mobilised in the town in 1801 each comprising 400 men exclusive of officers.[106] The most frequently occurring of the 31 different occupations represented among the 266 volunteers were weavers (162), followed some way behind by shoemakers (31) and flaxdressers (12).[107]

Loyal addresses, on the other hand, tended to be mainly subscribed to by members of the elites, which in Dundee meant mostly wealthy merchants. The loyal resolutions of February 1793 were signed by most of the important neighbouring landowners – Paterson of Castle Huntly, Hunter of Blackness, Duncan of Lundie, Laird of Strathmartine, Mylne of Mylnefield, Wedderburn of Ballindean – and prospering merchants – Jobsons, Pitcairns, Baxters, Morisons – as well as servants of the state.[108] A 'loyal' petition in opposition to a peace petition issued in Dundee in 1795 was signed by 347 individuals who were said by one correspondent to comprise a 'very great proportion of whatever is most respectable in the town, for character, opulence, or extent of dealing'.[109] For the lower orders, we have the evidence of the public loyal celebrations and spectacles of various kinds. Since these often provided free alcohol and food, no doubt motives for attendance varied greatly, and attendance might have been encouraged, to say the least, by employers and landowners. There were also those, at least in the early 1790s, who remained profoundly distrustful towards the political loyalties of the majority of the population.[110] However, opinions were also very susceptible to sharp shifts and fluctuations according to domestic and international conditions, and the evidence may be too slight to reach a firm conclusion.

THE UNITED SCOTSMEN AND THE LATER 1790s

Although supporters of the status quo appear to have been able to mobilise significant support from across society in the early 1790s, and again at critical moments in the later 1790s – notably 1797–98 – political dissent was never eradicated entirely. But it appears to have been embattled and sporadic. In 1795, a petition from Dundee called for an immediate peace in the war against France.[111] Contemporaries offered divergent views of the strength of local support for this initiative, but at least one frequent visitor to the town, Lord Kinnaird's gardener, was convinced that anti-war sentiment had taken a firm hold on the population of the town and neighbourhood.[112] There was, however, no protest against the so-called Gagging Acts, passed in 1795 by the Pitt ministry in a final effort to destroy domestic radicalism, such as occurred in Perth. In 1797, a general meeting of the incorporated trades of Dundee called for the dismissal of ministers as authors of 'all the miseries in which they and their countrymen are involved'.[113] There also seems to have been agitation to get up a peace petition, which one anonymous writer at least thought might well be supported by 'poor folks' owing to general ignorance, and also the 'scarcity of many and bad state of manufactures', a reference to the effects of a credit squeeze in the spring.[114] In the following year, the nine incorporated trades resolved to erect a bust of Charles James Fox in the Trades Hall 'as a testimony of their respect for that celebrated character'.[115]

In 1797, organised radicalism re-emerged in the clandestine form of the United Scotsmen. While the goals and scope of this organisation remain unclear, there were strong continuities with the earlier phase of radicalism, in terms both of personnel and aims.[116] There had always been a gap between the moderate leadership and a more extremist element amongst the rank and file, and radicals in Perth and Dundee had been implicated in the Watt Plot in 1794. In December 1793, an informant described George Mealmaker as a 'daring, dangerous fellow' for he seems to have been travelling through the north-east dispersing radical propaganda and, with fellow radicals in the town, was apparently openly boasting about plans to 'try their strength'. How far this went beyond talk is unknown, for the same informant noted that currently they had 'no arms'.[117] Mealmaker himself managed to persuade the authorities that he knew nothing of the Watt Plot, and was released without charge in 1794. A sermon printed in London in 1795 for the radical publisher John Smith, purporting to be by a certain 'G———— M————, M———— B———— C————n', may well have been by Mealmaker.[118] The sermon drew on and gave violent expression to a radical and apocalyptic strain in Presbyterianism which resurfaced under the impact of the French Revolution amongst some (although not all) Secessionist and independent congregations.

About the strength of the United Scotsmen in Dundee it is impossible to make an authoritative judgement, although the indications are that it was tiny. The provost of Perth refused to implement the Militia Act in 1797. Perthshire had been the site of violent and considerable anti-militia protests, which may have influenced his decision, but it appears that he was also concerned about the level of discontent and opposition in the town.[119] Much of Mealmaker's political activity in the later 1790s appear to have been focused on the Fife weaving communities, which had economic links to Dundee in the coarse linen trade, and the strength of the United Scotsmen regionally may have lain there rather than in Dundee itself. Fife, including Cupar, the county town, was the scene of violent anti-militia disturbances in 1797, as well as a petitioning campaign in favour of peace.[120] In Dundee, by contrast, the Act appears to have been implemented with neither opposition nor difficulty.[121]

Radicals were divided over whether to join the United Scotsmen, and certainly not all radicals who were still active in the later 1790s did so. Many of them were artisans, weavers and shoemakers, who had emerged as members of radical societies in late 1792, and whose political outlook was hardened by the experience of repression and frustration of their aims in the mid 1790s – men, in other words, like Mealmaker. Although their overall numbers were probably very small, they had continued access to radical newspapers and propaganda, and Dundee boasted a radical reading club in the later 1790s.[122] Local bookseller, Edward Lesslie was distributing similar material, including Paine's *The Age of Reason*.[123] In the earlier 1790s, he was one of two booksellers in Dundee who had received copies of the anti-war handbill issued by the Friends of Liberty; the other being Robert Miller.[124] Lesslie seems to have been an enterprising publisher as well as bookseller, for he was behind the production of a plan and a series of engravings of Dundee to accompany the separate and expanded publication of Robert Small's account of Dundee written for Sir John Sinclair's *Statistical Account of Scotland*. The engravings were also sold separately. He acted as an agent for the *Edinburgh Gazetteer* and later the *Scots Chronicle*, a paper founded in 1796 as the mouthpiece of the Scottish Opposition Whigs, as well as for several notable radical publications in the early 1790s.[125] In the early 1790s, he was identified by an informer as one of the main reformers in the town.[126] Whether he was a member of the United Scotsmen is unknown. His later career in the town was as a seller of cheap books. In

1809, he was librarian to the Rational Society, a reading and lecture club formed by a group of artisans. In this, his career may reflect a radical version of Enlightenment culture which took root in the town in the 1790s. In the early 1820s, he was again active politically, helping to organise a subscription for the then radical hero, Queen Caroline.[127]

About the activities of radicals at the end of the decade exceptionally little is known. There is no evidence that they were able to exploit the very serious social distress caused by the combination of unprecedented and sharp rises in food prices between 1799 and 1801 and trade depression as had been the case, for example, in Paisley.[128] Save a short-lived trade depression in 1793, and the food scares of 1795–96, economic conditions on Tayside remained relatively benign for much of the 1790s. In 1795–96, the authorities had taken very deliberate steps to prevent unrest and suffering created by high meal prices; in 1799–1801, even these efforts were exceeded.[129] In England, there is evidence of a subterranean shift in popular loyalties and of much 'passive dissidence'[130] by the end of the decade, and widespread agitation for peace revived. On Tayside at least, there is much less evidence of this, although the crisis of 1799–1801 remains one of the least studied periods in the history of later Georgian Scotland. There is evidence of a revival of the United Scotsmen in 1801–02, possibly linked to a British-wide conspiracy which was rendered abortive by the arrest of Colonel Despard in 1802.[131] In 1801, two trials for treason in Scotland were linked to this revival; one being of a Perth man, Thomas Wilson. A spy from Fife reported on supposed efforts to suborn the loyalties of Dundee's volunteers, but that is all we hear in the very scant records of the influence of the United Scotsmen in the town.[132]

By the end of the 1790s, little appears to have survived in Dundee of the radical politics which had emerged under the shadow of the early phases of the French Revolution. It had gained a foothold amongst sections of the skilled labouring classes, but was so quickly suppressed, cowed, or driven underground, that it is questionable just how well radicalism had ever been supported in Dundee during the 1790s. Even when the radical cause was at the height of its influence during the final months of 1792, the impression conveyed by the few extant sources is of a movement comprising only a committed minority. By the later 1790s, active radicals were a tiny group, probably significantly outnumbered by the volunteers (albeit there was a financial incentive for membership of the latter, as well as the benefit of exemption from militia service).[133]

Various factors account for this narrative of failure. Although repression was clearly very important, so was the degree of organisation and commitment of those who supported the political and social status quo. The propertied classes in Dundee rapidly closed ranks in defence of the existing political and social order in the 1790s, in part because it was more flexible than it was portrayed by reformers and radicals. But the political consensus which bound the propertied together was also, at bottom, a negative one, explained by the combination of domestic and international political conditions. The popular protests of late 1792 provided a focus for a deep rooted fear of the 'mob', which was steadily strengthening amongst the propertied classes during this period. Burgh reform had earlier attracted strong support in the 1780s, and was to do so again in the 1810s. By 1801, liberal forces were re-gathering in Dundee, signalled by the establishment of the *Dundee Weekly Advertiser* in that year, which was to become the major vehicle of middle-class protest politics in Dundee in the first two decades or so of the nineteenth century. One of its founders was that same Dr Robert Stewart who had been expelled from the Dundee Club in 1793 for his political views. It is very likely, moreover, that the experience of mobilising in support of peace and stability, and against the challenge posed by revolutionary France in the 1790s and Napoleonic France in the 1800s strengthened the political resolve and confidence of the middling ranks. Loyalism was not simply a conservative political force, as has been argued.[134]

Limited support for radicalism in the 1790s also had deeper-lying socio-economic roots.[135] The linen industry on Tayside and in Angus had generally prospered in the 1790s, partly owing to war-induced demand for sail cloth and brown linen. Supporters of the status quo in the early 1790s were happy to use the state of the industry and the role of a bounty on exports of coarse linen as a means of immunising local weavers against radicalism. Demand for labour was strong, which pushed wages higher. In 1792, tailors and weavers of household cloth increased their prices owing to recent wage increases among journeymen.[136] As James Donaldson wrote about the Carse of Gowrie, an area west of Dundee, in 1794:

> There is no doubt but the young people of both sexes, in this district, are induced to go into the manufacturing towns of Perth and Dundee, in consequence of the high wages they receive; and

therefore though it is evident that the vicinity of these towns is advantageous to this district in point of ready markets, yet it is also evident, that the same cause, has tended to raise the price of labour very considerably.[137]

There were periods of acute hardship for a labouring class with little margin for saving, especially in 1795–96 when food prices rose sharply – very sharply in 1799–1801. Yet it is remarkable how little success the radicals seem to have had in exploiting what hardship there was to draw support to their cause. In 1793, for example, reports from spies and the radicals themselves suggest that trade depression acted only to demoralise radicals and leave them critically short of funds.[138] Nor did the radicals appear to make much, if any, effort to politicise food protests. This may have partly been because the concerted efforts made to alleviate this hardship on the part of burgh authorities and wealthier townspeople served to deflect or discourage such attempts. The 1793 repeal of the duty on moving Scottish coal coastways, which reduced the price of coals for domestic use, was very enthusiastically greeted on Tayside.

Our knowledge, finally, of what happened to the tradition of radical politics represented by men such as Mealmaker is very limited. Tayside and Dundee fully participated in the revival of radical and reform politics which followed the end of the Napoleonic Wars, and in George Kinloch of Kinloch, the town boasted (if that is the right word) the only man of property arrested and charged for sedition in that period. Yet how much support there was for radical political reform and insurrectionary plots, as opposed to burgh reform, especially in the period 1819–20, is questionable. Kinloch claimed in a letter to the Lord Advocate written on 18 December that he had only attended the meeting on Magdalen Green after other 'gentlemen had refused to do so'. He went on: 'Dundee and all that part of Scotland is in a state of perfect tranquillity, although the poor are suffering great distress. There have been no training nor preparing of arms, nothing in short which indicates the smallest intention of resisting the laws in any way whatever'.[139] Kinloch obviously had an interest in saying this; however, there is little contemporary evidence of sustained radical agitation and arming outside of Renfrewshire and Lanarkshire.[140] The authorities thought likewise because the Seizure of Arms Act, one of the six acts passed in 1819 to suppress radicals, only applied in Scotland to these latter counties. The agitation surrounding the role of Queen Caroline in 1820 did, it is true, evoke a bigger response from Dundee and on Tayside, but this was partly because it was led by opposition Whigs and middle class reformers.[141] Why a revived popular radical tradition failed to establish a strong presence in Dundee and its hinterland is a question which only new research will answer.

NOTES

1 *Edinburgh Gazetteer*, 28 December 1792.
2 *Edinburgh Advertiser*, 14–18 December 1792.
3 Edinburgh University Library (EUL), Laing MSS II, 500, 554, Robert Dundas to Henry Dundas, 25 February 1794.
4 Blair Castle, Atholl Papers, 59 (1), 299, Paterson to Duke of Atholl, 5 September 1794. See also 261, Sir John Wedderburn, Balindean, to the Duke of Atholl, 19 July 1794; 283, same to same, 22 August 1794; 298, same to same, 4 September 1794; 301, Paterson to Duke of Atholl, 9 September 1794.
5 On Mealmaker's reputation, see e.g. E. W. McFarland, *Ireland and Scotland in the Age of Revolution: Planting the Green Bough* (Edinburgh, 1994), pp. 154–155.
6 James Maclaren, *The History of Dundee* (Dundee, 1874), pp. 136–138; Christopher A. Whatley, David B. Swinfen and Annette M. Smith, *The Life and Times of Dundee* (Edinburgh, 1993), pp. 128–130.
7 For convenient introductions to modern scholarship on Britain and Ireland, see H. T. Dickinson, *The Politics of the People in Eighteenth-Century Britain* (New York, 1994), ch. 7; Thomas Bartlett, David Dickson, Daire Keogh, Kevin Whelan (eds.), *1798: A Bicentenary Perspective* (Dublin, 2003), sections ii and iii.
8 National Archives of Scotland (NAS), RH 2/4/64, fols. 302–4b, Watt to Robert Dundas, 31 August 1792; fols. 318–319, Watt to Dundas, 21 Sept. 1792.
9 An annotated account of secret service monies drawn up in 1793 records a sum of £26 6s as having been paid to Graham of Fintry. Against this entry has been written 'Dundee'. (EUL, Laing MSS II, 500, 404–5: Accompt of money imprest in the hands of John Pringle Esquire His Majesty's Sheriff Depute of the County of Edinburgh on Account of Secret Services, 15 June 1793. See also EUL, Laing MSS II, 500, 566, memorandum for Mr Dundas [Henry] from Lord Advocate, April 1794, which shows that £33 were spent from the secret service funds at Dundee in the winter of 1792.)
10 NAS, Graham of Fintry Papers (microfilm copy), GD 151/11/3, James Mitchell, Dundee, to Graham of Fintry, 23 December 1793.
11 See e.g. EUL, Laing MSS II, 500, 1736, William Scott to Robert Dundas, 3 December 1797, which contains a list of 'citizens united' and 'citizens supposed to be united but not certain' from Perth.
12 NAS, High Court of Justiciary Papers, JC 26/281.
13 *Edinburgh Advertiser*, 2–5 October 1792, notice of 17 September.
14 *Edinburgh Advertiser*, 14–17 August 1792, notice of 14 August.
15 John Brims, 'The Scottish Democratic Movement in the Age of the French Revolution' (PhD thesis, University of Edinburgh, 1983), pp. 180–181, 228.

16 See EUL, Gen 1736, item 41, John Kinnear [on behalf of the Montrose Society of the Friends of the People for Constitutional Information] to the Earl of Buchan, 14 November. 1792; EUL, Laing MSS II, 500, 355, Andrew Dundas, Forfar, to Henry Dundas, 13 May 1793; NAS, RH 2/4/207, fol. 409, John Fyffe to Robert Graham of Fintry, Dundee, 25 November 1792; NAS, GD 151/11/39, James Watson, Arbroath, to Robert Graham of Fintry, 16 January 1793; *Edinburgh Gazetteer*, 7 December 1792, notice from Forfar, 1 December; *Edinburgh Gazetteer*, 14 December 1792, notices from the Friends of Liberty and of the People, Forfar, 6 December, and the Friends of the People, on account of Parliamentary Reform and Constitutional Information, for the Parishes of St Cyrus, Laurencekirk and Garvock; *Edinburgh Gazetteer*, 22 January 1793, which contains a further notice from the St Cyrus society, as well as an 'Address to the Inhabitants' which had been drawn up on 19 November 1792.

17 See e.g. Newton Castle, Blairgowrie, Macpherson of Clunie Papers, bundle 95, Allan Macpherson to David Smyth, 21 May 1793 [concerning the circulation of the *Edinburgh Gazetteer* amongst weavers in Blairgowrie]; Blair Castle, Atholl Papers, 59 (1), 252, Sir William Murray of Ochtertyre to Duke of Atholl, 7 July 1794; 297, Col. Andrew Macpherson, Blairgowrie, to the Duke of Atholl, 3 September 1794; 298, Sir John Wedderburn of Balindean to Duke of Atholl, 4 September 1794; 311, Sir William Ramsay, Bamff House near Coupar Angus, to the Duke of Atholl, 21 September 1794; 318, John Buchanan, ? of Auchlesstrie, ? Cambusmound, to Duke of Atholl, 27 September 1794.

18 Brims, 'The Scottish Democratic Movement', p. 55.

19 NAS, RH 2/4/209, fol. 13.

20 For contemporary comment on this process of political assimilation, see John Wilde, *An Address to the Lately Formed Society of the Friends of the People* (Edinburgh, 1793), p. viii. For modern analysis, see Dalphy I. Fagerstrom, 'The American Revolutionary Movement in Scottish Opinion 1763–1783' (PhD thesis, University of Edinburgh, 1951), esp. ch. 8; Donald E. Ginter, *Whig Organisation in the General Election of 1790* (Berkeley and Los Angeles, 1967). There is no satisfactory modern study of the Burgh reform movement, but see E. C. Black, *The Association: British Extra-Parliamentary Political Organisation 1769 to 1793* (Harvard, 1963), ch. 5.

21 For Stewart, see ch. 5.

22 *Edinburgh Advertiser*, 27–31 August, 31 August – 3 September 1790.

23 *Edinburgh Herald*, 20 July 1791.

24 See esp. NAS, RH 2/4/66, fol. 200, William Pulteney to Henry Dundas, 4 December 1792; fols. 202–203, Dempster to Pulteney, December 1792.

25 Both signed loyal resolutions agreed to in February 1792 (*Edinburgh Herald*, 6 March 1793).

26 EUL, Laing MSS II, 500, 248–249, George Paterson to Robert Dundas, 11 March 1793.

27 See the list of witnesses in the trial of Thomas Fyshe Palmer (*The Trial of Thomas Fyshe Palmer* (Edinburgh, 1794), pp. 13–14); NAS, JC 26/280/3, item 8; NAS, RH 2/4/73, fols. 228–230, list of visitors to the Rev. Thomas Fyshe Palmer in Perth Jail, 1793.

28 *Dumfries Weekly Journal*, 20 May 1777.

29 NAS, RH 2/4/73, fols. 212–217, report of spy, 'J.B.', 22 November 1793.

30 Published under the title *A Monitory Address to Great Britain* (1792).

31 Neil Douglas, *Britain's Guilt, Danger and Duty; Several Sermons, preached at Anderston,*

near Glasgow; Aug 23, 1795 (Dundee, 1795); Neil Douglas, *Messiah's Curious Rest in the Latter Days; A Sermon Delivered in the Associate Church, Before the Missionary Society, Dundee, May 1 1797 And in the Relief Church, Dove-Hill, Glasgow, May 21* (Dundee, 1797).

32 EUL, Laing MSS II, 500, 1033, George Hill, St Mary's College, St Andrews, to Duke of Atholl, 2 March 1797. See too Hill's speech as moderator in the General Assembly in 1797 (Laing MSS II, 500, 1039–43).

33 John R. McIntosh, *Church and Theology in Enlightenment Scotland: The Popular Party, 1740–1800* (East Linton, 1998), p. 32.

34 *Edinburgh Advertiser*, 13–16 April 1790.

35 See Colin Kidd, 'Conditional Britons: The Scots Convenanting Tradition and the Eighteenth Century British State', *English Historical Review*, 117 (2002), 1147–76; E. Vincent, 'The Responses of Scottish Churchmen to the French Revolution, 1789–1802', *Scottish Historical Review*, LXXIII (1994), pp. 191–215; John Brims, 'The Covenanting Tradition and Scottish Radicalism in the 1790s', in Terry Brotherstone (ed.), *Covenant, Charter and Party: Traditions of Revolt and Protest in Modern Scottish History* (Aberdeen, 1989).

36 Blair Castle, Atholl Papers, 59 (1), 370, Provost James Ramsay to the Duke of Atholl, 18 November 1794.

37 Perth and Kinross Council Archives (PKCA), PE 51/25, Petition to the magistrates of Perth anent Mr Sangster using seditious expressions, 1 March 1794, declaration of Alex Waterson [with respect to same], n.d., but presumably 1794.

38 The first Unitarian Church in Scotland was founded in 1782 by William Christie, who dominated the St Cyrus Society of the Friends of the People. Other Unitarian Churches in 1792 existed in Edinburgh, Arbroath, Montrose, Newburgh, and Dundee.

39 NAS, RH 2/4/64, fols. 318–319, Watt to Robert Dundas, 21 September 1792.

40 *The Trial of the Revd Thomas Fyshe Palmer Before the Circuit Court of Justiciary, Held at Perth, on the 12th and 13th of September, 1793, on an Indictment for Seditious Practices* (Edinburgh, 1794), p. 96, evidence of James Ellis junior.

41 *The Trial of the Revd Thomas Fyshe Palmer*, p. 91, evidence of James Ellis.

42 Brims, 'The Scottish Democratic Movement', p. 191.

43 A merchant, Jobson appears to have had radical sympathies, visiting Fyshe Palmer in jail in early October 1793 along with another Dundee merchant, James Small (NAS, RH 2/4/73, fols. 228–30).

44 *Glasgow Courier*, 15 January 1793.

45 See e.g. NAS, RH 2/4/66, fols. 258–259, Alexander Riddoch to Henry Dundas, Dundee, 8 December 1792.

46 Dundee City Archives (DCA), Dundee Town Council Minute Book (TCM), XII, 1779–93, entry for 29 November 1792, where Provost Riddoch, responding to the 'outcry of the inhabitants', requested several merchants to organise the shipping of three cargoes of coal from England.

47 NAS, RH 2/4/209, fol. 13, where anonymous author of a memorandum on Scottish radicalism writes, 'The Corn Laws are unpopular, the people say one part of the Country may be starved, before they can be assisted from another.'

48 NAS, RH 2/4/207, fols. 393–394, Riddoch to Robert Graham, 24 November 1792.

49 The following account of the riots is largely based on letters contained in NAS, RH 2/4/207, fols. 367–419.

50 K. J. Logue, *Popular Disturbances in Scotland, 1780–1815* (2nd edn, Edinburgh, 2003), p. 152.

51 They were dissuaded from attacking the building.

52 NAS, RH 2/4/207, fols. 389–391.

53 NAS, RH 2/4/207, fol. 410, James Mitchell to Mr Adam Pearson, Excise Office, Edinburgh, 25 November 1792.

54 DCA, GD/HF/M1/1, sederunt book belonging to the fraternity of maltmen at Dundee, 26 November 1791.

55 See the notice placed by the Glasgow brewers in the *Glasgow Advertiser*, 4 May 1787.

56 See further below.

57 See Mona Ozouf, *Festivals and the French Revolution* (Cambridge, MA, 1988).

58 Logue, *Popular Disturbances*, p. 150. For later evidence of Fyffe's active anti-reform stance, see EUL, Laing MSS II, 500, 532, Fyffe to Robert Dundas, 'Intrepid', Plymouth Sound, 31 December 1793.

59 NAS, RH 2/4/207, fols. 413–418, John Fyffe to Robert Graham of Fintry, 25 November 1792.

60 See esp. NAS, RH 2/4/66, fols. 258–259, Riddoch to Henry Dundas, 8 December 1792.

61 See e.g., *Edinburgh Evening Courant*, 29 November 1792.

62 NAS, RH 2/4/207, fol. 398, resolutions of the Society of the Friends of the Constitution, Dundee, 21 November 1792.

63 EUL, Gen 1736, 27, James Duncan, junior to Earl of Buchan, 23 November 1792.

64 EUL, Gen 1736, 41, John Kinnear, Montrose, to Earl of Buchan, 14 November 1792.

65 *Edinburgh Gazetteer*, 8 January 1793, notice of 2 January.

66 NAS, JC 26/270.

67 *Edinburgh Gazetteer*, 27 July 1793, notice of 26 June; 5 November 1793, notice of 16 October.

68 NAS, JC 26/280/3, item 16.

69 NAS, RH 2/4/73, fol. 204 v, James Mitchell to Robert Dundas?, 19 November 1793.

70 NAS, JC 280/2, item 21, William Anderson, Dundee, to Skirving, 14 November 1793.

71 Bob Harris, 'Scottish-English Connections in the British Radicalism of the 1790s', in T. C. Smout (ed.), *Anglo-Scottish Relations* (Proceedings of the British Academy, Oxford, 2005), n.62, p. 202.

72 The best modern account of the confusing Watt Plot is to be found in John Barrell, *Imagining the King's Death: Figurative Treason, Fantasies of Regicide, 1793–1796* (Oxford, 2000), ch. 9.

73 NAS, RH 2/4/83, fols. 41–49, A Narrative of the Arrest, Examination & Imprisonment of George Mealmaker, n.d.

74 NAS, GD 151/11/3, Susan Bean to Graham of Fintry, 8 July 1794.

75 Harris, 'Scottish-English Connections', pp. 204–205.

76 Michael T. Davis (ed.), *The London Corresponding Society, 1792–1799*, 9 vols. (London, 2002), vol. II, pp. 165–166.

77 Mary Thale (ed.), *Selections From the Papers of the London Corresponding Society* (Cambridge, 1983), pp. 306, 308.

78 NAS, JC 11/41, circuit court minute book – Perth, criminal letters against David Ross; JC 26/288, criminal letters against David Ross, late sail duck manufacturer in Dundee for riot; criminal letters against Jean Gordon and others; JC 26/282, justiciary court process papers – 1795 – south, criminal letters against John Rodger and others; decla-

ration of Jean Gordon, 21 Aug 1795; declaration of John Rogers, 21 August 1795.

79 *The Literary Correspondence of John Pinkerton, Esq.* (2 vols., London, 1830), vol. 1, p. 354, John Pinkerton to the Earl of Buchan, quoted in Emma Vincent Macleod, 'The Scottish Opposition Whigs and the French Revolution', in Bob Harris (ed.), *Scotland in the Age of the French Revolution* (Edinburgh, 2005), p. 83.

80 NAS, GD 151/11/3, William Douglas to Graham of Fintry, 26 November 1792.

81 NAS, GD 151/11/30, Archibald Neilson to Graham of Fintry, 31 January 1793; *Edinburgh Herald*, 15 February 1793; *Glasgow Courier*, 15 February 1793. There were 62 signatories to the resolution.

82 *Edinburgh Herald*, 6 March 1793.

83 British Library, Add MS 16,920, fols. 144–147, John Freeling to ?, 28 December 1792.

84 GD 151/11/15, John Fyfe to Graham of Fintry, 26 November 1792.

85 See esp. EUL, Laing MSS II, 500, 248–249, George Paterson to Robert Dundas, 11 March 1793.

86 NAS, GD 151/11/39, John Wauchope to Graham of Fintry, 13 February 1793.

87 NAS, GD 151/11/8, Dempster to Graham of Fintry, 7 March 1793.

88 *Glasgow Courier*, 5 July 1792.

89 *Edinburgh Advertiser*, 14–18 December 1792.

90 EUL, Laing MSS II, 500, pp. 248–249, George Paterson to Robert Dundas, 11 March 1793.

91 For William Brown, see Bob Harris, 'Scotland's Newspapers, the French Revolution and Domestic Radicalism (*c.* 1789–1794), *Scottish Historical Review*, 84 (April 2005), p. 53.

92 NAS, GD 151/11/36, Patrick Stirling to Graham of Fintry, 26 March 1795.

93 *Edinburgh Advertiser*, 22–26 March 1793.

94 *Edinburgh Advertiser*, 17–20 June 1794.

95 See *Edinburgh Advertiser*, 5–8 November, 27–31 December 1793.

96 *Edinburgh Advertiser*, 4–5 June, 8–12 November 1793; 6–10 June 1794.

97 *Edinburgh Advertiser*, 13–17 June 1794.

98 See Bob Harris, 'Popular Politics in Angus and Perthshire in the 1790s', *Historical Research*, 80 (2007), pp. 518–544.

99 Harris, 'Popular Politics in Angus and Perthshire'.

100 Ibid.

101 *Edinburgh Advertiser*, 6–10 January 1797.

102 NAS, GD 151/11/29, James Mylne to Graham of Fintry, 12 March 1797.

103 EUL, Laing MSS II, 500, 1835, Paterson of Castle Huntly to Duke of Atholl, 2 March 1798.

104 Angus Archives, M1/1/9, Montrose Town Council Minutes 1771–1794, entries for 13 August, 17 September 1794; M1/1/10, Montrose Town Council Minutes 1794–1817, entry for 27 September 1795.

105 NAS, Forfarshire Sheriff Court Papers, SC 47/72/3.

106 The information on numbers of volunteers is derived from *The History of the Town of Dundee* (Dundee, 1804), p. 135.

107 The other occupations are: barber; basketmaker; brewer; butcher; candlemaker; carpenter; cooper; copper smith; cotton works; drummer; flesher; founder; gardener; manufacturer; mason; merchant; merchant's clerk; painter; plasterer; plumber; ropespinner; servant; stocking weaver; tailor; tinman; upholsterer; watchmaker; and wright.

108 The signatories are listed in the *Edinburgh Herald*, 15 Feb., 6 March 1793.

109 *Edinburgh Magazine*, XXI (1795), p. 319.

110 See e.g. NLS, Melville Papers, 14,838, fols. 88–91, George Paterson to Robert Dundas, 21 January 1793.

111 *Edinburgh Magazine*, XXI (1795), p. 319.

112 PKCA, Kinnaird Papers, MS 100, Bundle 9, James Anderson to Lord Kinnaird, 15 February 1795.

113 *Edinburgh Advertiser*, 11–14 April 1797.

114 NAS, Buccleuch Papers, GD224/676/2/, 'Loyal Subject', Dundee, to the Duke of Buccleuch, 1 April 1797.

115 *Scots Chronicle*, 3–6 April 1798.

116 See E. W. McFarland, *Ireland and Scotland in the Age of Revolution: Planting the Green Bough* (Edinburgh, 1994), chapters 5 and 6.

117 NAS, GD 151/11/26, James Mitchell, Dundee, to Graham of Fintry, 23 December 1793.

118 *A Sermon Delivered in Dundee, February 20th, 1795* (London, 1795).

119 Blair Castle, Atholl Papers, 59 (4), 386a, Archibald Campbell of Clathick to Duke of Atholl, 1 September 1797; 392, Alexander Fechney, provost of Perth, to Duke of Atholl, 3 September 1797; 406, George Paterson of Castle Huntly to Duke of Atholl, 4 September 1797.

120 Logue, *Popular Disturbances*, pp. 94–95, 112; NAS, RH 2/4/81, fols. 97–98, Claud Boswell, Sheriff of Fife, to Robert Dundas, 8 September 1797.

121 EUL, Laing MSS II, 500, 1406, Lord Douglas, Bothwell Castle, to Robert Dundas, 3 September 1797.

122 Davis (ed.), *The London Corresponding Society*, IV, 67.

123 As recorded in the records of Edinburgh bookseller, Alexander Leslie (NAS, High Court of Justiciary Papers, JC28/293).

124 For Miller's radical activities, see also NAS, JC 26/280, bundle 1, 35, Robert Miller to William Skirving [?], 15 October 1793.

125 See Harris, 'Print and Politics', in Harris (ed.), *Scotland in the Age of the French Revolution*, p. 169.

126 NAS, RH 2/4/209, fol. 13.

127 For Leslie and the Queen Caroline collection, see *Dundee, Perth and Cupar Advertiser*, 1 December 1820.

128 For signs of the tension and distress in the town, see e.g. *Scots Chronicle*, 4–6 April, 29 April – 2 May 1800.

129 NAS, Court of Session Papers, CS229/R5/27, A. Riddoch v Mckenzie & Linsay, 1802 (case concerns purchase of meal by council in 1801); DCA, Dundee Council Minute Book, XIII, 1793–1805, entries for 10 February, 5 August, 20 August, 29 September 1795; 11 February, 18 February, 19 March 1796; 29 March 1800; 5 January, 23 February, 16 June 1801.

130 J. Dinwiddy, 'Interpretations of anti-Jacobinism', in Mark Philp (ed.), *The French Revolution and British Popular Politics* (Cambridge, 1991), p. 48.

131 Roger Wells, *Insurrection: The British Experience 1795–1803* (Stroud, 1986), esp. ch. 10.

132 NAS, RH 2/4/87, fols. 155–158, copy of an examination lately taken by the Sheriff of Fife, sent to the Lord Advocate from an informer, 2 April 1802.

133 Austin Gee, *The British Volunteer Movement, 1794–1814* (Oxford, 2003), p. 57.

134 Linda Colley, *Britons: The Forging of the Nation, 1707–1837* (New Haven and London, 1992).

135 See esp. T. M. Devine, 'The Failure of Radical Reform in Scotland in the Late
     Eighteenth Century: the Social and Economic Context', in T. M. Devine (ed.),
     Conflict and Stability in Scottish Society 1700–1850 (Edinburgh, 1990), pp. 51–64;
     W. Hamish Fraser, *Conflict and Class: Scottish Workers 1700–1838* (Edinburgh, 1988),
     esp. pp. 65–72.
136 *Edinburgh Advertiser*, 21–25 September 1792.
137 James Donaldson, *General View of the Agriculture of the Carse of Gowrie* (1794),
     pp. 21–22.
138 See the correspondence between radicals from this period in NAS, JC 26/280.
139 William M. Roach, 'Radical Reform Movements in Scotland from 1815–1822 with
     Particular Reference to the West of Scotland' (unpublished PhD thesis, University of
     Glasgow, 1970), p. 396.
140 Roach, 'Radical Reform Movements', esp. p. 147.
141 See Christopher A. Whatley, *Scottish Society 1707–1830: Beyond Jacobitism, towards
     industrialisation* (Manchester, 2000), pp. 325–326.

CHAPTER 9

Urban Order in Georgian Dundee *c.* 1770–1820

David G. Barrie

Following a prison tour of Scotland and the North of England in the early nineteenth century, the Quaker minister, and penal reformer, Joseph John Gurney, surprisingly concluded: 'At Dundee there are no criminals'.[1] He painted the town in a positive light based largely on the fact that he 'found not a single criminal' in the local jail.[2] Indeed, magistrates who accompanied Gurney on his visit claimed 'that there had not been a criminal in it *for seven months*'.[3] Dundee was singled out as being amongst the most orderly of the main Scottish burghs, largely due to what was perceived to be the strong influence of religious instruction, the absence of large factories and the good character of local inhabitants.[4] Others concurred with this view. In his *Statistical Account* of Dundee in 1793, Rev. Robert Small gave the impression of a fairly orderly burgh and law-abiding people, although he stopped short of making comparisons with other towns:

> Of persons belonging to Dundee, who have been condemned, banished from their country for life, or executed, upon account of felonies, the writer of this account cannot, after much inquiry, find more than three during the whole course of the present century.[5]

A few observers, however, expressed concern that the character of the town had deteriorated in the face of social dislocation, demographic change and commercial expansion. In 1799, for instance, 'Philetas' reported in the *Dundee Magazine* that 'Vice, manufactures and population' had 'kept a steady growth together', but offered no further evidence.[6]

These contrasting contemporary observations encapsulate opinion on order and stability in eighteenth-century Scottish society. The traditional school of thought portrayed Scots as passive, obedient, and easy to control, whereas the revisionist view paints Scots as, at times, being disorderly, rebellious and anti-authoritarian.[7] But, with a few notable exceptions, attention has focused more on protest, riot and godly discipline than upon day-to-day urban criminality.[8] What little research has been carried out on the latter has suggested that Scotland was a comparatively violent society; for instance, in the second half of the eighteenth century, indicted women in the Scottish lowlands were more inclined to have resorted to violence than their European counterparts.[9] Scholars have pointed to a hardening of attitudes towards crime in the eighteenth century,[10] an increase in female Justiciary Court indictments between 1750 and 1815,[11] fragmented social relations and growing demands for social segregation in Edinburgh from the mid eighteenth century,[12] and a sharp rise in the level of criminal prosecutions in the first half of the nineteenth century.[13] The trend, therefore, has been to argue that the middle ranks, imbued with heightened anxiety caused by urban growth and social dislocation, perceived crime to be on the increase.

Unfortunately, attempts to gain a full picture of urban order in Georgian Dundee were hindered by the nature of existing sources. National criminal returns for Scotland were not published until 1836, whilst local court records prior to this date are often incomplete and lacking in detail beyond civil disputes. The eighteenth-century records for Dundee Burgh Court (which dealt primarily with less serious offences) consist solely of an index of names, which makes it impossible to determine the types of offences brought before the court and long-term trends in prosecution.[14] The more serious criminal cases in Dundee were remitted to Forfarshire Sheriff Court whose records are far richer. However, the criminal affairs of the court did not become separated from the civil until the mid 1820s, and most of the court's business was taken up with civil affairs, which makes criminal research a time-consuming process for often little reward.[15] The records of the North Circuit High Court (whose jurisdiction covered Perthshire, Forfarshire and Fife) contain a wealth of information, although these reveal more about trends in prosecution and attitudes towards crime than the actual levels of crime committed, and this court dealt only with the most serious indictable crimes.[16]

Indeed, the flexible and fiscally-prudent manner in which local procurators and magistrates administered criminal justice ensured that the recorded level of crime bore no relation to the real level of criminality. High Court prosecutions were very much at the discretion of procurators, who would often base their decision on whether or not to prosecute on the likelihood of conviction or payment of legal fees.[17] Similarly, lower court magistrates often chose to impose non-custodial punishments and informal sanctions rather than pursue formal legal action, especially when there were insufficient funds to bring forward a prosecution.[18] In Dundee, for instance, magistrates often decided not to prosecute suspects under warrants in custody so long as the latter agreed to quit the burgh for varying periods of time.[19] Moreover, private prosecutions were extremely rare due to the time and expense involved in pursuing a case through the courts. It is extremely likely, therefore, that large numbers of offenders were never actually prosecuted.[20]

Conclusions about the level of crime and lawlessness in late Georgian Dundee, therefore, will have to be tentative, especially for periods when the evidence is patchy. Yet, if used cautiously, criminal indictments can yield interesting comparative results, providing illuminating insights into levels of urban order, as well as the changing ways in which local burgesses perceived and assessed social stability. This chapter will explore these themes over the pre-war era, 1770–1792, during the French Revolutionary and Napoleonic Wars, 1793–1815, and during the post-Napoleonic period, 1816–1820.

PRE-WAR 1770–1792

Late eighteenth-century Dundee has acquired the reputation of being a volatile burgh that was susceptible to outbreaks of food rioting, popular protest and smuggling – activities that were by no means exclusive to Dundee.[21] Less well known is the level of serious indictable crime which came before the North Circuit (Perth) Court. These records paint a different picture of the burgh, especially when compared with other towns and parishes within the region as a whole. The porteous rolls (lists of criminal prosecutions) for the North Circuit (Perth) were fairly small in any case, but the number of indictments was particularly low for the accused who gave Dundee as their residence. Between 1775 and 1792, 253 offenders were indicted at Perth; of these, just 4% (of the 201 whose residence is known) came from Dundee (see Figure 9.1). Given that Dundee accounted for approximately 6% of all inhabitants within Forfarshire, Perthshire and Fife, this was proportionately 50% below the regional average. Moreover, Angus had considerably fewer indictments – both numerically and in relation to population – than its neighbouring counties. Dundee, despite having upwards of four times the population of many burghs within the three counties, had a lower rate of indictments – lagging behind the smaller burghs such as Newburgh and Kirriemuir. Despite having around a third fewer inhabitants, the Angus burghs of Montrose, Arbroath and Brechin had collectively double the number of indictments as Dundee (see Figure 9.2).

However, these figures, to some extent, reflect the fact that no Dundonians were prosecuted for 'social crimes' such as mobbing, rioting and assaulting Customs officers, despite serious food rioting having occurred in the burgh in 1778.[22] This is significant as such offences accounted for just over a third of indictments brought before the Perth Circuit Court (see Figure 9.3) and usually involved groups of offenders. Indeed, in terms of the number of cases prosecuted – as opposed to offenders – Dundee's returns were roughly proportionate to the town's population within the region. The disproportionately high number of indictments in many of the smaller burghs was nearly always the result

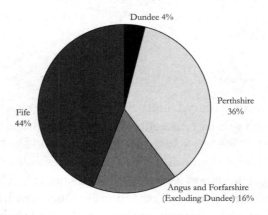

FIGURE 9.1
Residences of offenders indicted before North Circuit (Perth) 1775–92
(Based on 201 Cases where Residence is Known)

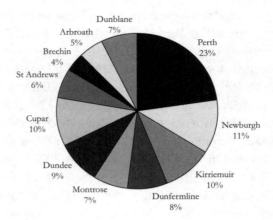

FIGURE 9.2
Burghs/parishes with highest indictment rates at North Circuit (Perth)
1775–92 (99 Cases)

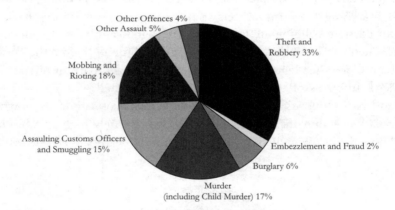

FIGURE 9.3
Offences for which accused were indicted at North Circuit (Perth) 1775–92
(244 Cases)

Sources for Figures 9.1 to 9.3: Returns collated from National Archives of Scotland (NAS),
'North Circuit Minute Books', JC11/31, 22 May 1775 to JC11/40, 2 May 1793.

of mobbing, rioting and assaulting Customs officers. These accounted
for all of the Newburgh indictments, all but one of Kirriemuir indictments, and around a quarter of Perth indictments. Why the Dundee
authorities should have been more reluctant than those in neighbouring
towns to prosecute those suspected of being involved in 'social protest' is

not clear,[23] for smuggling and mobbing were not uncommon in the burgh.[24] However, obtaining witness testimonies could be a problem, as revealed in a letter, sent in 1801 from the Sheriff Substitute of Forfarshire to the presiding judge, concerning recent riots over the transportation of barley in Dundee and Arbroath:

> On former occasions I have found it necessary to examine the witnesses as to the riots upon oath. Should your Lordship think any further investigations necessary I shall adopt that measure which will likely induce the persons examined to speak out which I have always found them very averse to do although no ways concerned in the mob.[25]

When considering indictments beyond 'social crimes', Dundee appears in a slightly less positive light. Within the three counties, only Perth had a higher indictment rate for crimes which did not involve a degree of social protest. Dundee's indictments involved serious offences such as murder, larceny, and assault and battery, often involving violence.[26] Nonetheless, the level of indictments for such offences was strikingly modest. Moreover, there were often fairly long periods of time, such as between 1784 and 1788, when no Dundonians were indicted before the Circuit Court at all. It was a similar story regarding indictments before the High Court in Edinburgh, with cases involving Dundonians being few and far between up to the late 1780s.[27]

The period 1775–80 saw the most indictments, but the numbers were too small to have any great significance.[28] The pattern of prosecutions concerning Dundonians remained fairly consistent – that is, sporadic and usually involving one or two offenders at a time. For the region as a whole, indictments at the Perth Circuit peaked between 1775 and 1778 and again between 1790 and 1792. These years saw a high number of prosecutions for mobbing and assaulting Customs officers, although there also appears to have been a significant increase in property crimes for the latter period.[29] This mirrored a similar trend in the Justiciary Court indictments for south-west Scotland.[30]

That few serious criminal cases involving Dundonians came before the Court of Justiciary is shown by the low number of offenders receiving capital convictions. Just two criminals from Dundee received the death sentence at the Perth Circuit between 1760 and 1792, and three more at the High Court in Edinburgh (based on those cases where the offender's residence is known).[31] This was slightly higher in relation to population than other burghs within the region, with the number of capital convictions at the Perth Circuit being fairly low (see Figures 9.4 and 9.5). However, the numbers involving Dundonians were still extremely small. These were very much in keeping with Scotland as a whole, which had fewer capital offences and a lower number of executions than other parts of the United Kingdom,[32] due mainly to contrasting legal systems rather than greater leniency on the part of Scottish courts. The capitally convicted in Dundee, as in other parts of Scotland, were less likely than their southern counterparts to have their sentences commuted to a lesser punishment, but the harshness of the Scottish system was mitigated by the fact that procurators were reluctant to prosecute under capital charges as it was difficult to secure a conviction.[33]

A more complete picture of urban order would require more research on the lesser courts, but the level of criminal indictments in these also appears to have been fairly low. Forfarshire Sheriff Court records in the 1780s reveal that references to fiscals as procurators rarely totalled more than twenty or thirty a year.[34] This suggests that the overwhelming majority of the court's dealings related to personal disputes and business transactions, given that private criminal prosecutions were extremely rare in eighteenth-century Scotland.[35] Sampled Sheriff Court processes confirmed this.[36] It is possible, however, that the absence of a Sheriff Court in the town (the local court was based in Forfar) reduced the willingness of victims to prosecute. Studies have suggested that the convenience of a local court encouraged victims to seek legal action as it reduced the time and travel involved in pursuing a case.[37]

Lawburrow Court returns were also fairly modest. Just 221 offenders,

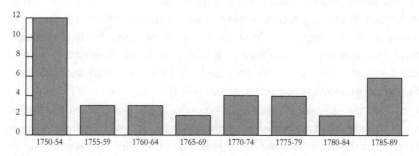

FIGURE 9.4: Number of capital convictions at North Circuit (Perth) 1750–89

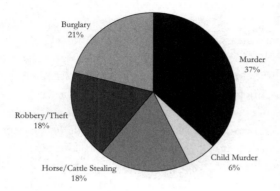

FIGURE 9.5

Offences for which offenders were capitally convicted at North Circuit (Perth) 1750–89 (33 Cases where offence is known: includes the capital convictions of Bruce, Ferguson and Dick at Edinburgh High Court in 1788 for breaking into the Dundee Banking Company).

Sources for Figures 9.4 and 9.5: Returns collated from NAS, 'North Circuit Minute Books', JC11/31, 22 May 1775 to JC11/40, 2 May 1793; 'Edinburgh Books of Adjournal', JC3/45 14 March 1788 to 24 March 1792; Perth and Kinross Council Archives (PKCA), B59/26/11, 'List of Sentences and Death Warrants'; and Alex F. Young, *The Encyclopaedia of Scottish Executions 1750 to 1963* (Kent, 1998).

or suspected offenders, were banished between 1775 and 1799, averaging less than ten a year.[38] Although some cases were fairly serious,[39] the majority were for relatively minor crimes, usually involving petty theft (see Figure 9.6). The expansion in the port and coastal shipping, with the influx of a large transient workforce, might have fostered an expansion in prostitution, but this is difficult both to substantiate and to quantify. The numbers banished for 'immoral practices' and 'keeping disorderly houses' were not large (see below), albeit the authorities might have turned a blind eye or dealt with them informally. Only the most hardened or 'notorious' offenders were banished, the majority of whom were eager to return and ply their trade.[40] This is perhaps indicative of the high demand for their services that one might expect in a flourishing port.

The number of Dundonians who claimed 'Lawburrows' to protect them from threats of bodily harm was not especially large either. This was a form of civil action which arose when two parties were in dispute,

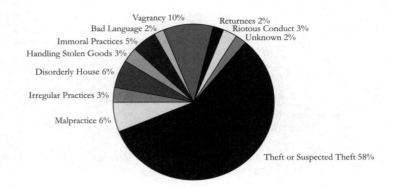

Vagrancy 10%
Bad Language 2%
Immoral Practices 5%
Handling Stolen Goods 3%
Disorderly House 6%
Irregular Practices 3%
Malpractice 6%
Returnees 2%
Riotous Conduct 3%
Unknown 2%
Theft or Suspected Theft 58%

FIGURE 9.6
Offences for which people were banished in Dundee Lawburrows Court 1775–99
(221 in total)

Source: Dundee City Archives (DCA), 'Lawburrows Books of Dundee, 1775 to 1799',
no reference numbers.

during which the petitioner would seek legal security that the defender
would not harm him or her, or the petitioner's family or property, under
financial penalty.[41] Between 1775 and 1790, just eighty Lawburrows
petitions were recorded.[42] Almost half of these involved disputes between
individuals who were both complainers and defenders. Such civil action
nearly always involved individuals from similar social and occupational
backgrounds (just over half involved artisans and retailers), indicating
that many of the disputes may have been business-related or quarrels
between neighbours.

Criminal indictments, of course, only measured crime which came
before the courts rather than crime committed. Nonetheless, other
indicators of urban order – such as attitudes towards crime, perceptions
of the labouring poor, and law enforcement and urban improvement
initiatives – also suggest that late Georgian Dundee was characterised by
long periods of relative calm. That is not to say, however, that there were
not significant periodic interruptions when fears of crime intensified and
attitudes towards it hardened. For instance, the moves to improve street
lighting in the early 1770s and 1780s (see Chapter 7) were indicative of
the fusion between a desire for improvement and increasing concern
with street crime.[43] Crucially, however, such heightened anxiety among

the propertied ranks tended to be confined to relatively short periods, which often coincided with downturns in the economy or the influx of large numbers of vagrants.[44] Voluntary subscription schemes for watching the streets at night became more prominent during short periods of mounting tension, and would then subside for much longer periods when urban order was more effectively restored. In 1772 and 1773, for instance, proposals were put forward to establish a paid night watch in the town in response to a reported rise in shop burglaries and riots.[45] Voluntary subscriptions were opened, but, significantly, contributions dwindled once tensions diminished. The system appears to have effectively collapsed, leaving a handful of town officers and part-time, unpaid constables for everyday policing.[46]

Vagrancy and food riots were the main concerns recorded in the minutes of the local council.[47] The latter have been well documented elsewhere,[48] but the disturbances during periods of scarcity and high prices which occurred in 1772–73 and 1778 arguably posed the biggest threat to urban order in this period. However, whilst the fear of the 'mob' was real,[49] it was by no means exclusive to Georgian Dundee. Other towns were also affected by rioting, and there is little evidence to suggest that those which occurred in Dundee in these years were any more threatening than those which occurred in other burghs. Concern with the wandering poor was more pressing. Once agricultural change in the region and the economic growth of the town combined to push and pull migrants to Georgian Dundee in ever increasing numbers, the streets and closes of the burgh were perceived as being 'infested' by hoards of beggars.[50] Much of the town's limited resources for maintaining urban order were therefore directed towards controlling them. In 1768 the council, 'considering the hardship the town labours under by the number of stranger beggars who are constantly therein', set up an inquiry to establish how many were native to the burgh and how many were migrants: the former were to receive begging badges, the latter were to be removed.[51] It had, however, little effect. A few years later councilors noted that 'the town has for these many years past been oppressed by beggars who do not belong to the town', which was a common complaint in many burghs during an era of rapid urban expansion.[52]

For much of the period between 1770 and the early to mid 1780s, therefore, the burgh's problems mirrored the experiences of other medium-sized towns. Short periods of heightened anxiety were separated by long periods of relative tranquility in which wandering poor, the 'mob' and crime rarely featured. Indeed, by contrast with Glasgow and Edinburgh, the only evidence of frayed social relations emerged in short bursts of violent protest during meal disturbances and periods of economic hardship.[53] In the main, the burgh does not appear to have been overly lawless.

There are a number of possible reasons for this. Gurney, following his visit to the burgh, argued that 'the small amount of crime' in the town was due to the universal religious education of the lower orders, and the pattern of small cottage industry which allowed for greater control and family supervision.[54] Although large numbers were employed in the expanding textile industries on the outskirts of town, the direct impact of industrial activity in the burgh was fairly limited in the late eighteenth century due to an insufficient supply of water power.[55] The local economy performed reasonably well,[56] and this long-term prosperity would have reduced any need to steal out of economic necessity.[57] Moreover, Dundee's rise in population from 12,426 in 1766 to 24,000 in 1800 was relatively modest when compared with many western burghs.[58] Dundee, therefore, was less affected by the social ills which demographic and industrial growth had brought to other towns. Furthermore, churches – traditionally an important mechanism of social control – appeared to have a stronger influence over the behaviour and morals of parishioners than in other large burghs.[59] That may partly be related to the town's large dissenting congregations, since church control was more effective in towns where dissent was strongest.[60]

However, from the mid to late 1780s and early 1790s, the character of the burgh began to change. The Church of Scotland in Dundee faced many of the challenges, not least keeping church provision in line with population growth, which were prevalent in other towns.[61] This made formal access to religious worship for the lower orders more difficult. As early as 1782, one Dundonian revealed that he attended dissenting services 'on Account of his not being able to pay for a seat in the established Church'.[62] In 1784, the Kirk Session complained that fornication was common in the port, with those involved increasingly refusing to pay fines because they belonged to different societies.[63] Moreover, Sabbath profanation appears with increasing regularity in the Session records from the third quarter of the eighteenth century: the Session reporting in 1782 that 'the profanation of the Lord's Day was becoming customary in this place'.[64] Rowdy behaviour of youths, disturbing the peace of the town and endangering the safety of property, also appeared to be on the increase.[65]

Indicative of this growing concern with a perceived rising tide of immorality, petty crime and disorder, was the employment of eight additional part-time constables in 1788[66] and the establishment of a network of religious organisations. These included a Sunday School in Hilltown in 1788, followed by another in Chapelshade a few years later and two more in Hawkhill and Blackscroft by 1794.[67] However, despite these, and Sabbath Evening and Bible Clubs, profanation of the Sabbath continued at an alarming rate, which added to middle-rank fears about urban order.[68]

Other indicators support the contemporary perception that crime rose in these years. Nine suspects from Dundee and its surrounding environs were indicted in Edinburgh between 1788 and 1789, the highest for ten years, and included high profile cases. In 1788, James Falconer, Patrick Bruce, both merchants in Dundee, and William Dick, shipmaster in Dundee, were found guilty of breaking into the Dundee Banking Company and stealing £423.[69] John Willox, innkeeper, and Thomas Howie, innkeeper, were also tried for the same offence but the jury returned a verdict of not proven.[70] Those found guilty were executed. In the same year, George Clark, James Caithness and Thomas Bisset, fishermen, West Haven near Dundee, were indicted for obstructing, assaulting and deforcing Dundee Customs officers in the nearby parish of Barry, one of whom was reported to have been beaten to the immediate danger of his life.[71] Indeed, Customs' records indicate that smuggling in the Tayside region was much more common than High Court records suggest.[72] Furthermore, between 1788 and 1793, the number of Dundonians who received capital convictions peaked over the period as a whole, with five death sentences being imposed – an unusually high number for the country as a whole.[73]

Returning soldiers from the American Revolutionary Wars (1775–83) are likely to have put a greater strain on the local economy and perhaps intensified fears of crime. Moreover, economic hardship and scarcity in the early 1790s resulted in heightened fears of local meal 'mobs'.[74] The last few years leading up to the Revolutionary and Napoleonic Wars, it seemed, had witnessed a slight change in the behaviour of the burgh's citizens, as was common in many burghs throughout the country.

WARTIME

The early years of the war heralded a return to a greater level of order. No Dundonians were indicted before the Edinburgh High Court between 24 January 1792 and 15 February 1796.[75] Prosecutions for sedition were common in other major burghs, often involving booksellers and publishers,[76] so the absence of Dundonians prosecuted is striking (see Chapter 10). There were food riots in 1795 and 1796, but in the main there is little telling evidence of heightened anxiety and increasing social tension up to the mid 1790s:[77] there was, for instance, a lull in law enforcement initiatives.[78] Such crime that was committed was more likely to be of a minor rather than serious nature, and no Dundonians received the death sentence between 1793 and 1798.

There are a number of reasons for this. The local economy flourished during the first few years of conflict, with the war increasing demand for sail cloth, hammocks and cheap shirtings.[79] At the same time, large numbers of young males, who were most likely to commit crime, were deployed overseas.[80] The *Dundee Advertiser* alluded to the absence of the burgh's 'dregs' in accounting for the streets being 'remarkably quiet' during long periods of wartime.[81] It is possible that a disproportionately high number of Dundonians might have been in the forces due to the efforts of the Impress Service, or Press Gang, which operated in Dundee and would seize able-bodied men to serve in the Navy. A small rendezvous, known as the 'Rondy', was stationed near the office house in the harbour under the authority of Captain Watson.[82] There are only a few recorded references to it in Customs and Excise records,[83] although there were occasional petitions to the council by the wives or relatives of those seized. It is possible that many debtors and petty criminals, who might otherwise have been formally charged, would have agreed to 'volunteer' rather than face prosecution. References to the Press Gang in the burgh's records often coincide with periods of economic downturn and a perceived rise in crime – as in 1790, 1803 and 1808 – when a larger pool of potential recruits was available.[84] This suggests that the Press Gang might also have been a mechanism for removing offenders during periods of escalating concerns with criminality.

The late 1790s and early 1800s (especially 1799 to 1801) saw widespread distress in the town due to a sharp rise in food prices and a downturn in trade.[85] Crime rose as a consequence,[86] and reports in the national press indicated increased social tension.[87] This was followed by further law enforcement initiatives and growing demands for police:[88] and additional constables were duly appointed.[89] Reports circulated in 1802 that magistrates, following a food riot in the previous year, were considering introducing a police bill.[90] Although a police force did not materialise, another fourteen constables were appointed in 1803.[91] Moreover, there was a sharp increase in the number of North Circuit (Perth) indictments in 1801–02 (see Figure 9.7), which rose to its highest level in thirty or so years. The overwhelming majority involved acts of theft or violence rather than mobbing or rioting (see Figure 9.8). Six of

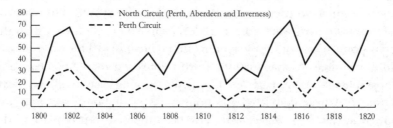

FIGURE 9.7
Number of annual returns of accused at North Circuit Court 1800–21

Sources: NAS, 'North Circuit Minute Books', JC11/44, 9 September 1799 to JC11/64, 7 April 1822.

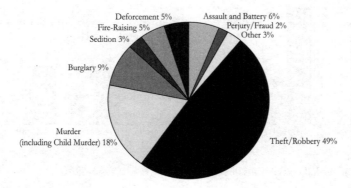

FIGURE 9.8
Offences for which accused were Indicted at North Circuit (Perth) 1800–05

Source: NAS, 'North Circuit Minute Books', JC11/44, 9 September 1799 to JC11/48, 21 April 1807.

these indictments in 1801 involved Dundonians – the highest number for the burgh for any year covered in this chapter. They included three indictments for robbery and burglary, and two for murder by duelling between soldiers on the beach east of Dundee.[92]

Capital convictions also increased to unusually high levels during this period, which is significant as courts were more likely to impose the death penalty during periods of 'moral panic' to serve as a deterrent to others. Five Dundonians were capitally convicted between 1799 and 1802 – two for robbery and three for burglary,[93] and the figure is likely to have been higher had the two soldiers indicted for murder after duelling in 1801 not absconded before the trial. Indeed, eight out of seventeen offenders who received capital convictions at Perth between 1793 and 1815, (whose residence is known) were from Dundee, proportionately higher than the burgh's population within the region (see Figure 9.9).[94] This was a greater ratio of criminals capitally convicted to population than Aberdeen, and comparable with Edinburgh and Glasgow.[95] Among them was John Watt, a Dundee weaver convicted for housebreaking, whose execution was reported in the *Scots Magazine* to have been the first to take place in the burgh for over a century (previously Dundee criminals had been executed either in Perth or Edinburgh).[96] It was believed that this move towards executing offenders in the locations where offences had been committed, bringing the Scottish system a little more in line with English practice,[97]

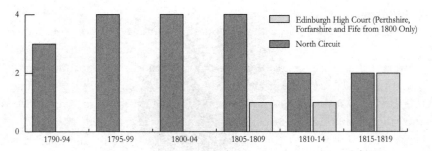

Figure 9.9
Number of capital convictions at North Circuit (Perth) 1790–1819

Sources: Returns collated from PKCA, B59/26/11, 'List of Sentences and Death Warrants'; Alex F. Young, *The Encyclopaedia of Scottish Executions 1750 to 1963* (Kent, 1998); NAS, 'North Circuit Minute Books', JC11/44, 9 September 1799 to JC11/61, 6 September 1820; and NAS, 'Edinburgh High Court Minute Books', JC8/1, 25 July 1799 to JC8/14, 14 February 1820.

would serve as a warning to local people (although the next execution in the burgh did not take place until 1826).[98]

For most of the Napoleonic War period, heightened anxiety over lawlessness was confined to particular issues and key events – one of which centred on theft from the workplace. In 1805, the *Dundee Advertiser* reported that local manufacturers had successfully prosecuted eighteen offenders for embezzlement and reset, which encouraged them 'not to compromise with such criminals in the future'.[99] They resolved to form an association and create a fund for the protection and punishment of all offenders.[100] This suggests a growing unwillingness to settle cases outwith the judicial system and was symbolic of a slackening in the ties between employers and employees. Two years later, the *Dundee Advertiser's* reported that several thefts had been committed at the shipping port. It concluded that 'exemplary punishment, in this instance, seems necessary', and implied that a short-term rise in criminality had resulted from rising unemployment and a periodic downturn in the linen trade.[101] According to a local mill manager, 'some of the spinners were put up in the Prison'.[102] Furthermore, a dip in the linen industry in 1811 seems to have stimulated a rise in property offences: for instance, increasing numbers of Dundonians were imprisoned in the local jail (see below); Circuit Court prosecutions increased (see Figure 9.7); and there were growing demands for more effective watching. This led to the employment of three 'stout men' to patrol the High Street and its immediate vicinity in 1814.[103]

Nonetheless, for most the period the burgh appeared remarkably quiet. Crime and disorder were rarely mentioned in the *Dundee Advertiser*. Even 'Letters to the Editor', a useful indicator of middle-rank perceptions of urban order, focused on relatively mundane issues.[104] The number of Dundee indictments at Perth and Edinburgh between 1800 and 1815 remained extremely modest, with no capital convictions between 1803 and 1813. An average of just nineteen prisoners per year were charged with criminal offences and committed to the local gaol between 1810 and 1815, almost half of whom were liberated without trial by order of the magistrates.[105]

Other indicators of urban order suggest that crime had not reached an intolerable level. Dundee was the only major burgh in Scotland not to introduce a salaried watch force under a local police act between 1800 and 1815. The uncoordinated efforts of different groups aimed at urban improvement proved to be sufficient in meeting the town's needs[106] (see Chapter 7). Moreover, the rate of urban growth in the burgh is likely to have helped keep the level of crime to a fairly tolerable level. It was much more modest than in many other towns, where watch forces had been introduced to deal with challenges posed by the influx of the wandering poor.[107] Furthermore, most urban expansion in Dundee appears to have taken place outside the city boundaries, in the industrial areas of Hawkhill and Scouringburn.[108] Significantly, the middle ranks continued to live in the town centre until well into the nineteenth century,[109] which might indicate that crime was more likely to be committed outwith the town boundary than within it. Finally, the relatively good performance of the economy, and the continuing enlistment of large numbers of young men into the forces, is also likely to have reduced pressure on the labour market and the need to steal because of poverty. Albeit with cyclical depressions, trade continued to boom during the war, with demand for hammocks, sail cloth and shirting increasing by almost 300% between the early 1790s and 1815.[110]

POST-WAR

The relative tranquillity which characterised many of the war years did not last. The end of the conflict heralded an escalation in social tensions and increasing fears about crime and its control. As an anonymous contributor to the *Dundee Advertiser* in 1815 noted, the post-war period had brought:

> an alarming increase in the number of nightly assaults and depre-
> dations committed in the streets of this town . . . [So long as
> foreign wars] 'drained the dregs' of our population, the streets . .
> . were in general remarkably quiet; but now indeed, the want of
> an inventive police begins to be felt severely.[111]

Crime, it seemed, had become more visible and attitudes towards it hardened. It was recorded with growing frequency, fuelling middle-rank anxiety about urban order. Much of the post-war alarm is likely to have been the result of media-generated 'moral panic' and sensationalist news reporting. Inflammatory language was used to portray the burgh as violent, lawless and out of control. The *Dundee Advertiser*, for instance, claimed in 1816 that 'depredations are becoming more and more frequent in our streets',[112] referring to the town as a 'den of danger'[113] infested by an 'organised army of thieves'.[114] Assault and robbery were so common, the paper reported, that 'numbers of citizens now carry loaded pistols for their defence at night'.[115] Much media attention was directed at vagrants, who were alleged to scar the streets in ever-increasing numbers, putting a further strain on a meagre poor law and charitable resources.[116]

Such reports were often exaggerated. They were designed to discredit self-appointed local officials and their management of local affairs, amidst widespread demands for burgh reform. Nonetheless, the evidence suggests that these claims were not completely without foundation. There was, for instance, an increase in the number of crime handbills, which is unlikely to have been solely the result of growing media interest and a hardening attitude towards crime.[117] Significantly, watching initiatives and demands for a system of police were more sustained than they had been previously. Between 1816 and 1823, at least five different watching schemes were introduced in Dundee; a Superintendent of Police was appointed in 1822; and the town acquired a Police Act in 1824.[118] At the same time, merchants and shopkeepers initiated measures to protect their own property, some employing watchmen to sleep in their shops,[119] whilst others erected iron bars over windows to protect them against the growing tide of burglaries.[120] A harbour watch was also established to protect shipping interests.[121] Whilst assaults, street robberies and riotous conduct took up much of the newspaper column inches, the watching initiatives which were introduced were very much driven by commercial interests rather than public safety as a whole.

Further concern with crime is illustrated by growing criticism of the system of prosecution which, it was reported, allowed large numbers of criminals to escape justice. News reports in the *Dundee Advertiser* claimed that it was extremely difficult to secure a criminal prosecution in the burgh due to a conflict of interest between local offices.[122] It was reported that magistrates rarely prosecuted criminals in the lesser courts so as not to burden the burgh with legal costs.[123] A letter to the editor of the *Dundee Advertiser* from 'a poor but honest man' summed up the correspondence of many: he complained that because he is poor 'he cannot obtain redress; [but] had a rich man, what is called a "respectable man", been insulted as I have been, 20 guineas of award in large characters would have graced the top of a hand bill'.[124]

What traditionally had been tolerated was increasingly frowned upon in the post-war period. Once a widely, although by no means universally, accepted form of social protest, a food riot in 1816 stimulated an unusually high level of concern and condemnation. The riot was reported in the local press as having 'shook the public peace and security of property'; Lord Justice Clarke described it as 'perhaps one of the greatest in modern times in this county'.[125] For short periods, the town had effectively been left at the mercy of the mob, which resulted in considerable damage to property with compensation claims amounting to over £300.[126] Although Provost Riddoch had been able to mingle with protesters in an attempt to allay their fears about food shortages, indicating that its danger should not be over-exaggerated, the disturbance did much to stimulate further demands for greater protection among the propertied classes.[127]

It may be significant that the 1816 riot followed press reports about the increasing level of disturbance in the town (albeit on a smaller scale).[128] These suggest that public peace was disturbed by rowdy behaviour on a regular basis.[129] Disorderly conduct and breach of the peace were amongst the most common offences brought before the local Police Court in the early nineteenth century.[130] Stobs Fair, the Lady Mary Fair and the king's birthday celebrations were all condemned for having descended into a cesspit of drunken debauchery, immorality and petty criminality, intensifying a process which had begun in the late eighteenth century.[131]

In keeping with national trends, the number of offenders imprisoned in the local jail grew significantly, greatly outstripping the rise in population (see Figure 9.10).[132] Although the rise may partly be explained

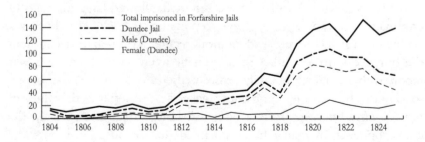

FIGURE 9.10
Number of prisoners committed to jail under warrants of magistrates, Sheriffs, Justices and Justiciary 1804–26

by changing attitudes, a growing willingness to prosecute, and more consistent recording (the returns for the early part of the century are suspiciously low), it is also likely to have reflected a change in behaviour. It coincided with a significant increase in Circuit and High Court prosecutions and a growing volume of Crown Office precognitions (available from 1812), the majority of which involved property offences.[133] Similarly, larger volumes of crimes came before local burgh and police courts following the introduction of the local Police Act in 1824,[134] the majority of which were for breach of local bye laws, petty thefts, misdemeanors, common assaults and riotous and disorderly conduct.[135] Nonetheless, it was further evidence that the character of the town was altering amidst a rising tide of criminality. Interestingly, Forfarshire had amongst the largest increase in recorded criminal investigations in the second quarter of the nineteenth century,[136] due in no small part to Dundee's rapid expansion after 1820.[137]

There were a number of reasons for the changing nature of the burgh. Demand for flax rose tenfold between 1815 and 1819, and ten new mills were built between 1818 and 1822 as Dundee geared up for industrial take-off.[138] Osnaburg production traded through the burgh, and the construction of new docks may have brought large numbers of labourers to Dundee and added to its transient workforce.[139] However, economic transition was far from smooth and periods of acute hardship were felt

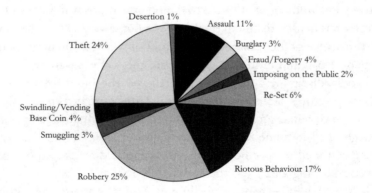

FIGURE 9.11
Offences for which offenders were imprisoned in Dundee Jail 1820 (99 in number)

Source for Figures 9.10 and 9.11: NAS, 'Calendar of Felons', Forfarshire, SC47/55/2.

by many. The immediate post-war years, in particular, were harsh for many Dundonians. That the overwhelming majority of offenders in the local jail were imprisoned for theft and robbery suggests that many crimes were committed out of economic necessity (see Figure 9.11). Peacetime brought an end to government contracts, falling real wage levels for many, and the return of young males looking for employment. At certain periods, the trade of the town was virtually stagnant which led to a rise in unemployment and mendicancy. These made the urban poor more visible, the streets appear less safe, and ultimately helped stimulate fears about law and order in the burgh.[140]

CONCLUSIONS

Given the level of 'dark crime' – crime which goes unreported, undetected, or is not prosecuted – conclusions about the level of urban order in late Georgian Dundee have to be offered tentatively. The growth in shipping and the large volume of sailors who passed through the port probably provided an environment conducive for prostitution, smuggling and petty theft. Moreover, Crown Office precognitions reveal a number of criminal investigations involving Dundonians which never came before the Circuit or High Court from 1812 onwards because of a lack of evidence and fiscal pressures.[141] Nonetheless, if much of its crime was hidden, Dundee was no different from other towns, so the comparatively low number of criminal trials and executions still suggests that the burgh was neither distinctively disorderly nor lawless. The generally good performance of the economy, the impact of war, a comparatively modest rate of urban and industrial growth and the – albeit waning – influence of godly discipline appear to have relieved the burgh of many of the social pressures faced in other large Scottish urban centres. Relations between different groups appear to have remained fairly harmonious.[142] Heightened awareness, anxiety and intolerance of crime and disorder were confined to specific periods of economic downturn, poor harvests in surrounding areas, and the ending of conflicts.

A final, and perhaps compelling, indicator of the relative orderliness of the burgh is provided by the middle-ranks' enthusiasm to continue living within the town centre alongside other social groups. In contrast to other burghs, social intermingling in Dundee continued until the mid nineteenth century.[143] Prior to this, there was no great desire for social segregation, largely due to the fact that the urban pressures were not as acute as they were in larger burghs. The middle ranks, in other words, perceived the town to be a relatively safe and orderly place in which to live, or, at least, one from which they were not desperate to escape. The 'urban crises' of crime and disease which affected other large Scottish cities had not blighted late Georgian Dundee to the same extent.[144]

NOTES

1 J. J. Gurney, *Notes on a Visit made to some of the Prisons in Scotland and the North of England, in Company with Elizabeth Fry; with some general Observations on the Subject of Prison Discipline* (London, 1819), pp. 25–26.

2 Ibid., p. 25.

3 Ibid.

4 Ibid., pp. 25–26 and 34.

5 *Old Statistical Accounts* [Online]. Available from: http://stat-acc-scot.edin.ac.uk/link/ 1791–99/Forfar/Dundee (hereafter: *Old Statistical Accounts*), p. 248.

6 Cited in C. A. Whatley, D. B. Swinfen and A. M. Smith, *The Life and Times of Dundee* (Edinburgh, 1993), p. 94.

7 See C. A. Whatley, *Scottish Society 1707–1830: Beyond Jacobitism, towards Industrialisation* (Manchester, 2000), pp. 142–149 for an overview of the traditional school of thought and passim for critique, but especially pp. 149–218.

8 See, for instance, C. A. Whatley, 'An Uninflammable People?', in I. Donnachie and C. A. Whatley (eds.), *The Manufacture of Scottish History* (Edinburgh, 1992); K. J. Logue, *Popular Disturbances in Scotland, 1780–1815* (Edinburgh, 1979); and T. M. Devine, (ed.), *Conflict and Stability in Scottish Society, 1700–1850* (Edinburgh, 1990).

9 Anne-Marie Kilday, *Women and Violent Crime in Enlightenment Scotland* (Suffolk, 2007), p. 148. Lenman and Parker, however, argue that Scotland was a more disciplined society in the years before the Industrial Revolution than has often been claimed. Bruce Lenman and Geoffrey Parker, 'Crime and Control in Scotland 1500–1800', *History Today*, 30 (1980), pp. 13–17.

10 C. A. Whatley, 'Labour in the Industrialising City, *c.* 1660–1830', in T. M. Devine and G. Jackson (eds.), *Glasgow. Volume I: Beginnings to 1830* (Manchester, 1995), pp. 382–383.

11 A. M. Kilday, 'Women and Crime in South-West Scotland: A Study of the Justiciary Court Records, 1750–1815' (PhD, Thesis, University of Strathclyde, 1998), pp. 347–352. Kilday tempers this increase by pointing out that demographic and legal changes make it impossible to say for certain that there was a long-term increase in the level of actual crime committed.

12 R. A. Houston, *Social Change in the Age of the Enlightenment: Edinburgh, 1660–1760* (Oxford, 1994), pp. 382–383.

13 I. Donnachie, ' "The Darker Side": A Speculative Survey of Scottish Crime during the First Half of the Nineteenth Century', *Scottish Economic and Social History*, 15 (1995), pp. 5–24 and Maurice C. Golden, 'Criminality and the Development of Policing in Dundee 1816–1833' (MPhil Thesis, University of Dundee, 2003), pp. 25–33.

14 Dundee City Archives (DCA), 'Burgh Court Records' (no reference numbers).

15 National Archives of Scotland (NAS), 'Forfarshire Sheriff Court Processes', SC47/22 series. Records of the Court's decrees – which might have illuminated the level of crime before the Court – are missing between 1750 and 1830. NAS, 'Forfarshire Sheriff Court Register of Decrees', SC47/7 series.

16 NAS, 'North Circuit Minute Books', JC11 series.

17 M. A. Crowther, 'Crime, Prosecution and Mercy: English Influence and Scottish Practice in the Early Nineteenth Century', in S. J. Connolly (ed.), *Kingdoms United? Great Britain and Ireland since 1500: Integration and Diversity* (Dublin, 1999), pp. 225–234.

18 See, for instance, DCA, 'Lawburrows Books of Dundee, 1775 to 1799', no reference numbers, and Whatley, *Scottish Society*, p. 286.

19 DCA, 'Lawburrows Books of Dundee, 1787–92'.

20 For problems using recorded indictments to measure and assess crime, see V. A. C. Gatrell, and T. B. Hadden, 'Criminal Statistics and their Interpretation', in E. A. Wrigley (ed.), *Nineteenth-Century Society. Essays in the Use of Quantitative Methods for the Study of Social Data* (Cambridge, 1972), pp. 372–378.

21 See, for instance, Whatley, Swinfen and Smith, *The Life and Times of Dundee*, although the authors emphasise that there were positive images of the burgh which should caution against overstating negative portrayals, pp. 95–102; S. G. E. Lythe, 'The Tayside Meal Mobs 1772–3', *Scottish Historical Review*, 46 (1967), pp. 26–36; and Frances Wilkins, *The Smuggling Story of Two Firths: Montrose to Dunbar* (Worcestershire, 1993), pp. 149 and 172–173.

22 Lythe, 'The Tayside Meal Mobs', pp. 26–36.

23 Whatley makes the same point. Whatley, *Scottish Society*, p. 204.

24 Whatley, Swinfen and Smith, *The Life and Times of Dundee*, pp. 95–102 and Wilkins, *The Smuggling Story of Two Firths*, pp. 149 and 172–173.

25 NAS, Letter dated 1801, 'Forfarshire Sheriff Substitute: Public Letter Book from 1795 to 1803', SC47/68/1.

26 These included George Smith, theft, 1775; William Maiden, murder, 1777–78; George Nicol and George Doctor, assault and battery, 1780–81; Archibald Stewart, theft, 1783–84; Duncan Fraser, theft, 1783–84; Andrew Yoal, theft, 1788; and Robert Brand, theft, 1789. See NAS, 'North Circuit Minute Books', JC11/31, 22 May 1775 to JC11/38, 27 September 1789.

27 See NAS, 'Edinburgh Books of Adjournal', JC3/45 series. Between 18 January 1785 and 13 August 1788, no Dundee criminal cases were uncovered in Edinburgh High Court Books of Adjournal. JC3/43, 18 January 1785 to 9 August 1786, and JC3/45, 14 March 1788 to 24 March 1792.

28 NAS, 'North Circuit Minute Books', JC11/31, 22 May 1775 to JC11/33, 25 September 1781.

29 Ibid., JC11/31, 22 May 1775 to JC11/40, 2 May 1793.

30 Kilday, 'Women and Crime', p. 345–352.

31 See Perth and Kinross Council Archives (PKCA), B59/26/11, 'List of Sentences and Death Warrants' and Alex F. Young, *The Encyclopaedia of Scottish Executions 1750 to 1963* (Kent, 1998), p. 48.

32 S. J. Connolly, 'Unnatural Death in Four Nations: Contrasts and Comparisons', in S. J. Connolly (ed.), *Kingdoms United?*, pp. 210–213.

33 Crowther, 'Crime, Prosecution and Mercy', pp. 229–235.

34 See, for instance, NAS, SC47/1/23.

35 NAS, 'Minute Book of Forfarshire Sheriff Court', SC47/1/23.

36 NAS, 'Forfarshire Sheriff Court Processes', SC47/22 series.

37 Peter King, 'Crime, Law and Society in Essex 1740–1820' (PhD, University of Cambridge, 1984), pp. 335–337; later published as *Crime and Law in England, 1750–1840* (Cambridge, 2006).

38 DCA, 'Lawburrows Books of Dundee, 1775 to 1799'.

39 Ibid.

40 Ibid.

41 *Encyclopaedia of the Laws of Scotland, Volume IX, Land Tax to Midwives* (Edinburgh, 1930), p. 53.

42 DCA, 'Lawburrows Books of Dundee, 1775 to 1790', No Reference Numbers.

43 B. Harris, 'Towns, Improvement and Cultural Change in Georgian Scotland: The Evidence of the Angus Burghs, *c.* 1760–1820', *Urban History*, 32 (2006), p. 209 and T. A. Markus, 'Buildings for the Sad, the Bad and the Mad in Urban Scotland 1780–1830', in T. A. Markus (ed.), *Order in Space and Society: Architectural Form and its Contexts in the Scottish Enlightenment* (Edinburgh, 1982), pp. 25–114.

44 See, for instance, DCA, Town Council Minutes (TCM), vol. XI, 1767–1779.

45 Ibid., 29 December 1772 and 25 October 1773.

46 There were no further references to subscriptions in the local records, with references to further watching initiatives in later years (outlined in main text) suggesting that the earlier schemes were only temporary.

47 See, for instance, DCA, TCM, 25 January 1773 and 11 March 1773.

48 Whatley, Swinfen and Smith, *The Life and Times of Dundee*, pp. 95–102 and S. G. E. Lythe, 'The Tayside Meal Mobs', pp. 26–36.

49 See B. Harris, 'How Radical a Town?', ch. 8 in this volume.

50 See NAS, Forfarshire Sheriff Court 'Note of Sentences Against Vagrants', SC47/55/1.

51 DCA, TCM, 27 October 1768.

52 Ibid., 11 March 1773.

53 For evidence of frayed social relations in Glasgow, see Whatley, *Scottish Society*, p. 159 and Whatley, 'Labour in the Industrialising City', p. 383. For Edinburgh, see Houston, *Social Change*, pp. 382–383.

54 Gurney, *Notes*, pp. 26 and 34. For a good overview of the views of penal reformers, see Joy Cameron, *Prisons and Punishment in Scotland from the Middle Ages to the Present Day* (Edinburgh, 1983), pp. 52–58.

55 Whatley, Swinfen and Smith, *The Life and Times of Dundee*, p. 64.

56 Ibid., p. 76.

57 Donnachie, ' "The Darker Side" ', p. 8.

58 *Old Statistical Accounts*, pp. 208 and 215.

59 Dundonians, for instance, were more likely than their counterparts in other burghs to admit fornication, illegitimate pregnancies were more likely to be detected, and the Kirk Session was less willing to accept money from sinners in lieu of appearance before the congregation as it would undermine the redemption principle enshrined in Calvinist doctrine. L. Leneman and R Mitchison, *Sin and the City. Sexuality and Social Control in Urban Scotland 1660–1780* (Edinburgh, 1998), pp. 35, 52–53, 72, 74, 77 and 95.

60 Ibid., p. 36. See also Ian McCraw, *The Kirks of Dundee Presbytery 1558–1999* (Friends of Dundee City Archives Publication No 3, 2000), Secession Congregations: pp. ix–xi.

61 For more on this, see Callum G. Brown, *Religion and Society in Scotland since 1707* (Edinburgh, 1997), pp. 96–97 and Harris, 'Towns, Improvement and Cultural Change in Georgian Scotland', p. 205.

62 Cited in Leneman and Mitchison, *Sin and the City*, p. 72.

63 NAS, 'Dundee Kirk Session Records', CH2/1218/6, 8 December 1784.

64 Ibid., CH2/1218/6, 7 November 1782.

65 Ibid., 18 April 1787 and 4 January 1792. Leneman and Mitchison, *Sin and the City*, pp. 17, 48–49.

66 DCA, TCM, 29 March and 7 October 1788.

67 NAS, 'Dundee Kirk Session Records', CH2/1218/7, 22 January 1794.

68 Ibid., and 13 February 1793, 10 April 1793 and 11 December 1799.

69 NAS, 'Edinburgh High Court Books of Adjournal', JC3/45, 13 August 1788 and 24–25 November 1788.

70 Ibid., 24–25 November 1788.

71 NAS, 'Edinburgh High Court Books of Adjournal', JC3/45, 1 December 1788.

72 Wilkins, *The Smuggling Story of Two Firths*, passim.

73 PKCA, B59/26/11, 'List of Sentences and Death Warrants'.

74 Whatley, Swinfen and Smith, *The Life and Times of Dundee*, p. 96 and 'Dundee Council Minute Book', 29 September 1792 and 29 November 1792.

75 NAS, 'Edinburgh High Court Book of Adjournal', JC3/46 24 January 1792 to 13 January 1794 and JC3/47 14 January 1794 to 15 February 1796.

76 Ibid.

77 For the response of local authorities and inhabitants, see DCA, TCM, 10 February 1795, 5 August 1795, 11 February 1796, 18 February 1796 and 27 November 1797.

78 DCA, TCM, vol. 13, 1793–1805.

79 Whatley, Swinfen and Smith, *The Life and Times of Dundee*, p. 65.

80 Clive Emsley, *Crime and Society in England 1750–1900*, Second Edition (London, 1996), pp. 32–33.

81 *Dundee, Perth and Cupar Advertiser*, 29 December 1815.

82 Thanks are owed to Malcolm Archibald who provided the information on the operation of the Press Gang in Dundee on which this discussion is based.

83 See, for instance, DCA, 'Customs and Excise Records', 14 October 1790, 25 November 1790, 1 April 1803, 24 April 1808 and 1 June 1808.

84 Ibid.

85 *Scots Chronicle*, 4–6 April and 29 April – 2 May 1800. See also C. A. Whatley 'Roots of 1790s Radicalism: Reviewing the Economic and Social Background', in B. Harris (ed.), *Scotland in the Age of the French Revolution* (Edinburgh, 2005), pp. 23–48.

86 See report by 'Philetus' in *Dundee Magazine in 1799* and also Whatley, Swinfen and Smith, *The Life and Times of Dundee*, p. 94.

87 *Scots Chronicle*, 4 – 6 April and 29 April – 2 May 1800.

88 Cited in Whatley, Swinfen and Smith, *The Life and Times of Dundee*, p. 94.

89 DCA, TCM, 6 October 1800 and 5 October 1801.

90 *Dundee, Perth and Cupar Advertiser*, 10 December 1802.

91 Ibid., 22 July 1803.

92 NAS, 'North Circuit Minute Books', JC11/45, 16 April 1801, 20 April 1801 and 23 October 1801.

93 PKCA, B59/26/11, 'List of Sentences and Death Warrants'; Young, *The Encyclopaedia of Scottish Executions*; NAS, 'North Circuit Minute Books', JC11/44, 9 September 1799

to JC11/46, 18 September 1802; and NAS, 'Edinburgh High Court Minute Books', JC8/1, 25 July 1799 to JC8/2, 7 March 1803.

94 PKCA, B59/26/11, 'List of Sentences and Death Warrants'; Young, *The Encyclopaedia of Scottish Executions*; NAS, 'North Circuit Minute Books, JC11/44, 9 September 1799 to JC11/55, 23 September 1816; and NAS, 'Edinburgh High Court Minute Books', JC8/1, 25 July 1799 to JC8/11, 6 April 1817.

95 Young, *The Encyclopaedia of Scottish Executions*, passim, cites 23 executions in Glasgow, 24 in Edinburgh and 3 in Aberdeen between 1793 and 1815.

96 *Scots Magazine*, June 1801.

97 The *Scots Magazine* in 1801 highlighted this, noting 'the determination of the Lords of the Justiciary, that in future all criminals who are sentenced to die shall be executed in the places where they committed the crimes for which their life is forfeited'. Ibid.

98 Jessie Sword, *They Did Wrong. Public Hangings in the Angus Area 1786 to 1868* (Friends of Dundee City Archives Publication No.5, 2005), pp. 40–43.

99 *Dundee, Perth and Cupar Advertiser*, 12 July 1805.

100 Ibid.

101 Ibid., 11 December 1807.

102 Cited in Whatley, Swinfen and Smith, *The Life and Times of Dundee*, p. 68.

103 *Dundee, Perth and Cupar Advertiser*, 9 December 1814.

104 See, for instance, 'Hints for preventing the destructive Caterpillar on Gooseberry Bushes', ibid., 7 June 1805.

105 'Returns of the Number of Persons Charged with Criminal Offences in England and Wales, Ireland and Scotland, 1822–3', Parliamentary Papers (P.P.), 1825 (197), XXIII, 523, mf. 27.184.

106 L. Miskell, 'From Conflict to Co-operation: Urban Improvement and the Case of Dundee, 1790–1850', *Urban History*, 29 (2002), pp. 356–358 and C. McKean, ' "Not even the trivial grace of a straight line" – or why Dundee never built a New Town', in L. Miskell, C. A. Whatley and B. Harris (eds.), *Victorian Dundee Image and Realities* (East Lothian, 2000), p. 22.

107 David G. Barrie, *Police in the Age of Improvement: Police Development and the Civic Tradition in Scotland, 1775–1865* (Cullompton, 2008), chapters 3 and 4.

108 Ibid.

109 Ibid., pp. 22–23.

110 G. Jackson and K. Kinnear, *The Trade and Shipping of Dundee, 1780–1850* (Dundee, 1991), pp. 6 and 77.

111 *Dundee, Perth and Cupar Advertiser*, 29 December 1815.

112 Ibid., 22 November 1816.

113 Ibid., 8 December 1820.

114 Ibid., 19 January 1821.

115 Ibid., 7 November 1822.

116 Ibid., 5 April 1816 and DCA, 'Minutes of Joint Meetings of the Magistrates and Town Council of Dundee and the Heritors and Kirk Session of the Parish of Dundee for the Administration of Poor Relief 1812–44'.

117 *Dundee, Perth and Cupar Advertiser*, 31 August 1821.

118 Ibid., 24 May 1816; 14 November 1817; 22 September 1820; 1 August 1821; DCA, TCM, 19 August 1817 and 5 George IV, cap. 129.

119 *Dundee, Perth and Cupar Advertiser*, 4 March 1824.

120 Ibid., 29 November 1816.

121 Golden, 'Criminality', p. 70.

122 *Dundee, Perth and Cupar Advertiser*, 21 May 1819.

123 *Dundee, Perth and Cupar Advertiser*, 29 November 1816.

124 Ibid., 21 May 1819.

125 Ibid., 28 March 1817.

126 DCA, TCM, 8 December 1819.

127 See, for instance, Council discussion on a proposal for a police bill, *Dundee, Perth and Cupar Advertiser*, 24 January 1817.

128 Ibid., 13 January 1815.

129 Ibid., 20 January 1815.

130 Golden, 'Criminality', p. 25.

131 Ian McCraw, *The Fairs of Dundee* (Dundee, 1993), pp. 41, 50 and 51 and Whatley, *Scottish Society*, p. 278.

132 'Returns of the Number of Persons charged with Criminal Offences in England and Wales, Ireland and Scotland 1822–3'.

133 NAS, 'Crown Office Precognitions', AD14 Series.

134 Golden, 'Criminality', pp. 25–26.

135 Whatley, *Scottish Society*, p. 287.

36 Donnachie, ' "The Darker Side" ', p .19.

37 Whatley, Swinfen and Smith, pp. 66–71.

138 Ibid., pp. 67–68.

139 Whatley, Swinfen and Smith, p. 79.

140 *Dundee, Perth and Cupar Advertiser*, 5 April 1816.

141 See NAS, AD14 series.

142 For growing tension in Glasgow, see Whatley, 'Labour in the Industrialising City', p. 383.

143 McKean, ' "Not even the trivial grace of a straight line" ' pp. 15–37.

144 Ibid., pp. 21–23 and Miskell, 'From Conflict to Co-operation', pp. 356–358. For Glasgow's urban crisis, see T. M. Devine, 'The Urban Crisis', in T.M Devine and G. Jackson (eds.), *Glasgow, Volume I: Beginnings to 1830* (Manchester, 1995), pp. 402–416.

CHAPTER 10

Merchants, the Middling Sort, and Cultural Life in Georgian Dundee[1]

Bob Harris

In the early eighteenth century, John Macky, erstwhile spy, adventurer, and Grub Street hack, remarked on the gentility of the merchants who presided over and whose ambition and activities forged the Georgian prosperity of Dundee and Montrose.[2] In the case of Montrose, such comments are unsurprising; the genteel credentials of Montrose were long-standing, and local gentry were an important component of the town's population, especially during the winter months.[3] However, Dundee has not latterly held the reputation of being fashionable town, and resident gentry were thin on the ground. The focus of this chapter is to examine changing patterns of cultural provision and changing cultural identities amongst the propertied classes of Georgian Dundee. As in previous centuries, Georgian Dundee's 'genteel' culture was one created by merchants and a small number of professionals (and their families), most of whom would have seen the town, and the town alone, as the proper stage for their ambitions and aspirations to status.

The chapter is divided into three. First, it charts the growing possession of new consumer goods and their display in the homes of especially wealthy merchants and other members of the middling sort. During the eighteenth century, possession and display of new luxuries became a key component of social identity amongst the middling ranks.[4] Many of these goods would have been bought in Perth, Edinburgh or even London; but from the final third of the eighteenth century, more local tradesmen and shopkeepers also began to supply them, and the second section of the chapter explores the development of this aspect of the burgh's economy. The third examines the emergence of new forms of

leisure and culture, especially in the public sphere. New types of entertainment, often involving new and distinctive patterns of association and
sociability, were notable aspects of urban change in this period[5], but ones
which are, as yet, poorly documented for most Scottish burghs.

However, evidence for such an investigation is patchy and uneven,
and tends to be heavily weighted in favour of the wealthy in society.
There is therefore a danger of offering an elitist portrayal of urban
cultural life and activities, and of neglecting the bulk of the middling sort
since its imprint in the historical record is much slighter.[6] Organisations
whose membership included a wider cross-section of the middling sort
(and even some artisans) – such as trades incorporations, Guildry and
freemasons' lodges and friendly societies of various types – often left only
an opaque or uninformative record of their social activities and importance. Whether such organisations had a diminishing if not residual,
importance in burgh life in the eighteenth century, as has been suggested,
requires more research, not just for Dundee but for Scotland in general.[7]
Speculative freemasonry, however, was one of the fastest growing organisations in Scotland from the 1730s, and its membership seems to have
encompassed a broad cross section of society, from landed gentry, at one
end, to artisans, at the other. By the end of the eighteenth century, there
were four lodges in Dundee; but we know, as yet, little about their
contribution to the burgh.[8]

Investigations of this kind are heavily reliant also on the press, for
there was a growing tendency for cultural entrepreneurs, brokers and
luxury tradesmen and shopkeepers to use the press to publicise their
activities. Yet far fewer did so than we might suppose. Before the second
half of the eighteenth century, much cultural activity took the form of
visiting entertainers whose activities, advertised using handbills or word
of mouth, are rarely documented. The Georgian burgh was a talking
town before it was one controlled by and through print. Indeed,
although several magazine-type publications were produced from the
1770s, the first Dundee newspaper to survive for any time was not
founded until 1801. So the existence of organisations is sometimes only
known through stray references. The sole mention, for example, of the
Dundee Scientific Society, from 1810, is to be found in sasines records.[9]
The extent of cultural provision may not only be under-recorded, but
even when sources are more abundant, straightforward questions such as
who, or how many, joined various societies are unanswerable.

Secondly, what was the composition of Dundee's elite and its middling sorts? Dundee's social elite was formed, in the main, from the ranks of prosperous local merchants. The term 'merchant' was used quite broadly in this period, but the elite group of merchants included individuals who were involved in manufacturing as well as trading in linen goods, and John Moir (fl. 1804–32) can stand as representative for them. He was involved in both manufacturing and trading in canvas, cotton and coffee bagging, sheetings, osnaburgs, sail and hammock cloth and yarn. A supplier for the Royal Navy, he was consigning goods to London, Liverpool, New York, Charleston and Jamaica, whilst importing flax from several Baltic ports.[10] The more successful merchants, like their counterparts in other ports in Britain, tended also to diversify into other activities, including banking (three banks had been founded by the early nineteenth century), whaling, sugar refining, brewing, cotton and woollen manufacturing, and, in one case, oil production.[11] Leading merchants traded regularly on commission for others.[12]

Dundee's merchant elite were defined primarily by their wealth and the scale and extent of their business interests. Quite a small body (of probably between 30 and 60 people), many of them were related either directly or through marriage (see also Chapter 1).[13] They were never a closed group, however, as the career of Alexander Riddoch illustrates. Riddoch, who rose to political dominance in Dundee in the final third of the eighteenth century, clinging on to power until 1817, was an incomer from the Perthshire parish of Monivaird. His wealth derived from diverse trading and business interests and some astute (some would say corrupt) speculation in urban property.[14] During the Georgian period, the urban elite changed quite markedly in composition, reflecting both the instability of commercial and manufacturing economies and demographic accident. Those who bought land and homes outside the town remained in a minority, and did not represent any departure from a wider pattern of diversifying assets.[15] The fact that relatively few purchased land may well reflect the relative modesty of their incomes and fortunes, when compared to, say, the merchant princes of Glasgow. It also probably reflects a habit, shared with other merchants in Britain, of purchasing villas on the edge of towns or a few miles from the town centre when looking to improve their domestic circumstances, as had been the case in the previous century. Ebenezer

Anderson originally occupied a tenement in the Cowgate – shop on the ground floor and living quarters on the first floor and in a garret. As he prospered in the early nineteenth century, he bought a villa on the south side of the Nethergate from the trustees of David Jobson junior[16] Isaac Watt, who seems to have had a keen sense of his self-worth, purchased and completely reformatted the house of Logie, before bankruptcy sometime in the early nineteenth century forced him to relinquish it, after which it quickly went through several hands, including David Fyffe's, a wealthy returnee from the West Indies.[17] Purchasers of estates in the town's hinterland in the later eighteenth century were more likely to be individuals who had had successful careers or prospered overseas in the West Indies or in the service of the East India Company (see Chapter 7) or in that of the British state. George Paterson, son of a Dundee corn merchant, who bought the Castle Lyon estate from the Earl of Strathmore in 1777 and returned it to its old name of Castle Huntly, had been a surgeon in the East India Company. David Laird, who bought the Strathmartine estate at about the same time, had enjoyed a successful career in the Royal Navy. Indeed, empire was also crucial to the revival of the fortunes of several local landed families – the Wedderburns, for example, the Fotheringhams of Powrie and Grahams of Duntrune.[18]

Dundee's merchant elite formed the apex of a much broader, diverse local middling class, which encompassed lesser merchants, shipmasters, numerous tradesmen and shopkeepers, as well as professionals of various kinds.[19] Dundee's shipmasters – around 100 such individuals are listed in first town directory (published in 1783) – prospered in the second half of the century (see Chapter 11). Yet the professional sector appears to have been relatively small for a town of Dundee's size, although there is currently a lack of comparative data to confirm this. This conclusion seems, nevertheless, to be borne out by Table 10.1.

The data tell us nothing about the incomes of professionals or the geographical range of their clientele which, if known, might cause us to read the totals in a different way. Several prosperous professionals made major contributions to the town's cultural life as, for example, the surgeon Robert Stewart – although his success may have been as much the consequence of his connections amongst the local landed elite as his practice in the town. Stewart was a key figure in the Speculative Society, Dundee's main Enlightenment club, and a supporter of the town's subscription library, founded in 1796. Together with the Rev. Robert

TABLE 10.1

Lawyers and medical practitioners, 1812–13

	Writers	Messengers at arms	Physicians	Surgeons	Apothecaries	Unclassified medical practitioners
Dundee	13	3	4	10	5	
Montrose	10	2	6	3	5	
Arbroath	7	3	2		2	2
Forfar	12	2				5
Brechin	5	3			1	5

Sources: *The Angus and Mearns Register for 1812* (Montrose, 1812); *The Angus and Mearns Register for 1813* (Montrose, 1813).

Small, he had been behind the formation of the town's dispensary in 1782. However, he had married into the gentry, his wife being one of two daughters of Charles Wedderburn of Pearsie, and the patronage of Sir Alexander Douglas seems to have been crucial to his success as a surgeon.[20] Stewart owned two houses, one a business address in the High Street, the other his main residence in Broughty Ferry,[21] then a fishing village with scattered villas. Judging by his estate, the physician Dr John Willison was another successful medical professional, although we know far less about him.[22] William Chalmers, town clerk and factor to Lord Kinnaird, whose main seat was on the Carse of Gowrie at Rossie, was probably the most successful of the Dundee's lawyers. He was one of very few individuals in the burgh to own, or at least be taxed for his ownership of, a gold watch in 1797–98.[23] These individuals set themselves apart through the strength of their links to local landed families. Thus, while Stewart's name, along with Willison's and Small's, appears in a dining book of Paterson of Castle Huntly's, no Dundee merchant or manufacturer was so honoured.[24] The boundary between town and country, frequently crossed in the Georgian period, remained very real for all that.

If there were, therefore, few professionals in the town, similarly small in number were resident gentry. Several gentry families did come to live in the town in the winter, but they were never at the front rank of landed society, and the habit faded in the later eighteenth century. William Murray of Ochtertyre spent the winter of 1733–34 in the town,[25] and Charles Wedderburn of Pearsie, recently returned from India, seems to have spent the winter of 1786–87 there. He and his wife later tended to go to Edinburgh or even, to the consternation of some friends and relations, remain in the freezing Angus braes.[26] In 1787, a friend of Wedderburn's wife declared, revealing at the same time the thinness of 'society' in the town: 'I hope you get a house in town next winter, I hear no word of Assemblies indeed I see nobody that is fit to appear at them.'[27] Hunter of Blackness was one of several landowners who maintained a property in the town at some point during the century, although the numbers doing so were never large.[28]

By the later eighteenth century, the 'pseudo gentry' included widows of wealthy merchants (an increasingly significant element in Dundee), wealthy returnees from the plantations, unmarried or widowed women from landed backgrounds living on a *rentier* income, and former officers in the armed services. As well as providing for their wives financially, in the form of an annual sum secured on their estate, merchants' wills usually contained provision for widows to have a life-rent in a property, as well as leaving household furnishings and goods to them.[29] Relatively few widows from landed families appear to have been resident in the town. When Robert Wedderburn of Pearsie died (in 1786), his wife gave up her life-rent in Pearsie House and appears to have lived in Dundee on an annual allowance of £200.[30] At around the same time, Mrs Fletcher, widow of Fletcher of Ballinshoe, was occupying one of the grandest houses in the town.[31] Even in the early nineteenth century, widows of landed gentry lived in several different parts of the town, including the Cowgate, which indicates how far the centre of the burgh retained a mixed social character.[32] The low number of such people is probably explained, from the later eighteenth century at least, by the existence of more attractive alternatives nearby. One was St Andrews, across the Tay in Fife;[33] but whereas George Dempster claimed for Broughty Ferry in 1810: 'The time is not very distant when this will be the winter Resort of most of us inland Lairds both for exercise & society',[34] that did not really transpire for another four decades. Prosperous landed families also tended to spend the winter in Edinburgh from the final third of the century, if not earlier.[35] Members of the gentry certainly visited Dundee on a fairly regular basis, but few of them normally resided there.

MATERIAL CULTURE

At the heart of far-reaching changes in the material culture of the middling ranks was the creation of much more richly and elaborately furnished domestic life, including the stricter demarcation of space within the home for different purposes such as display and hospitality.[36] One particularly significant development was the introduction of reception rooms into town houses, and in many Scottish homes, the principal reception room was the dining room.[37]

There is, unfortunately, very limited evidence on which to examine the extent to which Dundee's rich merchants and middling sort shared in this transformation. Notices of auctions of furniture and other household effects and of the rental or sale of houses that appeared in growing numbers in the newspapers suggest the quite widespread availability of genteel furnishings and accommodation from the end of the eighteenth century.[38] However, the potentially more revealing inventories of moveable estates, usually drawn up at the death of a householder, and the roup rolls of household furniture sold at the same point, are sparse and very unevenly distributed, especially before 1806.[39] Just sixty-four detailed inventories of household goods for residents of the town have been discovered for the period c. 1725–1820, too small and random a sample to attempt a serious statistical analysis. They are also heavily skewed towards the upper echelons of middling society – shipmasters, merchants, professionals, substantial brewers – although the odd minor tradesman is included.

Accepting such limitations, what do they reveal? First, by the early nineteenth century, reception rooms were becoming more common in the homes of the middling sort. Of the twenty-one inventories from the period 1800–20 which list furnishings in detail, ten houses had a dining room, and four a parlour; and their owners included an ironmonger, a millwright, a former Town Clerk, an architect (Samuel Bell), and several merchants.[40] The first inventory to include a dining room was recorded in 1767, belonging to the merchant, William Whiston.[41]

More homes contained fashionable drinking and serving utensils, such as crystal and glass decanters, punch bowls, ladles and glasses for the consumption of alcohol. William Chalmers had a particularly impressive cellar, including port, sherry, marsala, ginger wine, whisky, gin, rum, strong ale, and brandy, valued at £264 2s.[42] Chalmers' house had fourteen rooms – kitchen, dining room, drawing room, parlour, six bedrooms, sitting room, portico room, store room, and round room.[43] Fourteen-room houses, however, were certainly not the norm among the middling ranks in this period. Rather, most merchants and the middling sort lived in an apartment often above a shop or counting house. William Sturrock, for example, occupied an apartment of two bedrooms, pantry, and dining room off which there was a closet, a kitchen and cellars.[44] Even in the early nineteenth century, individuals of middling status were still living in quite modest circumstances, implying that the division between the elite and the rest may well have been a widening one, not least in terms of lifestyles.[45] John Wemyss, a merchant who died in 1799, left household goods valued at around £40, which included two dining tables, three easy chairs, four mirrors, a modest amount of china ware, and three decanters.[46] Thomas Muat, a confectioner who died in 1821, dwelt in a three roomed apartment above his shop, but his dining room was still well furnished with, inter alia, eight mahogany chairs and a Pembroke table.[47] In the households of tradesmen, it was a case of the purchase of a few, relatively inexpensive, newer pieces. By the final decades of the century, even weavers and other craftsmen might boast a few such objects in their houses.[48]

Fashionable high-status items regularly appear in the inventories only from the third quarter of the eighteenth century, although there were several exceptions. The household effects of Patrick Balneavis, for example, a merchant and former bailie who died in 1735, included feather beds, six fashionable Russia leather chairs, other upholstered chairs, and a large mirror. The household goods of James Hamilton, almost certainly a shipmaster rather than the sailor he was described as, were valued in 1758 at over £400, and included mahogany furniture, silverware, a mirror, and five pictures. By the third quarter of the century, genteel merchants, shipmasters, and professionals had become a part of Dundee society (see Chapter 11). In 1775, shipmaster John Martin left chinaware of various kinds, silver spoons, a mahogany table and chest of drawers, and a range of prints including the king and queen (presumably George III and Queen Charlotte).[49] Patrick Yeaman, a former provost who died in 1767, left an extensive array of household goods, including mahogany furniture (a 'very large' table, drawers, a bed stead), sixteen prints, chintz window curtains, a great deal of silver, china and glass ware, and a very substantial wine cellar.[50] These leave no room for doubt about the value that he placed on being able to offer fashionable hospitality to visitors. Other inventories from the subsequent two decades reinforce this picture. Merchant James Guthrie left household goods valued at well over £100, including a large mahogany dining table, prints, four carpets – including a 'France' carpet, three mirrors and a very substantial and quite diverse library.[51]

It is impossible to tell how typical such individuals were, or how typical it was of other Scottish burghs. In England, new consumer items had spread rapidly through propertied society from the later seventeenth century.[52] Similar developments appear in general to have occurred later north of the border, reflecting the country's relative lower level of urbanisation.[53] The question is how much later. Dundee's excellent sea communications with Edinburgh and particularly London meant that access to such goods was never a problem. Inventories imply that fashionable goods such as mirrors and mahogany furniture spread more slowly to and in Dundee than to towns like Montrose and Perth, which had a long and continuous history of gentrification – but only by a decade or two. This conclusion is consistent also with the evidence of the development of luxury trades in the town.

RETAILING GENTILITY:
THE RISE OF THE LUXURY SECTOR

Locating and identifying luxury trades and services in mid eighteenth century Dundee is difficult. The town contained a coffee house of some pretension in 1721 and specialist book sellers from a relatively early date – including Thomas Glass, publisher of the first book to be printed in the town in the eighteenth century (in 1768).[54] Probably in the early 1780s, Robert Nicoll opened the first commercial circulating library in the town, although he had been active as a bookseller in the town a decade earlier.[55] Burgess admissions record the presence of a staymaker in 1761; a stationer in 1765; a gunsmith in 1773 (continuing a traditional occupation of Renaissance Dundee); a periwig maker in 1773; an architect and a seedsman in 1783.[56] Although the town's first trade directory lacks sufficient detail to make a systematic assessment of the size and scope of Dundee's luxury trades, it contained two upholsterers, a jeweller, a small number of mantua makers and milliners, a music master, a singing master, and three dancing masters.[57] At least one cabinet maker was working in the town in 1781, although he is not listed in the directory.[58]

The luxury sector becomes much more visible several decades later, partly after 1801 when there was now a newspaper to provide a means of publicity. A clear expansion and increase in the capitalisation of luxury trades and services had taken place, one symptom of which was the rise of larger, more elaborate shops. By 1820, the book trade had grown considerably and diversified, and included a circulating library for French language books (opened in 1807), a dealer in part-number books, and a periodical publication warehouse (opened in 1816). Robert Donaldson's bookshop was one of the first retail establishments in the town to be lit by gas, in 1817. By 1825, the town also boasted an expanded educational sector, including four ladies academies.[59] Instruction in polite accomplishments such as dancing, drawing and painting, and elocution had become more widely available, and there had been a further development of music teaching. In 1807, in collaboration with the bookseller James Chalmers, Charles Duff, a musician, opened a music shop in Castle Street, selling instruments, including pianos, and music.[60] Those desiring it could readily find instruction on the piano, violin, viola, cello, and flute.[61]

Notable too was the increase in the numbers and diversity of luxury craftsmen and tradesmen. There were twenty-two cabinet makers by 1825, and trades new to the town included a carver and gilder, confectioner, perfumer, umbrella maker, watch and clock maker, coach maker, chair maker, portrait painter, engraver, lapidary, and toy dealer. Advertisements indicated a luxury sector of some buoyancy, and the existence of a market keenly attuned to national (usually meaning London in this period) fashions.[62] In April 1806, John Butterworth announced that he had returned from 'the principal manufacturing towns' having purchased 'a new and beautiful assortment of Goods for the Summer trade'. His goods included printed cambrics and calicoes, ginghams, muslins, dimities and cambric, furniture dimities and printed furnitures, shawls, stockings and laces, new arrivals of Adelphi cotton thread and a box of London-made hats in the newest shapes.[63] Most of the fashionable shops were clustered in the High Street, Crichton Street, and Castle Street (there were four 'elegant' shops below the Theatre Royal).[64] There were also periodic visits to the town from portrait painters and miniaturists.[65] In 1818, a new cookery shop opened at the head of the Seagate whose proprietor, Helen Lindsay, taught cooking and pastry, and advertised the provision of mock turtle and brown soup for dinner parties.[66]

Retailing luxury and genteel behaviour were thus important components of Dundee by the early nineteenth century, and there was strengthening demand for those goods and services deemed fashionable by contemporaries. Yet even by 1825, the luxury sector played only a minor part in the town's economy, employing a tiny number of people compared to the provision of more basic goods and services, and it was less important relative to other towns that enjoyed greater gentry patronage. It was also considerably less important than in several English manufacturing towns.[67] This almost certainly reflected differences both in wealth, and in its distribution within the urban population.

CULTURAL LIFE

If Dundee was home to relatively few luxury tradesmen and services, at least before the later eighteenth century, it also boasted few novel cultural attractions to tempt visitors and entertain its residents. There are isolated references to cock fights in Dundee in the 1720s and there was a substantial coffee room by the same decade.[68] There were brief visits by dramatic companies from Edinburgh in 1734 and 1755, and there is a reference to a musical society in 1757.[69] Only one record of any assembly being held before the final quarter of the century has been found, that being in 1735 – twelve years after regular assemblies had been established in the Scottish capital.[70]

One factor which inhibited cultural development was the influence of the Kirk and religiously-inspired opposition – especially to the theatre. The authority of the Church appears, unlike in other larger burghs, to have remained strong until the 1780s.[71] Dundee's most important minister in the first half of the eighteenth century was John Willison, an influential member of the popular wing of the Church, whose writings continued to be very widely read during the later eighteenth century; in the decades after 1760 the town was to become an important centre for religious dissent, including the Relief Church, Unitarianism, Secessionist churches, Quakers, Methodism, and, most famously, the Glasite Church. As late as 1784, the burgh authorities were still striving to prevent a theatre opening in the town.[72] After the 1760s moderates had, however, gained a firm foothold, following the appointment of ministers such as Rev. Dr Robert Small. A man of pronounced and broad intellectual interests, including astronomy, Small also appears to have been liberal in his theology and ecclesiology. In 1800, along with another Dundee minister, David Davidson, he was forced to defend his conduct before the local presbytery and then the General Assembly of the Kirk for admitting elders without requiring them to subscribe to the Westminster Confession.[73] The growing influence of such moderate ministers removed an important brake on cultural liberalisation.

One result was that Dundee, like other burghs in Scotland, saw significant cultural change during the final third of the century, a process which accelerated markedly in the opening decades of the nineteenth. Regular concerts and assemblies were held from the 1770s and '80s; touring companies staged plays and entertainments regularly from the 1760s, while the first permanent theatre emerged in 1800. By 1820, a cultural world of a new depth and range had come into existence, a world which sought to present itself in terms of its rationality and respectability, as well as its fashionability.

By the early nineteenth century, there were usually around eight assemblies per season – quite select gatherings sponsored by neighbouring gentry or the urban pseudo gentry. In addition to them, attendees probably came mostly from the ranks of the wealthy merchants and professionals. In 1809, a second series of subscription assemblies was organised in the Sailors' Hall, which probably drew on a slightly different cross-section of local society, although the 'respectability of the assembly' was still closely guarded.[74] However, the development of the Valentine Club in the later 1810s, which staged several balls a season, threatened the viability of the subscription assemblies.[75] The club appears to have operated on the basis of blackballing inappropriate members, and may have been an attempt to reinforce the social exclusivity of balls in the town. The first masquerade ball in Dundee, held in the Theatre Royal in 1820 (which after 1810 had taken over from the Exchange Coffee Room as the largest venue for such events in the town, and remained so until the construction of the Thistle Halls in 1826) was slightly spoilt by the fact that all the participants were readily identifiable, something which reinforces the impression of a small fashionable elite.[76]

It was not just the assembly room which drew the landed classes to the burgh. Clubs – the Dundee Club, for example, membership of which spanned urban and rural elites or freemasonry – provided other opportunities for county and urban notability to socialise.[77] Throughout the 1800s, one or other of the town's inns hosted the annual dinner of the Camperdown Club to mark the anniversary of Admiral Duncan's famous naval victory at the battle of Camperdown in 1797.[78] Dinners to celebrate the anniversaries of Fox's and Pitt's birthdays similarly involved rural and urban elites.[79] The Centre Bowmen, who have left little record of their activities, were probably drawn from the town's business elite and from among the neighbouring landed classes. They dined on an almost monthly basis, especially during the summer months, and held an annual archery competition.[80] During the 1790s and early 1800s, the rage for volunteering also provided regular occasions for dinners and balls, often sponsored by a landed notable.

The theatre, the circus (present in Dundee during the winters of 1806–07 and 1807–08, and again in 1814), and music all benefited from the patronage of landed gentry, in addition to ministers and professionals from the surrounding communities. In association with the circus, in 1808, Mr Humphreys, a riding master, offered instruction in the 'Polite Art of Riding and Managing . . . horses on the Road or in the Field'.[81] In 1810, the audience for the opening of the Theatre Royal in Dundee was described as 'numerous and genteel' and having included 'many strangers from Perth, Forfar, Arbroath, Cupar Fife, and the surrounding country'.[82] The nearest race course to Dundee was at Monifieth to the east of the town, and annual summer races were staged there. These drew to them members of the landed classes and, it appears, many other sections of Dundee society, perhaps drawn too by the foot races and pig chases.[83]

The expansion in cultural life was a consequence of growing numbers of outside cultural entrepreneurs – touring musicians, actors, exhibitors, as well as theatre managers – searching out new markets or rather audiences. Many of them were operating on a British-wide basis, or retailing London credentials to provincial audiences.[84] Alongside their activities, however, must be placed the efforts and ambitions of a series of important cultural brokers within the town, many of whom were employed in education. Dancing masters staged annual balls showcasing the efforts of their star pupils, as did music masters concerts. In England, church organists had long played a key role in musical life in provincial towns and cities. In early 1800s Dundee, much musical life in the burgh appears to have revolved around a Mr Rodgers, organist at the new Episcopalian Chapel in Castle Street. He gave and organised concerts in Montrose as well as Dundee. In 1815, Rodgers sought to leave Dundee, but following entreaties from local people and the amateur musical society, the Concord Club, he changed his mind.[85]

There was also significantly increased investment in cultural infrastructure from the 1790s. By 1800 there were two substantial inns in the town. The New Inn in the High Street incorporated a ballroom and six parlours. The second, Merchant's Inn and Hotel located on the corner of Castle Street, was described in 1813 as having been 'fitted up in a superior style', probably in response to the facilities on offer at the other.[86] Other spaces for meetings and entertainments included freemasons' lodges, which were regularly hired out as venues for this purpose.[87] Other cultural facilities were funded by subscription, drawing on the rising cultural aspirations of the merchant elite and other members of the middling sort. In 1812, a subscription was opened to create a public walk on Magdalen Green in Dundee, partly motivated by the closure of the Ward as an area of recreation in the town, and the long-standing use of the Meadows as a drying and bleaching green.[88] Proponents of the scheme argued that 'the inhabitants had long felt the want of public walks, and urged that 'Magdalen Yard might, at an expence of comparatively little trifling, be converted into one of the most convenient and beautiful places of public recreation in Scotland'.[89] The most striking example, however, of this type of investment in Dundee was the construction of the New Theatre in Castle Street, begun only a decade after the establishment of Dundee's first permanent theatre. Initially funded by a subscription of over £3,000, it was designed as a prominent statement of the refinement and cultural standing of the burgh.[90] The strength of local excitement and willingness to contribute financially to the project is indicated in a letter sent to Charles Wedderburn soon after the subscription was launched: 'Provost Riddoch has sold an area in Castle Street for a Theatre – in an hour or two 36 shares were subscribed at £25 each – next day 10 more – in short I suppose the whole £3,500 is already fill'd – Plan & Elevation hung up in the Coffee Room and if you don't make hast [sic] you will be too late.'[91]

The influence of Enlightenment rationalism and scientific culture is much more readily discernable by the early nineteenth century, and print in its myriad and multiplying forms was the crucial agent of change and

(*Left*). Couttie's Wynd. The principal route between the Nethergate and the Shore, curving through the densest of the Maritime Quarter. It exemplified the tightly woven and densely populated urban fabric which the later eighteenth century was beginning to perceive as not just insalubrious but rather alarming. (Dundee Central Library)

(*Below*). View of Dundee from Dudhope in 1818. This view, effectively from Dudhope Castle, shows Dundee just before its nineteenth-century expansion. However, industrial expansion was already taking place along the water course of the Scouringburn beyond the burgh boundary, rising up to the right. (Lamb's *Old Dundee*).

(*Bottom*). Polite recreation. The Ward Lands, to the north-west of the town centre, had formed part of Mary Queen of Scots' gift to the town, and had remained agricultural. In the later eighteenth century, they were planted and laid out with tree-lined walks for polite recreation. (Small)

(*Right*). George Clark was the 'gley-eyed' shipowner who led the opposition of the Council's short-sighted proposals for the harbour in 1814. This somewhat simian caricature is extracted from Harry Harwood's 1822 lampoon 'The Executive'.

(*Below*). The Exchange Coffee House, completed in 1828 on the edge of the Earl Grey Dock, was built for subscribing merchants who moved down here from the Trades Hall to be nearer the harbour. Designed by George Smith at the new shore level, it was constructed upon pre-existing vaulted storage at the original shore level 12 feet below. (Dundee University Archives)

transmission. A subscription library had been established in 1796,[92] the bulk of whose membership came from the ranks of local merchants, professionals, teachers and shopkeepers. Merchants, professionals, and tradesmen were well represented amongst the 159 subscribers identified in the Library's minute book, although there was also a small number of artisans.[93] The Library's management committee – elected every six months from the subscribers – included two merchants, a manufacturer, a shipmaster, and two shopkeepers in 1797; whereas three years later, it included a dyer, hosier, two watchmakers, baker, one of the ministers of the town, a merchant, a manufacturer, a schoolmaster, and an auctioneer. By 1807, the Library contained 1,873 volumes, including many Enlightenment classics, and important political as well as literary works.[94] Substantial private libraries were probably limited to members of the pseudo gentry, professionals, ministers, and a few wealthy merchants.[95] A corn merchant left a library in 1822 comprising 378 volumes, while slightly earlier, merchant James Guthrie left books which included religious, philosophical and many literary works, including the *Spectator* and *Female Spectator*.[96] Books were relatively expensive, however, and becoming more so in the early nineteenth century. Partly for this reason, private libraries were increasingly supplemented by circulating libraries. By 1813, there were four in Dundee, including that of James Chalmers in Castle Street, who boasted that it comprised around 5,000 volumes (although no catalogue survives). The catalogue of John Hamilton's circulating library in the High Street, in existence by January 1819,[97] contained 1,389 books in 1826, well over two-thirds of which were novels, a burgeoning literary form in this period, and the mainstay of many such libraries.[98]

The emergence of several societies, albeit often as an evanescent presence, also reflected the quickening circulation from the later eighteenth century of Enlightenment culture and values. The Dundee Speculative Society, in existence by the early 1770s, was apparently the first debating society in Scotland to admit women to its debates. The Rational Society, founded in 1809 and folding in 1821, appears to have had a membership comprising younger tradesmen and artisans. It may also have been a manifestation of a more radical current of Enlightenment culture which took root amongst a minority of professionals, artisans and shopkeepers. Closely associated with the Society was the radical bookseller Edward Lesslie, purveyor of cheap books.[99] The

Society held lectures on scientific subjects – in January 1814 a Mr James Nicol, a smith, gave 'a very ingenious essay on the properties and phenomena of steel', established a museum of scientific curiosities and instruments, and a modest library of British and European Enlightenment scholarship. George Don, the Forfar botanist who had created a botanic garden of considerable scale and contemporary interest outside Forfar, was elected an honorary member of the society in 1809.[100] A growing number of peripatetic scientific lecturers visited the burgh by the 1800s, retailing natural philosophy, mystery, and entertainment in equal measure.[101]

The membership of these societies was relatively modest, typical of such bodies elsewhere. There were twenty-six members of the Speculative Society in 1782, mostly drawn from the town's professional and mercantile elite.[102] Of the Dundee Scientific Society nothing is known, except that it existed, while the only piece of information we possess about the Dundee Botanical and Horticultural Society is that in 1814 it planned to create a library.

Although cultural life and habits in Dundee were therefore changing increasingly quickly by the early nineteenth century, the town remained, however, first and foremost, a port and manufacturing town. Its merchants and other members of the middling sort did indeed share in the important cultural changes that were transforming urban society. They were, moreover, possessed of sufficient confidence to develop their own new cultural horizons and forms of genteel living, no longer dependant on local gentry to show them how. At the fringes of landed society, there was little to separate the mercantile elite and lesser landed families, other than perhaps psychologically. David Laird of Strathmartine, being neither fully of the town nor country, highlights the ambiguities which could arise. A long-time resident of the town, he married one of the daughters of Dundee merchant George Yeaman of Balbeuchly (a member of one of Dundee's historic mercantile dynasties). Although local landowners may have provided patronage and support to various social activities, their influence overall appears to have been a waning one from the final third of the eighteenth century.

Much about this process of change still remains hidden from view, and it is very difficult to determine precisely how much changed and how fast, especially in the earlier period. Few Dundee merchants appear to have been trading overseas in the early eighteenth century. What they read and consumed and how they lived is largely unknown; although George Dempster, son of one of them, could declare to Henry Dundas in 1788: 'From a dirty Hole in which I was born, it [Dundee] has grown into a beautiful city'.[103] Whether Dundee's luxury sector was really a relatively small one, or Dundee's elite merchants more or less gentrified than, say, their Greenock counterparts, only further research will answer. There is ample evidence that Dundee and its elites wished to foster a reputation for cultural refinement and modernity in its eighteenth century sense, of wishing to position the town, in short, in the mainstream of Enlightenment urban cultural development. There is, however, a final important point to be made. Just as the new forms of entertainment and living were spreading, so too were new social challenges arising – growing poverty and disorder – and new ways of responding to these (see Chapters 6 and 9). From the 1790s or there-abouts, a growing number of associations and institutions (Sunday schools, missionary societies) were founded which, more or less directly, sought to re-impose order on society. The values these bodies stood for played a growing role in the construction of urban social identities, central to the process of forging the 'middle class' identity of the nineteenth century.[104] So ideals of respectability, commonly associated with the Victorian era, were already casting their long shadow over Dundee's elites and middling sort by 1800. The theatre, for example, staged benefit concerts for local charities.[105] A rising tide of respectability, therefore, closely associated with both evangelical currents of religion and increased economic instability (one aspect of accelerating industriali-sation of linen production), may have caused the cultural expansion and liberalisation enjoyed by Dundee in the later eighteenth and early nineteenth century to stagnate, if not go into reverse, in the succeeding decades.

NOTES

1 Two research assistants, Dr David Barrie and Vivienne Dunstan, have made a major contribution to this chapter. The latter's employment was made possible by a grant from the Leverhulme Trust to fund a pilot project on the late Enlightenment Scottish burgh.

2 John Macky, *A Journey Through Scotland. In Familiar Letters from a Gentleman Here, to his Friend Abroad. Being the Third Volume which Completes Great Britain* (2nd edn,

1732), pp. 95–96, 101; Daniel Defoe, *A Tour Through the Whole Island of Great Britain*, abridged and edited with an introduction and notes by Pat Rogers (London, 1986), p. 651.

3 For later comment on this, see National Library of Scotland (NLS), MS 3294, Alexander Brown, 'Journey in Scotland with Sketches of Some Picturesque Ruins in that Interesting Country in Two Volumes' (1787), vol. I, pp. 131–132.

4 See Charles Saumarez Smith, *The Rise of Design and the Domestic Interior in Eighteenth Century England* (London, 2000) and Maxine Berg, *Luxury and Pleasure in Eighteenth Century Britain* (Oxford, 2005).

5 Peter Borsay, *The English Urban Renaissance: Culture and Society in the Provincial Town 1660–1760* (Oxford, 1989); Peter Clark, *British Clubs and Societies 1580–1800: The Origins of an Associational World* (Oxford, 2000).

6 Jonathan Barry, 'Provincial Town Culture, 1640–1760: Urbane or Civic?', in J. Pittock and A. Wear (eds.), *Interpretation and Cultural History in Eighteenth-Century Britain* (Basingstoke, 1991), pp. 198–234; Rosemary Sweet, *The English Town 1680–1840: Government, Society and Culture* (Harlow, 1999).

7 See T. M. Devine, 'The Merchant Class of the Larger Scottish Towns in the Seventeenth and Early Eighteenth Centuries', in George Gordon and Brian Dicks (eds.), *Scottish Urban History* (Aberdeen, 1983), pp. 93–97.

8 But see Clark, *British Clubs and Societies*, ch. 9. The nearly completed research of St Andrews PhD student Mark Wallace promises to shed much-needed light on eighteenth-century Scottish freemasonry. A list of the members of the Dundee Kilwinning Lodge survives from 1745. It includes several members of the nobility, several professionals and public officials, and a smattering of artisans. The largest occupational group, however, were merchants.

9 National Archives of Scotland (NAS), Dundee Burgh Register of Sasines, B19/4/2, 24 July 1810, fols. 62–68 v.

10 NAS, Court of Session Records, CS 96/4208.

11 Dundee Bank (1763); Dundee New Bank (1802); Dundee Union Bank (1809).

12 As revealed in NAS, Court of Session Records, 360; 35, '4 Feb. 1794, Petition of William Wilson, Merchant in Dundee'.

13 In pursuit of a case in the Court of Session, concerning payment of dues as a freeman on commissioned goods, William Wilson cited in his support a petition from twenty-four merchants 'composing', he or his lawyers claimed, 'almost every merchant of any consequence (ibid., p. 3).

14 Information from unpublished research by Mrs Marilyn Healey. See also NAS, CC3/3/16, pp. 1–24, testament of Alexander Riddoch, 1823; CC3/5/7, pp. 299–325, inventory of the late Alexander Riddoch. Moveable estate valued at £12,000. The Register of Sasines shows 43 property transactions involving Riddoch between 1781 and 1819.

15 A conclusion based on a preliminary survey of the sasines records for Angus for the period 1780–1820, as well as wills and testaments of merchants. For a similar position earlier in the century, see Devine, 'The Merchant Class', pp. 105–106.

16 NAS, Brechin Commissary Court, CC3/5/5, inventory, marriage contract, trust disposition and settlement of Ebenezer Anderson, 2 July 1818.

17 For Watt and Logie, see A. J. Warden, *Angus or Forfarshire, The Land and People, Descriptive and Historical*, 5 vols. (Dundee, 1880–85), vol. IV, p. 193. Watt's keen sense of his social dignity is hinted at in NAS, Court of Session Productions, 271; 10, '1 Dec.

1812, Answers for Alexander Gruar, John Smith, and others, feuars at Scouring-burn near Dundee', p. 8.

18 See Warden, *Angus or Forfarshire, a Land and People*; Douglas J. Hamilton, *Scotland, the Caribbean and the Atlantic World 1750–1820* (Manchester, 2005), esp. pp. 59–61.

19 For the social structure of the town's population, see ch. 6, table 6.2 in this volume.

20 Dundee City Archives (DCA), GD/We/SRO 131, Box 5, Bundle 3, David to Charles Wedderburn, 26 Jan. 1782.

21 NAS, Forfar Register of Sassines, 1781–1820, 125 [for property in the High Street]; NAS, CC3/3/13, testament of Robert Stewart, surgeon in Dundee, 26 April 1804.

22 Willison's moveable estate at his death (in 1811) was valued at over £3,000, and included shares in the Dundee Sugar Refining Company, the Dundee Banking Company, a whaling ship, and the Dundee and Perth Shipping Company (NAS, CC3/5/2, pp. 259–260).

23 NAS, E326/12/2, clock and watch returns, 1797–1798, Scottish counties, E–L.

24 NAS, Paterson of Castle Huntly Papers, GD 508/3/116, 'An Account of What Company is Kept at Castle Huntly, 1780–1783'. This pattern of close relationships between certain professionals and local landed families was long-standing. William Rait, a physician from the mid century, was at one time tutor to William Douglas of Brigton.

25 Blair Castle, Atholl Papers, Box 46 (7), 70, William Murray of Ochtertyre, Dundee, to the Duke of Atholl, 16 Nov. 1733; 80, same to same, Dundee, 16 December 1733.

26 DCA, GD/We/SRO 131, Box 5, Bundle 3, David to Charles Wedderburn, 9 Jan. 1799.

27 DCA, GD/We/SRO 131, Box 8, Bundle 4, Anne Crawford, Invergowrie, to Mrs Charles Wedderburn, 25 [no month] 1787.

28 See NAS, E326/3/20, inhabited house tax, Dundee, 5 July 1778 – 5 April 1779. Members of landed society who paid this tax, and were therefore occupying houses in the town, include Sir John Wedderburn; Mungo Murray [of Lintrose]; John L'Amy [of Dunkenny]; John Guthrie of Guthrie; George Blair of Adamston; and Alexander Hunter of Blackness. Captain David Laird of Strathmartine also appears to have owned a house, with a garden, in the Seagate. In 1807, Patrick Carnegy of Lour purchased a new tenement on the north side of the Nethergate (NAS, B19/3/32, 16 May 1807, fols. 152–155 v).

29 See e.g. NAS, CC3/3/16, pp. 1–24, testament of Alexander Riddoch (wife was left possession of all furniture and goods, together with an annual annuity of £200, and an additional annuity fund to cover all burdens and debts to secure possession of her home); CC3/5/4, testament of William Webster, jun, merchant in Dundee, 1816 (wife provided with life-rent in all heritable property and goods).

30 DCA, GD/We/SRO 131, Box 5, Bundle 3, David to Charles Wedderburn, 23 June 1786.

31 She also, unusually, had for a period in the 1780s two male servants (a gardener and a house servant) (NAS, E326/5/6, 8, 10, male servants tax, burghs, 1785–86, 1786–87, 1787–88).

32 Mrs Guthie sen. of Guthrie had a house in the Cowgate (*Dundee, Perth and Cupar Advertiser*, 11 May 1810). Mrs Read sen. of Logie one in Tay Street before 1807 (ibid., 3 April. 1807).

33 DCA, GD/We/SRO 131, Box 7, Bundle 12, Dempster of Dunnichen to Charles Wedderburn, 20 January 1816.

34 DCA, GD/We/SRO 131, Box 6, Bundle 2, Dempster of Dunnichen to Charles Wedderburn, 16 December 1810.

35 See DCA, GD/We/SRO 131, Box 8, Bundle 6, Mrs Henry Scrymgeour to Mrs Charles Wedderburn, 2 February 1805, where she writes: 'Powrie [ie of Fotheringham] had an immense party at supper (and I believe a dance too) last night at which, I heard, there were the whole of Angus and a piece of Fife . . . the town [of Edinburgh] is crowded past belief.'

36 See n. 4, above.

37 S. Nenadic, 'Middle-Rank consumers and Domestic Culture in Edinburgh and Glasgow, 1729–1840', *Past and Present*, 145 (1994), p. 141.

38 See e.g. notices of sales in the *Dundee, Perth and Cupar Advertiser*, 24 May 1811 and 5 March 1813.

39 Scottish executors were not required to list the moveable contents of testaments until 1804. Testaments before 1806, which list moveable contents in any detail, are rare and distributed very unevenly over time. Roup rolls appear in Warrants of Testaments. Usually, it is only where testaments were not registered that warrants were preserved. Registers of Testaments tend to record only the total value of goods sold at auctions.

40 NAS, CC3/5/1, pp. 174–185, Margaret Kerr, relict of Peter Chalmers, excise officer, North Ferry, near Dundee, 1807 (kitchen, dining room, two rooms identified by location); CC3/5/3, pp. 2–33, John Leslie, ironmonger, Dundee, died in 1812, registered 1813 (kitchen, dining room, bedroom); CC3/5/3, pp. 35–39, Samuel Bell, architect, Dundee, 1813 (kitchen, dining room, bedroom, parlour); CC3/5/3, pp. 2–33, James Campbell, merchant, Dundee (kitchen, dining room, parlour, bedroom, one room identified by location); CC3/5/3, pp. 494–498, William Thomson, merchant and manufacturer, Dundee, 1815 (kitchen, dining room, four bedrooms, nursery); CC3/5/4, pp. 258–261, John Crystal, postmaster, Dundee, 1816 (kitchen, dining room, two bedrooms); CC3/5/4, pp. 269–271, William Dick, Millwright, Dundee, 1817 (kitchen, dining room, and two bedrooms); CC3/5/4, pp. 393–409, William Chalmers, Town Clerk, Dundee (kitchen, dining room, drawing room, parlour, six bedrooms, sitting room, portico room, store room and round room); CC3/5/5, p. 403, Susan Keay, occupation not stated, 1819 (kitchen, and three rooms identified by location); CC3/5/6, pp. 226–230, George Wilkie of Auchleshie, merchant in Dundee, 1820 (dining room, parlour, and two bedrooms); CC3/5/6, pp. 446–453, Thomas Muat, confectioner, Dundee, 1821 (kitchen, dining room, and bedroom).

41 DCA, TC/JI/63, inventory of William Whiston, merchant, 1767. The room was furnished with six chairs, two elbow chairs, two mahogany tables, a chimney, a mirror, eleven prints, a grate, fender, poker, tongs and a shovel. But see NAS, CC3/3/11, pp. 226–227, testament of Margaret Machern, relict of Robert Philip, shipmaster, Dundee, 1758, where there is a reference a 'mirror in the dining room'.

42 The size of Chalmer's cellar may well reflect his official position. Compare, for example, the cellar of John Colville, Town Clerk of Arbroath, who died in 1812 (CC20/7/5, inventory of the personal estate of John Colville, Town Clerk of Arbroath, d. 26 Oct. 1812). Colville's cellar included 33 bottles of rum; 145 bottles of strong beer; 66 bottles of whisky; 155 bottles of port; 160 bottles of porter; as well as smaller numbers of bottles of gin, Madeira, currant wine, sherry and brandy.

43 See n. 40, above.

44 NAS, CS 96/408, sederunt book of William Sturrock, merchant, Dundee, 1802–3.

45 See e.g. NAS, CS96/394, sederunt book and inventory of William McIntyre, merchant in Dundee, 1801 (furniture in house valued at only £25, although it did include a large mahogany table, mirror, and tea apparel); CC3/5/1, pp. 13–16,

inventory of Henry Jack, manufacturer in Dundee, 1806 (furniture appears to have included no mahogany items, a small looking glass, square oak table, and a small tea tray); CC3/5/4, pp. 6–7, inventory of Janet and Jean Doig, Dundee, 1815; CC3/5/4, pp. 6–7, inventory of John Proctor, shipmaster in Dundee, 1816 (household inventory valued at total of £32 9s).

46 NAS, CC3/4/32, pp. 5822–5831, inventory and roup roll of John Wemyss, merchant in Dundee, 1799.

47 NAS CC3/5/6, pp. 446–453, inventory of Thomas Muat, confectioner in Dundee, 1821. See also CC3/5/4, pp. 258–261, inventory of John Crystal, postmaster in Dundee, 1816 (household inventory valued at total of £38 10s 8d); CC3/5/4, inventory of William Dick, millwright in Dundee, 1817 (total value of household goods £63 15s).

48 See e.g. NAS, CC3/4/27, pp. 384–385, inventory of David Bowman, weaver in Dundee, 1772; CC3/4/28, inventory of Janet Binny, relict of David Simpson, weaver in Dundee, 1777.

49 NAS, CC3/10/3, pp. 250–251, testament of Patrick Balneavis, 1735; CC/3/3/11, pp. 205–207, testament of James Hamilton, 1757; CC3/3/12, pp. 151–154, testament of John Martin, shipmaster, Dundee, 1775.

50 DCA, TC/JI/64, inventory of the means and effects pertaining and belonging to Patrick Yeaman, merchant and sometime provost of Dundee, 1767.

51 DCA, TC/JI/83, inventory of James Guthrie, merchant, Dundee, 1786.

52 See esp. Lorna Weatherill, *Consumer Behaviour and Material Culture in Britain 1660–1760* (London, 1988).

53 Although several recent books on this topic purpose to cover the whole of Britain, in reality they are about England.

54 NAS, CC3/3/11, testament dative and inventory of Thomas Glass, bookseller, Dundee, 1758. Also active in the town in this period were Thomas Lundie, bookseller, and Henry Galbraith, printer. The first MS reference to a coffee house is a receipt dating from 1721 (DCA, TC/Mis. 112/4/1/5–7, protest of Alex. Ferriar, merchant, Bailie and former Treasurer of Dundee, to David Crichton, junior maltman in Dundee, to pay to either him or his successor in the 'coffie house in Dundee the sum of fifty merks as payment of your burgess ticket', 4 October 1721). The household goods left by Patrick Scot, shipmaster and former bailie of the town, appear to be those for a coffee house; they include a billiard table and various other games (NAS, CC3/3/10, pp. 289–293, testament of Patrick Scot, 1737). The coffee house was probably located in Old Coffee House Close off the Overgate.

55 Dundee Central Library, Lamb Collection 6 (7), *A Catalogue of the New Circulating Library . . . Which are Lent . . . By R. Nicoll, Bookseller, Stationer and Printseller, Dundee* (Dundee, n.d.; but probably early 1780s). Nicoll was certainly present in the town in 1770, when he ordered copies of Walter Ruddiman's *Weekly Magazine* from Ruddiman in Edinburgh (Edinburgh University Library, Laing MSS III, 752, Weekly Magazine Accounts, 1768–73).

56 DCA, 'Lockit Book'.

57 *The Dundee Register of Merchants and Trades, with all the Public Offices for M,DCC,LXXXIII* (Dundee, 1782), pp. 16, 24, 39. It is likely that dancing masters were present significantly earlier, although no record to date has come to light to confirm this.

58 NAS, Forfarshire Particular Register of Sasines, 1781–1820, printed abridgements, 29, 19, 7 Nov. 1781 (in favour of John Miles, cabinet maker, Dundee).

59 There was a boarding school for young ladies in the town at least by the 1770s, for
which see the notice placed by a Miss Thompson in the *Edinburgh Advertiser*, 21
October 1777. The school taught needlework and 'necessary accomplishments'; it also
provided employment to music, dancing and writing masters. The notice indicates
that Thomson's establishment was replacing an existing one.

60 *Dundee, Perth and Cupar Advertiser*, 29 January 1807. The partnership was dissolved in
1815, and Duff opened a new music warehouse in Castle Street next to the Theatre.
Chalmers opened the Music and Stationary Warehouse, which sold music and musical
instruments. Duff's business appears not have endured, at least in original form. By
1816, he had moved to the Musical Saloon in the Nethergate (*Dundee, Perth and
Cupar Advertiser*, 16 August 1816).

61 See e.g. *Dundee, Perth and Cupar Advertiser*, 6 November 1812 [Andrew Pirie, includes
class for young ladies on piano]; 2 December 1814 [Adam Clarkson, teacher of music,
esp. violin, intends to reside in Dundee; 25 May 1817 [Miss Stewart, instruction on
piano]; 20 February 1818 [Professor of Music, H. Smith, instruction in piano, violin
'thorough bass, and singings'; 27 February 1818 [D. Crabb from Manchester,
instruction in piano, violin, violincello, viola, flute plus private tuition in fashionable
dancing]; 4 June 1819 [Mr Taylor from Perth to open classes for vocal music]. Mr
Rodgers, the organist at the Episcopal Chapel in Castle Sreet also offered instruction
in the violin and several other instruments during the 1810s. For the importance of
accomplishment in the construction of feminity in this period, see Ann Bermingham,
Learning to Draw: Studies in the Cultural History of a Polite and Useful Art (New
Haven and London, 2000), esp. ch. 5, 'Accomplished Women'.

62 *Dundee, Perth and Cupar Advertiser*, 2 November 1804 [Miss Gibson, milliner, south
side of High Street]; 8 February 1805 [Eugene Marzorati, carver, gilder and print seller,
Castle Street]; 25 October 1805 [Miss Henderson, mantua maker and dress maker];
4 April 1806 [Misses M. and C. Saunders, mantua makers and milliners]; 23 May 1806
[D. Manson, silversmith and jewellery business in Crichton Sreet]; 19 September 1806
[William Thoms, haberdasher, Trades' Hall]; 16 January 1807 [William Constable,
watchmaker, north side of High Street]; 31 July 1807 [John Sturrock, clothier and tea
dealer, High Street]; 6 May 1808 [J. Souter, haberdasher and draper]; 24 June 1808
[London and Dundee Straw Chip and Fancy Hat Ware-House, opposite the English
Chapel]; 22 July 1808 [Mrs J. Crichton, straw hats and bonnets, 2 Castle Street];
9 September 1808 [China and Glass Ware-House, opposite Exchange Coffee House];
19 May 1809 [Robert Tobet, Upholstery Warehouse]; 8 June 1810 [J. Gowans, carver
and gilder, also sold London prints]; 9 April 1813 [Frederick S. Innes, perfumery and
fancy goods]; 14 May 1813 [Stalker, ladies and gentlemen's hairdresser and ornamental
hair manufacturer]; 14 May 1813 [Bowman and Crichton, High Street haberdashers;
I. and E. Black, High Street, milliners and dress makers]; 19 February 1819 [J. Meek,
gentlemen's hairdresser and cutter, formerly assistant to late Mr Bowman of New
Bond Street, London]; 26 November 1819 [H. Smith opened New London Hat
warehouse, 40 Murraygate]; 5 May 1820 [R. Young, Muslin Warehouse]; 13 October
1820 [India and British Shawlwarehouse, north-west corner of Trades' Hall];
17 November 1820 [E. Miller, Ladies' Fashionable Hats, Crichton Street].

63 *Dundee, Perth and Cupar Advertiser*, 4 April 1806. Butterworth's shop was in the
High Street.

64 *Dundee, Perth and Cupar Advertiser*, 12 March 1813. See also the article in the *Dundee,
Perth and Cupar Advertiser*, 30 May 1817 on 'High Street Beaux'. 'Union Hall, High

Street, Dundee' (1847), an oil painting by George McGillivray in the McManus Galleries, Dundee, conveys a strong impression, albeit for a later period, of the position of high status shops at the heart of the burgh, as well as the High Street as a site of elite display.

65 *Dundee, Perth and Cupar Advertiser*, 29 August 1806, 1 January 1808 [Mr Harvie, miniaturist from Edinburgh]; 4 May 1810 [E. Gerard, portrait painter, had been to Montrose, Brechin and Forfar before Dundee]. 20 September 1811 [R. Hardie, trained at RA, several years practice in London, miniaturist]; 7 October 1814 [Mr Nairne, portrait painter]; 29 October 1819 [Mr Simson, portrait painter, will resume portrait painting and classes for drawing early next year]; 6 October 1820 [Alexander Milne, school of drawing and portrait painting, south-west corner of Chapelshade].

66 *Dundee, Perth and Cupar Advertiser*, 4 December 1818.

67 See relevant comment in Jon Stobart, 'In search of a leisure hierarchy: English spa towns in the urban system', in P. Borsay, G. Hirschfelder and R. Mohrmann (eds.), *New Directions in Urban History, Aspects of European Art, Tourism and Leisure since the Enlightenment* (Munster, 2000), pp. 18–40.

68 Glamis Castle, Angus, Strathmore Papers, 260/44, John Wedderburn, Dundee to Earl of Strathmore, 14 February 1727. This letter refers to a cock fight in Dundee involving one of Strathmore's birds.

69 Frank Boyd, *Records of the Dundee Stage, From the Earliest Times to the Present Day* (Dundee, 1886), pp. 5–7; David Johnson, *Music and Society in Lowland Scotland in the Eighteenth Century* (London, 1972), p. 44.

70 *Caledonian Mercury*, 18 November 1735.

71 Leah Leneman, *Sin in the City: Sexuality and Social Control in Urban Scotland 1660–1780* (Edinburgh, 1998).

72 DCA, Dundee Town Council Minute Book, entry for 9 August 1784.

73 *Scots Chronicle*, 30 May–3 June 1800. *A Defence Delivered by R. Small D.D. At the Bar of the Last General Assembly* was being sold by Edward Lesslie in early August (*Scots Chronicle*, 1–5 August 1800).

74 *Dundee, Perth and Cupar Advertiser*, 15 December 1809.

75 *Dundee, Perth and Cupar Advertiser*, 17 October 1817; 30 January, 19 February, 23 July, 6 August 1818; 17 March 1820.

76 *Dundee, Perth and Cupar Advertiser*, 1 and 29 December 1820.

77 For the Dundee Club, see *Edinburgh Evening Courant*, 16 February 1792.

78 *Dundee, Perth and Cupar Advertiser*, 5 October, 12 October 1804; 3 October, 17 October 1806; 2 October, 16 October 1807; 29 September 1820.

79 *Dundee, Perth and Cupar Advertiser*, 26 January, 1 June 1810; 18 January, 31 May 1811; 29 April 1814; 19 May 1815.

80 Notices of their meetings were regularly placed in the local paper from their foundation in 1809, which may indicate a membership which was regional rather than purely local to the burgh. For a discussion of archery clubs in England and Wales in this period, see Martin Jones, 'Archery, Romance and Elite Culture in England and Wales, *c.* 1780–1840', *History*, 89 (2004), pp. 193–208.

81 *Dundee, Perth and Cupar Advertiser*, 15 February 1808.

82 *Dundee, Perth and Cupar Advertiser*, 17 August 1810.

83 *Dundee, Perth and Cupar Advertiser*, 26 July 1805; 13 June 1806; 17 July 1807; 21 October 1808; 21 July 1809; 17 May 1810; 16 August 1811; 14 August 1812; 23 April 1813; 5 November 1813; 22 April 1814; 1 July 1814; 12 August 1814; 18 August 1815; 9 August

1816; 15 August 1817; 31 July 1818; 21 July 1820.

84 See e.g. Mr Dwyer of the Theatre Royal, Drury Lane and Edinburgh, recitation and songs (*Dundee, Perth and Cupar Advertiser* 29 August 1806; Messrs Elliot, Beale and Evans, London, vocal concert, Dundee & Montrose (*Dundee, Perth and Cupar Advertiser*, 29 January 1808; 29 January 1809; 26 January 1810; 18 January 1811; 25 January 1811; 8 February 1811; 29 March 1811; 28 June 1818).

85 *Dundee, Perth and Cupar Advertiser*, 24 March 1815; 5 May 1815.

86 For the New Inn, see the description in the *Edinburgh Advertiser*, 11 December 1792. For the Castle Street Inn and Hotel, see *Dundee, Perth and Cupar Advertiser*, 1 January 1813.

87 See e.g. the 'large and elegant lodge' of the Dundee Operative Masons in Guillans Close, Overgate, Dundee which was supposedly 'well adapted for a ballroom' (*Dundee, Perth and Cupar Advertiser*, 22 May 1812).

88 In 1804, the Ward was described as 'a large spot of grass, inclosed by a thorn hedge, shaded with trees, and encircled by a pleasant walk, which is well frequented during the salubrity of summer' (*History of the Town of Dundee* (Dundee, 1804), p. 113). For the subscription and subsequent legal action, see *Dundee, Perth and Cupar Advertiser*, 25 October 1811; 7 February, 6 March, 15 May, 3 July, 14 August 1812; 11, 30 June 1813.

89 NAS, Court of Sessions papers, CS 313:7, Maule v Watt (1816–18), 'Advocation for William Maule, 12 November 1813', p. 3.

90 See *Dundee, Perth and Cupar Advertiser*, 13, 20 May 1808; 17 August 1810; 11 December 1812.

91 DCA, GD/We/SRO 131, Box 9, Bundle 4, Col. Rattray, Downie Park, to Charles Wedderburn, 16 May 1808.

92 By 1824, the West-Port (Chapel) Library was also in existence, but may well have been founded earlier. It comprised mostly religious works, but by no means all. There were several histories, including Hume and Smollett's *History of England* and William Robertson's *History of Scotland*, travel volumes, literary works and collected editions of the *Spectator*, the *Adventurer*, and the *Tradesmen; or Commercial Magazine*. Dundee Central Library Collection 6 (11), *Regulations and Catalogue of the West Port Library* (Dundee, 1824).

93 DCA, 316 (6), Minutes of the Dundee Public Library.

94 DCL, Lamb Collection 8 (16), Regulations of Dundee Public Library.

95 Important private libraries sold at auction in the early nineteenth century, and advertised in the *Dundee, Perth and Cupar Advertiser*, included those of Dr Robert Stewart, surgeon (30 November 1804); James Ballingall, merchant (26 September 1806); Patrick Duff, writer (25 December 1807); R. Douglas Esq. (9 February 1810); Rev. J. Black (20 January 1815). A sale of books and prints formerly belonging to Thomas Mathewson, painter, included volumes of the *Encyclopedia Britannica*, the *Spectator*, the *Literary Magazine*, and William Robertson's *History of Scotland* (3 May 1816). The druggist John Jolly was described as having possessed a 'large and very valuable collection of books on chemistry and medicine, history, voyages, travels, novels &c' (*Dundee, Perth and Cupar Advertiser*, 28 June 1811).

96 NAS, CC3/5/7, pp. 128–136, articles of roup of property belonging to Thomas Rattray, corn merchant in Dundee, 1822; DCA, TC/JI/83, inventory of James Guthrie, merchant, Dundee, 1786. See also NAS, CS 96/408 and 409, sederunt books of William Sturrock, merchant, Dundee, 1802–03, 1803–24; CS96/3692, sederunt book of Robert Duff, merchant, Dundee, 1820–26.

97 Hamilton's library is depicted in Henry Harwood's 'The Executive' (1822) at first floor level in the High Street, on the corner of Castle Street and above an ironmonger's shop.

98 *Dundee, Perth and Cupar Advertiser*, 1 January, 23 July 1819; DCL, Lamb Collection 6(4), *Catalogue of the Circulating Library of John Hamilton, High Street, Dundee* (Dundee, 1826).

99 Lesslie's political involvement can be traced back to the 1790s, when he appears to have been disseminating radical literature in and around Dundee. He was also involved in the upsurge of radicalism which coincided with the end of the Napeolonic Wars. In 1820, his name was given as the person to receive subscriptions for a service of plate to be given to the current heroine of the radicals, Queen Caroline (*Dundee, Perth and Cupar Advertiser*, 1 Dec. 1820).

100 DCL, Lamb Collection, Catalogue of effects of Dundee Rational Institution, to be sold by public roup, 1821. The library comprised 134 books. See also *Dundee, Perth and Cupar Advertiser*, 21 April 1809; 14 December 1810; 28 January 1814; 24 February 1814. For Don, see *Portrait Gallery of Forfar Notables, From Drawings by John Young, Letterpress by Alexander Lowson* (published by subscription, Aberdeen, 1893), pp. 39–52.

101 See e.g. *Dundee, Perth and Cupar Advertiser*, 28 July 1806; 19 December 1806; 17 January 1812; 17 November 1815; 18 July 1817; 7 January 1820; 2 June 1820; *Montrose Review*, 1 May 1818; 14 August 1818; 30 October 1818; 5 February 1819; 19 March 1819; 31 December 1819; 7 January 1820.

102 *The Dundee Register, of Merchants and Trades, with all the Public Offices, &c. For M,DCC,LXXXIII* (Dundee, 1782), pp. 41–42.

103 NLS, MS 653, Dempster to Henry Dundas, 31 January 1788. Dempster was writing in support of the extension of the bounty on exports of coarse linen, critical to Dundee's economic prosperity from the middle of the century.

104 R. J. Morris, 'Voluntary societies and British urban elites, 1780–1850: an analysis', in Peter Borsay (ed.), *The Eighteenth-Century Town* (London, 1990), pp. 338–360.

105 DCA, GD/Mus 32, Account Current Book of Thomas Watt, manager for proprietors of Dundee New Theatre, Castle Street, which shows that the proprietors usually reserved the right to hire out the theatre on a temporary basis to other people for 'Assemblies, Balls, Concerts, school orations or other charitable purposes'.

Maritime Dundee and its Harbour *c.* 1755–1820

Charles McKean and Claire Swan,
with Malcolm Archibald

INTRODUCTION

Dundee's prosperity as a seaport had always depended upon its shipping, but its location on the Tay estuary made the maintenance of its harbour a perpetual economic drain. The harbour's problems were perceived as coming from upstream. Virtually every decade since the late fifteenth century, the council had had to contemplate undertaking repairs, following the constant undermining and eroding of its west bulwark by the powerful currents of the river, and the perpetual silting up its basin with mud. Few major improvements had been undertaken since the repairs following the disastrous storms of 1668, albeit the port's reception area had been smartened in the Vault – with the construction of Strathmartine's Lodging and arcaded apartments lorded over by the new Town House, one of whose pedimented facades towered south over the harbour. The burgh's storage girnals of Packhouse Square, however, completed in 1644, had become worn out by 1755. Just as work to repair and reroof them was beginning, the council decided that they were no longer sufficient for the town's growing trade, and appointed William Robertson, architect of Leven, to design a replacement.[1]

Before work began on site, however, what became known as the Lisbon earthquake struck near the coast of Portugal at 9.30 a.m. on the morning of 1 November 1755. It was followed by a destructive tsunami that caused near-total devastation in Lisbon and south-west Portugal, killing an estimated 60,000 to 100,000 people, its after-effects reaching as far away as Helsinki and Barbados.[2] It was possibly on 3 November[3] that the ensuing tidal wave entered the Tay estuary. It ripped away the large timber buoy fixed by the Seamen's Fraternity to the rocks as the harbour's principal navigation aid, obliterated the massive stone east bulwark of the harbour, and drove the buoy up against the west bulwark.[4] Attacked from its least expected quarter, Dundee's harbour was effectively obliterated.

The following April, presumably because no action had been taken, the Seamen's Fraternity petitioned the council to rebuild the eastern side of the harbour.[5] When doing so, Dundee recast its shoreline once again. It raised the dock level and located its new baroque Packhouses lining the quayside, with a gated enclosure behind. So Dundee's second major public building of the eighteenth century was also designed to awe visitors as they arrived by sea – as it did. To prevent such damage recurring, the street levels of the New Shore (later renamed Butcher Row after the Shambles were moved there in 1775), Fish Street and neighbourhood were raised 5 to 12 feet depending upon location, relegating the original entrance storeys to semi-basements.[6]

Dundee was and fundamentally remained a seaport,[7] and this chapter will examine how the port's trade evolved during the eighteenth century, and how it developed a distinctive maritime identity.[8] Dundee was never a dockyard town,[9] but seems to have balanced the concept of 'inport' and 'outport' very successfully in that it developed the industries required for the processing of imports and exports, to the extent that each trade required. Indeed, its profile of blubber boiling, and processing sugar, candles, tanned hides and liquor fits the profile of a town that is *predominantly* a port, rather than a town with a harbour, like a glove.[10] By the end of the century, however, the success of osnaburg manufacture and of whaling had come to overshadow the coloured thread, glass and shoe manufacture, shipbuilding and the sugar refining that had grown up since mid century.

Its increasing trade added to the pressure on a largely unimproved and relatively shallow harbour; and it was the failure of the burgh council to invest in a harbour sufficiently large and deep enough to satisfy its merchants' ambitions that led to the bitter 1810 dispute between the shipping interest and the town council – a dispute that culminated in terminating the leadership of the burgh's longest-serving provost, Alexander Riddoch.[11]

THE HARBOUR

The great natural advantage of Dundee's harbour was, as it always had been, its 'roads' or safe estuarial anchorage for shipping which provided shelter from storms in the North Sea. In December 1790, for example, the brig *Christian* arrived 'under stress of weather' and unloaded her cargo of coal at Dundee rather than continue to her destination.[12] Whereas the Fraternity of Seamen was responsible for maintaining the great buoy and the two lighthouses that marked the entrance to the firth of Tay, the condition of the harbour itself remained the responsibility of the council and, in particular, that of the shoremaster. Since there was 'no back water' to sluice out the silt, 'which it wants very much' observed John Macky in 1723,[13] it could only just cope with ships of up to 300 tons – and sometimes not even that, for in at least one instance, a vessel ran aground on a 'sandbank in the middle of the harbour'. As early as the 1760s, larger vessels were being forced to discharge part of their cargo into lighters, in order to lessen their draught before they could approach the quays;[14] and it was common for casks of whale blubber to be floated ashore from ship direct to the boiling yards in the Seagate and Roodyards, or for timber to be ferried by raft from ship to woodyards.[15] Although shipping also had to negotiate shifting sandbanks, the most prominent being the Ballast Bank downstream from Magdalene Point, and the Middle Bank, directly opposite the harbour entrance,[16] it was the increase in size and number of vessels that underlined the essential inadequacy of the harbour so far as both shipmasters and merchants were concerned.

In 1768, finding that their repairs to the harbour after the tsunami were insufficient, the council agreed to appoint a 'proper skilful person' to advise on harbour strategy.[17] The architect John Adam (son of the designer of the Town House) duly reported, followed by the prominent English civil engineer John Smeaton a year later. Adam recommended the removal of an obstructive rock from the western entrance, and sealing the east entrance to allow the ebbing tide to 'clear away the mud' from the harbour. He suggested that if the small bay upstream of the west bulwark were reclaimed and filled in, it would also increase the force of the Tay's current.[18] This, the second major land reclamation in Dundee's history, was thereafter used as Dundee's largest woodyard (highly convenient for the adjacent shipbuilding yards).

The burgh had created a tidal basin which filled up with water at high tide, to be released through sluices at 15 minute intervals thereafter to aid workers employed to dig channels through the silt. Smeaton thought this entirely inadequate. Famous for his innovative design for the third Eddystone lighthouse, he was then designing the new bridge over the Tay at Perth (opened in 1771), and had been working on the Forth and Clyde canal. He visited Dundee on 4 August 1769 during spring tides, and concluded that the harbour was too much enclosed, and the mud bank at its centre greatly diminished the space available for larger vessels. He recommended excavating two pairs of three tunnels from the west, each 12 feet wide; and that the west bulwark be extended outwards to direct the river current through these tunnels. The river would therefore flush its own silt from within the harbour. The tidal basin was to be maintained, but its water was to be let out all at once, and its sluices redirected to scour along the pier walls; even then, some men would probably still be required to dig. Smeaton's report was couched in terms of making the best of a bad job.[19]

The Old Fort and the chapel of St Nicholas, which the town had purchased in 1737,[20] were duly demolished;[21] the council cut the necessary tunnels and arched them over to create a platform for the Craig or Ferry Pier.[22] The capital needed for such extensive alterations was borrowed from Dempster's Bank.[23] Save for the addition of an east pier in 1782,[24] the shape was set for the next fifty years: a harbour with 14 feet of water at spring tide, and the capacity for about two hundred sail.[25] To recoup its outlay, in 1770 the council increased the shore dues from every vessel using the facilities for cleaning and graving;[26] but the fact that even then it had to borrow capital for regular repairs and maintenance, never mind the new east pier,[27] lent credence to later accusations that it had been diverting harbour income away into other burgh purposes. Whenever major harbour works were required, the burgh was driven into indebtedness; and that blinded the council to the continuing conflict between the harbour and the growing volume and scale of the shipping.

Early foreign-trading vessels had been small – the sloop *Penelope* that arrived from Campvere in December 1753,[28] for instance, was only 25 tons, and the brigantine *Mary* that departed for Christiansand (now Oslo) only fifty.[29] The *Merry Ploughman*, a regular trader with the Baltic, weighed 54 tons,[30] the *Elizabeth*, a sloop on the Norway trade, only 45 tons,[31] and the brigantine *Margaret*, arriving from Gothenburg, a mere 30.[32] These diminutive vessels made the 100-ton snow *George* of Dysart, which arrived from Riga, appear positively gargantuan.[33] By 1777, Dundee vessels trading internationally were about double the size of the 1740s, averaging *c.* 68 tons, and coasting vessels 33. By comparison, Glasgow had 1,209 ships weighing less than 60 tons, and 117 weighing between 60 and 80. If whalers were taken out of the equation, the vessels operating from both Dundee's and Glasgow's harbours were broadly similar in size, although Glasgow had nine times more of them.[34] It was a pattern of inexorable growth. By 1805, the size of Dundee's international traders had risen by another 40%, and by a further 40% to 139 tons by 1810. Coastal vessels increased in size by about the same proportion. Size was crucial. The 176-ton *Rodney* was considered to be small for Arctic seamanship and therefore insufficiently large for the bounty (see p. 260), whereas the 364-ton whaler *Dundee*, however good for whaling, was really too large for the harbour.

INTERNATIONAL TRADE

During the eighteenth century, Dundee continued to enjoy the limited direct trade with ports in and around the Mediterranean that it had for centuries, importing mainly wine, salt, vinegar and cork. A ship trading with the Mediterranean needed to purchase a Mediterranean Pass (which cost of £1 15s 6d in 1759), for the protection it offered from the Barbary Pirates, who attacked vessels from Christian countries to sell their crews into the North African slave markets. Britain bought immunity with an annual bribe or tribute, and issued passes that could be showed to any attacker. There is no record of Barbary pirates capturing a Dundee vessel, but the usual other maritime risks had a disproportionate effect in the context of Dundee's smallish fleet. When *Dubray* was 'put ashore on the English coast' when outward bound for the Canaries and the coast of Barbary;[35] a French privateer captured *Phoenix* on her voyage to Lisbon in April 1758;[36] and the *Kinnoul*, was ordered into Inverkeithing bay for quarantine for fear of disease on her return from Leghorn,[37] there was a significant impact upon the town; and the war towards the end of the century caused the frequency of Mediterranean voyages to dip sharply.

In the 1750s, some six vessels were sailing annually to ports such as Bilbao, Lisbon, Gibraltar, St Lucar (Seville's port), Leghorn, and the

Canary Islands, with an occasional voyage to Venice or the Cape Verde Islands off the western coast of Africa as well.[38] The volume of imported wine may not have been exceptional – George Glen's *Dolphin* carried eighteen pipes and four hogsheads wine[39] and Robert Patullo's *Buxton* fifty-six hogsheads of Spanish wine, in addition to reeds and cork[40] – but the trade was steady, and excess wine was shipped coastwise to England.[41] A greater quantity of alcohol probably entered Dundee illicitly, smuggling and ports customarily going hand in hand, for the Customs Office regularly advertised in the *Edinburgh Advertiser* Excise sales of illegally imported alcohol – hundreds of gallons of Geneva, or brandy, aquavit and rum, and substantial quantities of wine never mind tea – at Dundee's Customs House.[42] The principal importer from the Mediterranean in the late eighteenth century was John Rankine, but others included Ann Robertson and her sisters who refused to accept a cargo of Portuguese cork in 1777 since it was 'of a mean quantity'.[43] Citrus fruit was a continuing import, the *Merry Plowman* (James Smith, Master) docking in 1754 with a cargo of Spanish wine, lemons, oranges, raisins, figs and nuts.[44] Dundee vessels traded wine from Iberia with ports in northern Europe – the 54-ton brigantine *Merry Plowman*, for instance, carrying wine from Cadiz up to Danzig in 1755,[45] and the *Two Brothers* returning tea, iron and tar from Stockholm down to Lisbon.[46]

TABLE 11.1
Wines and spirits landed in Dundee from abroad in 1813

Spirits Quantity (gallons)	type	Wine Quantity (gallons)	type
25,272	Rum	7,078	Portuguese red
312	Brandy	3,962	Spanish white
474	Gin	121	French red
1,561	Rum shrub	421	Madeira
		97	French white

Source: CE 70/1/14: 5 January 1814.

Historically, Dundee's principal trading links had been with ports in and around the Baltic, particularly the import of constructional timber from

Norway,[47] and this trade remained of crucial importance, serving not just the many wood merchants and shipbuilders, but also the cabinet makers of the town.[48] In the eighteenth century, however, the Baltic trade developed a new character, namely the import of raw Ratziger flax from St Petersburg and Riga for processing into osnaburgs in Dundee and Angus, prior to its export to markets in America and the West Indies.[49] Keen to encourage linen production in Scotland, the government had introduced a bounty for quality-stamped osnaburgs exported across the Atlantic in 1742, and renewed it periodically until the early nineteenth century. The government's Board of Trustees offered training and encouragement, the British Linen Company offered capital, and the traditional linen outworking patterns in the Forfar area provided historic weaving expertise.[50] By 1757, Angus-woven osnaburgs had reached the required quality to be shipped to London for onward sale to the West Indies, and the British Linen Company appointed Richard Neilson as its agent in Dundee to oversee its operations.[51] These factors combined to transform Angus into by far the largest centre of osnaburg manufacture in Scotland. However, despite the encouragement of home-grown flax, over half Scotland's flax was imported by the mid 1770s, presumably for reasons of reliability of supply, and that figure rose to over 80% by the turn of the century.[52] Most of it was imported through Dundee (which also diverted some St Petersburg flax and Riga hemp codilla to its two thriving rope works).[53] By the end of the century, Dundee had also become a major manufacturer of sailcloth.[54]

Whilst some osnaburgs were exported directly to America, most were dispatched to the British Linen Company's warehouses in London – even though America and the West Indies remained their ultimate destination. That has led to the erroneous conclusion that Dundee's international trade was in recession between 1780 and 1810.[55] Far from it. Osnaburgs were booming, reaching their peak only in 1817. The misunderstanding arose from the fact that they were being exported coastwise to London first.

International trading vessels generally arrived between spring and late autumn, and the average return Baltic voyage took ten weeks. There were few voyages during the winter when many of the Baltic ports were closed by ice, for the voyage was often dangerous. In 1800 *Fame*, a regular trader, was reported 'lost in the Baltic on her voyage here from St Petersburgh [*sic*]',[56] while in early 1802 *Britannia* was 'lost in the Baltic' and the *Euphemia*, 'lost on the coast of Finland'.[57] A small number of Dundee vessels ventured the daunting journey around the North Cape north to Archangel in the White Sea, one being the *Riga Merchant*, which returned with tar, timber and maritime stores in 1803,[58] although bad weather forced its shipmaster, Thomas Elliot, to jettison forty of his 854 barrels of tar on his next voyage.[59]

Whaling became significant in Dundee's economy in the 1750s,[60] following the introduction of the 1750 Bounty Act. The Act was intended to create a reservoir of seamen 'hardy beyond most others' that could be tapped in time of war, and guaranteed a payment of £2 sterling for every ton weight of a whaling ship that exceeded 200 tons.[61] Ironically, since Dundee whaling men carried a protection to keep them free of the Dundee press gang that preyed on unwary seamen, comparatively few actually served on board warships.[62] A decent sized whale could produce 9 tons of oil and a ton and a half of whalebone. Baleen from its mouth was used for bonnets and hooped skirts, stays and whips, brush-bristles and bodices, and was supplied to the dressmakers, umbrella-makers, cutlers and brush manufacturers that clustered nearby – not to mention the numerous hat makers who congregated farther out in the town.[63] Whale blubber was boiled down to oil, and then used for street lighting, batching flax, tanning, and in soap making. Dundee's manufacture of soap had its roots in the early seventeenth century, and William Mitchell, of the Peep o' Day Soap Works (just outside the burgh boundary to the east), used whale oil to manufacture soap for the American market.[64] He consigned three separate shipments of it on the *Fame's* voyages to Charleston in the early 1770s.[65] Other portions of the animal were auctioned – as, for example, the sale of 200 whale fins from Greenland rouped in 1792.[66]

With this incentive to dare the Arctic without risk of major financial loss, Dundee merchants entered a trade that endured for over 150 years. In 1793, the port sent four whaling ships into the Arctic – adapted to wartime conditions by being armed,[67] and the fleet had doubled by 1815. In time, the burgh became Britain's largest whaling port. Whalers greatly increased Dundee's average vessel tonnage, for whaling required relatively huge vessels, carrying up to ten times more crew than the average Atlantic trading vessel.[68] The whaling companies all grouped together on the south side of the Seagate near the Sugar House, where they could have their own jetties and space for their boiling yards.

Direct trade to and from America had been sporadic in the early eighteenth century, limited to a few ships to or from Boston and Virginia,[69] leaving in early spring or late summer, and almost always returning in late summer.[70] However, between 1751 and 1775, that changed. Twenty-five direct voyages were made from Dundee to America with nineteen returning, and since it is difficult to ascertain the dependability of the records, there may have been others that went unrecorded.[71] Three-quarters of them were made to Charleston, South Carolina, and the principal export was linen – the bulk of it osnaburgs. Whereas their Louisiana counterparts opted for cotton for their slaves, South Carolinian planters preferred osnaburgs, and the prominent Carolina planter Henry Laurens provided each slave with 3 yards of it, in addition to 5 yards of plain linens, a linen handkerchief, a blanket and a hat.[72] Thus in September 1757, the *Mercury* sailed for Charleston laden with 21,534 yards of plain linen and 2,134 yards of chequered linen.[73] Slave supplies were also evident on the *Fame* that left for Charleston, via Cape Fear, in 1773. Alongside the customary linen, it carried 360 hats, 342 printed linen 'hankies', 854 checked linen hankies and 6 pairs of blankets.[74]

Trading between Dundee and the Americas was specific, opportunistic and informal, with methods reminiscent of a century earlier. Unlike the well-established transatlantic trade of the Glasgow merchants, Dundonians were exploiting a small niche market, responding to very specific mail orders, and dispatching one-off consignments to meet them. John Rankine consigned cargoes of both Dundee manufactures and other supplies to his representatives in North Carolina, South Carolina and Georgia on the understanding that he would receive payment once a buyer had been found on its arrival. The only recorded voyage from Dundee to Philadelphia, set up by Rankine in 1765, carried general linen and coal goods, leather shoes and boots, Scots salt, oatmeal, sheepskin britches and barrels of salmon.[75] Return goods, all products of the British plantations, included turpentine, tar and pitch. In 1767, James Syme and John Richardson & Son, for example, imported 1,220 barrels of turpentine, nine barrels of tar and seven of pitch from Port Hampton, Virginia.[76] The *Adventure* sailed to Norfolk, Virginia, in 1771 containing hats, thread, woollen cloths, blankets, 3,000 quills, 1 ton of cheese, copper kettles, muskets and barrels of gunpowder.[77] Because the value of such goods was relatively low, large quantities were required to make the voyage profitable.

Between 1767 and 1775, John Rankine commissioned fourteen voyages to the Southern colonies, twelve touching at Charleston. Outbound, he dispatched linen and leather supplies, receiving cargoes of rice on return[78] which had had to be bought by Rankine's associate in Charleston since, as a rule, South Carolina planters disliked consigning rice still owned by them by sea.[79] Once in Dundee, the rice acted as a remittance for the linen and leather, and was then exported to its principal markets in Holland and Germany.[80]

Between 1750 and 1775, the firm of John Jobson & Company commissioned three journeys to North Carolina. In 1764 the *Two Friends of St Christopher* carried over 20,000 yards of plain and chequered linen, with sundries including thread, books, snuff and silk.[81] Two years later, they dispatched the *Peggie* laden with over 10,000 yards of plain linen, a variety of clothing, coal, ale and Portuguese wine, returning with eighty-one barrels of plantation tar.[82] These journeys were unusual, however, for Jobson's were more focused upon Arctic whaling and the Baltic trade. Its principal interest was importing flax from Riga, where they perpetuated the preference for dealing with kin. To that end, they dispatched Robert Jobson (known as Riga Bob[83]) to live in Riga to control the family investment.[84]

Dundee vessels also traded between Charleston and Lisbon. Typically, linen supplies would be off-loaded in Charleston, the ship then laden with rice headed for Lisbon before returning to Dundee with both rice and wine. Although it was rare on the outward voyage, almost half of the nineteen return voyages from America to Dundee between 1750 and 1775 stopped at Lisbon. The exception was *Fame* which stopped at Madeira in 1771 to exchange millinery for a cargo of wine before continuing to Charleston.[85] The particular nature of the cargoes and irregularities of the journeys indicate that Dundee merchants were responding to their American agents' needs on demand. The bulk of Dundee's transatlantic trade, however, passed through London.[86]

Dundee also had a long-standing trade of a similar nature with the West Indies – particularly the Caribbean islands of Grenada, Jamaica and Antigua. In November 1753, the *Dolphin* left for Jamaica only carrying linen,[87] beginning a trade that, by 1815, had grown to the annual export of over 300,000 yards of linen direct to Jamaica (in addition to regular supplies of soap, nails and thread[88]). On 6 February 1764, the *James and Margaret* left for Antigua carrying a cargo of linen, cast iron, French wine, candles, sailcloth and leather, returning in July with brown muscavado sugar and rum.[89] By 1813, Dundee was importing over 25,000 of rum from the West Indies – by far the most sought after alcoholic commodity to arrive in Dundee judging by quantity: not surprisingly given the burgh's nature as a seaport filled with mariners.[90]

The demand for the large cargoes of leather saddles and bridles, stirrups and whips from America boosted Dundee's long-standing tanning and shoemaking industries. Its tanneries had grown from three in 1775 to nine by the 1790s,[91] and leather merchants, saddlers and harness-makers now used whale oil to tan their leather. Local merchants Smith, Strachan & Company commanded a large majority of the Charleston trade up to the early 1760s,[92] and it was through such commission agents that their cargoes were consigned. There is some evidence, however, that the leather may have been supplied by Native Americans. In 1759, Dundee had dispatched a quantity of coloured thread to Charleston together with a consignment of iron tools. The Cherokees, then the dominant tribe in Charleston's hinterland, used coloured thread for wampum, a valued decorative Indian gift that required a variety of coloured and white threads; and tools represented an important bargaining commodity. The *Mercury* returned the following year with 100lbs of draped Indian deer skin. In May 1762, the *Mercury* again docked from Charleston carrying 100lb of dressed Indian deer skin, returning again with 179lbs of coloured thread. Shoe manufacturers did particularly well from the export of shoes and boots.[93] The 30,000 yards of staple linen carried by the *Mercury* that sailed for Charleston in September 1761 were accompanied by over 10,000 pairs of shoes, four pairs of boots, and forty-nine leather saddles and bridles, with leather stirrups and spare tanned leather.[94]

In 1765, local merchant James Crawford set up a Sugar House[95] and attracted a master sugar maker from London to run it. The seven-storied sugar house, long the predominant landmark of eastern Dundee, was situated on the north side of the Seagate. Sugar was imported largely by one of Dundee Sugar House's owners, the prominent merchant, Alexander Strachan, frequently in exchange for linen. In 1767, the Sugar House passed to Crichton, Strachan & Company, which then sold it back to James Crawford and James Fairweather junior, in 1779[96] – implying that it may not initially have been hugely prosperous. During the Fairweathers' reign as sugar refiners, however, imports to Dundee rose from 62 tons in 1786 to 583 tons in 1791,[97] and by 1800, they were exporting refined sugar to the Baltic through Isaac Watt and William Baxter. Exports rose from over 437 hundredweight in 1801 to a peak of 4,083 hundredweight in 1805, before the firm of Bell and Young sold the company in 1806, and exports slumped.[98] Although Dundee's sugar adventure remained minimal when compared to Glasgow's (in 1805, the latter exported 311,343 hundredweight, 93% of the national total), Dundee's commanded 20% of the non-Glasgow sugar trade in Scotland.[99]

At the end of 1774, the Continental Congress made the importation and consumption of British goods and manufactures and the exportation of American commodities to Britain illegal,[100] and the last eighteenth century ship to sail from Dundee direct to America was the *Fame*, which left in January 1775. Perhaps in response, Dundee's merchants opposed the colonists, as witness the address to the Earl of Suffolk in November 1775 by the Gentlemen, Clergy, Merchants, Manufacturers & Incorporated Trades, & Inhabitants of Dundee. It expressed their surprise at the 'ungrateful conduct of many . . . American subjects', and advocated 'vigorous measures' to persuade them of their 'obstinacy' until they 'appear sensible'.[101] The following year, America took only around 9% of Scottish linen exports, as compared to 66% the previous year.[102] As one Virginian merchant complained,

> We have had little or no trade here for some time past occasioned
> by the extreme scarcity of all kinds of coarse goods and I am at a
> loss to see how the poorer sort of people and negroes are to be
> provided with Clothing and Linen in future, when what they
> have at present here is worn out.[103]

Yet osnaburg production in Angus barely registered a dip.[104] As the petitioners informed Suffolk, 'it is with great pleasure we can assure your Majesty that our trade hath as yet suffered nothing by the American ports being shut against us'.[105] With goods consigned coastwise to London or to Glasgow,[106] Scottish manufactures found their way through Canada, Nova Scotia, Newfoundland or the West Indies. The Scots also created new trade links with East and West Florida, and latterly with New York.[107] But the American War of Independence (1775–83) severed the Dundee merchants' direct access to the American economy, and direct shipments to America did not resume until 1801 – even then being neither regular nor stable.

Since the council was forced in 1790 to offer mariners a bounty of two guineas each to persuade them to join the navy, the port appears to have been at full stretch.[108] But once the French Revolutionary War was under way, flax vessels could only travel safely from the Baltic in convoys. In April 1794, thirteen docked together,[109] six vessels arrived simultaneously in November 1797,[110] and a further thirteen Baltic traders arrived together in April the following year.[111] Although the port lost five vessels between January and March 1806 – *William* rammed by a collier, the *Providence*, *Clarence* and the *Two Brothers* foundered, only the *British Tar* was burnt by the French – indicating that Poseidon was a far greater danger than Boney.[112] Attacks by the enemy increased. Danish privateers captured three of the six Dundee vessels lost in 1808[113] compared to only one the previous year.[114] Of the twenty-three vessels that arrived in Dundee from foreign ports, only one was from Russia and seven from Sweden. Although foreign-going vessels leaving the port of Dundee declined by about 30%, they had increased in size to about the same proportion. Nonetheless, the Collector of Customs lamented, in September 1809, that 'trade at this port has been very inconsiderable since the ports of Denmark, Prussia and Russia were shut against us'.[115]

THE MARITIME QUARTER

During the eighteenth century, the shore side of the burgh – roughly defined as the district lying between the Town House and the High Street/Nethergate and the sea (extending eastwards up the Seagate out to the Roodyards) – consolidated a distinct maritime identity.[116] Still dominated by the habitations of shipmasters, it was becoming home to a growing number of trades that supplied the colonies, or – more precisely – that provisioned the ships and their crews, and, presumably, catered for sailors. Fish Street, Butcher Row and the surrounding locality comprised dense-packed, high-status tall tenement/apartment blocks, sometimes rising to more than six storeys, cut through by innumerable closes and wynds. As the port developed, however, so did the quarter become more business-like.

First, the reclamation of the bay of mudflats upstream of the west bulwark upstream of St Nicholas Craig and the creation of West Shore provided new space for woodyards and shipbuilding. Accordingly, in 1764, William Mitchell, William Stormont and David Anderson, ships carpenters, took land for shipbuilding at Plout's Well, Craig, at a rent of 4 pence sterling for each ton of vessel built.[117] Sailors boiled tar in the nearby Shore Walk.[118] Despite the fact that some fashionable new dwellings were erected at the sea end of the long rigs that extended down from the ancient properties facing the Nethergate, much of the flat land was used for storage yards and warehouses, and also for the miscellaneous urban activities inappropriate for a town centre location. Here therefore, alongside warehouses, was the 500 seater St Andrew's Episcopalian Chapel, whose congregation was 'most of the gentlemen of the County'[119] and later, Robert Cowie's Yeaman Shore Theatre that was advertising plays by 1803.[120]

The shore, with its 'Pleasant Walk pav'd with flagstones, and Rows of Trees on each side, which serves for an Exchange to the merchants and masters of ships', that John Macky had praised so fulsomely in the 1720s,[121] was changing character. In pursuit of civic improvement for the town centre – albeit in the teeth of opposition from the Fleshers – the council decided to remove the burgh's fleshmarket from the High Street to be next to the fish market in 1775. Here it constructed 'one of the Neatest [fleshmarkets] of its kind in this Nation',[122] and the New Shore was renamed Butcher Row in consequence. Yet the shore had not yet lost its quality or attraction. In 1790, the Seamen's Fraternity, which had received its royal charter sixteen years earlier,[123] constructed the Seamen's Hall (or Trinity House) just east of the harbour, to designs by Samuel Bell. The principal civic monument of the shore, the sumptuous first floor hall of this elegant pavilion was frequently used for civic functions, routs and balls, and on the ground floor offices a School of Navigation where aspirant shipmasters were required to attend lessons (used as a church on Sundays).[124]

Access to the harbour down steep and narrow closes, exemplified by Scott's, Kay's, Key's and Whitehall Closes and Couttie's and Tyndall's Wynds, no longer suited the developing port, and three new streets were cut through – St Andrew's Street in 1775, Crichton Street between the High Street and the Customs House conceived in 1777, and the even wider and smarter Castle Street between the Trades Hall and the harbour in 1795 (albeit not fully open for another thirteen years). Castle Street was the most distinctly modern of them all, planned with individual terraced houses in mind, and soon graced both by the Theatre Royal, opened in 1810, and another English Chapel. But Dundee's preference remained apartment-living in the European manner (see Chapter 6), their interiors beautifully refashioned and panelled in the most fashionable manner.[125]

In 1782, the maritime quarter was inhabited by a mixture of seafaring, shipping, crafts and trade people. It accounted for over half of Dundee's fifty two shipmasters, a sixth of its merchants, two thirds of the burgh's taverns and innkeepers, and all of its wood merchants.[126] Shipmasters had nothing like the wealth of the Baltic merchants, but although their furniture was not large in quantity, it tended to be of good mahogany, and the seadogs were usually well supplied with silver, porcelain and prints (never mind chests, punchbowls, and bottles).[127] There was also a concentration of tailors, the second largest congregation of shoemakers, a third of the town's chaise and horse dealers (presumably as carriers), fifteen maltmen, three each of wrights, masons and barbers, twelve weavers (clustered in the Seagate) and, inter alia, a writer and a blockmaker. The vast majority of butchers had followed the new flesh-market to that quarter.[128] The Shore and West Shore, where Dundee's two shipbuilders and three of the town's twenty-one taverns were situated, were thriving.

Seamen remain invisible in town directories, although 380 sailors were employed in Dundee-registered coastal vessels alone in 1806 (i.e. excluding whalers, international traders and visiting vessels),[129] and the harbour provided employment for twelve dockers – men who 'unloaded vessels'.[130] Since 1759, Dundee's sailors had been harassed by the Press Gang, when an impress boat was first stationed in the harbour.[131] The Press fixed on the Necessary House on the east bulwark of the harbour as their customary rendezvous and lock up, from which its gangs set out to sweep the streets of the maritime quarter.[132] From time to time, the council took pity on wives of 'several sailors impressed' who were in severe want, and received petitions from boatmen for protection against the Press Gang.[133] In 1802, the Gang, then under the command of a zealous Captain Watson,[134] was prosecuting its task with such vigour that many of the burgh's fishermen had to apply for Certificates of Protection against it. Perhaps this zealotry explains the minor scandal in 1808 when William Tasker, a Customs official, 'contributed toward the effecting an escape' of shipmaster Robert Low, who had been illegally impressed.[135]

Forty years later, the maritime quarter showed as much continuity as change. Dundee's seventy-two shipmasters now represented the burgh's largest single group of the elite with a specific trained skill,[136] and over two thirds of them remained based there – ten in Tyndal's Wynd, nine in Fish Street, and eight in St Clement's Lane, providing the market for a third of the port's hairdressers. The port's nautical interests were met by agents, brokers, coopers, three blockmakers, excise officers, landwaiters, ships' painters, rope makers, sailcloth manufacturers, shipmakers, ship brokers, ships' biscuit manufacturers and ship owners. But there were no longer the concentrations of the other trades in the maritime quarter. They had spread more evenly round the town – there was a Master of Marine and Commercial Academy in the High Street for instance – implying, perhaps, that the influence of Dundee's port was permeating the entire burgh.[137] Judging from the location of shipowners, agents, brokers and merchants, however, the mercantile heart of the town was firmly in Murraygate/Cowgate, beside the Baltic Exchange. Castle Street had finally begun to attract professional classes – six each of writers and shipmasters as residents.

This enhanced activity had its downside. The Seagate, to the east of the docks, with its blubber storehouses and boiling-sheds had become a 'filthy neighbourhood . . . surrounded by . . . noisome manufactories, such as foundries . . . ' with 'the only dwellings . . . of a very inferior description, chiefly occupied by persons directly connected with . . . these manufactories'.[138] The quarter was gaining a reputation that, in time, would impel those with any choice to move further out, as was fairly typical of other ports at the time.[139] Although having a good supply of ships in the harbour enabled the Theatre Royal's manager to fill his seats in Castle Street, 'sailors are good hands at filling the gallery' he reported,[140] sailors did not represent an elite audience. The Craig area had retained two shipbuilders and two shipowners, but barely a year later, shipbuilding was displaced by Dundee's new wet docks, and relocated to the new shipbuilding parade by Panmure Dock. The new docks represented the port's third wave of foreshore land reclamation. The fourth wave occurred when the railways arrived through foreshore and mudflats – from the east in 1838, and from the west in 1847. The maritime quarter was now remote from the sea and began to be regarded as an inconvenient nuisance. The Seamen's Mission that emerged in Fish Street was symbolic of its social decline, and the latter's demolition *c.* 1885 caused considerable civic satisfaction.

THE LIBERATING OF THE HARBOUR

As the century closed, the bulk of Dundee's shipping may have remained coastal, but it was increasing rapidly in volume, causing the Customs staff to complain in 1790 that their duty was 'severe from the increase in the coasting trade'.[141] By 1805, shipping was 350% greater than in 1777,[142] and the number of mariners directly employed by Dundee-registered vessels had risen to 380. Two years later, the number of vessels had risen by a further 26%, and the mariners by a further 40% (for coastal vessels had also increased in average size[143]). Dundee's first joint-stock coastal shipping company, the Dundee, Perth & London had been established in 1798, and owned 12 vessels which sailed twice-weekly to their destinations.[144] Its popularity duly led to the Kirk Session attempting in 1810 to stop London sailings from leaving on a Sunday and, a decade later, trying to prevent the 'great crowds' that were now gathering on a Sunday to watch the ships leave.[145]

In 1801, Dundee had opened direct trade with New York once again, dispatching large cargoes of linen products and other popular British goods and sundries[146] on one or two ships per year (larger in tonnage than their predecessors). Andrew Peddie's cargo was typical: 120 tons of coal as well as 'bounty linen and other goods not under prohibition . . . manufactured in this country'.[147] In 1802, *Jean* carried 2,000 bolts of linen to Norfolk, Virginia,[148] and in May the following year, the 250-ton United States vessel *Lydia* loaded goods for New York.[149] Following the end of the French wars, the trade flourished in an unprecedented manner, beginning a highly profitable and expansive business connection that continued for the rest of the century.[150]

A secondary cause of the increase in shipping was the port's growing fishing industry. Salmon had long been a principal export from the port, for the burgh owned the salmon fisheries between Invergowrie and the Gaw of Barry,[151] but it was now involved in the herring and white fish industry, and exporting both dried ling to Newcastle and salmon to London.[152] In 1801, one hundred boats (including the relatively large buss *Nelly*[153]) were herring fishing in the Tay, for which the Dundee fish curer James Davidson seems to have been the principal merchant.[154]

Records are silent about the maritime interest's view of local politics in the later eighteenth century: more is known about their employers – the Baltic merchants and commission agents who ran the town's economy. Possibly because they remained aloof from burgh politics – and were explicitly excluded from them by provost Alexander Riddoch from 1800 – they were dismissed contemptuously by him as a 'Combination of Murraygate Merchants'.[155] Riddoch had first been elected provost in 1789, and he, his crony Andrew Peddie (normally appointed burgh treasurer when Riddoch was provost), and their coterie remained in unchallenged political control of the burgh for the next forty years.[156] At about the same time as Riddoch's election, the Baltic merchants established a coffee house in the recently built Bain Square, on the corner of the Cowgate and Wellgate, next to where they were wont to discuss trade in the open air in front of St Andrew's church. That habit earned them the collective nickname of the 'Coogate'.[157] The 'Coogate' appears to have given the Riddoch regime a decade to develop an appropriate strategy for the harbour before concluding that the council was not going to do so. They then formed an informal committee of merchants, manufacturers and shipowners to champion the maritime interest. The Committee pressurised the council to protest to London about the navy's near destruction of the port's trade with the West Indies and the Spanish colonies 'whereby a great stock of those linens remain unsaleable on the hands of the merchants'[158] and then, two years later, sought to have Dundee declared a free port, since its trade was otherwise being restricted.[159] Neither had much effect; but this new political power continued to meet.

In 1810, when otherwise pursuing a programme of reactive and minor civic improvement, the council had been compelled to seek an Act of Parliament by an obdurate baker who opposed the widening of the 8-foot wide narrows of the Nethergate. The council then tacked a codicil on to its street-widening Bill authorising the raising of capital for harbour improvements, finally accepting that the harbour was 'too confined, and the depth . . . too small for . . . many of the vessels'. Far from welcoming this, the Baltic merchants regarded it as the last straw. The credibility of the council on harbour matters had already been damaged by the appointment of Andrew Peddie as shoremaster who, with Riddoch, had blocked the opening of Castle Street to the harbour over eighteen years whilst they had haggled over compensation for losing part of their jointly-owned woodyard.[160] Peddie, furthermore, was to be charged with renting public ground on an illegal length of lease at far too low a rent.[161] But to attempt to deal with the harbour by way of a codicil to something completely different illustrated the complete lack of under-standing of shipping issues in the council.

The maritime fraternity had had enough. Inspired by shipowner George Clark –

> . . . Geordie, the gleyed shipowner
> Wha a statue expects for his pains,
> To grace our new pier when we get it,
> And show that a tar may have brains[162]

and chaired by Robert Jobson ('red Rob that went out to Riga and cam' home a Russian bear'), the committee of merchants, manufacturers and shipowners met on 2 February 1814 and agreed to oppose the plans.[163] The improvement of the harbour, they claimed, was 'a public work of such magnitude and importance that on the manner of its execution depends the future prosperity perhaps the very existence of this town as a flourishing sea port'.[164] The engineer appointed by the council, Robert Stevenson, agreed that the harbour was in a 'ruinous state and unfit for the accommodation of the shipping resorting to the port',[165] but his proposals were limited, and because he had allowed Riddoch to retain servitude over a key part of it, his report was unacceptable to the Committee. They opposed the act formally on two grounds: first that the council could not be trusted to devise adequate harbour improvements; and secondly, that it could not be trusted to spend the money raised for harbour improvements upon the harbour. After all, only a quarter of the shore dues collected between 1764 and 1814 had been reinvested in the harbour itself.[166] There was also probably lingering resentment that it had been the refusal of the frantic petition by Dundee's glass works at Carolina Port in 1790 seeking exemption from these shore dues that had led to its closure, with a hundred people thrown out of work.[167]

It was the opening salvo of such a miserable saga of non-engagement and denial between the council and its burgh elite that the latter felt impelled to publish the correspondence to justify their actions to the wider population. The upshot was that control of the harbour was removed from the council in 1815, and placed in the hands of a new harbour commission with a twenty-one year life. Whilst still giving the council a considerable role, the commission gave a larger one to the merchants and mariners of Dundee. In 1828, when plans for the new

Exchange Coffee House facing the new dock were published, the *Directory* commented: 'By the united efforts of the Merchants and Shipowners, the Harbour has been brought to its present state of perfection'.[168] In 1830, responsibility for the harbour was placed in the hands of a Dundee Harbour Trust in perpetuity, rather than reverting to the council as originally intended. Once construction began on the first wet dock, designed by Thomas Telford, the maritime trade of Dundee increased exponentially. The King William IV dock was duly followed by the Earl Grey dock and, later, the Victoria and Camperdown docks, in almost a half century of continuous dock construction.[169] Latent demand, suppressed by the inadequacies of Dundee's unimproved harbour, must have played a large a part in the following decades of continuous dock construction.

CONCLUSION

Whereas histories of Dundee during the long eighteenth century have tended to focus upon the burgh's linen manufacture, the burgh's character can be equally well appreciated in terms of a seaport – and its activities, industries and its physical form can best be understood in that light. Its merchants had showed themselves to be adventurous and flexible in seeking out changing markets, and its fleet grew accordingly both in size and number of vessels. All hinged, however, on the support that could be provided within the maritime quarter, and upon the adequacy of the docks. It was not the enemy that was holding back the port of Dundee so much as its own council's ineptitude. It was, therefore, the other victory of 1815 – that of the maritime interest over Dundee's town council – that had at least equal significance in the burgh's history.

NOTES

1   Dundee City Archives (DCA), Town Council Minutes (TCM) 20 May 1754, 20 March 1755.
2   The National Information Service for Earthquake Engineering, University of California, Berkley [Online]. Available from: http://nisee.berkley.edu/lisbon/ .
3   Calculation by Professor Rob Duck.
4   DCA, Shoremaster's Accounts Martinmas 1757–58: money was paid to re-anchor 'the buoy carried off by the Tide to the westward side of the harbour'.
5   TCM, 19 April 1756.

6   See, for example, photographs of Fish Street in Dundee City Council's website *Photopolis* [Online]. Available from: www.dundeecity.gov.uk/photodb/main.html. The most striking difference was that the fine arcades lining the base of the Pierson building, now the Customs House, were truncated and appeared squat.

7   G. Jackson with K. Kinnear (eds.), *The Trade and Shipping of Dundee, 1780–1850* (Dundee: Abertay Historical Society, 1991), p. 5; B. Lenman, *From Esk to Tweed: Harbours, Ships and Men of the East Coast of Scotland* (Glasgow, 1975), p. 25.

8   Lenman, *Esk to Tweed*, p. 25.

9   See P. Corfield, *The Impact of the English Town 1700 – 1800* (Oxford, 1982), ch. 3.

10 See G. Jackson, 'Ports 1700 – 1840' in P. Clark, (ed.), *Cambridge Urban History of Britain Vol. II* (Cambridge, 2000), pp. 706–721.

11 C. McKean, ' "Not even the trivial grace of a straight line" – or why Dundee never built a new town', in L. Miskell, C. A. Whatley and B. Harris (eds.), *Victorian Dundee: Image and Realities* (East Lothian, 2000), p. 28; M. Healey, 'The Legacy of Alexander Riddoch' (unfinished MPhil Thesis, University of Dundee, 2003).

12 DCA, Records of the Customs and Excise (hereafter, CE), 70/1/7, 1789–1796, 29 December 1790.

13 J. Macky, *A Journey through Scotland* (London, 1723), p. 95.

14 DCA, CE 70/1/4, 10 May 1765.

15 DCA, CE 70/1/6, 17 April 1773.

16 G. Buchan, *Dundee Harbour; Its History and Development: A lecture delivered to the members of the Dundee Institute of Engineers on the 14 December 1899*, (Dundee, 1899), p. 18.

17 TCM, 27 June 1768.

18 TCM, 10 October 1768.

19 DCA, *The Report of John Smeaton, engineer, upon the Harbour of Dundee*, 15 March 1770.

20 *Charters, Writs and Public Documents of the Royal Burgh of Dundee* (Dundee, 1880), p. 178.

21 A. H. Miller (ed.), *The First History of Dundee* (Dundee, 1923) p. 139.

22 TCM, 4 July 1776.

23 TCM, 27 June 1770.

24 TCM, 17 June 1782.

25 *First History*, p. 78, cited in in H. Robertson, *Mariners of Dundee: Their City, Their River, Their Fraternity* (Dundee, 2006), p. 73. The *Statistical Account* was equally sanguine about the harbour, stating that it could accommodate vessels of 'up to 300 tons'.

26 TCM, 25 August 1770.

27 TCM, 19 April 1784.

28 DCA, CE 70/1/3, 21 December 1753.

29 DCA, CE 70/1/3, 22 December 1753.

30 DCA, CE 70/1/3, 6 August 1755.

31 DCA, CE 70/1/3, 2 April 1756.

32 DCA, CE 70/1/3, 13 September 1758.

33 DCA, CE 70/1/4, 19 July 1766.

34 Letter to Thomas Telford, *Clyde Reports*, 1824, p. 15, cited in Andrew Gibb, *Glasgow: The Making of a City* (London, 1983), p. 85.

35 DCA, CE 70/1/3, 15 January 1757.

36 DCA, CE 70/1/3, 28 April 1758.

37 DCA, CE 70/1/6, 23 April 1776.

38 DCA, CE 70/1/3, 1 August 1753; 22 August 1753; 14 September 1753; 5 December 1753; 26 September 1753; 7 May 1755; CE 70/1/4: 1 August 1766; 12 February 1767.

39 DCA, CE 70/1/3: 7 May 1755.

40 DCA, CE 70/1/3: 28 November 1753.

41 DCA, CE 70/1/3: 24 August 1753.

42 *Edinburgh Advertiser*, 9 January 1787 and 9 November 1792.

43 DCA, CE 70/1/6, 22 March 1777.

44 DCA, CE 70/1/3, 18 December 1754. It gives the lie to another enduring Dundee myth about the accidental origins of marmalade: see W. M. Matthew, *Keiller's of Dundee: The Rise of the Marmalade Dynasty* (Dundee: Abertay Historical Society, 1998), pp. 4 and 17.

45 DCA, CE 70/1/3: 16 July 1755.

46 DCA, CE 70/1/3: 29 August 1755.

47 Kate Newland, 'What was the Role of Norwegian and Baltic Timber in the Scottish Building Industry in the Seventeenth Century?' PhD in progress (University of Dundee).

48 *The Dundee Register of Merchants and Trades with all the offices etc.*, (Dundee, 1783); *Dundee Directory*, 1821–22.

49 We are indebted to Anne Law for a sight of her MPhil thesis 'Why Forfar Became the Centre of Osnaburg Manufacture' (University of Dundee, 2009).

50 Law, ibid.

51 C. W. Boase, *A Century of Banking in Dundee*, (Edinburgh, 1867) p. 39; Letter from the Linen Company, Edinburgh, to William Tod, London, 18 October 1757, cited in A. Durie, *British Linen Company (1745–1775)*, (Edinburgh, 1996), p. 87.

52 Flax importation increased from 150 tons in 1746 to 3000 tons by 1800, Durie (ed.), *The British Linen Company*, p. 107.

53 Robertson, *Mariners of Dundee*, p. 88.

54 A. J. Warden, *Linen Trade: Ancient and Modern* (Dundee, 1967), p. 548.

55 G. Jackson and K. Kinnear, *The Trade and Shipping of Dundee 1780–1850* (Dundee, 1991), p. 77.

56 DCA, CE 70/1/7, 6 January 1800.

57 DCA, CE 70/1/10, 26 February 1802.

58 DCA, CE 70/1/10, 23 November 1803.

59 DCA, CE 70/1/10, 24 October 1804.

60 In 1756, the Earl of Strathmore first took out shares in the Dundee Whale Fishing Company. Glamis MSS Box 102, Bundle 2.

61 *Extracts from Convention of the Royal Burghs of Scotland 1759–1779* (Edinburgh 1917), 26 November 1766.

62 DCA, CE 70/1/10, 11 July 1805.

63 Mudie, *Dundee Delineated* (Dundee, 1822), pp. 92–93; *Dundee Directory*, 1821–22.

64 There was a second soap-works in the Meadows. Mudie, *Dundee Delineated*, p. 97.

65 National Archives of Scotland (NAS), E504/11/8, Collectors Quarterly Returns.

66 *Edinburgh Advertiser*, 9 November 1792.

67 DCA, CE 70/1/10, 11 July 1805.

68 Mudie, *Dundee Delineated*, pp. 81–87.

69 Scotland's principal trading destination was Virginia, taking over 60% of Scottish linen exports in 1765. It was not, however, Dundee's main trading partner. On the two known voyages to Virginia in 1751 and 1771, Dundee exported over 6,000 yards of plain linen among other general goods including hats, woollen blankets, weapons and Portuguese wine. However, considering that Virginia was importing £21,000 of Scottish linens in 1774 alone, and it is most probable that Dundee was manufacturing the majority of this, it is clear that these materials were being exported through other Scottish ports. NAS RH2/4/12, Import Export Ledgers.

70 See Appendices 1 and 2; NAS E504/11/2–9, Customs Quarterly Returns.

71 NAS E504/11/2–9, Customs Quarterly Returns. Some ships may have entered illegally and others may not have been required to be recorded for tax purposes. It also depended on the Customs Officer's reliability. They often wrote up their ship logs only at the end of each quarter, and there was one instance when a boat to Liverpool was noted as a transatlantic voyage.

72 R. S. DuPlessis, 'Cloth and the Emergence of the Atlantic Economy', in P. Coclains, *The Atlantic Economy* (Cambridge, Massachusetts, 1995), p. 80.

73 This was alongside 16 tons of great coals, small coals, 69 pairs of white thread stockings, 12 shirts, 1,392 pairs of leather shoes and unknown quantities of saddles, bridles, tanned leather, white thread and iron spoons. The supplying merchants were Alexander Strachan and Smith, Strachan & Company. NAS E504/11/8, Collectors Quarterly Returns.

74 NAS E504/11/8, Collectors Quarterly Returns.

75 NAS E504/11/5, Collectors Quarterly Returns.

76 NAS E504/11/6, Collectors Quarterly Returns.

77 NAS E504/11/8, Collectors Quarterly Returns.

78 NAS E504/11/6–9, Collectors Quarterly Returns.

79 S. Max Edelson, 'The Characters of Commodities: the reputations of South Carolina rice and indigo in the Atlantic world', in Coclains (ed.), *The Atlantic Economy*, p. 348.

80 R. Nash, 'The Organisation of Trade and Finance in the British-Atlantic Economy, 1600–1830', in P. Coclains (ed.), *The Atlantic Economy during the Seventeenth and Eighteenth Century: New Perspectives on Organisation, Operation, Practices*, (South Carolina, 2005), p. 104.

81 NAS E504/11/5, Collectors Quarterly Returns.

82 NAS E504/11/6, Collectors Quarterly Returns.

83 J. M. Beatts, *Reminiscences of a Dundonian* (Dundee, 1882), p. 68.

84 The Jobsons, farmers of the Mains of Foulis, who first appeared as shipmasters in Dundee in the seventeenth century, became as influential a dynasty in eighteenth century Dundee as the Wedderburns had been earlier. Charles Jobson was burgh treasurer in 1745, and another David, a Writer (lawyer), was elected to the Tailors, Hammermen, Glovers, Bakers, Weavers Cordiners and Book Scriveners. The merchant John Jobson was a dyer and deacon of the Waulkers in 1768. His son David was elected a dyer in 1749. David Jobson, a cordiner, became Cashier of the Dundee Bank, D. and J. Jobson were bakers, Andrew Jobson a tailor, and Riga Bob a merchant. Jobsons were significant in the council, the infirmary, Trinity House (the Seamen's Fraternity), the Trades Hall and in the Kirk.

85 NAS E504/11/8, Collectors Quarterly Returns.

86 DCA, CE 70/1/6, 1789–1792.

87 NAS E504/11/5, Collectors Quarterly Returns.

88 Jackson and Kinnear, *The Trade and Shipping of Dundee*, pp. 19 and 85.

89 NAS E504/11/6, Collectors Quarterly Returns.

90 DCA, CE 70/1/14, 5 January 1814.

91 Miller, *First History*, p. 158 and Mudie, *Dundee Delineated*, p. 93.

92 NAS E504/11/2–9, Collectors Quarterly Returns.

93 Mudie, *Dundee Delineated*, p. 95.

94 Although this was a typical cargo in terms of commodities, this was by far the largest quantity of leather shoes reported. Throughout the 1750s and '60s, the average amount would have been just over 1,000 pairs.

95 *Articles of Co-Partnery*, 20 October 1779.

96 *Articles of Co-Partnery*, 20 October 1779.

97 Robertson, *Mariners of Dundee*, p. 81.

98 DCA, CE 70/1/11, 14 July 1808.

99 Gordon Jackson, 'New Horizons in Trade' in T.M Devine and Gordon Jackson, *Glasgow Volume I: Beginnings to 1830* (Manchester, 1995), p. 29.

100 M. L. Robertson, 'Scottish Commerce and the American War of Independence', in *The Economic History Review*, New Series, vol. 9, No. 1 (1956), p. 124.

101 Address of the Gentlemen, Clergy, Merchants, Manufacturers & Incorporated Trades, & Inhabitants of Dundee, transmitted to the Earl of Suffolk, His Majesty's Principal Secretary of State, *Dundee Weekly Magazine*, 17–24 November, 1775.

102 Durie, *Scottish Linen Industry*, p. 152.

103 T. Devine, *The Tobacco Lords* (Edinburgh, 1975), p. 126.

104 *Dundee Magazine and Journal of the Times*, 1799.

105 Address, *Dundee Weekly Magazine*, 17–24 November, 1775.

106 DCA, CE 70/1/6, 1789–1792.

107 Robertson, 'Scottish Commerce', p. 125.

108 TCM, 16 September 1790.

109 DCA, CE 70/1/6, 8 April 1794.

110 DCA, CE 70/1/6, 8 November 1797.

111 DCA, CE 70/1/6, 28 April 1798.

112 Robertson, *Mariners of Dundee*, p. 89.

113 DCA, CE 70/1/12, 5 January 1808.

114 DCA, CE 70/1/11, 5 January 1807.

115 DCA, CE 70/1/12, 6 September 1808.

116 The district came to include Seagate and its closes, Commercial Street, Castle Street, Tyndall's Wynd, The Vault, Crichton Street, Couttie's Wynd, Castle Wynd, Union Street, the closes – Whitehall, Scott's etc – between Nethergate and the Shore, Fish Street, Yeaman Shore, and Butcher Row.

117 TCM, 29 November 1764.

118 Miller, *First History*, p. 177.

119 R. Pococke, *Tours in Scotland* (Edinburgh, 1887), p. 223.

120 Dundee Central Library, Lamb Collection 252 (18). We are grateful to Stephen Fraser for this information. Also *Edinburgh Advertiser*.

121 Macky, *Journey*, p. 96.

122 Miller, *First History*, p. 253

123 This had occurred on 17 September 1774. H. Robertson, *Mariners of Dundee: Their City, Their River, Their Fraternity* (Dundee, 2006), p. 74.

124 Robertson, *Mariners*, p. 78.

125 The quality of these apartments has recently been revealed by the discovery in the Wellgate Library of over 600 drawings by Charles Lawson undertaken *c.* 1850–1880. Many of them depict elaborate and sophisticated interiors.

126 *The Dundee Register of Merchants and Trades with all the offices etc.* (Dundee, 1783), p. 12.

127 For example, the testament of John Martin, 1775. NAS/CC3/3/12, pp. 151–155.

128 *Dundee Register.*

129 CE 70/1/10 1802–06: 5 January 1806.

130 TCM, vol. 11, 13 November 1776.

131 CE 70/1/3 25 April 1759.

132 TCM, vol. 14, 28 April 1808.

133 TCM, 17 July 1755, 2 January 1758.

134 DCA, CE 70/1/8 (9), 1800 – 1802.

135 DCA, CE 70/1/11, 1 June 1808; TCM 28 April 1808.

136 Mudie, *Dundee Delineated*, 'principal inhabitants', pp. 213–240. Numerically, there were both more manufacturers and merchants; but the manufacturers varied from shoemaking to linen shirting, and the merchants from potato merchants to wholesalers and stoneware merchants. Shipmasters represented a single discipline with specific training.

137 *Dundee Directory*, 1809, 1821–22.

138 *Statement concerning the Whale-Fishing Trade at Dundee in Reference to its Proposed Introduction into Burntisland* (Burntisland, 1830)

139 Jackson, 'Ports', p. 724.

140 DCA, GD/NMS/32 Henry Johnston, Theatre Manager's diary entry 6 December 1821.

141 DCA, CE 70/1/7, 3 August 1790.

142 DCA, CE 70/1/10, 5 January 1806; CE 70/1/12, 5 January 1810.

143 Robertson, *Mariners of Dundee*, p. 83.

144 NAS Kirk Session Records CH2/12/1218/8, 22 October 1810; and 1218/9, 24 September 1823.

145 NAS E504/11/17–18, Collectors Quarterly Returns; Dundee University Archives (DUA) MS 73, Ingram Shipping lists, vols. 9–13.

146 DCA, CE 70/1/8 (9), 1800–02, 31 March 1801

147 DCA, CE 70/1/8 (9), 7 October 1801.

148 DCA, CE 70/1/10, 1802–06.

149 NAS E504/11/18–21, Collectors Quarterly Returns; DUA, MS73, Ingram, vol. 11.

150 Robertson, *Mariners of Dundee*, p. 48.

151 DCA, CE 70/1/7, 8 July 1792; CE 70/1/8, 9 July 1794 – 3 July 1795.

152 DCA, CE 70/1/7, 29 May 1798.

153 DCA, CE 70/1/9, 17 January 1801.

154 Letter A Riddoch to Robert Graham of Fintry, 21 Nov 1789. NAS/GD 151/11/28ff.

155 There have been many varying opinions of the influence of Provost Riddoch over Dundee's harbour at the turn of the century, but all agree that there was a need for improvement: McKean, 'Not even the trivial grace of a straight line', p. 28; W. Kenefick, 'The Growth and Development of the port of Dundee in the nineteenth and early twentieth centuries', in Miskell *et al.*, *Victorian Dundee*, pp. 41–42; E. Gauldie, *One Artful and Ambitious Individual: Alexander Riddoch, 1745–1822* (Dundee, 1989), p. 35; Healey, 'The Legacy of Alexander Riddoch', ch. 1, p. 11.

156 Dundee Chamber of Commerce *Centenary Memorial* (Dundee, 1936), p. 62.

157 TCM, 7 May 1801.

158 TCM, 13 December 1802.

159 TCM, 22 May 1806.

160 TCM, 14 and 28 September 1815, 3 October 1815.

161 Verse extracted from a contemporary poem on the harbour affair in James Cox's Journal. DUA MS/6/2/5/1.

162 *Proceedings of a Committee of Merchants, Manufacturers, Shipowners and Others for the Improvement of the Harbour of Dundee.* (Dundee, 1814).

163 DCA, *Minute Book of the Harbour Committee,* 5 March 1814, cited in Healey, 'The Legacy of Alexander Riddoch', ch. 3, p. 7.

164 *Memorial for Merchants, Manufacturers and Shipowners* (Dundee, 1813).

165 Kenefick, 'The Growth and Development of the port of Dundee', pp. 40–41.

166 *Municipal History of Dundee* (Dundee, 1878), p. 129. Also The Old Statistical Account, p. 29.

167 *Dundee Directory* (Dundee, 1828) p. v.

168 See L. Miskell and W. Kenefick, 'A Flourishing Seaport – Dundee Harbour and the Making of the Industrial Town' in *Scottish Economic and Social History* 20, part 2 (2000).

Appendix 1

Export voyages from Dundee, 1750–1775

Date	Ship	Port of origin	Destination
25/01/1751	*Delight of Dundee*	Dundee	Virginia
12/07/1753	*Mercury of Dundee*	Dundee	Charleston
24/07/1756	*Mercury of Dundee*	Dundee	Charleston
15/09/1757	*Mercury of Dundee*	Dundee	Charleston
22/08/1759	*Mercury of Dundee*	Dundee	Charleston
24/04/1760	*Mercury of Dundee*	Dundee	Charleston
18/09/1761	*Mercury of Dundee*	Dundee	Charleston
02/11/1762	*Dolphin of Dundee*	Dundee	Charleston
06/09/1763	*Dolphin of Dundee*	Dundee	Charleston
25/06/1764	*Two Friends*	Dundee	North Carolina
20/04/1765	*Saint Johnstone of Perth*	Dundee	Philadelphia
30/04/1765	*Minerva of Dundee*	Dundee	Charleston
12/09/1765	*Dolphin of Dundee*	Dundee	Charleston
27/02/1766	*Peggie of Dundee*	Dundee	North Carolina
20/10/1766	*Success of Dundee*	Dundee	Charleston
17/03/1767	*Peggie of Dundee*	Dundee	Cape Fear, North Carolina
19/10/1767	*Elizabeth of Dundee*	Dundee	Charleston
10/12/1767	*Fame*	Dundee	Charleston
22/11/1769	*Fame*	Dundee	Charleston

Date	Ship	Port of origin	Destination
18/12/1770	*Europa of Dundee*	Dundee	Charleston
22/03/1771	*Fame*	Dundee	Charleston
02/10/1771	*Adventure of Perth*	Dundee	Norfolk, Virginia
24/10/1771	*Fame*	Dundee	Charleston
20/01/1773	*Fame*	Dundee	Charleston
20/01/1775	*Fame*	Dundee	Charleston & Savannah

Source: NAS E504/11/2–9, Collectors Quarterly Returns: Dundee.

Appendix II

Import voyages to Dundee, 1750–1775

Date	Ship	Port of origin	Via	Destination
23/05/1754	Mercury of Dundee	Charleston	Lisbon	Dundee
01/09/1756	Mercury of Dundee	Charleston		Dundee
09/05/1757	Mercury of Dundee	Charleston	Lisbon	Dundee
19/08/1757	Mercury of Dundee	Charleston		Dundee
24/04/1760	Mercury of Dundee	Charleston		Dundee
23/06/1761	Mercury of Dundee	Charleston	Lisbon	Dundee
04/05/1762	Mercury of Dundee	Charleston		Dundee
26/07/1762	Dolphin of Dundee	Charleston		Dundee
10/08/1763	Dolphin of Dundee	Charleston		Dundee
16/05/1764	Dolphin of Dundee	Charleston		Dundee
17/10/1766	Peggie of Dundee	North Carolina		Dundee
16/09/1767	Nancy of Northfolk	Port Hampton, Virginia		Dundee
05/12/1767	Fame	Charleston	Lisbon	Dundee
10/08/1769	Fame	Charleston	Lisbon	Dundee
22/10/1770	Fame	Charleston	Lisbon	Dundee
15/04/1772	Europa of Dundee	Charleston	Lisbon	Dundee
30/04/1773	Fame	South Carolina	Lisbon	Dundee
11/11/1774	Elizabeth	Edenton, NC		Dundee
16/10/1775	Elizabeth	Edenton, NC		Dundee

Source: NAS E504/11/2–9, Collectors Quarterly Returns: Dundee

Bibliography

ARCHIVAL SOURCES

Angus Archives
Montrose Town Council Minutes

Blair Castle
Atholl Papers

Centre for South Asian Studies, Cambridge
Duncan Papers

Dundee Central Library
The Charles Lawson Collection
The Lamb Collection

Dundee City Archives
Auchterhouse Session Minutes. CH2/23
Book of Acts and Decrees of the Council
Charters and Writs: 'Decreet by King James
    VI and the Lords of Council deciding
    the dispute between the towns of Perth
    and Dundee respecting their privileges
    on the Tay and the precedence'. CC1/79
Dundee General Session Minutes.
    CH2/1218
Dundee Presbytery Minutes. CH2/103
Dundee Register of Ships
Dundee Treasurer's Accounts
Guildry Sederunt, 9 May 1735
Land Tax Register, 1826–30
Lawburrows Books of Dundee, 1775 to 1799
Lockit Book, 1740–60
Minute Book of the Harbour Committee

Minutes of the Dundee Public Library
Sederunt book belonging to the fraternity of
    maltmen at Dundee, 26 November 1791.
    GD/HF/M1/1
Shoremaster's Accounts Martinmas 1757–8
*The Report of John Smeaton, engineer, upon
    the Harbour of Dundee*, 15 March 1770
Town Council Minutes (TCM)
Wedderburn of Pearsie Papers

Edinburgh City Archives
Accompt of the State and condition of the
    Burgh of Striline, 1700. SL 30/223
Convention of Royal Burghs: Report of the
    Commissioners Appoynted for visiting
    the Burgh of Dundee, 13 June 1700.
    SL 30/223
Information to the Right Honourable
    Convention of Burrows anent the Caice
    of the Royall Burghs in the shire of
    Angus, 1716. SL 30/227
Petition by the Burgh of Elgine, 1697.
    SL 30/216
Petitions for the Burgh of Dundee.
    SL 30/221
Petition by the Merchants of Dumfries,
    4 July 1704. SL 30/223
Report of the State of the Towne of Dundie,
    6 June 1710. SL 30/223

Edinburgh City Library Special Collections
Andrew Armstrong's Journal, 1789–93.
    DA 1861.789

Edinburgh University Library
Laing Papers

Glamis Castle
Glamis papers
Strathmore Papers

Huntington Library
Stowe Collection. ST57/30

National Archives of Scotland
Abercairney Muniments. GD24/1/464
Acts of Parliament. PA2
Alexander Piper of Newgrange Papers.
    RH15/101
A Narrative of the Arrest, Examination &
    Imprisonment of George Mealmaker.
    RH2/4/83
Brechin Commissary Court: Registers of
    Inventories and Settlements. CC3/5
Papers of the Montague–Douglas–Scott
    family, Dukes of Buccleuch. GD224
Calendar of Felons, Forfarshire, SC47/55/2
Papers of Clerk family of Penicuik,
    Midlothian. GD18
Colonel Charles Hotham to Lieutenant-
    General George Carpenter, Dundee,
    18 October 1716. RH2/4/312/219(B)
Register of Acts and Decreets of Court of
    Session, CS7
Court of Session Papers. CS229/R5/27
Court of Session Records. CS96/4208
Demographic and occupational profile of
    Dundee, 1811. SC47/71/4
Dundee Burgh Register of Sasines. B19/4/2
Dundee Entry book: Imports and exports
    (1681–1682). E72/7/9
Edinburgh High Court Books of Adjournal.
    JC3
Edinburgh High Court Minute Books. JC8
Female Servant Tax in Scottish Burghs,
    E326/6/3, E326/6/7, E326/6/11, E326/6/15,
    E326/6/19, E326/6/23 and E326/6/27
Female Servant Tax in Scottish Counties,
    E326/6/1, E326/6/5, E326/6/9, E326/6/13,
    E326/6/17, E326/6/21 and E326/6/25.
Forfarshire Particular Register of Sasines,
    1781–1820
Forfarshire Sheriff Court Records. SC47
Graham of Fintry Papers (microfilm copy).
    GD151/11/3

High Court of Justiciary Papers.
    JC28/293
Import Export Ledgers. RH2/4/12
Inhabited House Tax in the Burgh of
    Dundee, 5 July 1778 to 5 April 1797,
    E326/3 Series.
Inhabited House Tax, Forfarshire, 1778-98,
    E326/3/18 Series.
Inventory of Samuel Bell, architect in
    Dundee, 1813. CC3/5/3
John Leslie, ninth earl of Rothes to […],
    Edinburgh, 5 February 1716.
    RH 2/4/309(90)
Male Servant Tax in Scottish Burghs,
    E326/5/2, E326/5/4, E326/5/6,
    E326/5/8, E326/5/10, E326/5/12,
    E326/5/14, E326/5/16, E326/5/18,
    E326/5/20, E326/5/22, E326/5/24 and
    E326/5/26.
Male Servant Tax in Scottish Counties,
    E326/5/1, E326/5/3, E326/5/5, E326/5/7,
    E326/5/9, E326/5/11, E326/5/13,
    E326/5/15, E326/5/17, E326/5/19,
    E326/5/21, E326/5/23 and E326/5/25.
Memorial Concerning the Present State of
    Angus and Mearns, Brechin,
    31 May 1716. RH2/4/311/20
Montrose Manuscripts.
    GD220/5/453/13
North Circuit Minute Books. JC11
Ogilvie of Inverquharity Manuscripts.
    GD205
Papers of the Dundas Family of Melville.
    GD51
Papers of the Gordon Family. GD44
Paterson of Castle Huntly Papers. GD508
Privy Council: Register Of Acta, 1696–99.
    PC 1/51
Register of Seisins (Forfar)
Report of spy, 'J.B.', 22 November. 1793.
    RH 2/4/73
Schoolmaster returns of militia names for
    year 1801. SC47/72/3
State Papers Scotland: Case of the Toun of
    Dundie. RH 2/4/308
Window Tax, E326/1/50, E326/1/51,
    E326/1/52, E326/1/53, E326/1/149,
    E326/1/150 and E326/1/151.

National Register of Archives (Scotland)
Papers of the Earl of Strathmore

National Library of Scotland
Alexander Brown, 'Journey in Scotland
    with sketches of some Picturesque
    Ruins in that Interesting Country
    in Two Volumes', vol. 1.
    MS 3294
Dempster to Henry Dundas, 31 January
    1788. MS 653
Fletcher of Saltoun. MS 16538
Melville Papers
Saltoun Papers. MS 17567
Travel journal of unidentified Irish visitor,
    1818. MS 2795
Yester Papers. MS 7026

Newton Castle
Macpherson of Clunie Papers

Perth and Kinross Council Archives
Act of convention of burghs, 1582.
    B59/26/1/9/7/1
Baron Kinnaird of Inchture, Rossie Priory
    Papers. MS 100
Hunters of Glencarse Papers. MS 177
James VI to the earl Marischal, 30 May
    1594. B59/26/1/9/1
Letteris for Perth for the superioritie of
    place Perth aganis Dundie, 16 June 1582.
    B59/26/1/9/2
List of Sentences and Death Warrants.
    B59/26/11
Lord Gray to the Provost of Perth anent
    Stamping of Linen etc, 15 December
    1726. B59/24/8/4
Perth Burgh Records, Address by the Burgh
    of Perth to the Parliament, 1700.
    B59/34/12
Petitions, 1689–1739. B59/26/4
Perth Town Council Papers. PE 51
Register of Acts of the Council, 1601–1602.
    B59/16/1
Sederunt of the Committee of Freeholders
    of the Shire of Forfar, 10 November
    1726. B59/24/8/4

St Andrews University Library
Hay of Leyes Muniments. MS36220

Tamil Nadu State Archives
Mayor's Court Records, Private
    Miscellaneous xii (c): 'Diary of George

Bruce, 9 November 1776 to
    18 September 1777'
University of Dundee Archives Services
John P. Ingram Collection. MS 73
Mr James Guthrie's Diary.
    BRMS 3/DC46
Papers relating to Naughton Estate and
    Castle and the Crawford Family.
    MS15/218/4

NEWSPAPERS, PERIODICALS
AND DIRECTORIES

Caledonian Mercury
Dumfries Weekly Journal
Dundee Magazine and Journal of the Times
Dundee, Perth and Cupar Advertiser
Dundee Weekly Advertiser
Dundee Weekly Magazine
Edinburgh Advertiser
Edinburgh Evening Courant
Edinburgh Gazetteer
Edinburgh Herald
Glasgow Courier
The London directory for the year 1778.
    Containing an alphabetical list of the
    names and places of abode of the
    merchants and principal traders
    (London, 1778)
Scots Chronicle
Scots Magazine

PRIMARY SOURCES

Adair, J., *The Mappe of Straithern,*
    Stormont & Cars of Gourie (1683)
Baldwin, R., *Baldwin's New Complete*
    Guide to all persons who have any
    trade or concern with the City of London,
    and parts adjacent (London, 1768)
Barclay, J., *The Voyages and Travels of*
    James Barclay, containing many surprising
    adventures, and interesting narratives
    (London, 1777)
Beatts, J. M., *Reminiscences of a Dundonian*
    (Dundee, 1882)
Beveridge, J. (ed.), *Register of the Privy*
    Seal of Scotland Vol. IV (RSS),
    (Edinburgh, 1952)

Buchan, G., *Dundee Harbour; Its History and Development: A lecture delivered to the members of the Dundee Institute of Engineers on the 14 December 1899*, (Dundee, 1899)

Burton, J. H., (ed.), *The Darien Papers: Being a Selection of Original Letters and Official Documents relating to the Establishment of a colony at Darien by the Company of Scotland* (Bannatyne Club, 1849)

Calderwood, D., *The Historie of the Kirk of Scotland*, (Edinburgh, 1842)

Campbell, A., *Journey from Edinburgh* (2 vols., London, 1802)

Chambers, W. R., *Domestic Annals of Scotland Vol. 3* (Edinburgh, 1874)

Defoe, D., *A Tour through the whole Island of Great Britain* (London, 1725)

Donaldson, J., *General View of the Agriculture of the Carse of Gowrie* (London, 1794)

Douglas, N., *Britain's Guilt, Danger and Duty; Several Sermons, preached at Anderston, near Glasgow; Aug 23, 1795* (Dundee, 1795)

Douglas, N., *Messiah's Curious Rest in the Latter Days; A Sermon Delivered in the Associate Church, Before the Missionary Society, Dundee, May 1 1797 And in the Relief Church, Dove-Hill, Glasgow, May 21* (Dundee, 1797)

Durie, A. (ed.), *The British Linen Company, 1745–1775* (Edinburgh, 1996)

Edward, R., *The County of Angus 1678* (reprint Edinburgh, 1883)

Ferguson, J. (ed.), *The Letters of George Dempster to Sir Adam Fergusson, 1756–1813* (London, 1934)

Gillies, J., *Historical Collections Relating to Remarkable Periods of the Success of the Gospel and Eminent Instruments Employed in providing it*, 2 vols. (Glasgow, 1754)

Gurney, J. J., *Notes on a Visit made to some of the Prisons in Scotland and the North of England, in Company with Elizabeth Fry; with some general Observations on the Subject of Prison Discipline* (London, 1819)

Hay, D. (ed.), *The Letters of James V* (Edinburgh, 1954)

Heron, R., *Scotland Delineated, or a Geographical Description of Every Shire in Scotland, including the Northern and Western Isles* (2nd edn, Edinburgh, 1799, reprinted Edinburgh, 1975)

Historical Manuscripts Commission, *Report on the Manuscripts of the Earl of Mar and Kellie* (London, 1904)

Lettice, J., *Letters on a Tour through various parts of Scotland for the year 1792* (London, 1794)

Loch, D., *A Tour through most of the Trading Towns and Villages of Scotland: Containing notes and Observations Concerning Trade and Manufacturers* (Edinburgh, 1778)

Macky, J., *A Journey Through Scotland. In Familiar Letters from a Gentleman Here, to his Friend Abroad. Being the Third Volume which Completes Great Britain* (2nd edn, 1732)

Masson, D. (ed.), *Register of the Privy Council of Scotland Vol. VIII, 1607–1610* (Edinburgh, 1887)

Millar, A. H. (ed.), *Compt Buik of David Wedderburne* (Edinburgh, 1898)

Pococke, R., *Tours in Scotland* (Edinburgh, 1887)

Renwick, R. (ed.), *Charters and other Documents relating to the Royal Burgh of Stirling AD 1124–1705* (Glasgow, 1884)

Renwick, R. (ed.), *Extracts from the Records of the Royal Burgh of Lanark* (Glasgow, 1893)

Skrine, H., *Three Successive Tours in the North of England, and a Great Part of Scotland, Interspersed with Descriptions of the Scenes they Presented, and Occasional Observations on the State of Society* (London, 1795)

Snodgrass, J., *The Means of Preserving the Life and Power of Religion in a Time of general Corruption. A Valedictory Sermon to the Inhabitants of Dundee* (Dundee, 1781)

Thomson, T. (ed.), *The Acts of the Parliaments of Scotland (APS), Vol. X* (Edinburgh, 1823)

Wilde, J., *An Address to the Lately Formed Society of the Friends of the People* (Edinburgh, 1793)

An Account of the Present Persecution of the Church in Scotland in Several Letters (London, 1690)

A Monitory Address to Great Britain (1792)

A Select Collection of Letters of the Late Rev George Whitefield, 3 vols. (London, 1772)

The Darien Papers (Bannatyne Club, Edinburgh, 1849)

The Dundee Register of Merchants and Trades (Dundee, 1783)

Encyclopaedia of the Laws of Scotland, Volume IX, Land Tax to Midwives (Edinburgh, 1930)

The Literary Correspondence of John Pinkerton, Esq. 2 vols. (London, 1830)

Memorial for merchants, manufacturers and shipowners (Dundee, 1813)

The Municipal History of Dundee (Dundee, 1878)

Proceedings of a Committee of Merchants, Manufacturers, Shipowners and others for the Improvement of the Harbour of Dundee (Dundee, 1814)

A Sermon Delivered in Dundee, February 20th, 1795 (London, 1795)

Statement concerning the Whale-Fishing Trade at Dundee in Reference to its Proposed Introduction into Burntisland (Burntisland, 1830)

The Trial of the Revd Thomas Fyshe Palmer Before the Circuit Court of Justiciary, Held at Perth, on the 12th and 13th of September, 1793, on an Indictment for Seditious Practices (Edinburgh, 1794)

The Traveller's Guide through Scotland and its Islands, 2 vols. (7th edn, Edinburgh, 1818)

SECONDARY SOURCES

Airs, M. and Tyack, G. (eds.), *The Renaissance Villa in Britain* (Lincoln, 2007)

Bannerman, J., *The Beatons: A Medical Kindred in the Classical Gaelic Tradition* (Edinburgh, 1986)

Barber, W. J., *British Economic Thought and India, 1600–1858* (Oxford, 1975)

Barrell, J., *Imagining the King's Death: Figurative Treason, Fantasies of Regicide, 1793–1796* (Oxford, 2000)

Barrie, D. G., *Police in the Age of Improvement: Police Development and the Civic Tradition in Scotland, 1775–1865* (Cullompton, 2008)

Bartlett, T., Dickson, D., Keogh, D., Whelan, K. (eds.), *1798: A Bicentenary Perspective* (Dublin, 2003)

Bayly, C. A., *The Birth of the Modern World, 1780–1814* (Oxford, 2004)

Berg, M., *Luxury and Pleasure in Eighteenth Century Britain* (Oxford, 2005)

Bermingham, A., *Learning to Draw: Studies in the Cultural History of a Polite and Useful Art* (New Haven and London, 2000)

Black, E. C., *The Association: British Extra-Parliamentary Political Organisation 1769 to 1793* (Harvard, 1963)

Boase, C. W., *A Century of Banking in Dundee*, (Edinburgh, 1867)

Bogle, K. R., *Scotland's Common Ridings* (Stroud, 2004)

Borsay, P., *The English Urban Renaissance: Culture and Society in the Provincial Town 1660–1760* (Oxford, 1989)

Borsay, P. (ed.), *The Eighteenth-Century Town* (Harlow, 1990)

Borsay, P., Hirschfelder, G. and Mohrmann, R. (eds.), *New Directions in Urban History, Aspects of European Art, Tourism and Leisure since the Enlightenment* (Munster, 2000)

Bowen, H. V., *Revenue and Reform: The Indian Problem in British Politics, 1757–1773* (Cambridge, 1991)

Bowen, H. V., *The Business of Empire: The East India Company & Imperial Britain, 1756–1833* (Cambridge, 2006)

Boyd, F., *Records of the Dundee Stage, From the Earliest Times to the Present Day* (Dundee, 1886)

Brotherstone, T. (ed.), *Covenant, Charter and Party: Traditions of Revolt and Protest in Modern Scottish History* (Aberdeen, 1989)

Brown, C. G., *Religion and Society in Scotland since 1707* (Edinburgh, 1997)

Brown, K. M. and Mann, A. J. (eds.), *The History of the Scottish Parliament 1567–1707*, Vol. 2 (Edinburgh, 2005)

Buddle, A., Rohatgi, P. & Brown, I. G., *The Tiger and the Thistle: Tipu Sultan and the Scots in India* (Edinburgh, 1999)

Cage, R. A. (ed.), *The Scots Abroad: Labour, Capital, Enterprise, 1750–1914* (London, 1985)

Cain, P. J. & Hopkins, A. G., *British Imperialism: Innovation and Expansion, 1688–1914* (London, 1993)

Cameron, J., *Prisons and Punishment in Scotland from the Middle Ages to the Present Day* (Edinburgh, 1983)

Chaudhuri, K. N., *The Trading World of Asia and the English East India Company, 1660–1760* (Cambridge, 1978)

Clark, P. (ed.), *The Cambridge Urban History of Britain Vol. II: 1540–1840* (Cambridge, 2000)

Clark, P., *British Clubs and Societies 1580–1800: The Origins of an Associational World* (Oxford, 2000)

Coclanis, P. *The Atlantic Economy during the Seventeenth and Eighteenth Century: New Perspectives on Organization, Operation, Practices* (South Carolina, 2005)

Colley, L., *Britons: The Forging of the Nation, 1707–1837* (New Haven and London, 1992)

Connolly, S. J. (ed.), *Kingdoms United? Great Britain and Ireland since 1500: Integration and Diversity* (Dublin, 1999)

Connolly, S. J., Houston, R. A. and Morris, R. J. (eds.), *Conflict, Identity and Economic Development: Ireland and Scotland, 1600–1939* (Preston, 1995)

Corfield, P. J., *Power and the Professions in Britain, 1700–1850* (London, 1995)

Corfield, P. J., *The Impact of the English Town, 1700–1800* (Oxford, 1982)

Cowan, I. B and Easson, D. E., *Mediaeval Religious Houses Scotland* (London, 1976)

Cruickshanks, E., Handley, S. and Hayton, D. W. (eds.), *The History of Parliament, The House of Commons, 1690–1714*, 5 vols. (Cambridge, 2002)

Cummings, A. J. G. and Devine, T. M. (eds.), *Industry, Business and Society in Scotland since 1700* (Edinburgh, 1994)

Cunninghame, I. (ed.), *The Nation Survey'd* (East Linton, 2001)

Davis, M. T. (ed.), *The London Corresponding Society, 1792–1799* (London, 2002)

Dennison, P., (ed.), *Conservation and Change in Historic Towns* (York, 2000)

Dennison, E. P., Ditchburn, D. and Lynch, M. (eds.), *Aberdeen before 1800: A New History* (East Linton, 2002)

Devine, T. M., (ed.), *Conflict and Stability in Scottish Society 1700–1850* (Edinburgh, 1990)

Devine, T. M., *The Transformation of Rural Scotland: Social Change and the Agrarian Economy, 1660–1815* (Edinburgh, 1994)

Devine, T. M., Lee, C. H. and Peden G. C. (eds.), *The Transformation of Scotland: The Economy since 1700* (Edinburgh, 2005)

Devine, T. M. and Jackson, G. (eds.), *Glasgow. Volume I: Beginnings to 1830* (Manchester, 1995)

Devine, T. M. and Young, J. R. (eds.), *Eighteenth-Century Scotland: New Perspectives* (East Linton, 1999)

Dickinson, H. T., *The Politics of the People in Eighteenth-Century Britain* (New York, 1994)

Dingwall, C., 'Dr Patrick Blair and Dundee's first Botanic Garden' (Unpublished research paper, Dundee, 1987)

Dingwall, H. M., *A History of Scottish Medicine: Themes and Influences* (Edinburgh, 2003)

Dingwall, H., *Physicians, Surgeons and Apothecaries: Medicine in Seventeenth-Century Edinburgh* (East Linton, 1995)

Dobson, D., *The Jacobites of Angus, 1689–1746* (St Andrews, 1995)

Donald, D. and O' Gorman, F. (eds.), *Ordering the World in the Eighteenth Century* (Basingstoke, 2006)

Donnachie, I. and Whatley, C. A. (eds.), *The Manufacture of Scottish History* (Edinburgh, 1992)

Donnison, J., *Midwives and Medical Men: A History of Inter-Professional Rivalries and Women's Rights* (London, 1977)

Dow, D. A. (ed.), *The Influence of Scottish Medicine: An Historical Assessment of its International Impact* (Carnforth, 1988)

Drummond, A. L. and Bulloch, J.,
The Scottish Church 1688–1843
(Edinburgh, 1973)

Duffy, C., *The '45* (London, 2003)

Dumett, R. E. (ed.), *Gentlemanly
Capitalism and British Imperialism:
The New Debate on Empire*
(London, 1999)

Duncan, A., *Memorials of the Faculty of
Physicians and Surgeons of Glasgow
1599–1850* (Glasgow, 1896)

Durie, A. J., *The Scottish Linen Industry in
the Eighteenth Century* (Edinburgh, 1979)

Ehrenreich, B. and English, D., *Witches,
Midwives and Nurses: A History of
Women Healers* (New York, 1973)

Emsley, C., *Crime and Society in England,
1750–1900* (London, 1996)

Evenden, D., *The Midwives of Seventeenth-
Century London* (Cambridge, 2000)

Farrington, A., *A Biographical Index of East
India Company Maritime Service Officers,
1600–1834* (London, 1999)

Fawcett, R., *Scottish Mediaeval Churches*
(Stroud, 2002)

Ferguson, T., *The Dawn of Scottish Social
Welfare* (London, 1948)

Fittis, R. S., *The Perthshire Antiquarian
Miscellany* (Perth, 1875)

Flinn, M. (ed.), *Scottish Population History
from the Seventeenth Century to the 1930s*
(Cambridge, 1977)

Forster, R. and Ranum, O. (eds.), *Biology of
Man in History: Selections from the
Annales, économies, sociétés, civilisations*
trans. E. Forster and P. M. Ranum
(Baltimore, 1975)

Foyster, E. and Whatley, C. A. (eds.),
Everyday Life in Scotland Vol. 2 1600–1800
(Edinburgh, 2009)

Fraser, W. H., *Conflict and Class: Scottish
Workers 1700–1838* (Edinburgh, 1988)

Fry, M., *The Dundas Despotism*
(Edinburgh, 1992)

Fry, M. *The Scottish Empire*
(Edinburgh, 2001)

Gauldie, E., *One Artful and Ambitious
individual: Alexander Riddoch, 1745–1822*
(Dundee, 1989)

Gee, A., *The British Volunteer Movement,
1794–1814* (Oxford, 2003)

Geyer-Kordesch, J. and Macdonald, F.,
*Physicians and Surgeons in Glasgow:
The History of the Royal College of
Physicians and Surgeons of Glasgow
1599–1858* (London, 1999)

Gibb, A., *Glasgow: The Making of a City*
(London, 1983)

Ginter, D. E., *Whig Organisation in the
General Election of 1790* (Berkeley and
Los Angeles, 1967)

Goodare, J., *State and Society in Early
Modern Scotland* (Oxford, 1999)

Gordon, G. and Dicks, B. (eds.), *Scottish
Urban History* (Aberdeen, 1983)

Gordon, G. (ed.), *Perspectives of the
Scottish City* (Aberdeen, 1985)

Gowing, L., *Common Bodies: Women,
Touch and Power in Seventeenth-Century
England* (London, 2003)

Graham, E. J., *A Maritime History of
Scotland, 1650–1780* (East Linton, 2002)

Graham, M. F., *The Uses of Reform: 'Godly
Discipline' and Popular Behaviour in
Scotland and Beyond, 1560–1610*
(Leiden, 1996)

Gupta, A. D. & Pearson, M. N. (eds.),
India and the Indian Ocean, 1500–1800
(Calcutta, 1987)

Haldane, J. A. L. (ed.), *The Haldanes of
Gleneagles* (Edinburgh, 1929)

Hamilton, D., *The Healers: A History of
Medicine in Scotland* (Edinburgh, 1981)

Hamilton, D. J., *Scotland, the Caribbean
and the Atlantic World 1750–1820*
(Manchester, 2005)

Harris, B. (ed.), *Scotland in the Age of the
French Revolution* (Edinburgh, 2005)

Harris, B. and MacDonald, A. R. (eds.),
*Scotland: The Making and Unmaking of
the Nation c. 1100–1707*, Vol. 2
(Dundee, 2007)

Hatton, R. and Anderson, M. S. (eds.),
*Studies in Diplomatic History: Essays in
Memory of David Bayne Horn*
(London, 1970)

Hay, W. (ed.), *Charters, Writs, and Public
Documents of the Royal Burgh of Dundee*
(Dundee, 1880)

Hodson, V. C. P., *List of the Officers
of the Bengal Army, 1758–1834,*
(London, 1927)

Hoppit, J. (ed.), *Parliaments, nations and identities in Britain and Ireland, 1660–1850* (Manchester, 2003)

Houston, R. A., *Social Change in the Age of the Enlightenment: Edinburgh, 1660–1760* (Oxford, 1994)

Houston, R. A. and Whyte, I. D. (eds.), *Scottish Society, 1500–1800* (Cambridge, 1989)

Jackson, G. and Kinnear, K., *The Trade and Shipping of Dundee, 1780–1850* (Dundee, 1991)

Jackson, G. and Lythe, S. G. E. (eds.), *The Port of Montrose: A History of its Harbour, Trade and Shipping* (New York and Tayport, 1993)

Jenkinson, J., *Scottish Medical Societies 1731–1939: Their History and Records* (Edinburgh, 1993)

Johnson, D., *Music and Society in Lowland Scotland in the Eighteenth Century* (London, 1972)

Kilday, A. M., *Women and Violent Crime in Enlightenment Scotland* (Suffolk, 2007)

Lamb, A. C., *Dundee, Its Quaint and Historic Buildings* (Dundee, 1895)

Landsman, N. C. (ed.), *Nation and Province in the First British Empire: Scotland and the Americas, 1600–1800* (London, 2001)

Lawson, P., *The East India Company: A History* (London, 1993)

Lenman, B., *The Jacobite Risings in Britain 1689–1746* (Aberdeen, 1995)

Lenman, B., *From Esk to Tweed: Harbours, Ships and Men of the East Coast of Scotland* (Glasgow, 1975)

Leneman, L. and Mitchison, R., *Sin in the City: Sexuality and Social Control in Urban Scotland, 1660–1780* (Edinburgh, 1998)

Lindsay, J., *The Scottish Poor Law: Its Operation in the North-East from 1745 to 1845* (Ilfracombe, 1975)

Livingstone, A., Aikman, C. W. H. and Hart, B. S., *No Quarter Given: The Muster Roll of Prince Charles Edward Stuart's Army, 1745–46* (Glasgow, 2001)

Logue, K. J., *Popular Disturbances in Scotland, 1780–1815* (Edinburgh, 1979)

Luscombe, E., *Across the Years, Episcopacy in Forfar 1560–2000* (Dundee, 2006)

Lynch, M. (ed.), *The Early Modern Town in Scotland* (London, 1987)

Lynch, M., *Edinburgh and the Reformation* (Edinburgh, 1981)

Mackie, J. D. and Pryde, G. S., *The Estate of the Burgesses in the Scots Parliament* (St Andrews, 1923)

Markus, T. A. (ed.), *Order in Space and Society: Architectural Form and its Contexts in the Scottish Enlightenment* (Edinburgh, 1982)

Marland, H. (ed.), *The Art of Midwifery: Early Modern Midwives in Europe* (London, 1993)

Marland, H. and Pelling, M. (eds.), *The Task of Healing: Medicine, Religion and Gender in England and the Netherlands 1450–1800* (Rotterdam, 1996)

Marshall, P. J., *East Indian Fortunes* (Oxford, 1976)

Marshall, P. J., *The Making and Unmaking of Empire: Britain, India and America, c. 1750–1783* (Oxford, 2005)

Marshall, T., *Murdering to Dissect: Grave-Robbing, Frankenstein and the Anatomy Literature* (Manchester, 1995)

Marwick, J. D., *Index to the Records of the Convention of the Royal Burghs of Scotland* (Edinburgh, 1890)

Marwick, J. D. (ed.), *Extracts from the Records of the Convention of the Royal Burghs of Scotland, 1615–1676* (Edinburgh, 1878)

Marwick, J. D. (ed.), *Extracts from the Records of the Convention of the Royal Burghs of Scotland, 1677–1711* (Edinburgh, 1880)

Mason, R. A., *Kingship and Common Weal* (East Linton, 1998)

Matthew, H. C. G. and Harrison, B. (eds.), *Oxford Dictionary of National Biography* (Oxford, 2004)

Matthew, W. M., *Keiller's of Dundee: The Rise of the Marmalade Dynasty* (Dundee, 1998)

Maxwell, A., *Old Dundee Prior to the Reformation* (Edinburgh, 1891)

Maxwell, A., *History of Old Dundee Narrated out of the Town Council Register with Additions from Contemporary Annals* (Edinburgh, 1884)

M'Crie, C. G., *Scotland's Part and Place in the Revolution of 1688* (Edinburgh, 1688)

McCarthy, A. (ed.), *A Global Clan: Scottish Migrant Networks and Identities since the Eighteenth Century* (London, 2006)

McCraw, I., *The Kirks of Dundee Presbytery 1558–1999* (Dundee, 2000)

McCraw, I., *The Fairs of Dundee* (Dundee, 1993)

MacDonald, A. R., *The Burghs and Parliament in Scotland c. 1550–1651* (Aldershot, 2007)

McFarland, E. W., *Ireland and Scotland in the Age of Revolution: Planting the Green Bough* (Edinburgh, 1994)

McIntosh, J. R., *Church and Theology in Enlightenment Scotland: The Popular Party, 1740–1800* (East Linton, 1998)

McKean, C. and Walker, D., *Dundee: An Illustrated Introduction* (Edinburgh, 1984)

McNeill, P. G. B. and MacQueen, H. L. (eds.), *Atlas of Scottish History to 1707* (Edinburgh, 1996)

Maclaren, J., *The History of Dundee* (Dundee, 1874)

Miller, A. H. (ed.), *The First History of Dundee* (Dundee, 1923)

Miskell, L., Whatley, C. A. and Harris, B. (eds.), *Victorian Dundee: Image and Realities* (East Linton, 2000)

Mitchison, R., *The Old Poor Law in Scotland* (Edinburgh, 2000)

Namier, L. and Brooke, J. (eds.), *The House of Commons, 1754–1790*, 3 vols. (London, 1964)

Nicholas, D., *Urban Europe 1100–1700* (Basingstoke, 2003)

Nightingale, P., *Fortune and Integrity: A Study of Moral Attitudes in the Indian Diary of George Paterson, 1769–1774* (Oxford, 1985)

Ottenheym, K. and Mignot, C. (eds.) *Bâtiments Publiques – le Gouvernement, la Justice, et l'Économie* (forthcoming)

Ozouf, M., *Festivals and the French Revolution* (Cambridge, 1988)

Pagan, T., *The Convention of the Royal Burghs of Scotland* (Glasgow, 1926)

Paton, H. M. (ed.), *Accounts of the Masters of Works for Building and Repairing Royal Palaces and Castles. Vol. 1, 1529–1615* (Edinburgh, 1957)

Paton, H. (ed.), *Register of the Privy Council of Scotland (RPCS)*, Vol. 13 (Edinburgh, 1932)

Pelling, M., *The Common Lot: Sickness, Medical Occupations and the Urban Poor in Early Modern England* (London, 1998)

Perry, D., *Dundee Rediscovered* (Perth, 2005)

Philips, C. H., *The East India Company, 1784–1834* (Manchester, 1961)

Philp, M. (ed.), *The French Revolution and British Popular Politics* (Cambridge, 1991)

Pittock, J. and Wear, A. (eds.), *Interpretation and Cultural History in Eighteenth-Century Britain* (Basingstoke, 1991)

Pittock, M. G. H., *The Myth of the Jacobite Clans* (Edinburgh, 1995)

Pollock, L., *With Faith and Physic: The Life of a Tudor Gentlewoman, Lady Grace Mildmay, 1552–1620* (London, 1993)

Pryde G. S., *The Burghs of Scotland: A Critical List* (Oxford, 1965)

Rait, R. S., *The Parliaments of Scotland* (Glasgow, 1924)

Reid, L., *Scottish Midwives: Twentieth-Century Voices* (East Linton, 2000)

Risse, G. B., *Hospital Life in Enlightenment Scotland: Care and Teaching at the Royal Infirmary of Edinburgh* (Cambridge, 1986)

Robertson, H., *Mariners of Dundee: Their City, Their River, Their Fraternity* (Dundee, 2006)

Rollo, J. A., *Dundee Historical Fragments* (Dundee, 1911)

Rosner, L., *Medical Education in the Age of Improvement: Edinburgh Students and Apprentices 1760–1826* (Edinburgh, 1991)

Rousseau, G. S. and Porter, R. (eds.), *Sexual Underworlds of the Enlightenment* (Manchester, 1989)

Sanderson, E. C., *Women and Work in 18th-Century Edinburgh* (Basingstoke, 1996)

Saunders, A. and Davidson, P. (eds.), *Visual Words and Verbal Pictures* (Glasgow, 2005)

Scott, A. M., *Bonnie Dundee* (Edinburgh, 2000)

Scott, A. M., *Discovering Dundee: The Story of a City* (Edinburgh, 1989)

Scott, A. M. (ed.), *Miscellany of the Scottish History Society* (Edinburgh, 1990)

Sedgwick, R. (ed.), *The House of Commons, 1715–1754*, 2 vols. (London, 1970)

Shaw, J., *Water Power in Scotland, 1550–1870* (Edinburgh, 1984)

Sinclair, J. (ed.), *The Statistical Account of Scotland 1791–1799* Vol. 13: Angus (Wakefield, 1976)

Skinner, W. C., *The Barronie of Hilltowne of Dundee* (Dundee, 1927)

Slack, P., *The Impact of Plague in Tudor and Stuart England* (Oxford, 1990)

Slaven, A., *The Development of the West of Scotland, 1750–1960* (London, 1975)

Small, R., *Statistical Account of the Parish and Town of Dundee* (Dundee, 1793)

Smith, A. M., *The Nine Trades of Dundee* (Dundee, 1995)

Smith, A. M., *The Guildry of Dundee: A History of the Merchant Guild of Dundee up to the 19th Century* (Dundee, 2005)

Smith, C. S., *The Rise of Design and the Domestic Interior in Eighteenth Century England* (London, 2000)

Smout, T. C., *A History of the Scottish People, 1560–1830* (London, 1987)

Smout, T. C., *Scottish Trade on the Eve of the Union* (Edinburgh and London, 1963)

Smout, T. C. (ed.), *Anglo-Scottish Relations from 1603 to 1900* (Oxford, 2005)

Stavert, M. L. (ed.), *The Perth Guildry Book, 1452–1601* (Edinburgh, 1993)

Stevenson, D., *The Scottish Revolution 1637–1644: The Triumph of the Covenanters* (Newton Abbot, 1973)

Stevenson, D., *Revolution and Counter Revolution, 1644–1651* (Edinburgh, 2003)

Sunter, R. M., *Patronage and Politics in Scotland, 1707–1832* (Edinburgh, 1986)

Sutherland, L., *The East India Company in Eighteenth Century Politics* (Oxford, 1962)

Sweet, R., *The English Town 1680–1840: Government, Society and Culture* (Harlow, 1999)

Sword, J., *They Did Wrong: Public Hangings in the Angus Area 1786 to 1868* (Friends of Dundee City Archives Publication No.5, 2005)

Symonds, D. A., *Weep Not For Me: Women, Ballads and Infanticide in Early Modern Scotland* (Pennsylvania, 1997)

Szechi, D., *1715 The Great Jacobite Rebellion* (London, 2006)

Terry, C. S., *John Graham of Claverhouse, Viscount of Dundee 1684–1689* (London, 1905)

Thale, M. (ed.), *Selections From the Papers of the London Corresponding Society* (Cambridge, 1983)

Thomson, J., *The History of Dundee* (Dundee, 1847)

Thomson, J. and MacLaren, J., *The History of Dundee* (Dundee, 1874)

Thorne, R. G. (ed.), *The House of Commons, 1790–1820* (London, 1986)

Torrie, E. P. D., *Medieval Dundee: A Town and its People* (Dundee, 1990)

Warden, A., *The History of Old Dundee* (Dundee, 1884)

Warden, A. J., *Burgh Laws of Dundee* (London, 1872)

Warden, A. J., *Angus or Forfarshire, the Land and People Descriptive and Historical*, Vol. 5 (Dundee, 1885)

Warden, A. J. *Linen Trade: Ancient and Modern* (Dundee, 1967)

Watson, N., *Dundee: A Short History* (Edinburgh, 2006)

Weatherill, L., *Consumer Behaviour and Material Culture in Britain 1660–1760* (London, 1988)

Wedderburn, A., *The Wedderburn Book* (Printed Privately, 1898)

Wells, R., *Insurrection: The British Experience 1795–1803* (Stroud, 1986)

Whatley, C. A., Smith, A. S. and Swinfen, D. B., *The Life and Times of Dundee* (Edinburgh, 1993)

Whatley, C. A., *Onwards from Osnaburgs: The Rise and Progress of a Scottish Textile Company, Don & Low of Forfar 1792–1992* (Edinburgh, 1992)

Whatley, C. A., *Scottish Society: Beyond Jacobitism towards Industrialisation* (Manchester, 2000)

Whyte, I. D., *Scotland Before the Industrial Revolution* (Harlow, 1995)

Wilkins, F., *The Smuggling Story of Two Firths: Montrose to Dunbar* (Worcestershire, 1993)

Wilson, A., *The Making of Man-Midwifery: Childbirth in England, 1660–1770* (Cambridge MA, 1995)

Withrington, D. J. and Grant, I. R. (eds.), *The Statistical Account of Scotland* (Wakefield, 1983)

Wrigley, E. A. (ed.), *Nineteenth-Century Society. Essays in the Use of Quantitative Methods for the Study of Social Data* (Cambridge, 1972)

Young A. F., *The Encyclopaedia of Scottish Executions 1750 to 1963* (Kent, 1998)

Young, M., *The Parliaments of Scotland: Burgh and Shire Commissioners*, 2 vols. (Edinburgh, 1992–3)

Anon, *The House of Binny* (Madras, 1969)

Year Book of the Grand Lodge of Ancient Free and Accepted Masons of Scotland (Edinburgh, 2007)

JOURNAL ARTICLES

Bowen, H. V., 'The Little Parliament: The General Court of the East India Company, 1750–1784', *The Historical Journal*, 34 (1991)

Brown, D. J., 'The Government of Scotland under Henry Dundas and William Pitt', *History*, 83 (1998)

Bryant, G. J., 'Scots in India in the Eighteenth Century', *Scottish Historical Review*, 64 (1985)

Buist, R. C., 'Dundee Doctors in the Sixteenth Century', *Edinburgh Medical Journal*, 37 (1930)

Cain, P. J. and Hopkins, A. G., 'Gentlemanly Capitalism and British Expansion Overseas, I: The Old Colonial System, 1688–1850', *Economic History Review*, 2nd Series, 39 (1986)

Coleman, D. C., ''Proto-industrialisation': A Concept too Many', *The Economic History Review*, New Series, 36 (1983)

Crawford, C., 'Patients' Rights and the Law of Contract in Eighteenth-Century England', *Social History of Medicine*, 13 (2000)

Dean, D. M., 'Public or Private? London, Leather and Legislation in Elizabethan England', *Historical Journal*, 31 (1988)

Dennison, E. P. and Lynch, M., 'Crown, Capital, and Metropolis. Edinburgh and Canongate: The Rise of a Capital and an Urban Court', *Journal of Urban History*, 32 (2005)

Dingwall, H. M., ' "To be insert in the *Mercury*": Medical Practitioners and the Press in Eighteenth-Century Edinburgh', *Social History of Medicine*, 13 (2000)

Donnachie, I., ' "The Darker Side": A Speculative Survey of Scottish Crime during the First Half of the Nineteenth Century', *Scottish Economic and Social History*, 15 (1995)

Goodare, J., 'The Scottish Parliament and its Early Modern "Rivals" ', *Parliaments, Estates and Representation*, 24 (2004)

Harris, B., 'Popular Politics in Angus and Perthshire in the 1790s', *Historical Research*, 80 (2007)

Harris, B., 'Scotland's Newspapers, the French Revolution and Domestic Radicalism (c. 1789–1794)', *Scottish Historical Review*, 84 (2005)

Harris, B., 'Towns, Improvement and Cultural Change in Georgian Scotland: The Evidence of the Angus Burghs, c. 1760–1820', *Urban History*, 33 (2006)

Houston, R. and Snell, K. D., 'Proto-industrialisation? Cottage Industry, Social Change, and Industrial Revolution', *The Historical Journal*, 27 (1984)

Jones, M., 'Archery, Romance and Elite Culture in England and Wales, c. 1780–1840', *History*, 89 (2004)

Kidd, C., 'Conditional Britons: The Scots Convenanting Tradition and the Eighteenth-Century British State', *English Historical Review*, 117 (2002)

Kümin, B. and Würgler, A., 'Petitions, *Gravamina* and the Early Modern state: Local Influence on Central Legislation in England and Germany (Hesse)', *Parliaments, Estates and Representation*, 17 (1997)

Lenman, B. and Parker, G., 'Crime and Control in Scotland 1500–1800', *History Today*, 30 (1980)

Lythe, S. G. E., 'The Origin and Development of Dundee: A Study in Historical Geography', *Scottish Geographical Magazine*, 54 (1938)

Lythe, S. G. E., 'The Tayside Meal Mobs 1772–3', *Scottish Historical Review*, 46 (1967)

MacDonald, A. R., 'Deliberative Processes in Parliament, *c.* 1567–1639: multicameralism and the Lords of the Articles', *Scottish Historical Review*, 81 (2002)

MacDonald, A. R., ' "Tedious to rehers"? Parliament and Locality in Scotland *c.* 1500–1651: the Burghs of North-East Fife', *Parliaments, Estates and Representation*, 20 (2000)

Miskell, L., 'From Conflict to Co-operation: Urban Improvement and the Case of Dundee, 1790–1850', *Urban History*, 29 (2002)

Miskell, L. and Kenefick, W., 'A Flourishing Seaport – Dundee Harbour and the Making of the Industrial Town' in *Scottish Economic and Social History*, 20 (2000)

McGilvray, G. K., 'Post-Union Scotland and the India Connection: Patronage and Political Management', *Cencrastus*, 37 (1990)

Mackillop, A., 'Accessing Empire: Scotland, Europe, Britain, and the Asia Trade', *Itinerario*, 29 (2005)

Nenadic, S., 'Experience and Expectations in the Transformation of the Highland Gentlewoman, 1680–1820', *Scottish Historical Review*, 80 (2001)

Nenadic, S., 'Middle-Rank Consumers and Domestic Culture in Edinburgh and Glasgow, 1729–1840', *Past and Present*, 145 (1994)

Nenadic, S., 'The Impact of the Military Profession on Highland Gentry Families, *c.* 1730–1830', *Scottish Historical Review*, 85 (2006)

Porter, A., ' "Gentlemanly Capitalism" and Empire: The British Experience since 1750', *Journal of Imperial and Commonwealth History*, 18 (1990)

Razzell, P. E., 'Social Origins of Officers in the Indian and British Home Army: 1758–1962', *The British Journal of Sociology*, 14 (1963)

Rice, F. J., 'The Origins of an Organisation of Insanity in Scotland', *Scottish Economic and Social History*, 5 (1985)

Robertson, J., 'The Storming of Dundee, 1651', *History Scotland*, 3 (2003)

Robertson, M. L., 'Scottish Commerce and the American War of Independence', *The Economic History Review*, New Series, 9 (1956)

Sanz, P., 'The Cities in the Aragonese Cortes in the Medieval and Early Modern Periods', *Parliaments, Estates and Representation*, 14 (1994)

Smout, T. C., 'The Burgh of Montrose and the Union of 1707', *Scottish Historical Review*, 66 (1987)

Soltow, L., 'Inequality of Wealth in Land in Scotland in the Eighteenth Century', *Scottish Economic and Social History*, 10 (1990)

Tittler, R., 'Elizabethan Towns and the "Points of Contact": Parliament', *Parliamentary History*, 8 (1989)

Vincent, E., 'The Responses of Scottish Churchmen to the French Revolution, 1789–1802', *Scottish Historical Review*, 73 (1994)

de Vries, J., 'The Industrial and the Industrious Revolution', *The Journal of Economic History*, 54 (1994)

Whatley, C. A., 'Economic Causes and Consequences of the Union of 1707: A Survey', *Scottish Historical Review*, 68 (1989)

Whatley, C. A., 'The Union of 1707, Integration and the Scottish Burghs: The Case of the 1720 Food Riots', *Scottish Historical Review*, 78 (1999)

Whatley, C. A., 'Salt, Coal and the Union of 1707: A revision article', *Scottish Historical Review*, 66 (1987)

DISSERTATIONS

Brims, J., 'The Scottish Democratic Movement in the Age of the French Revolution' (PhD thesis, University of Edinburgh, 1983)

Bryant, G. J., 'The East India Company and its Army, 1600–1778' (PhD thesis, King's College, 1975)

Cameron, A., 'From Ritual to Regulation? The Development of Midwifery in Glasgow and the West of Scotland, c. 1740–1840' (PhD thesis, University of Glasgow, 2003)

Fagerstrom, D. I., 'The American Revolutionary Movement in Scottish Opinion 1763–1783' (PhD thesis, University of Edinburgh, 1951)

Flett, I. F., 'The Conflict of the Reformation and Democracy in the Geneva of Scotland 1443–1610: an intro-duction to edited texts of documents relating to the burgh of Dundee' (MPhil dissertation, University of St Andrews, 1981)

Golden, M. C., 'Criminality and the Development of Policing in Dundee 1816–1833' (MPhil dissertation, University of Dundee, 2003)

Healey, M., 'The Legacy of Alexander Riddoch' (MPhil dissertation, University of Dundee, 2003: imcomplete)

Kilday, A. M., 'Women and Crime in South-West Scotland: A Study of the Justiciary Court Records, 1750–1815' (PhD thesis, University of Strathclyde, 1998)

King, P., 'Crime, Law and Society in Essex 1740–1820' (PhD thesis, University of Cambridge, 1984)

Law, A., 'Why Forfar Became the Centre of Osnaburg Manufacture' (MPhil dissertation, University of Dundee, 2008)

Mee, S., 'Perth and Worcester: How Similar were Two British Towns in the Late Eighteenth Century?' (MPhil disser-tation, University of Dundee, 2007)

MacQueen, E. E., 'The General Assembly of the Kirk as a Rival of Parliament' (PhD thesis, University of St Andrews, 1927)

McGilvray, G. K., 'East India Patronage and the Political Management of Scotland, 1720–1774' (PhD thesis, Open University, 1989)

Monaghan, S. J., 'The Dundee Shipping Lists as a Record of the Impact of the Union upon the Dundee Shipping Industry, 1705 to 1710' (MA dissertation, University of Dundee, 1988)

Newland, K., 'What was the Role of Norwegian and Baltic Timber in the Scottish Building Industry in the Seventeenth Century?' (PhD in progress, University of Dundee)

Parker, J. G., 'The Directors of the East India Company, 1754–1790', (PhD thesis, University of Edinburgh, 1977)

Roach, W. M., 'Radical Reform Movements in Scotland from 1815–1822 with Particular Reference to the West of Scotland' (PhD thesis, University of Glasgow, 1970)

Wemyss, C., 'Some Aspects of Scottish Country House Construction in the Post-Restoration Period; Patrick Smyth and the Building of Methven Castle, 1678–1681' (MPhil dissertation, University of Dundee, 2002)

Young, M., 'Rural Society in Scotland from the Restoration to the Union: Challenge and Response in the Carse of Gowrie, circa 1660–1707' (PhD thesis, University of Dundee, 2004)

ONLINE RESOURCES

Old Statistical Accounts: http://stat-acc-scot.edin.ac.uk/link/ 1791-99/Forfar/Dundee

Photopolis: www.dundeecity.gov.uk/photodb/main. htm

Survey of Scottish Witchcraft Database: www.arts.ed.ac.uk/witches/

The National Information Service for Earthquake Engineering, University of California, Berkley: http://nisee.berkley.edu/lisbon/

Index